EVERY STICK AND STONE THAT STANDS
KILKENNY

BY
SEAN KENNY
2003

ISBN
0 9545741 0 9

PUBLISHED BY SEÁN KENNY
2003

DESIGN AND PRINT
KILKENNY PEOPLE PRINTING LIMITED
PURCELLSINCH, KILKENNY, IRELAND
056 63366

All sculptures shown in this book, and on front and back covers, were sculpted by the author, Seán Kenny, for the Art Exhibitions held in Saint Kieran's College, Kilkenny, during the years from 1966 to 1971. I know that the sculpture, An Spailpín Fánach, was first exhibited in 1966.

The Saint Kieran's College Exhibitions were said to be the inspiration and forerunner of our present Kilkenny Arts Festival. These were the brainchild of Rev. Fr. Joe Delaney, now attached to Saint John's parish in the city.

I dedicate this book to my mother and father, Ann and Bob Kenny,
sisters and brothers: Kitty, Christy, Patty, Richie, Mickey and Betty,
who taught me everything good that I know.

To my wife Ann for her steadfast support and encouragement
and to our family: Ann-Marie, Cathy, Bob, Fintan and Colette,
for their forebearance and help in deciding grammatical correctness
and spellings, etc, and some great sketches by Cathy.

To my friends who believed in me and praised my feeble efforts to write,
reading me early and late, and to the source of my inspiration:
the fine, decent, honest-to-God people from the Marble City
and county of Kilkenny, on the banks of the river Nore.

Seán Kenny

CONTENTS

FOREWORD

Seán Kenny has produced this most fascinating book which will capture the imagination of Kilkenny people, both at home and abroad. In it he has struck a rich vein of local history, and in his own rare and sensitive manner highlights the humour of our local "characters" of yesteryear.

Those of us who have lived through the age of mass emigration from Ireland, will relive those times in Sean's "The Irish in London", which is an integral part of his book. Few people who lived through the '40s, '50s and even the early '60s, escaped the scourge of emigration, either on a personal level or by saying goodbye at the railway station to some close friend or relative who was heading for an English city seeking employment.

In Seán Kenny's description of "The Irish in London" he describes vividly what many exiles experienced while working in London.

We in Kilkenny are fortuitous that Seán's skill with the pen has bound together conduits of personal experience with folklore, which would have been lost in the mists of time, had it not been printed for the benefit of posterity in this fine book.

I believe that it is only fair to say that Seán Kenny has now joined the illustrious company of the many great writers Kilkenny has produced. Names which come to mind are John Banim, Jonathan Swift, Canon Carrigan, and closer to home, the late and great Dan MacAuley.

There is a similarity in style between Seán and Dan – both of whom hail from the approximate locality – and tell their tale with a unique talent.

In his book Seán Kenny combines his knowledge and love of Kilkenny and its people to give us a unique inheritance. I sincerely hope, that you the reader, will enjoy and cherish this book which comes as a result of many years of research by the author.

I wish Seán every success, and quote the sanguine words of an old Kilkenny character who once said "there's the makings of a book in every Irishman – but most of us are too lazy to sit down and work at it"!

Seán Ó Ciarmhaic

ACKNOWLEDGEMENTS

Some writings by the following literary champions were considered in the presentation of this book: May Sparks, Tom Lyng, Sean J. White, James Delahunty, Dónal Mac Auglaigh, Dr. Robert Wyse Jackson, Frank McEvoy, Hubert Butler and Canon Carrigan, historian.

SPONSORS

Eamon Langton, Langton House Hotel
Tom Cantwell, T.C. Tyres, Patrick Street
Vivian Good, Goods of Kilkenny
Dunnes Stores, P.R.O. Mr. O'Reilly
Watergate Theatre, Kilkenny
Ger Cody, Manager Watergate Theatre
Duggans Monster House
J.D. Murphy Investment, Friends First
Richard Dore, Optometrist, High Street
Peter Dore, Bacon Butcher, High Street
Saint Canice's Credit Union
Smithwick's Brewery
James Travers, The Garage, Ormonde Road
Vincent McIntyre, The Village Inn
Aileen Hehir, William Street

PREFACE

I wrote a little book some years ago which I called *Sounds of Sadness*. It was a light-weight attempt in the short story, poetry and pen and ink drawing world of letters. Some pieces from that little book are included in this book – I hope with some success: "I read something belonging to you once upon a time. Why don't you write a ...?"

And so I did and here it is. I can only hope that you like it. It is the best that I am capable of. Just like my father before me said: "I love every stick and stone that stands Kilkenny". Thank you for reading me.

Seán Kenny

The Irish in London

IRISH EMIGRANT
BY SEAN KENNY

THE IRISH IN LONDON
LIST OF CHARACTERS

ALLEN HUNT	PROTAGONIST
PAT HUNT	HEAD BARMAN, 'THE CHAMPION'
NANCY BLACKMORE	PAT'S FIANCE
ROSIE TAYLOR (KEEGAN)	WIFE OF BILL TAYLOR
PATRICIA	ROSIE'S DAUGHTER
BILL TAYLOR	ROSIE'S HUSBAND
MATT RYAN	HEAD BARMAN, 'THE POPPY'
IVOR DAVIES	BARMAN, 'THE POPPY'
LUKE BRANNIGAN	BUILDING CONTRACTOR
JACK BOLAND	BUILDING CONTRACTOR PARTNERS
PEGGY O'SHEA	NURSE–FRIEND OF ALLEN
EILEEN MURPHY	IVOR'S FIANCÉE

EPISODE ONE

LAID OFF
LONDON BOUND
SAILING
READING TO EUSTON

LAID OFF

"You won't be missing much, Allen. This place is running downhill faster than a frightened foal for its mother. 'Tis more like a "Sweat Shop" than a factory since they brought in the time and motion men", said old Jack.

"I'm not too pushed about getting the sack. I wasn't going anywhere, anyhow. It's four years wasted as far as I'm concerned, Jack".

"What'll you do lad, sign on or take the mail-boat?"

"I'll pack me bag and sail for merry old England".

"Is it to be Manchester, Liverpool or Birmingham?"

"None of them. I'm heading for the big smoke, where there's gold in the streets". "You'll be the first to find it then of all the Kilkenny men that left for London town. There's about as many Irish men and women working in London as there are in the whole of Dublin".

"Then one more won't make much difference."

"They say 'tis a pagan land, where a body could lose the run of itself in a hurry". "That's all eye-wash Jack. If there wasn't England to go to we'd be eating grass here for the past twenty years".

"You'll need an address to go to or a friend to put you on the right track when you land. And don't forget references from the factory here and from your parish priest. Without them you're a gonner, Allen"

"It's all taken care of. My older brother Pat has been working over in London for the past five years. He's the head barman in a pub called "The Champion", on the Bayswater Road. He'll be there at Euston Station to meet me."

"Oh well, you're sitting pretty so lad. And you have youth on your side and a bit of schooling. Still and all you'd better mind yourself. The women over there are so well walked they know more at sixteen than they do over here getting married".

On the previous Friday morning as Allen clocked-in at the factory, he saw his name in bold print on the notice board:

Will Mr. Allen Hunt please call to the Manager's office this Friday morning at 10 a.m.

"Sorry to loose you Allen, but the factory is going through a difficult period right now. You have been a diligent worker and a good time keeper but it's union rules as you know; last man in is first man out. If things should pick up we'll send for you right away. Good luck". The manager shook Allens hand.

One week later Allen collected his 'cards', a reference and three weeks pay. On the way out he said goodbye to old Jack. "I'll say a prayer for you lad. More than likely you'll need it". Leaving home wasn't half as harrowing as he had thought it might be. The fact that he was going to be met and advised by his big brother took most of the heartbreak out of it for his parents.

"Be sure to go to Mass every Sunday and attend the Sacraments once a month, Allen. That's all any of us have in this life" advised his mother.

"Depend on no man but yourself", said his father.

LONDON BOUND

Kilkenny railway station was crowded when Allen arrived with his overcoat over one arm, his tweed cap on the Kildare side and his suit-case bound with a heavy leather strap. He got into a thirty foot queue for the ticket office. The man behind him was talking to someone. "Biggest crowd I've ever seen in all my years. Oh well, Irelands loss is England's gain, as they say".

Allen was at the ticket office. "London one way please". "That'll be seven pound eighteen shillings Sir." "Mile maith agat", he answered without thinking. The clerk shot a glance and smiled uneasily. As he wound his way up the platform through the crowd the far off whistle of the Waterford train pierced the din of conversation. Shouts of "here she is", "She's running on time" and "don't forget to write" and such like exclamations echoed like a well rehearsed song.

The train was in. The station clock told it was 7 p.m. and the last farewells were said. "Take your seats ladies and gentlemen. The train will leave for Waterford in ten minutes time. Get on board now please. Will those who are not travelling please stand back from the doors."

The station master was shouting into the loud-speaker.

IRISH EMIGRANT
BY SEAN KENNY

14

A young lady looking over her shoulder, crying, bumped into Allen and let her suitcase fall.

"It's my fault", he said. "I should have seen you coming. Let me carry that on to the train for you". "'Twas my fault, I should have been looking where I was going, Thanks." Sitting beside him on the train she dried her eyes with a handkerchief that had the initials POS embroidered on it in pink.

"How far are you going, Miss?"

"I'm bound for London, a place called Hammersmith. And yourself?"

"First stop Bayswater Road", "The Champion". "I'll remember that. My name is Peggy O'Shea, I'm from Callan".

"And I'm Allen Hunt, Kilkenny City. You've been over before then?"

"Yes, I just came home to bury my mother".

"Sorry for your troubles, Peggy". He could think of nothing else to say and silence overtook them."

At Waterford the boat-train for Rosslare was behind schedule. There would be a delay of not more than forty five minutes – an hour at the most- less with any luck said the Porter.

"Percy Ffrench is not dead yet". He was glad to have found something to say.

"Are you right there Michael are you right?" She answered with a smile. Little by little the passengers were evacuating the platform and spilling into the lounge bar."

"No pints gentlemen, only large bottles and spirits and ham sandwiches and mineral waters of the ladies. Time wandered off unnoticed as the empty large bottles mounted up and the plates of ham sandwiches disappeared. Given the circumstances it would have been most unusual if somebody hadn't burst into song. A powerfully built middle aged man was on his feet::

"I watched last night the rising moon upon a foreign strand,
'Till memories came like flowers in June of home and fatherland".

SAILING

It was "The Moon Behind The Hill", written by William Keneally and known for generations as the Kilkenny Anthem. The boat-train had arrived at last. And the hubbub of conversation increased in proportion to the amount of refreshments consumed. Suddenly everybody was telling everyone else the innermost state of their private affairs. "I'm with McAlpine's Fusilier's – a tea boy. I make more money carrying bets to the bookie's than I get in me pay packet".

"Me! I have myself down as a married man with six kids. If I'm ever caught I'll be in jail for life". They bartered stories that were fantastic for ones that were true and felt the better for it. At Rosslare the mail-boat sat on the water waiting patiently. The old regulars knew her by sight.

"Oh God, 'tis the old Princess Maud. We'll have thrown up our guts long before we reach Fishguard."

"She doesn't have any stabliser's – tosses you about like cement in a mixer."

The smiling fresh-faced man sitting beside Peggy and Allen, pushed plastic bags into their hands. "What's that for?" Allen asked anxiously.

"You'll soon find out", said he still smiling.

"The bag is for getting sick in", Peggy whispered.

"What about yourself?" Allen asked the man, "you don't have one".

"I don't need one. I've made this trip a dozen times. I have me sea-legs"

Forty-five minutes out the "Princess Maud" was rolling like a drunken sailor having lost a boot and most of the passengers were violently sick. Peggy had given her plastic bag to the fresh-faced man, just in time. She had seen his complexion change to a duckegg green. Allen gave his bag to a man behind him, who was praying for the ship to go down.

Peggy smiled at Allen. "You're a cool one, and on your first crossing at that".

"And you seem to have everything under control, yourself young woman."

"Just for that I am definitely calling to see you at "The Champion" on the Bayswater Road, Allen Hunt, and you had better be there".

The 'Maud' sailed into Fishguard and disgorged her passengers who were sick, sore and sorry. Across the tracks the train for London was ready and waiting. Allen carried the two suit-cases and Peggy slung his overcoat over her shoulder and put his tweed cap upon her head.

Porters were busy loading freight – their barrows squealing up and down the platform like a stuck pig. The passengers were mostly silent, some sullen. The station master put the loud-hailer to his lips: ""All aboard for Swansea, Cardiff, Reading and London. Take your seats ladies and gentlemen please."

Allen fixed their cases on the overhead rack and putting his hands on Peggies shoulders gently pushed her down into the seat in front of him. "Oh, you like to boss people then" she said in mock displeasure.

"Only those who need guidance" he said with a grin.

At Swansea about a dozen people got off and porters ran to and fro with parcels and hardware. Within minutes they were on their way. At Cardiff there was a delay of fifteen minutes as passengers poured from the train, – "there's a large contingent of Irish living in Cardiff, Allen." The green flag went up and they were on their way once more.

READING TO EUSTON

"The next stop is ours", a young woman told her daughter who had fallen asleep. She shook her anxiously. "Come on Cathy wake up. Put your coat on and get you bag. We're pulling into Reading station any minute now." The daughter was sitting beside Allen, the mother beside Peggy.

He took their bags down off the rack. "Thank you Sir". He smiled. "You're welcome". They were alone now. "Have you ever read the "Ballad of Reading Goal" Peggy?" "Can't say I have." "It's a long narrative poem by Oscar Wilde."

"I read one or two of his poems at school but never heard of the Reading Goal one. Recite one verse of it. I dare you. Just for me."

"Yet each man kills the thing he loves,
By each let this be heard,
Some do it with a bitter look,
Some with a flattering word
The coward does it with a kiss,
The brave man with a sword!"

"That's very interesting. How would you do it, Allen?"

"With a blunt instrument". He laughed

"I'd say with a sword – definitely".

"We'll never know, - will we?"

"Stranger things have happened".

"Next stop Euston station, London Town", a happy go lucky young Irishman called out at the top of his voice. And the train slowed down noticeably and began to whistle itself into the station. Amid loudspeakers blaring and blinding lights, a sea of faces flooded the platform.

Allen felt his guts tighten as he got to his feet. Peggy was reaching for her suitcase. "I'll get that", he said. "Will there be someone here to meet you?" No, there won't be anyone" and she looked at him closely as she took the case out of his hand. The train had come to a halt with a jolt and the doors were pulled open. It had been a long haul (twelve hours since they had left Kilkenny) and the passengers were anxious to dismount and meet their kit and kin.

When Allen stepped out onto the platform, Peggy was nowhere to be seen. It was as if she had been swallowed up by the clamouring throng. He called out her name, "Peggy, Peggy O'Shea" but there was no reply. Then suddenly he quickened – someone was calling his name. "Allen old son, 'tis good to see you". Standing beside him was his brother Pat. After they had exchanged greetings and inquiries about their parents health, Pat took Allen's suitcase and made straight for a restaurant. He shouted over his shoulder at Allen, "Come on man, don't be standing there gaping, you need to get a bit of grub into you." Allen ate bacon and egg with bread, butter and a pot of tea. Pat lit a cigarette.

"Who was that you were calling out to when I came upon you on the platform?" "Oh 'twas just a young lady I travelled over with. I was going to carry her case to the taxi for her, that's all".

"I see, gallant as always. It's not that but this young man, - as soon as you're ready we'll take the tube to Bayswater Road and "The Champion".

EPISODE TWO

THE CHAMPION
NANCY BLACKMORE
ROSIE TAYLOR

"THE CHAMPION"

"I'm ready if your are, Pat." Allen and Pat boarded the Circle Line at Euston Square underground and travelled to Bayswater Road via Great Portland Street, Baker Street, Edgeware Road and Paddington. They walked up the Bayswater Road with Kensington Gardens on their left.

"It's only a ten minute walk, there's not point taking a bus."

"That's all right by me, you are carrying the case. Is it always like this – the crowds of people: It's like coming out of Croke Park after an All-Ireland final."

"You have to remember there are eight and a half million people living here. This can be a tough town Allen. You've got to be able to take care of yourself. And another thing, don't talk Irish revolutionary politics over here. You could land yourself in big trouble."

"I'll be a good boy and say my prayers, morn' and night, Pat"

"It's not bloody-well funny, Allen. And tell me, have you any idea what you're going to do over here?"

"I'll take just about anything to get started and then I'll look around for something suitable". "That sounds sensible enough. I could probably get you a start as a trainee barman, the money wouldn't be great but you'd be living in – all-found.". "That would suit me fine". "This is it, The Champion".

The building stood three storeys high. A bright oak façade covered the ground floor front except for the huge plate-glass window, which was opaque. Across its centre in bold six inch red lettering was the legend, "Watney Man, Red Barrell". The matching oak-panelled doors displayed ornamental, highly polished brass letter-boxes at each side of window. The door to the left for the lounge bar and the door to the right for the public bar. Above the huge front window in twelve inch Celtic gold letters trimmed in black, the name of this famous hostelry was written.

Whether on foot, in car or travelling by bus, the passing multitudes could not fail to appreciate that this was truly "The Champion".

"This is my humble abode" said Pat with a bow. "Kindly step inside". They walked into the lounge bar and Pat deposited Allen's suitcase behind the counter. The lounge was decked out in brown leather seats and bright oak tables and chairs. Decorative tiles covered the floor and the walls were clad with oak panelling. The ceiling which was fifteen feet high was painted daffodil yellow and a plaster moulding painted in mint green surrounded it and a brass candelabra hung down.

"Is this a pub or a millionaire's mansion?"

"This is a Watney Man, House. It's brewery owned and the principal drink sold here is Red Barrell."

It was all double Dutch to Allen.

There were about forty or fifty people dispersed throughout the lounge. Some sat at tables, others sat on stools at the bar and the strange part about it was most of them were women and something else most of the men wore hard hats, black overcoats and striped grey trousers.

"It's like something out of Dickens," Allen said. "I'm having a culture shock here".

"Never mind, you'll get used to it. What'll you have to drink?"

"I'll try a pint of your Red Barrell and see how it compares to the home brew".

NANCY BLACKMORE

"There, get that inside your shirt and have a good look at the head-line on the Daily Mirror". "John Fitzgerald Kennedy elected President of the U.S.A." In smaller print underneath it read "Irish American Catholic in the Whitehouse, swept into power by landslide victory."

"Wonders will never cease after that. The Irish-American vote is colossal – as big as forty million they reckon."

"The lady behind the bar insisted on buying that drink for you."

Allen looked across and right enough there she was waving her hand and smiling broadly at him.

"I'm getting this treatment because I am the head barman's brother – right?"

"That, and a little something else. Nancy come on over here and meet this opinionated young brother of mine. This is Nancy Blackmore. Well, what do you think?"

"She's a stunner"

"You're embarrassing me Pat," she said with delight.

"Don't get any ideas brother. This is the woman who's going to have my children".

"Do you like it" she asked, holding out her diamond ring for inspection. "We got engaged last week. Had the biggest party ever seen at The Champion." She spoke with a polished English accent but Allen detected a slight Dublin inflection.

"It's beautiful – must have cost a stack. I wish you joy".

Allen thought her to be about twenty eight and above average height. She had green eyes full of light and her hair was black and glossy like polished ebony. She wouldn't be easy to please and there was something cold and calculating about those eyes.

"Nancy is working with me here at The Champion".

"That's nice and cosy", Allen said with a grin.

"This fellow is going to be a handful Pat", she joked and winked at Allen.

"He'll be all right as soon as we get the hay out of his hair".

"Listen Pat I was going through the vacancies in the morning papers. They are looking for a capable barman at 'The Green Man' and there's a vacancy for a trainee at 'The Poppy' on the Edgware Road." She turned to Allen. "We know the Governor of 'The Poppy' pretty well".

"So if the job's not already gone it's as good as yours, brother" said Pat.

"I'll ring The Poppy right now" she said and left them.

The Governor of 'The Poppy' is a big Tipperary man called Mike O'Hara. It's a busy house and can be a bit tough at times but it will be a start hopefully."

"I really appreciate this Pat. I won't forget it."

"That's what brothers are for, brother".

Nancy Blackmore was off the phone and heading towards them.

"Mike O'Hara has gone home to Ireland with the wife and family for two weeks holidays. He will not be back until next week. There is a couple named Bill and Rosalie Taylor doing relief work for them at The Poppy. I spoke with the wife and she said to send Allen over right away.

The funny thing about it is that she seemed to know you Pat. Pat looked up at the ceiling "Rosalie Taylor, no, it doesn't ring a bell."

"But the strangest thing of all is that I could have sworn I recognised her voice, myself, but couldn't put a face on it."

NANCY BLACKMORE
BY SEAN KENNY

20

ROSIE TAYLOR

"Never mind, the main thing is that Allen has high hopes of a job. I'll take you over to "The Poppy" myself just as soon as I've seen to the shelves being stocked-up. Then we'll see who this mystery woman is".

"No you won't, I'll take Allen over to "The Poppy" for the interview. You'll be needed here, Watney Man are due to arrive this morning with a large consignment of bottled beer".

Allen was looking from one to the other. "I can find my own way there just point me in the right direction."

"'Tis not as simple as all that. You'll need to take the 'underground', the tube, and it takes a bit of getting used to. Nancy will take you there. Her feminine curiosity is getting the better of her, anyway."

Allen Hunt and Nancy Blackmore took the tube at Bayswater and went first to Paddington and then to Edgware Road.

"'The Poppy' isn't far from here Allen, just a few minutes walk."

They walked through the right hand side entrance into the lounge bar.

"What can I get you?" asked a middle aged, red faced man in a distinctly west of Ireland accent.

"We've come in connection with the advertisement for a trainee barman in the morning papers", Nancy said.

"Then you'll need to see the Governor".

"Actually it was Mrs. Rosalie Taylor I spoke with on the phone".

"Oh right. I'll get her for you."

Upstairs Rosalie Taylor had just finished putting on her face. She had combed her auburn hair and was wearing her best skirt and blouse. The middle aged, red faced barman knocked on the room door. "There's people downstairs in the lounge, wants to see you mam."

"Thanks Matt, I'll be right down". Again she brushed her hair, adjusted her nylons and turned sideways to examine in the full-length mirror her bodily proportions. Coming downstairs she saw that the door which led to the lounge had been left partly open. She pushed it out until only a few inches of it remained open. Rosalie knew she could study her visitors without being seen. Suddenly her face changed colour. She went deadly pale and gasped in disbelief. Then she looked again to make sure. The young man was definitely Pat Hunt's brother, the resemblance was uncanny. But it was the woman who had frightened her. And there was no mistaking her identity, with that jet black shining hair and those bright green calculating eyes.

Roselie's knees were knocking as she turned and slowly climbed the stairs, where she got physically sick.

Rosalie Taylor sat on the wickerwork laundry basket and wiped her forehead. She had never been strong. "As weak as a June Robin" her mother used to say.

All her life she had been plagued with bouts of asthma. And now the thought that this highly dangerous woman was in some way connected with Pat Hunt and his brother, shattered her. Surely Pat would never get involved with such a person, she thought. He would see through her. But would he? After all, hadn't she fooled Madam Kaan the Beautician, Trevor Briggs the Goldsmith and even herself Rosie Keegan. That was her name when she and Pat went out together, before she met and married Bill Taylor. It was Bill who always called her Rosalie.

Rosie Keegan first met Nancy Blackmore when she worked at Whighteleys of Bayswater. At that time it was one of London's most prestigious stores. Rosie was cashier in the accounts department. To the right of accounts was the beauty salon and to the left was the jewellers shop.

"We have taken on a new hair-care girl and she is positively splendid, you'll have to meet her Rosie," said Madame Kaan.

About three weeks later a wealthy old patron of the salon discovered her purse was missing when she went to pay her bill. Nobody suspected a thing. One month later a pair of gold earrings valued at seventy five pounds disappeared from the jewellers. Nor was the accounts department free from larceny. Small sums of money seemed to vanish from the petty cash box usually left unlocked on Rosie's desk. After she locked it the key went missing. Still no one dreamed of coupling Nancy Blackmore with the thefts. She had so ingratiated herself with all and sundry that to suspect her was unthinkable.

Until one Thursday at closing time she accidentally let fall from her overcoat pocket a small sheet of pink paper. Printed across the top of the page was the name and business of the proprietor. ZACHARY WINEBURG PAWNBROKER, FINCHLEY ROAD, LONDON. Underneath and written in free hand;

"Pair of Diamond shaped earrings – 24 cwt gold. £50 = advanced.
ZW

Madam Kaan found the docket and showed it to Trevor Briggs, who told Rosie Keegan. Together they figured they were hot on the trail of the thief. They were strengthened in their suspicions when Nancy Blackmore was observed going through the waste-paper basket and sweeping under the furniture. She had lost a letter from a dear friend, she told Madam Kaan. To confront her with the Pawnbrokers docket would not suffice. She was far too clever and would deny ownership. They would have to set a trap.

EPISODE THREE

THE TRAP IS SET
THE POPPY
BILL TAYLOR
IVOR DAVIES

THE TRAP IS SET

At five fifty-five on the Friday night the plan was put into motion. The days takings in the Beauty Salon were painstakingly counted into a large unsealed envelope. Madam Kaan pretended she did not have the time to count the money and casually asked Nancy Blackmore to deposit it at the Accounts Department. The temptation proved too much for her. She took forty pounds, sealed the envelope and handed it to Rosie Keegan. The store detective was at her elbow.

In court, Rosie's evidence was crucial in getting a conviction. When she counted the money in front of Nancy Blackmore and the store detective there was three hundred and sixty pounds whereas four hundred had been put into it in the presence of the detective. Further the prosecution showed that Nancy Blackmore had a criminal record going back years. She was given a three months jail sentence in Pentonvil prison which was increased to six months after she threatened she'd "come looking for" Rosie when she got out. The whole experience was so traumatic for Rosie that her health broke down, and she was advised by her doctor to take time off work and go home to Ireland. Her bags were packed on the Friday night that she reluctantly went with a friend to an "Irish Nite Out" It was at "The Angel" in Hammersmith. Three famous Kilkenny musicians were on stage that night: Billy Tyrrell on Saxophone, Joe Connick on Piano and Harry Tunstan on Drums. She would remember that night all the days of her life. It was there she met the man who would change the whole course of her life. His name was Pat Hunt. When she got back to her lodgings she unpacked her bags and wrote a cheerful letter to her mother. Her health had improved overnight. Pat became the be-all and end-all of her existence. But she never dared to tell him of her growing fears for Nancy Blackmore's release. As the months went by her happiness with Pat flowered but her anxiety was likewise on the increase. Her health once again went into decline.

A week before her tormentor was set free she collapsed and was taken to hospital. She knew she had to get away. But she couldn't bring herself to tell Pat about Nancy Blackmore and her threat. She was afraid he would think her silly. She was afraid of loosing him. And now she was becoming seriously ill. But Pat could not understand her leaving him.

"Why can't you convalesce here in London? The best doctors and the finest hospitals in the world are here".

"But I've got asthma Pat. I need the pure air of Ireland, not the smoke and smog of London." And there was something else that she desperately wanted to tell him but she wasn't sure about it. Her ill health had thrown all her natural bodily functions into confusion.

"I suppose if you are determined to go, there's nothing I can do about it", he said on the way to Euston Station.

"I'll write as soon as I get home Pat. Be sure to answer my letters".

THE POPPY

Allen Hunt and Nancy Blackmore were waiting for Rosalie Taylor in the lounge bar at The Poppy on the Edgware Road. Matt Ryan, the middle aged red faced barman had told Rosalie that two people were waiting to see her downstairs. Allen found the aroma of hot coffee, wax polish and frothy beer almost breathtaking. The horse-shoe shaped counter stood four feet high and measured about fifty feet around. Jars of pickled onions and hard boiled eggs beside bowls of salted peanuts were placed haphazardly along the counter top. And two trays, one at each end of the horse-shoe had side plates and steel knives and forks. The walls were clad with heavily embossed gold and crimson paper. And from the cream coloured ceiling a huge propeller-like fan swished intermittently. It reminded Allen of the great wooden propeller which hung in the Motor Company at John Street Kilkenny. It was the main source of power in Godwin Swifts first 'Aerial Chariot".

Twenty five or thirty people sat at tables. Most of them were reading in near silence except for the occasional rasp of crisp newspaper pages being turned and the alternate swish of the fan. The quietude contrasted strangely with the loud buzz of conversation that came across over the seven foot cedarwood partition from the public bar.

"Would you like something to drink while you're waiting?" Matt Ryan asked.

"Not for me thanks but perhaps Nancy would?"

"Why not, I'll have a G & T with a slice of lemon. 'Gordons' will be fine Matt". He stood there looking at her. "I thought I recognised you. You're Pat Hunts girl and this can only be Pats brother. You're a dead ringer for him", and he gave Allen his hand. "I'm Matt Ryan, Cork".

"And I'm Allen. Nice to meet you Matt." Allen reached to pay for the drink.

"That's all right – it is on the house." There was a crashing of noise from the public bar as someone knocked over a couple of glasses. "Leave it Paddy, I'll get it. You have enough taken. Go home and sleep it off". The barman's voice told the story. Matt Ryan was grinning. "It gets a bit tough in there be-times. Nothing you couldn't handle Allen. It's as easy as knocking snow off a rope". He winked and moved away like a well oiled machine.

"They're a different bloody breed", she said, indicating the public bar.

"They have to live too."

"They're just riffraff," she said sarcastically. "Thugs and bums".

"That may be your opinion but it's certainly not mine". He wasn't going to be brow-beaten by her. He was his own man. Something close to a sneer played about her mouth, then disappeared.

"Forget it, – we're friends for Christ's sake – almost family."

There was a disconcerting pause.

"She's taking her bloody time in coming to see us", she said. Just then Allen caught sight of someone peering at them through the slit of a slightly open door at the back of the lounge.

"We are being sized up".

"Who? Where?!

"The door to your right. Don't look." But she did and saw the shadow move behind the door. "There's something going on here" she said. "More than meets the eye".

It was ten minutes later when a tall silver haired seventy year old man came through the door. You could tell that he had once been a dashing virile specimen of manhood.

"So sorry about that. My wife had a little turn just then. I'll take over from here. Would you like something to drink?" he addressed himself to Allen.

"I'll have a G & T with a slice of lemon" she said. He acknowledged her request with a nod and turned to Allen.

"I'll have a glass of beer, please."

BILL TAYLOR

"Fine, we'll sit over here, then".

Matt Ryan was at the table and had the chairs pulled out before they reached it. Bill Taylor was smiling broadly. "That's service for you", and he gave Matt the order.

"So you are the young man who is interested in the job!"

""Yes Sir I am."

"And you have just arrived over from Ireland – Kilkenny City I am told"

"Have you been to Kilkenny, Sir?"

"Yes I have been. You could say I earned by bread there for a time."

"What did you work at?"

"I was a soldier. As a young Lieutenant in the British Army. I was there when we handed Kilkenny Army Barracks over the Irish Provisional Government forces in 1922."

"Did you see much action in Kilkenny"

"There were but a handful of die-hards in the city but they kept us busy".

"That's good", Allen said and they both laughed.

"I have references from the P.P. and former employer." He handed over the papers and Bill Taylor gave them a cursory glance. "These are first class".

"And his brother is head barman at "The Champion". I believe Mrs. Taylor knows Pat", she cut across them.

"Quite so", he said without looking at her. "It makes it that much easier to say the job is yours young man."

"Thank you kindly Sir".

"You will be living-in, paid union rates and work union hours. My wife Rosalie and I are merely doing relief work here. The Governor Mike O'Hara will be back next week from Ireland, you will need a day to settle in. Bring your gear over tonight or tomorrow – which ever suits you. You can start Monday morning at 10 a.m. in the Public bar. Matt Ryan will show you the ropes." He got on his feet gave a nod, 'cheerio' and was gone.

Allen thought it would be better to take his suitcase over to 'The Poppy' on the night rather than wait for the morrow. He felt elated about landing the job, but he knew in his heart he was trading on his brothers reputation. "That's what brothers are for", Pat had said. But he would have to make his own way, for better or worse.

He took his suitcase from behind the counter at 'The Champion'. Pat was tending bar.

"Do you know how to get there on your own?"

"I'll take the District Line from Bayswater to Paddington and on to the Edgware Road".

"You're learning fast brother. Matt Ryan had better watch-out if he's to remain head barman at 'The Poppy'," said Pat smiling.

As Allen Hunt climbed the back stairs he surprised a little girl playing with her doll on the top step. Frightened by his sudden appearance she dropped the doll and it tumbled down at his feet. "What's your name?" he asked as he returned the doll. She ran to where another stairs went up to the second floor, calling out in a clear voice as she went: "Patricia, Patricia, Patricia."

PATRICIA, PLAYING WITH HER DOLL
BY SEAN KENNY

26

IVOR DAVIES

Halfway down the narrow corridor to his right Allen heard a door open and saw a tall thirty year old man step out and stand in the passage. He was smiling broadly and said: "I thought I heard someone. You must be the new recruit Matt Ryan spoke of. I'm Ivor Davies." He extended a hand. "I'm in charge in the Lounge Bar of 'The Poppy', for my sins." His grip was like a clamp and his hands were large and muscular which surprised Allen because the man's frame was almost skinny and his face though full of vitality was near fleshless. "I'll take that", he said and without hesitating he took the big suitcase from Allen and walked into the room. Over his shoulder he spoke in his sing-song Welsh accent, with the last word in each sentence a few octaves above the rest. "You're well on your way now lad to making your first million". He threw the suitcase on the bed in a corner of the room. "What in Christ's name do ya have in it, the kitchen sink?" He laughed.

"Mostly books".

"Better than guns"

"I'm Allen Hunt, over from Ireland".

"I know. You're welcome. Any relation of Pat's is alright with me. I know you are a "Kilkenny Cat". Allen looked at him curiously. How could a Welshman be so intimate with the traditional story concerning the natives of Kilkenny? "And I attended by invitation, last years A.G.M of the Kilkenny Men's Association at "The Swan" in Stockwell, – Tim Walsh's place.

That man's name conjured up memories. Like a clarion call summoning sleeping troops. The name Tim Walsh surfaced into Allen's thinking. He instantly recalled how his brother had written home in praise of that staunch Kilkenny man who was regarded by many job seeking and down-at-heel Kilkennyites, as a latter day Saint Christopher.

"I trust you won't mind me asking Ivor, but what is your connection with the "Kilkenny Men's Association?"

"It's no secret Allen, I'm engaged to a Kilkenny girl".

"Congratulations. I wonder if I might know her".

"Your brother Pat does. Her name is Eileen Murphy. She's from Kilkenny City.

"It doesn't ring a bell. That's not to say I don't know her".

"You'll meet her soon enough. I'm sure you realise that Bill Taylor and his wife Rosalie are only here while Mike O'Hara and his wife are away on holidays."

"Yes I do. He seems to be a nice fellow. I didn't get to meet his wife though".

"That was her little girl that you met on the stairs. Patricia, that's Irish isn't it?"

"Yes, it's the female version of Patrick, or Pat."

EPISODE FOUR

WHO HAS BEEN SLEEPING IN MY BED
TO GO AND MISS HIM OR STAY AND MEET HIM
MYSTERY WOMAN

WHO HAS BEEN SLEEPING IN MY BED

"That's your doss over there Allen, and this one is mine". Ivor Davies sat upright on the side of his bed in "The Poppy", pointing at the single bed that was neatly dressed in a yellow and brown candlewick spread in the corner. Allen Hunt's suitcase lay on top of it where Ivor had thrown it.

"The last man to sleep in that bed is doing five years in Wormwood Scrubs."

"O yeah, and he had scabies and a wooden leg as well. Why don't you pull the other one?"

"It's no joke lad. He was lifted for possession of a loaded revolver. Billy McNeill was his name. He was a Gaelic speaker and came from Connemara. Not much older than yourself, Allen. He was taken out of here at seven one morning by two policemen and a detective. A few days later he was tried at the Old Bailey and sentenced to five years for membership of the Provisional IRA."

Allen bit his bottom lip "Was that the reason you said; 'better than guns' when I told you it was books that I had in the suitcase a moment ago?"

"Something like that, lad. I was real sorry for Billy. He seemed like a nice bloke, but he was a fool for himself. Once in, there's no way out, that's I.R.A. policy."

Allen looked intently at Ivor, like a mason might examine a corner-stone, searching for a structural fault. And Ivor felt the scrutiny of his gaze but didn't flinch. Instead, he took out a twenty packet of 'Senior Service' cigarettes and was soon blowing expanding smoke rings towards the ceiling.

Allen walked to the window next his bed. Damask cotton curtains hung half open from a bamboo pole. They almost touched the faded orange and green linoleum that covered the floor. With both hands he pulled the curtains apart "Let there be light", Allen said as he looked wide-eyed out onto the jam-packed Edgware Road.

Throngs of people were travelling on foot towards the underground tube station while a similar number were sieving through them in the direction of Marylebone. With eyes wide open and mouths shut tight, they showed no signs of recognition, nor made any attempts to communicate. They came and they went, wave upon wave, a tide of resolute humanity that never seemed to wane. And always their feet rising and falling like pistons and their unceasing multitudinous thoughts whirling in unseen eddies about their heads.

"Where in the name of God are they all hurrying to?"

"Nobody knows but themselves."

"How long have you worked at The Poppy, Ivor?"

"Since the first day I arrived in London, four years ago next September."

"I was a textile worker myself back home, – in a factory called Greenvale Woolen Mills. But when some far Eastern countries got a foothold in the textile industry and set up their infamous 'Sweat Shops'. That was the death knell for the centuries old, Irish Mills."

"I worked down the mines, did I. Aye, when a lad of fourteen, went down with Dada and my two bothers Ianto and Cedric. Ianto lost his nerve after a roof fell-in in forty five – we had to dig him out. Me I got my two lungs crocked after ten years cutting at the coalface. I was diagnosed as a victim of 'Silicoses'. It's known as miners T.B." Allen looked at him with surprise and apprehension. "Do you mean tuberculosis? Should you be smoking then?"

Ivor smiled and blew the biggest smoke ring that Allen had ever seen, "of course I shouldn't smoke – no one should. But there's no need to worry, it's not contagious. Silicoses is an industrial disease."

"What part of Wales do you come from Ivor?"

"Glamorganshire, – it's in the south-east and lies between Brecknock and the Bristol Channel. My people come from the Rhondda Valley region. It's a bleak landscape that's pockmarked with coal pits and slagheaps and capped by bare mountains. Yet for all it's grime and roughness 'tis a beautiful place."

"Have you ever gone back?"

"No. Dada and Mama are both dead."

"You have my sympathy."

"And you have my thanks".

IVOR DAVIES BLOWING SMOKE RINGS
BY SEAN KENNY

"What's it like working in the public bar here in 'The Poppy'?"

"It's tough enough at times. But if you're a brother of Pat Hunt, I reckon you can take care of yourself. In any event you'll have the best barman in London at your elbow. They don't come any better than Matt Ryan."

Ivor was grinning; "it just occurred to me that you'll be alright once you've learned when to duck."

"As bad as that is it? Maybe I should take boxing lessons or join a Judo club?"

Ivor got serious. "Listen Allen, that was only a joke." He got to his feet, straightened his tie and combed his thick shock of brown hair.

"I'm due back on in the lounge bar in a few minutes. Nice talking to you. Best of luck." See you soon."

TO GO AND MISS HIM OR STAY AND MEET HIM

"And you are quite sure it was she?" Bill Taylor sat at breakfast with his wife Rosie, (whom he affectionately called Rosalie) and her three year old daughter Patricia. Bill and Rosie were having boiled eggs, tea and toast with 'Olde English' marmalade. Patricia sat between them wielding a large table spoon over a bowl of steaming porridge which she kept hitting like an overanxious learner might hammer out her first notes on a xylophone.

"Please eat your porridge Patricia and stop behaving like a little monkey." Patricia began to sulk. "Oh yes it was her alright. I'd know her skin on a bush."

Bill Taylor smiled, took the spoon from Patricia and began feeding her.

"I could never forget that arrogant face, those piercing eyes and that phony English accent."

Rosie's eyes were fixed on the pot of marmalade with its colourfully painted label: the black iron pot suspended over the open fire. The cat sitting on its hunkers, soaking up the heat – peace and tranquility. It reminded her of her childhood on holidays in her grandmother's house in west Cork.

"Do you think it might be nice if we were to go over to Ireland for a few weeks when Mike and Mary O'Hara return from their holidays, dear? It would do Patricia a world of good, don't you think?"

Rosie wondered if Bill had been reading her thoughts. She hoped not. He would be bitterly disappointed if he were to apprehend them now. And he was always so considerate, so kind. She knew there was nothing he wouldn't do for herself and Patricia, and yet, in the depths of her soul she yearned to see another, to meet with him, to speak with him, to be with him, once more, – for the heart is a merciless hunter. Bill Taylor wiped Patricia's mouth with a napkin and gave her a table spoon. The bowl was empty except for a few blobs of milk which Patricia began to poke at with her spoon. "At least one of us is eating breakfast. Shall I clear the table Rosalie. You seem to be done?"

"Yes, I think you are right. A few weeks in Ireland will do us all good. I never want to meet that horrible woman again. But what worries me is what's going to become of Pat Hunt by the time she has finished with him. She'll destroy him Bill. She'll bring him to his knees or worse. He doesn't deserve that"

"Could it be that he knows who you are?"

"Not a chance. After all he hasn't seen me in years and has only heard of me as Rosalie Taylor and not Rosie Keegan."

"Yes, but wasn't it strange that it was she who came with Allen for the trainee barman's job and not his brother Pat? "

Her catlike curiosity was roused from the moment I innocently said on the phone that I had known Pat Hunt. She won't rest now until she has discovered who I am and if I might be a threat to her plans. No matter what the outcome, Pat must be told she is a convicted vicious criminal and a jailbird."

"But how do you suppose he should be told and by whom?"

MYSTERY WOMAN

"Isn't that really something; he's been in London one half day and already he knows how to use the Underground." Pat Hunt wore a grin like the bottom half of a circle.

"He's a sharp one alright – I'll grant you that. Maybe too sharp."

"What's that supposed to mean?" Pats forehead became a river of wrinkles that flowed into a frown, puncturing his broad smile.

"He picks up on everything. He event caught the mysterious Mrs. Taylor spying on us from behind a half closed door at 'The Poppy'. The one who told me on the phone she knew you. I can't put a face on that friggin voice, but I know that whinging tone from somewhere. There's something hostile about it."

"How can you be sure that the person you saw watching from behind the door was one and the same that you heard on the phone?"

""I could feel it in my guts. There's something going on here that needs close watching – something weird and underhanded."

"Your imagination is running away with you. The next thing you'll be saying is that this mysterious Mrs. Taylor and me are having a secret affair!"

"Then how does she know you for Christ's sake? How? She told me she knows you. She told her husband she knows you and she told Allen she knows you. It seems you are the only one in this equation she hasn't told. Of course there would be no reason for her to tell you if the two of you were having an affair. It could well be to her you've been going on your nights off."

Pat was incredulous. He stood there stiff as a plank and seething with rage. He was staring at her but couldn't see her through the blood-shot blinding fury inside his head. "I can't believe I'm hearing this." His voice cracked with passion.

"If I don't get out of here now, I won't be accountable for what might happen." So saying, Pat Hunt palmed open the swing doors out of the lounge at 'The Champion' and walked out onto the Bayswater Road. He turned left and walked a hundred yards to the pedestrian crossing. A small bundle of people stood anxiously watching the signal on the other side. Pat stared at the angry red light; 'DON'T WALK'. In a second it turned green; 'WALK NOW'. On the other side of the road he went left and walked in double quick time to Kensington Gardens, where he sat anxiously looking into the Round Pond.

Luke Brannigan sat straight as a plumb-line in an antique cedar-wood chair behind his cedar-wood desk. The room measured fifteen feet by twelve and the ceiling capped it, nine feet above the floor. A bookcase measuring seven feet by six and made of similar wood was packed with books of General Knowledge, Ancient History, National Geographics, Old Masters and Modern Classics. Standing on its own projecting pedestal outside the case was a leather bound copy of The Jerusalem Bible. Beside that hung a three foot by two detailed map of Ireland, showing the six Northern counties separated by a thick border line that resembled a barbed wire fence more than perimeter lines. The map was set in a brass frame that was screwed to the wall. Behind that map, a miniature safe was built into the wall. Its location was known to two men, as was its combination. Next to the map of Ireland hung an Ordinance map of Greater London, showing: Bus Routes, Main Line Stations, Underground Stations, Hotels, Theatres, Churches, Cinemas, Embassies and Government Departments. On the other side of the room two pale blue filing cabinets stood side by side and wide as the back of a bus. Under the side window lay a Morocco covered Chaise-longue and beside it an armchair of the same French period was similarly upholstered.

The green shaded desk lamp made of ornamental brass was lighting and shining directly down on a letter from the Development and Environmental Department, Westminster. The auspicious communication was addressed to: Brannigan and Boland, Building Contractors, 9 & 10 Lamb Street, Spitalfields, London.

Luke Brannigan removed his reading glasses and proceeded to polish them vigorously with a snow-white starched handkerchief. He looked hard at his foreman and junior partner Jack Boland, first through the left lenses, then through the right one. Jack didn't bat an eye lid but looked Luke straight in the face.

"We got the contract Jack. We are up there with the best of them now." He took a deep breath and went on: "But can anyone tell me who in God's name gave the loaded revolver to young Billy McNeill?"

EPISODE FIVE

EARLY MORNING RUSH
ANY OLD SOUVENIR OF LOVE
BROTHERS IN DEED

EARLY MORNING RUSH

Allen Hunt wore a well-ironed duckegg-blue shirt with flowing sleeves buttoned at the wrists. Under his seventeen-inch collar, a navy-blue paisley tie was perfectly fashioned into a Windsor knot, with the tip of the wide front petal touching his navel. His black worsted pants with a thirty four-inch waist was belted with a Sheffield buckle on japanned leather. There was a crease down the front of the thirty two-inch legs, sharp enough to shave the beard of Absolom. Standing erect he stood six feet tall in his well-polished Padmore and Barnes all leather black Moccasin shoes.

Allen was set like a coiled trap, ready to spring into action. He contemplated his surroundings in the public bar. Straight in front of him and about twenty feet from the bar counter an eight feet by six plate glass window looked out onto the Edgeware Road. Reading from right to left, letters reversed, the name of the establishment was painted across the middle, in gold trimmed with black; 'The Poppy'. Beneath it, near the bottom, the name of the Brewery that owned the premises was in reduced letters; A Whitbread House. The window glistened like a signalling mirror in the sun. It was the trademark of Matt Ryan, who according to Ivor Davies, was the best barman in London.

Matt, now in his forty ninth year was powerfully built. His shoulders were wide and thick set and his hands were large like spoon shaped oars. His eyes manifested his humanity and good humour as much as the square jaw and dimpled chin professed his manliness. But despite his weight and strength, his speed and dexterity were legend.

When Matt Ryan saw Allen Hunt look at his watch he did likewise. "It's ten twenty two," he said. "Eight minutes to opening time, Allen". He looked all around the public bar. "The shelves are stocked, the glasses steamed and polished and the pumps are primed. We're in ship shape lad."

Allen smiled nervously like a shy man going on a blind date. To get to know by name, all the bottled beers and stouts and their different prices seemed like a job for a memory man, just then. Matt rubbed his huge hands together like a pipe smoker crushing slivers of cut plug-tobacco.

"This is the inside story of opening time at "The Poppy", Allen. When I open the front doors there will be a stampede of ten or twelve men to get to the counter. They will be boisterous and even threatening, especially when they see you are new. They'll test you to see how far you'll let them go. Keep a cool head and be firm. All of these men will have had several drinks already. They are early morning drinkers who will have come from a pub across the road called "The Red Lion". It's a speak-easy Cider house. They sell 'Scrumpy', and it's lethal. It's a raw alcohol that burns your guts. They come in here to cool down. Don't serve them anything other than Stout and Mild or Mild and Bitter. Remember Allen, if any of them get out of hand, show them the door."

ANY OLD SOUVENIR OF LOVE

Pat Hunt felt exasperated, but he had begun to gather his thoughts about him and was reasoning things out. Because he had a practical mind he was able to assemble all the whys and wherefores of his present predicament.

He sat now on one of the park benches close to the Round Pond in Kensington Gardens. A few children had gathered with their mothers or Nannies and were triumphantly sailing their toy boats on the sky-grey waters around the statue of Peter Pan. His mind lingered for a while on the story of the type of person who never grows up. Could there be a connection here? He smiled to himself. One never knows.

He had been too trusting in his dealings with others, especially with Nancy Blackmore, his fiancé. How quick she was to accuse him of an extramural affair. And he knew from experience that those who are themselves capable of doing the deed are the first to accuse others of it. Also he saw a side of her that he had never seen before; jealousy with violence. In one fiery revelation the cat had shown its teeth and claws. With hindsight he could see that what had happened was inevitable. It was she who had engineered their engagement. She had taken him to a jewellers shop at Earls Court on the pretence of having her watch strap repaired. But he ended up buying her an engagement ring for almost two hundred pounds. And he knew now that he had never really loved her. She had exercised some kind of come-hither over him and he was fascinated by her physical presence. All that would end now, – end in pain and recriminations. So be it. It was sad.

The sorrowing heart unable to bear the pain of parting, will search through the attic of the memory for any old souvenir of love that might refresh and renew it. "What ever became of Rosie Keegan?", Pat Hunt asked himself.

She had resurrected herself in his memory, for she had been worrying about him long and hard. "Is she dead or alive? I wonder did she marry and raise a family? Is she still living in Ireland or did she return to London? God it would be great to see her again. But I don't suppose I ever will." Pat didn't believe in mental telepathy, he was too practical for that, but Rosie Taylor alias Rosie Keegan, did.

Nancy Blackmore sat drinking a large gin and tonic in a chic bar off the Edgeware Road on Upper Berkeley Street. It was close to the Heinz Gallery, but she wouldn't be visiting there, – it wasn't her style. For hours she had been drinking and pondering over how she might get the information she was looking for. She hit on a plan and went to the public phone which was in a wooden kiosk inside the front door. She lifted the phone and dialled the appropriate number. The phone was ringing at the other end. She slid a diamond shaped lozenge into her mouth to conseal her identity. The phone rang once, twice, three times and a mans voice answered:

"Hello, this is "The Poppy", a Whitbread house. How can I help you?"

"Could I talk to Mrs. Rosie Taylor?"

"Who is calling please?"

"I'm an old school pal of Rosie's. We haven't met for years."

"Would you hold for a moment?" "Rosalie, you are wanted on the phone by a lady who says she is an old school pal of yours."

"That's strange – I wonder who it can be? Hello, who is calling please? My husband didn't catch your name."

"I just hope I've got the right person. I don't want to make a nuisance of myself. You are Rosie Keegan aren't you?"

"Yes I am – and you are?" Nancy Blackmore left down the phone. She was grinning like the evil matrons did when gathered around the guillotine to witness murder during the French Revolution.

Rosie looked puzzled. "The line went dead, Bill. Either that or the phone was put down in a hurry. She said the latter as if to herself. "Did she give you her name?" "No. Her only reason for ringing was to discover my identity. I see that now. If you ask me it was none other than the infamous Nancy Blackmore"

Rosie shuddered and left down the phone. Then she called Patricia to her and lifted her up into her arms. Bill Taylor looked at the two of them, his face covered with concern. The needle in the temperature gauge inside his head had suddenly gone into the red.

BROTHERS IN DEED

Luke Brannigan looked hard at Jack Boland and was waiting for an answer to his question which was: Who in the name of God had given a loaded revolver to young Billy McNeill?

"The entire matter is under investigation. I have my suspicions but I don't wish to say anymore for the present?"

"Right, I'll leave it with you, then. Down to business so. Do you think we might have any problems getting the financial backing to build those five hundred houses? And how about manpower and equipment?"

"I think the financial backing will be easy to secure once we produce this communication from the Development Department Westminster. The equipment will follow on the heels of the Bank Draft and as regards labour; if we give them a little over the odds they'll flock to us. And we can always let out a little subcontracting to friends that we can depend upon."

"My sentiments entirely Jack. You're as good as a tonic. But there's a mountain of work to be done with the estimates and the plans. 'Tis like the good Lord said, "we must earn our bread by the sweat of our brow." Genesis, Chapter 3 Verse 19."

Jack shook his head and smiled.

Luke Brannigan and Jack Boland were like brothers, though not physically so. In fact they had once been brothers, – brothers-in-law. Luke had been married to Jack's sister and had lost her to breast cancer some years earlier. Although he was only in his middle thirties at the time of the bereavement, he never remarried. Neither did he once go out with another woman in all of those eleven years. Perhaps if there had been children he might have remarried to give them a mother, but that was not the case.

Three years earlier Luke and Jack were working for McAlpine on a massive shopping development in Piccadilly. The work was running behind schedule so things were being rushed. As a result some difficulties had arisen concerning the laying of sewage pipes. The levels were all wrong. The company engineer with the works foreman and Jack Boland went down in the twenty-foot cutting to remedy the fault. Luke Brannigan was on the surface and had gone to the storeman to collect some lagging equipment. When he came back he instantly saw the shuttering had shifted, and slid further in front of his very eyes. Luke went as close to the edge as he dared and called out in a loud, steady and authoritative voice: "Come up out of the cutting NOW. The shuttering has shifted and is near collapse. Come up now in God's Name."

LUKE BRANNIGAN SHREWD BUT SINCERE
BY SEAN KENNY

There was no mistaking the urgency and sincerity in his voice. The three men dropped what tools they had in hand and began to climb the ladder quickly but without panic. The foreman who was nearest came up first. Next the engineer and as Jack Boland put his foot on the ladder, the shuttering groaned and shifted again. Luke had spotted a loose rope from a hoist lying on a makeshift table a few feet behind him. Like lightening he grabbed it and slung the ringed end down into the grasping hands of Jack.

"Hold on to that for dear life," he shouted as the shuttering slipped down further. The two saved men got on the rope with Luke, and pulled with might and main, as the sides began falling in. They could see only his head and shoulders and then his arms above his head, holding on, – holding on in terrible desperation. As the cutting caved in and the shuttering went crashing down the twenty-foot vertical drop, the siren was sounded and the workers came running to help in any way they could.

Had it not been for the alertness, promptitude and calm display of courage by Luke Brannigan the life of Jack Boland would most certainly have been lost. In fact it was readily believed that all three men would have been buried alive under the enormously crushing weight of the shuttering and the very many tons of earth.

With the help of half a dozen powerful men, Jack was lifted up from under the earth that covered his lower body. Though half unconscious he still held onto the rope with a grip like a vice. The ambulance had arrived and the stretcher was brought over.

"Are you alright old son?" Luke asked Jack as they carried him to the ambulance. He did not expect him to reply.

"I'm alive thanks to you Luke. I owe you my life, old friend."

Jack's injuries were serious but were not permanent. But he was unable to work for almost a year. McAlpine's paid out a very large sum by way of compensation. Luke went regularly to visit Jack while convalescing and met Jack's sister Elizabeth whom he later married.

EPISODE SIX

LOVE HAS NO TETHERS
A TETE-A-TETE WITH TART
A REVELATION: CAUGHT ON THE REBOUND
INTRODUCED BY PAT

LOVE HAS NO TETHERS

"When a woman makes up her mind, rightly or wrongly, to do something, neither God nor the Devil could hunt it out of her head until she sees it through" said Matt Ryan to Ivor Davies. Both men were finishing breakfast in the staff dining room at 'The Poppy' on the Edgware Road.

"You've just made that up, Matt – haven't you? I'm right is it. You should come to preach in our Chapel some day". Ivor burst out laughing. That's an Irish yarn if I ever heard one". Matt could only smile at the whole-heartedness of Ivor's laughter.

The truth was that he was trying to put Ivor on his guard about the lewd goings on of a certain young lady sitting on the throne of Ivors affections. He would have to be told, but this wasn't the time nor the place.

On the top floor in the same house Rosie and Bill Taylor were reading in the sitting room of the living quarters. Rosie's three year old daughter Patricia was sitting on the floor with crayons and a colouring book, making apples blue and bananas black. Bill was engrossed in a war magazine. The feature story with pictures was 'The Battle of Britain'. Douglas Bader waved at him from a photo as he stood on two artificial legs beside his fighter aeroplane. The caption read: 'Reach for the Sky'. Bill was in his element studying the art of war.

Rosie was browsing through a periodical publication called Women to Day. She had just finished reading an article by the socialite and feminist writer Dorothy Sawyers, with the long-winded questioning title: 'Was there ever a One Man Woman?'

And the well-informed feminist began her story with a one-word sentence: Never. Rosie felt threatened by the article but wouldn't admit it even to herself, even though she had already decided on a course of action that wasn't a thousand miles away from Ms. Sawyer's erroneous conceptions.

"I was just thinking, Bill, it might be a good idea if you were to go over to Knightsbridge and check all is well with the house. And while you're at it collect the post. I'm expecting a letter from Ireland."

"But you had a letter two days before we left, dear."

"Never mind that Bill. Please go over and see that everything is all right – no break-ins, or burst pipes. I mean you never can tell."

"When shall I go dear?"

"After lunch will be fine, love."

A TETE-A-TETE WITH TART

Allen Hunt arrived at 'The Poppy' at approximately 2.00 p.m. He had been to Madame Tussaud's and the London Planetarium on the Marylebone Road. He was aesthetic about what he had seen, especially the Planetarium. It was a breath- taking experience to see images of the celestial bodies projected upon the vast dome and witness their relative paths and speeds through the night sky. It was pure magic. Wouldn't it be brilliant to meet and speak with the genius who had thought out and constructed the mind-boggling adventure. He was delighted to be in London.

Allen turned the key in the side door and entered the long red tiled hallway leading to the stairs. He folded the Daily Mirror into a baton and began climbing the red and blue linoleum covered stairs.

Suddenly he became aware there was someone standing on the first landing. It was Rosie Taylor and she was holding her daughter Patricia in her arms.

"Is that you Allen? I was about to take Patricia next door to the Bijou for some 'Lemmons Pure Sweets."

"I can do that for you Mrs. Taylor. Stay right where you are." Allen turned and was walking towards the door when Rosie shouted after him: "Here's the money Allen," and she held up a purse. Allen just waved his hand above his head without turning. The Bijou was a sweet and fruit shop, two doors down from 'The Poppy'. Although he didn't have much money, yet he bought a little box of Lemmons Pure Sweets for three shillings and sixpence. "O but you shouldn't have gone to such expense Allen. It's really too much." She was genuinely concerned and surprised. He was Pat Hunt's brother for certain – generous to a fault. And he looked so much like him. His voice, his movements and his captivating smile.

BIG BEN
BY SEAN KENNY

"Why don't you come upstairs and I'll make us a cup of tea. There's an apple tart made with Irish pippins, fresh from the bakery."

"It's very kind of you but there is something that I was hoping to do before going on duty this afternoon."

"But you've got loads of time Allen. You won't be going on duty until 4.00 p.m." She blushed, having said it.

Allen was surprised. She must have familiarised herself with the roster. "We promise not to eat him, only the tart. Isn't that so Patricia?" Patricia was busy biting the plastic cover off the box of sweets, like a puppy gnawing at its first lead."

"I thank you for your kind invitation Mrs. Taylor. I'd be delighted."

"Make yourself comfortable while I put on the kettle. Over here they say; I'll put on kettle. They don't seem to need the definite article."

"But they do need the kettle, I hope."

They both laughed and Patricia joined in because Allen had taken off the plastic and opened the box of sweets.

"How well, may I ask, did you know Pat?" It seemed the right thing to say, as he believed it was because of his brother that she had invited him upstairs.

"O, very well. We went out together for quite some time. We truly had some great times," and her voice became almost inaudible; "truly wonderful times." Then she reached out for Patricia and gave her a hug.

"How long ago was that?" She began to fidget and combed Patricia's hair with her fingers.

"O about four years ago, – when we were all young – young and foolish, I suppose one could say. How do you like the apple tart?"

"It's very nice, – lovely, thanks".

There was an awkward pause and Allen offered his hand to Patricia. She ran to him and stood close by him with eyes sparkling like diamonds against black satin.

"There's something I wanted to talk to you about. What do you think of Nancy Blackmore, Allen?"

"I was right", Allen said to himself, "here it comes – the burning question."

"You couldn't possibly know this but she has a criminal record and has done time in Pentonville Prison. I helped to send her there. She is dangerous."

"It doesn't surprise me, but does Pat know all this?"

"No. It's Pat I'm worried about. She'll destroy him Allen, if he doesn't get away from her, – before it is too late."

Her eyes were swimming in tears, – tears that burst their banks and flowed sadly down the contours of her sorrowful face.

Allen offered her his handkerchief which she accepted with a brief smile that surfaced and sunk back again, overcome by sobbing.

"What's to be done, Allen?"

"I don't really know but I'll broach the subject with Pat, carefully and play-it-by-ear after that."

"What beats me is, how did she fool Pat?"

"She probably caught him on the rebound."

A REVELATION: CAUGHT ON THE REBOUND

As he walked out of Kensington Gardens, Pat Hunt's step was lighter. He had left all his indecision and self-pity behind him on a park bench near the Round Pond. By now he hoped those murky thoughts had jumped in and drowned themselves in the calm clear waters of the artificial lake. He had decided once and for all, that Nancy Blackmore was more trouble than she was worth. It wasn't the first time he had misgivings about her conduct. He had covered for her on many occasions. There was her absenteeism, drinking on the job and shortages in the 'Till'. And there were other indiscretions of a dubious nature, which he had pushed into his subconscious, not wanting to confront them. But all that was finished now. Suddenly he stopped walking along the footpath on the Bayswater Road. "Good Christ!" he said aloud. "I was caught on the rebound after Rosie Keegan." Two women close to him, elbowed each other and sniggered. Pat neither saw nor heard them, but began walking again, back to "The Champion".

Nancy Blackmore walked sheepishly towards Pat as he went behind the bar.

"Pat I just want to say sorry. We can talk this over, can't we – like we always do?"

"Not this time Nancy. We're all washed up. There's nothing left to work on". He looked at her hand. She wasn't wearing her engagement ring. "And I'll have my ring back too if you please."

"You bloody bastard." Nancy Blackmore was frothing at the mouth. Her whole appearance had altered until she looked more like a mad-woman than a rational human being.

"Get this straight mister, – you haven't heard the last of me, – and I lost the fn ring." She put on her jacket saying: "I'll be back later with company. Have my cards and money ready."

INTRODUCED BY PAT

Allen stepped into the lounge bar at "The Champion", on Bayswater Road. He stood for a moment and looked all around like a hawk scanning the terrain. Fully informed he moved smoothly towards the bar counter and ordered a pint of "Best Bitter" from a barmaid who was obviously new to the game. She became flustered and filled the glass with froth. "Sorry Pat," she said, "I'll get it right this time."

"Not if you keep calling me Pat," Allen said while nodding in the direction of where his brother Pat was sitting at a table, in lively conversation with a customer. She looked from Allen to Pat and back again.

"You're twins, for heavens sake!"

"No we're not, – just brothers." He knew that Pat had seen him the moment he darkened the door. The man with whom he was speaking looked across at Allen, smiled, and nodded briefly. Pat was on his feet and walking toward Allen. His face was fixed in a smile but his eyes couldn't hide the sadness beneath. Life is truly paradoxical, Allen thought. He knows he is better off without her and bad and all that she was, he still misses her.

"Well old son, its good to see you. I'm told you're fitting in at "The Poppy"' like a three speed sprocket on a racing bike."

"I'm doing alright. How are you?"

"Fine thanks. There's someone over here who would like to meet you. He's an engineer in the building business."

"But why would he want to meet me? I don't know the man from Adam, nor he, me."

"He knows more about you than you might think, brother. Come on over and meet the man."

Allen followed Pat across the Lounge, like Achilles on the heels on Phoenix, doing as he was told.

The man at the table stood up as they approached. He was about forty-five years of age and of medium build. He had an oval face with a tight mouth that told of one who knew, but never blabbed. His fair hair was turning grey and receding at the temples. When Pat introduced him to Allen, his pale blue eyes lit up with intelligence.

"Allen, this is Jack Boland, a good friend. Jack, this is my brother Allen." They shook hands and sat down together.

EPISODE SEVEN

A LITERARY INVITATION
PEGGY O'SHEA GOES SEARCHING FOR ALLEN HUNT
IVOR DAVIES' FIANCÉE
READING TO EUSTON

A LITERARY INVITATION

Pat Hunt introduced his brother Allen and good friend Jack Boland (Building Contractor) to each other at 'The Champion', on the Bayswater Road. As they shook hands, Allen felt a surge of sincerity and good will flow from his warm grasp. And there was an air of self-confidence about him that made Allen think to himself: This man has been through the mill and is nobodies fool. As he parked his pint of Best Bitter on the lounge table he observed that Jack Bolands weathered countenance was lined with character. "This introduction", he thought again "might well prove to be interesting."

"How are you settling in, in 'Perfidious Alban', – the land of the ancient foe?" Jack's pale blue eyes narrowed like a bow that had shot it's arrow. Even so their lit-up awareness remained turned on and Allen felt he could almost hear him listening for a reply. The question was fired like a shot in the dark. If there was anything there it would hit it. If not, it would return like a boomerang, – nothing lost. Although he felt he was being tested, Allen wasn't sure if Jack Boland was being philosophical or political. Either way his answer would need to be relevant.

"To answer that question adequately I would need to explain where I'm from. That would help put things into perspective. I'm a Kilkenny man first and foremost, as were my parents before me. The city of The Confederation and capital of Ireland from 1642-1649 and recognised as such by Spain, France, Italy, Holland, Sweden and Denmark. The Parliament at Kilkenny made the Laws for the thirty-two counties of Ireland. It raised four armies, one for each province and one of the greatest swordsmen in Europe Owen Roe O'Neill was Commander in Chief. But our own betrayed us and they poisoned Owen Roe on his way to confront Cromwell at Drogheda. Thereby leaving us at the mercy of that tyrant, who massacred our people and plundered our property remembered in that monster's fiendish command:

HOUSES OF THE CONFEDERATION PARLIAMENT OF IRELAND AT KILKENNY
BY SEAN KENNY

'To hell or to Connaught, and all that that employed. We have been an emigrant nation ever since." The Famine in 1846, '47 and '48 brought about a terrible Exodus, in the Coffin Ships to America and light sailing ships to England and the Continent. The population was reduced from eight and a half million souls to five million." Allen paused to take a sip from his pint. Pat was looking at Jack Boland who was intently listening with obvious admiration to Allen's explanatory discourse.

"And yes, I'm settling in very nicely thank you. There's so much to be seen and learned about, here. I'm truly glad that I came over to work in London."

Jack Boland couldn't hide his delight.

"That was most informative Allen and very convincing. You should consider doing a turn at 'Speakers Corner' in Hyde Park, some Sunday afternoon. It's a fantastic platform for democracy. On Sundays the park is always crowded and it is then the famous tub-thumping public orators get up on rostrums and soap boxes to air their views. You'd gather a crowd in no time at all, Allen, – an intelligent, questioning crowd."

Pat was beaming. "There's an idea for you old son. But you wouldn't want to get too political. He pushed his chair back from the table, saying.:

"It's alright for some people, but there are those who must work." Pat was gone when Allen spoke again.

"I'm puzzled by something Pat said earlier, Jack. He said you wanted to meet me and then went on to say, that you knew me better than I thought. How come?"

Jack Boland sized up Allen as though he was looking through him. A secret smile played around the corners of his mouth. It flickered and disappeared as he spoke, slowly and thoughtfully: "Well, Allen, I feel I know something of you, through your poetry and prose."

When Allen gave him a puzzled look, Jack quickly added, "Pat was good enough to let me see some of your writings."

Allen wanted to ask him what he thought of them, but dared not. Instead he took inspiration from a paperback edition of "Sons and Lovers" lying on the table beside Jack's drink. Jack caught Allen's eyes as they rested upon the Novel. "What do you think of D.H. Lawrence?"

"He was a marvelous story teller, a middling poet and a run-of-the-mill dramatist."

Jack sat up straight and brought his top dentures down on his bottom lip. "I would have to say I believe Lawrence to have been one of the most innovative writers of the twentieth century."

"That's a large claim, but I suppose he was, after James Joyce, that is."

"Personally, I thought that sections of Ulysses' were offensive."

"But wasn't "The Rainbow" confiscated and banned because of its obscenity. And where do you leave, 'Lady Chatterley's Lover?"

Jack was visibly enthralled. "A few of us have got together and invited the Monaghan Poet, Patrick Kavanagh to come over and do a reading for us in the Empress of Russia Pub at Sloan Square. The Reading is advertised and booked for Saturday night week, at eight thirty. That's why I came over from Spitalfields, hoping to meet you, after Pat phoned me saying you were coming here at this time." Jack paused to emphasize what he was about to say next. "How would you like to read with Patrick Kavanagh, Allen?" Allen just sat there, speechless, his eyes nearly closed, looking out of his mouth.

PEGGY O'SHEA GOES SEARCHING FOR ALLEN HUNT

She had been thinking about going to see him since she had taken up her new position in Hertfordshire. The job had been advertised in the 'Medical Journal'. "A vacancy exists for Wards Sisters at Leaveston Hospital Abbot's Langley Watford Herts. Only those with full Nursing Credentials need apply." One week later the letter arrived at Hammersmith General Hospital. "We are happy to inform you that your application has been successful. Please reply by return if you wish to take up this position."

It would mean an increase of ten pounds per month on her present salary. Her father lived alone since the death of her mother in Callan, Co. Kilkenny.

He suffered from severe arthritis and the few extra pounds would get him a little local help about the house. But Watford and Hertfordshire were a long way off from where she lived and worked in the heart of London. She felt like she was leaving a part of her own heart behind when she boarded the train to Watford.

"Am I just kidding myself" she asked, "when I only met the man once – even if it was for a twelve hour sea and train trip from Kilkenny to London? He probably wouldn't know me if I stood in front of him right now. He has long since forgotten my name. What of it if he has? I won't die of fright. I'll just say; I was passing by and thought I'd drop in. How are you anyway? I'm having a wonderful time out in Hertsfordshire. The social contacts leave nothing to be desired.

I will, I won't. I will, I will, I will." Peggy O'Shea boarded the Bakerloo Line train at Watford station bound for 'The Champion' public house on the Bayswater Road London.

"Here goes," she said, "for better or worse." The train sped towards Croseby, Moor Park, Northwood, Pinner and North Harrow, Northwick Park and Preston Road. She was familiar with the stops as far as here, but there was a long way to go to Baker Street, where she would have to change to the Circle Line to get to Bayswater.

From there a brisk walk would land her at the front door of 'The Champion'. Where, she felt as nervous as Amy Johnson contemplating her first solo flight from London to Australia.

When Peggy walked into 'The Champion' she had no cognisance of her surroundings and her legs seemed to loose their rhythm. She felt she was in danger of toppling over, like a child learning to walk. Pat Hunt and the blond trainee barmaid were both behind the counter and chatting amicably while serving the customers. There he was as large as life and looking at her with a welcoming smile. She had to control herself for fear of running towards him.

"Yes Miss what can I do for you?" He was looking straight at her, but there wasn't a flicker of recognition. "I was right all along" she said to herself.

He has completely forgotten me. There's nothing for it now but to brazen it out.

"Could I have a glass of Light Ale please?" She'd let him see he wasn't the only one who had other things on his mind. He put the drink down in front of her. "I was looking for a man named Allen Hunt, " she said as she placed a shilling on the counter.

"Well Miss, Allen Hunt doesn't work here but I can direct you to where he does work. Are you familiar with the Underground?" Peggy was aghast. What kind of game was he playing at?

"I hope you don't mind me asking but are you a friend of Allen's?"

"I only met him once, but it's not important. I was in the neighbourhood and thought I might drop in and say hello. If you should see him in the near future, tell him Peggy O'Shea called." She couldn't risk stepping up on the rung to sit on the stool. She was afraid she might slip.

Instead she took one sip from the Light Ale and turned to go.

"I can do better than that. I'll phone Allen at 'The Poppy' over on the Edgware Road. That's where he works. If he isn't on the premises I'll leave word that Peggy O'Shea called to see him. I'm his brother Pat."

"O thanks be to God", she thought "his brother – that's why. He must be his twin."

"Come to think of it, I'm sure I heard him speak of you not so long ago."

"Wonder of wonders – he hasn't forgotten about me after all," she told herself. "Will I wait while you phone to see if he's there," she asked?

"But of course I'll do it right away. Please take a seat."

Within minutes Pat was back all smiles: "Allen asked me to say hello and wonders if you would be so kind as to drop over to 'The Poppy' on Edgware Road. He would come over to see you himself but unfortunately he can't get away." Peggy was ecstatic. If she had won the Irish Hospital's Sweep Stakes, together with the Irish Dawn Beauty Contest, she could not be happier. "I'd be delighted to go over and see him. Please tell him I'm on my way. Thank you kindly." She extended her hand: "It was lovely meeting you Pat. Perhaps we'll meet again." She went out the door in a hurry and turned left down the Bayswater Road. She kept looking straight ahead like a blinkered filly in her first maiden hurdle.

The blonde trainee barmaid was looking after her, wide-eyed with curiosity and bursting to let Pat have the benefit of her female intuition. She turned to him saying: "Did you ever heart the likes of it? She was just passing, and dropped in to say hello – in my eye she did! Allen had better watch out, for that one. She's got it bad."

IVOR DAVIES' FIANCÉ

Eileen Murphy climbed the seven, steep and broken steps, up from her dingy basement flat on Chesterton Road in the Ladbroke Grove area of London. She was in her late twenties but looked much older because of the amount of paint and powder, plastered like a mask over her face. Her sable coloured three-quarter coat was a cheap imitation of the large South African antelope's fur. Smoking a Marleborough cigarette through a plastic holder and standing five feet ten inches in her roaring red high heels, she was a sight for sore eyes.

EPISODE EIGHT

JOCK DUNDEE
HEART ATTACK
SUICIDE
A SECRET RENDEZVOUS

JOCK DUNDEE

Allen Hunt was coming off duty from the public bar at 'The Poppy' on the Edgware Road, London. It was now four o'clock in the afternoon and he would not be due back on duty until eight o'clock that night. He was glad of the break as the morning had been hectic. The early morning drinkers coming over from the speakeasy Scrumpy house known as The Red Lion, had somehow of late doubled their numbers. The state of their intoxication had likewise increased. Following on the heels of this there was plenty of 'argy bargy' and loads of abusive language especially amongst themselves. When drink pours in, common sense flows out, Allen thought to himself.

It wasn't that Allen couldn't handle the extra hassle but he needed to be more vigilant and on his toes at all times. He was required to be a dispenser of justice and a peace maker, rolled into one. He told his highly amused brother, Pat: "At 'The Poppy' I'm a cross between a Policeman and a Parish Priest." Allen reckoned that as many as sixty percent of these misfortunates were Irish born or of Irish descent. In saying that it must be remembered that the Irish were by far the largest ethnic group of emigrants in London. Some, who were born in Ireland left school at fourteen years and went to work as messenger boys or runners for local businesses.

JOCK DUNDEE
BY SEAN KENNY

Once they reached the ripe old age of seventeen years they were dismissed, and another batch of fourteen year olds took their places. It was a simple case of economics, but for the dismissed it was a case of crossing The Herring Pond to seek their fortunes. Others who got little or no schooling and could neither read nor write, emigrated and joined the building crews of Murphy or McAlpine as Navvies. Many of these had no ambition to hold down a steady job or make a home for themselves. Often the worry of being found out as an illiterate haunted them and they dropped out of society in shame. Then there were those who claimed their lives had no purpose, no excitement. After working a hard day on the building site they were left looking at the four walls of an undecorated and cheaply furnished room, for the long and lonely nights. More often than not they went out to meet their fellow workers and had a few drinks to be part of something – part of life. But if this became habitual one could easily become addicted and loose one's way.

There was a different set of circumstances for those who were born in England of emigrant Irish parents. Many of those who were born in Liverpool, Manchester or Birmingham drifted into London to seek anonymity. There they would find better cover, where they could do menial works for small remunerations and at the same time sign-on and collect their Social Welfare payments.

But it was amongst those who were born in Ireland and had little or no education that the worst cases of deprivation existed. These were unable to form friendships because they suffered from inferiority complexes or had poor self-esteem. Where alcohol was concerned these people were the most vulnerable. Like the old maxim says; it gave them Dutch Courage. But if they became addicted the second saying became equally true: One drink was too many and ten wasn't enough.

It isn't easy to understand or explain the Irish psyche and it's affinity with alcohol. More than one psychologist has suggested that our Celtic temperament lends itself to the stimulating powers of intoxicating liquors. One way or another all those who relied on the consumption of alcohol to sustain them, were eventually consumed by it.

Allen was probably right when he estimated that about sixty percent of the London addicts were Irish. The other forty percent were made up of Jocks and Taffies and down and out Cockneys, and there were always the few shell shocked, British ex-army men who couldn't cope.

Allen, who was nearing the peak of his mental and physical powers wasn't really tired but he was weary. His patience had been tried on a number of occasions this morning. There was this rugged fiftyish Scot whose face was so battered that had he gone back home to Dundee his own mother would have had him evicted as an imposter. He was known to all and sundry as Jock Dundee.

On his third pint of Stout and Mild, Jock got to his feet and called on Allen to come out from behind the bar and have a go. With his chin tucked into his right shoulder, his fists in front of his face and his feet wide apart one could tell he had at some time or other boxed as a Southpaw in the square ring.

"Come on out Paddy and I'll show ya wha Joe Lewis did to Billy Conn. Do ya ken wha he tauld im afore he nailed im to the flure?" He said: "ya can run Billy bu ya no can hide."

"I'll tell you once more Jock, sit down and shut up. If I have to come out from behind this bar you had better be able to run faster than the Wild Man from Borneo. Be a good fellow now and don't make me clear this counter. If you put me to it, I'll clear you out of here once and for all. You'll be barred. Have you got that Jock?"

That did it. Allen knew Jock Dundee was not afraid of him, but he didn't want to be barred from 'The Poppy'. It was an important part of his everyday life.

HEART ATTACK

Allen went into the long hallway by the side door and ran up the stairs two at a time. He was about to turn down the corridor to the staff dining room when he heard a knocking sound on the floor over his head. He stopped and listened as the tapping went on, rat-tat-tat, rat-tat-tat.

It was a signal. Something was wrong. He could sense it. That tapping meant someone was trying to make contact. Without further hesitation he ran up the stairs to the living quarters on the top floor. The door to the kitchen was partly open. It was from there the tapping came. Cautiously he pushed in the door. Sitting on the floor with his back to the wall, Bill Taylor was beating a tattoo on the wooden floor with a ladle. He looked distressed and disheveled. When he saw Allen he smiled faintly and stopped the clamour. Allen knelt down beside him and was about to help him to his feet but Bill shook his head. In a feeble voice he told Allen: "There are tablets in the inside pocket of my jacket on the back of the door." Allen got them and squeezed one out of a sachet. Bill took it and placed it under his tongue.

"I'll be alright in a few minutes Allen, thank you." When he extended a hand, Allen gently got him onto a chair, saying "take it easy Mr. Taylor. Do you wish me to phone for a doctor or an ambulance."

"Please don't Allen, it was only a slight turn, – nothing to worry about really. I'm fine now. I want you to promise me one thing Allen, that you wont say a word to Mrs. Taylor or any member of the staff about this little affair. As you can see it wasn't serious". Allen nodded his consent but insisted: "I think you should tell Mrs. Taylor yourself. Wouldn't it be better than having her find you as I did, just now? The fright might be too much for her. You should think about it sir." Bill Taylor smiled a smile of gratitude that was smothered in sadness.

SUICIDE

Luke Brannigan stood up from the table to answer the phone. His housekeeper who was a woman in her sixties beat him to it.

"Yes it is. Mr. Brannigan is having supper at the moment, – could you call back?" Luke was standing beside her, smiling with open hand thrust out to receive the phone. Molly who was a first cousin once removed, saw herself as the guardian of Luke's unencumbered hours. "You should take advantage of every pause," she told him over and over again. Luke knew the genesis of that advice. It was a catch-phrase used by British army sergeants for their troops at the front, when a lull came in fighting during the First World War. By resting them at every break the sergeants were sure to get the best out of them when the fighting resumed. Molly had no such ambitions. She merely wanted Luke to take things easy. He almost had to wrestle with her to get the phone.

"Hello, who is speaking? O it's you Jack. Is everything all right?"

"I'm afraid not Luke. I've got some bad news."

"Bad news you say. How bad is it Jack? Is it the contract for the housing estate? Or is it something personal?"

"I've just got news that Billy McNeill is dead." There was a killing pause. "He committed suicide in Wormwood Scrubs."

"O merciful Jesus, what are we going to do? What will I tell his poor mother? When did it happen?"

"About an hour ago. Apparently he had been sewing mail bags in the prison workshop. Shortly after going back to his cell, the guards found him hanging by the neck from a leather strap." Luke left the phone down as if it were a sack of desolation. He put on his jacket and loosened his necktie. As he left his home he shut tight the front door and walked out from Hayes' Mews opposite Berkeley Square. He walked quickly towards Farm Street and the Church Of The Immaculate Conception. Father Dan O'Driscoll was the Parish Priest. At the priest's house Luke's ringing was answered by a white haired pink faced old lady dressed in black. "O 'tis yourself Mr. Brannigan. Won't you come on in sir. His Reverence will be delighted to see you. Come into the kitchen. He's listening to the news from Radio Eireann."

A SECRET RENDEZVOUS

Smoking a Marlborough cigarette through a plastic holder and standing five feet ten inches in her roaring red high heels, she was a sight for sore eyes.

"More bloody steps, I'll break off a feckin' heel if I'm not careful. It would be just my luck 'n all – to be like Long John Silver. Winston wouldn't like it, one bit. I hope he's there now. I'm so looking forward to seeing him again. If anything happened to him I think I'd die." Eileen Murphy was on the platform at Ladbroke Grove station waiting for the Metropolitan Line train to Hammersmith Broadway.

"O come on for Christ's sake, what's keeping ya. It's always the same; the more hurry the less speed. Here it is limpin' inta the station. Three friggin' cheers. A wheelbarrow id be quicker." She sat beside a window and shook her shoulders to loosen up. Latimer Road, Shepherds Bush and Goldhawk Road. "The next stop is Hammersmith. This is it. How do I look?" She took a mirror from her handbag, a tube of lipstick and a comb. "A quick fix an' I'm all set." She was so pleased with herself that she winked at the mirror and gave a little giggle. He told her he loved her dearly and she said she loved him truly. She had returned her running repairs outfit to her handbag and stepped down onto the platform. She walked through the tunnel under the Hammersmith Broadway and up the twelve steps at the other side. She was standing outside "The George", public house, lounge bar and restaurant. It was a beautiful Victorian Limestone building. One of the finest of it's kind in London.

"Here goes nothing," she said and bowled into 'The George', like Mata Hari, bowing with bouquet in the Café – Concert at the Ambassadeurs. The special aroma of roasted coffee beans blended with the spicy fragrance of polish and cigar smoke, pervaded the room. From the far end of the bar counter, swing doors shot out open from the kitchen, bringing with them the odour of grilled steak and onions. A rather slovenly waitress shuffled out carrying a large silver tray laden with food. She wore a wrinkled black satinette suit with a white yellow-stained blouse and her hair in her eyes like an English Sheepdog.

"O yes, there he is – the handsome brute. Yew whoo, Winston". She crossed the room to where a big black South African in his early thirties, sat at a table with a glass of spirits and a tankard of larger beer in front of him. The very first words he spoke were: "Did you get the money?"

EPISODE NINE

LOVERS OR JUST FRIENDS?

LOVERS OR JUST FRIENDS?

Bayswater Underground station was less than a quarter mile walk from The Champion. As she briskly covered the ground, Peggy O'Shea found herself humming; "O' What A Beautiful Morning, O' What A Beautiful Day." And to think that Allen Hunt had actually asked for her to call and see him at The Poppy. Meeting his look-a-like brother Pat, was an added bonus. She felt like a friend of the family, well, almost.

People were going into and coming out from Kensington Gardens in droves. She knew that Kensington Palace was in the Gardens and that Queen Victoria had been born there. She who married her cousin Prince Albert and bore him nine children. But her Prince died a young man. Later in 1876 her favourite minister Disraeli, proclaimed her Empress of India. She reigned for 63 years, – had nine children and loved Disraeli. "I've got a wonderful feeling everything is going my Way. At long last I feel alive."

The Circle and District lines run though Bayswater Underground Station. As she went down the iron stairway the Circle line train was pulling into the platform. She jumped for joy down the last two steps as doors opened automatically with a loud mechanical swish. Six minutes would see her in the Edgware Road station. She knew her way around London. Why wouldn't she? Prior to her taking the nursing job out at Leaveston Hospital, Watford Herts, she had lived and worked as a nurse in Hammersmith General Hospital for three years. Like most of the London Irish, Peggy knew the Underground railway systems like a rabbit knows every interconnecting tunnel in the miles of subterranean passages known as burrows.

Paddington was the first stop. Four different lines ran through Paddington, the District, the Circle, the Metropolitan and the Bakerloo lines. Next stop was Allen Hunt, at 'The Poppy' on the Edgware Road.

Ivor Davies came into the Public Bar and walked in a circuitous direction towards Matt Ryan. As he went past Allen, he asked out of the corner of his mouth "Are we expecting a visit from a female friend?"

"News travels fast in 'The Poppy,'" Allen answered.

Ivor spoke with Matt "Mr. Taylor would like to have a word with you upstairs, Matt." Matt frowned. "What's that about? I spoke with him this morning. Something must have come up. O.K. thanks Ivor. Back in a jiffy," he told Allen and went out the hall door that led to the stairs.

"Don't forget to introduce her now, the minute she arrives. Will it be alright if I give her a little peck on the cheek just to make her feel welcome?"

"I don't even want you to look at her. You might frighten the life out of the poor girl," Allen said in jest. "Go on get out of here before Matt comes back." Ivor went back into the Lounge all smiles.

Five minutes later Peggy O'Shea walked hesitantly into the Public Bar of 'The Poppy'. She stepped warily like a young deer out of its territory, – trembling, yet determined to discover. Allen looked up from where he was washing glasses under the bar counter. She was positively charming in her two piece Summer suit of lavender and white brocade. Her off white leather shoulder bag was slung low and in her matching high heel shoes, she cut a dash that would capture the admiration of all but the most disinterested and unimaginative members of the male sex. He was exactly as she remembered him, tall, broad shouldered, smiling that friendly smile, full of life and vitality. Looking straight at him now, he was not as much like his brother as she had thought earlier. No, he looked just like Allen Hunt, who had accompanied and escorted her so manfully from McDonagh Station Kilkenny to Euston Station London.

"You look great Peggy. It was nice of you to come over." He dried his hands, whipped the towel over his shoulder and came out from behind the bar.

"You don't look too bad yourself. It's good to see you Allen."

They shook hands and Allen kissed her on the cheek. Ivor had opened the connecting door between the Lounge and the Public Bar. He stood there ogling the pair of them like a fond father enjoying his only sons first attempts at walking.

Allen felt Peggie's distraction as she looked over his shoulder. When he turned to see the source of her concern he saw Ivor beaming like a search-light in a fog with his long face fashioned into a broad smile.

"What the hell are you looking at Taffy?"

"Certainly not you Paddy. Will I give her that welcoming kiss now or would you like me to meet her later, seeing as how you'll be working?" Smiling Allen beckoned Ivor to come and meet Peggy.

"This is my good friend Ivor Davies. He's from Glamorganshire in Wales. He swears he's not a Brit but insists that he's a Celt."

"I'm delighted to meet you Ivor." She turned her face to allow him kiss her on the cheek, "Of course you're as much a Celt as the Irish and the Scots are."

"That's Matt Ryans heavy step coming down the stairs," Allen said to Ivor. "Get back into the Lounge quickly."

"Nice to meet you Peggy. I've got to go." Ivor was back inside with the connecting door closed before Matt opened the hall door into the Public Bar. He looked concerned, almost worried but he brightened up when he saw Allen and Peggy.

"Who have we got here Allen?"

"Peggy, this large gentleman is Matt Ryan. He's my boss here at 'The Poppy', and he's a good friend even if he is from West Cork." Matt acknowledged the joke with a nod and a smile while extending a hand as big as a malthouse shovel.

"Matt, this is Peggy O'Shea. She's a nurse working here in London and comes from Callan, Co. Kilkenny". Matt cradled her hand in his palm. It was like an infant lost in a four-poster bed.

"Callan, you say. I once worked for a man named Jack Walsh from Callan. He was a builder in Cambridge." A fine decent man, he was. "

Peggy shook her head. "Can't say I ever heard of him."

Matt was smiling. "You know, old Jack had a saying about his home town: You can walk through Ireland but you'll run through Callan. 'Contentious Callan' he called it."

"That may well be Mr. Ryan, but did you know that some of Irelands greatest sons came from Callan. Ignatius Rice, founder of the Christian Brothers, who are now teaching world wide, he came from Callan. And the Architect of the White House in Washington D.C., James Hoban he came from Callan, also. That is to name but two, who are world famous, Mr. Ryan."

"This young lady is bright but better than that she's brave. You'd do well to hold on to her. She'd be a good one to have in your corner."

"I think I'm beginning to like your boss Allen. He sounds like a very intelligent man."

"What are you two setting up here, a mutual admiration society?" All three were enjoying the banter.

"What time are you going off duty Allen?" asked Matt.

"I'll be finishing for the day at four o'clock, Matt."

Matt looked at his watch: "It's 2.30 p.m."

"I'll tell you what: I'll entertain Peggy while you slip upstairs and change. I'm giving you the rest of the day off, on the town, – the two of you. What would you like to have to drink Peggy?"

"I'll have a glass of Larger beer thank you very much."

He turned to Allen: "What's keeping you – get going young man."

As they were ready to walk out the door, Matt said to Allen: "I need to have a talk with you when you get back. It's important. Something has happened that has changed how things stand, here at "The Poppy". I don't expect you to come back in a hurry. Whatever time it is I'll be on the premises. Enjoy yourselves and take care. Nice meeting you Peggy."" he called after them at the door.

"You too Matt," – and the door closed. Ivor silently closed the connecting door between the Lounge and the Public Bar.

"What was all that about?" Peggy asked Allen. "Sounds serious don't you think?"

"Very strange to say the least. He looked quite worried when he first came down stairs and then he lightened up after a few minutes."

"Did you not notice," she parried, "the second he saw me he was all smiles."

"There's confidence for you," he said and gave her a slap on the backside.

"He could have his eye on me, – who knows."

"Alright, alright, that's enough of blowing your own trumpet." They laughed together happily rejoicing in their reformed friendship.

"Have you been down the Victoria Embankment, Allen? It's a beautiful thoroughfare, full of historical monuments and sculptures. It's lined with all kinds of trees and it runs for more than a mile. It stretches from Westminster Bridge to Black Friars Bridge."

"We've got a Black Friars Bridge across the river Breagagh in Kilkenny city. Did you know that?"

"No I didn't but I don't expect it's as big as this one here."

"How can you tell if you've never seen it?"

"O all right the Black Friars Bridge in Kilkenny is twice as big as the one here in London. Is that to your satisfaction Sir?"

"Seriously Allen, the Victoria Embankment is really worth seeing."

"Right lead on McDuff. It's on your head. How do we travel, – by Underground or by bus?"

"We'll go by Underground. If we went by bus we would have to make at least two changes. By Underground we can go straight through from where we are at the Edgware Road to Westminster. The District or Circle lines will take us there."

"Do you know something?"

"No, what?"

"You're a mine of information. You should give up that old nursing job and become a tour guide with London Transport."

THE POET PATRICK KAVANAGH
BY SEAN KENNY

"Would you ever dry up and get out the money."

"O sorry, I thought this was for free."

Peggy laughed like she hadn't laughed for ages. The more she saw him, the more she liked him.

The Circle line train was first into the station. Allen kept her talking and laughing all the way from the Edgware Road to Westminster. Most of all she found herself thinking how nice it was to be with him. To be part of his conversation, his good humour and his unassuming manner.

After leaving the Edgware Road the next stop was Paddington, then Bayswater, Notting Hill Gate, High Street Kensington, Gloucester Road, South Kensington and Sloane Square. As Allen read the destination on the tunnel wall and on the support walls behind the platform, he looked at her, hesitated then said; "Peggy I hope you won't think me boastful but this is where I'll be reading my own Poetry and Prose with the Great Monaghan Poet, Patrick Kavanagh – at the Empress of Russia Pub, Sloane Square.

A lump came into Peggy's throat and tears flooded her eyes. She was unable to speak. She caught his hand and held it tightly. "O God," she said, "I think I'm going to cry."

"It's not as if it was a sentence of death," he said while laughing.

"When is the Poetry and Prose reading set for, Allen?" She shook his hand rather roughly for fear he might brush off her question with a joke. When he realised how in earnest she was, he told her: "Next Saturday night at 8.00 p.m. Admission ten shillings. If you would like to come I'll try and get you a free Pass."

"Allen, a free Pass would be the least of my worries. I only hope I can get off work in time. It's a long way from Watford to Sloane Square."

"It's not as if you'll be going to see W.B. Yeats collect the Nobel Prize for Poetry."

"No, - it will be much more important than that."

Allen looked at her thoughtfully as the train ran on to Victoria, Saint James's Park and Westminster.

EPISODE TEN

URGENT PHONE CALL
NANCY BLACKMORE RETURNS IN FORCE

URGENT PHONE CALL

Pat Hunt, head barman at 'The Champion' on the Bayswater Road, woke on his day off duty. Normally he would be in high spirits on such a day. Instead he felt gloomy and out of sorts. Something was nagging at him and he couldn't quite figure it out, and then it dawned on him. It was the conversation he had had with his brother Allen, on the telephone last night. It all came flooding back now:

"It is of great importance that you and I should meet for a chat, brother. Unless I miss my guess you will be greatly surprised with what I have to tell you. The fact is there are three matters that I need to talk to you about. Two of them directly apply to yourself. The third which is of no great importance concerns me. The first and by far the most important revolves around the lives of Mrs. Rosie Taylor and her daughter Patricia. The second concerns the character of Nancy Blackmore and the third stems from the situation that has arisen just now at 'The Poppy'. I know you will understand when I tell you it would not be feasible or proper to discuss these matters further over the phone. As we both have time off tomorrow, perhaps you would suggest some out of the way place, where we could meet."

That's a mouthful brother, – but I wouldn't doubt you. You have certainly got me guessing. I feel I'm already on tenter-hooks. You seem to have done a Sherlock Holmes job on a whole series of events. I must say you've got me puzzled. Look, I'll tell you what we'll do: Let's meet tomorrow morning at eleven o'clock at the Marble Arch. Do you know where it is and how to get there?"

Yes I do. It's at Oxford Street and close to Speakers Corner, Hyde Park, where Jack Boland said I should get up on a soap box and do some public speaking. Am I right?"

"You've hit the nail on the head, brother. That's where it's at."

"By the way Pat, what part of Ireland does Jack Boland come from?"

"Dundalk, – a few miles from the Border."

"I thought so. He sounds like he might have crossed over once or twice after dark."

"That's enough said about that sort of thing, brother. The walls have ears, you understand. But tell me this, how did you get on with Peggy O'Shea? She looks to be quite a woman."

"We got on famous, – had a whale of a time. I'll tell you all about that tomorrow, brother. See you then. Slán." "Watch how you go."

NANCY BLACKMORE RETURNS IN FORCE

Pat Hunt looked at the wall clock over the Lounge door at 'The Champion;, on the Bayswater Road. It was half past ten, Thursday night, thirty minutes before closing time. He had just been on the phone to his brother Allen, and was wondering about their conversation. Not to worry, he'd have it all laid bare before him tomorrow, like an intimate love story by Liam O'Flaherty. Allen should have apprenticed himself to Scotland Yard and not to the beer trade in a Whitbread House.

Pat glanced under the bar counter. The chain and padlock were there. The padlock was fastened onto the chain and the key was in his pocket. He called Gwen, the new barmaid: "Have you seen the wooden mallet that was under the counter, Gwen?

"Yes Pat, – I put it in the store, on one of the kegs. Did you want it?"

"Please leave it back where you found it, like a good girl."

Gwen retrieved the mallet and put it back exactly where she had found it, beside the lock and chain.

At approximately ten forty Nancy Blackmore walked into the Lounge bar. She was accompanied by two thugs who were as ugly as gargoyles and probably as brainless, Pat reckoned. One was coloured, and one was a greasy white. Pat had them under observation from the moment they entered the Lounge. Nancy made for the section of counter where Pat was serving, her two bodyguards followed. He pretended not to see them. He could tell that all three had been drinking, and the evil of their intentions registered upon their faces.

"Hello sweetheart, I heard you've been missing me. That's your hard luck, Mr. I prefer real macho men, just like Nelson here and Horse. I'll have my three weeks pay and my cards, up front and in a hurry, – like now." Pat paid them no heed but kept on serving. "And I'll have a large G and T and two pints of Best Bitter for me mates. An' don't you try any rough stuff either or my friends here will take you apart."

Pat looked at the two thugs scornfully. "Your wages and cards have been here for the past week – but first where is my ring?"

She thrust out her hand, almost hitting him in the face. "See, I told you, I lost the fn thing." She slapped the counter with the palm of her right hand and shouted: "Give me my cards and my money, NOW."

Pat was finishing an order for a customer when he saw her greasy white heavyweight accomplice shake a knife down his sleeve and into his hand. As he did so, Pat reached under the counter like lightening. The thug released the lethal steel blade with a menacing flick. As he raised the deadly weapon chest high, Pat swung the padlock by the chain and caught the would-be assassin on the butt of the ear. He went down as if poleaxed. Still holding the end of the chain, Pat grabbed the wooden mallet and jumped the counter. He turned and moved towards the black thug who held a black-jack with the attached strap around his wrist and he wore a knuckleduster on the other hand.

"Strangle him Nelson" she screamed as the black man advanced towards Pat. Pat was swinging the padlock like David wielded his sling-shot just before he shattered Goliath's forehead and killed him instantly.

Once again the thug moved in, trying to avoid the circular motion of the padlock at the end of the chain. On the ear it sounded a little like the whine of a circular saw. In sheer desperation the thug made a wild swing with his leather covered club which Pat warded of with the mallet. Then Pat aimed his spinning missile at the hand that wielded the club. The padlock crashed, with bone breaking force on the back of the thug's hand. The recipient let out a roar like a wounded lion and turned to run from the Lounge. As he ran clutching his broken hand, Pat struck him on the shoulder with the mallet and he spun around like a ballet dancer doing a pirouette. On his second twirl, Pat dropped the mallet on the thugs foot and he went down on his back like a spancelled ass. Nancy Blackmore looked like she had been poisoned. She was clutching her throat like Lucrezia Borgia might have done any evening after dinner at her brothers mansion. But now the fight was over. Pat Hunt had brought it to a spectacular conclusion. The two notorious thugs were down and out, at least for the present. They lay on their backs like all the original horizontal heavyweights.

Nancy Blackmore knew that Pat Hunt was as tough as they came. But how could anyone believe that one man could handle two proven street-fighters, armed with knives, blackjacks and knuckledusters? Pat was the last word in resourcefulness. He had had that wooden mallet, together with padlock and chain, under the counter, ready and waiting for her return. She had warned him she would be back with reinforcements.

Pat went to the office and collected the wage packet plus, the employment insurance cards belonging to Nancy Blackmore. She snapped them out of his hand without a word and tore open the wage-packet and began counting the stiff, mint fresh notes in front of him. Pat knew there wasn't a chance in hell he would ever get back the engagement ring. 'So be it.'

When she had done counting she tore the packet into a dozen pieces and threw the fragments into his face.

"Go now before I call the Police." The dazed thugs were scrambling to their feet and looking fearfully at Pat who had already confiscated their weapons, down to taking the knuckleduster off the blackman's hand. These two were now slinking towards the door. They had been well and truly beaten, and at their own game into the bargain. Whoever else might try it, they would not be back. Not so Nancy Blackmore, who had regained her composure. She walked unconcerned and unrepentant out the door and onto the Bayswater Road. Would she try something else at some time in the future? In any event Pat Hunt wasn't convinced he had seen the last of her. It had been a costly relationship in matters of time and money. The time that had been lost and the money that had been squandered. He had learned his lesson and paid dearly for it.

The customer's one hundred and twenty eyes followed his every movement, the men's with envy and the women's with admiration. Another forty or so had left in fear when Pat had felled the greasy white thug who was about to use the deadly flick-knife.

During the fracas the new barmaid Gwen had nothing to do but stand and stare in disbelief and trepidation. She had seen a totally different side of Pat Hunt whom she had grown to like and wonder about.

Don't serve anyone else, Gwen. He looked at his watch on the shelf where he had put it the moment Nancy and company came through the door.

There were two people drinking in the Lounge who watched anxiously from the first moment the confrontation became obvious. Both were in their late twenties. One was from Cashel, county Tipperary and the other was a born Londoner, whose parents came from Oranmore, county Galway. These were ready to intervene at the drop of a hat. But they would not do so unless asked or it became absolutely necessary to save Pat Hunt's life.

THE TWO VOLUNTEERS
BY SEAN KENNY

61

They were thrilled though not surprised how Pat had disposed of his would be assassins. For them it was like a ringside seat for the main event at the London Palladium. But of course it meant much more than that. Here was a man upon whom their very life's might one day depend. Not only theirs but the lives of their comrades too. Theirs was a perilous game of life and death.

"Time, ladies and gentlemen, please. The show is over. It's time to drink them up or leave them behind. Tomorrow is another day. Come along ladies and gentlemen, please – have you no homes to go to?"

Pat walked between the tables as he exhorted the customers to drink up and go. He nodded briefly as he passed by the table of the two men who had watched the contest so closely and so anxiously.

The customers began to vacate the Lounge in rapid succession. Everybody wanted to speak to Pat – to congratulate him, – to shake his hand. Some of the men clapped him on the back while many of the women sought to touch him on the arms, chest or backside. For they saw him as a hero, – someone to look up to, – to respect. They desperately needed to let him know he was a man apart.

"See you soon Pat." "Ta-ra, for now Pat." "'E's a lovely bloke 'e is."

When Pat put the padlock and chain on the outside front door which leads to the Lounge, only two men were left on the premises.

"You can go now Gwen. I'll clean up. Thanks, and safe home."

"Thanks Pat, - you're very kind. Good night."

Pat pulled three pints of Best Bitter and carried them to where the two men were sitting. He sat down beside them.

"This is the crunch: I do not want my brother, Allen, drawn into this under any circumstances."

EPISODE ELEVEN

A BLOOD SACRIFICE
PEGGY GIVES ALLEN A GUIDED TOUR DOWN THE VICTORIA EMBANKMENT
A CHANGE COMES TO "THE POPPY"

A BLOOD SACRIFICE

"O 'tis yourself Mr Brannigan. His Reverence will be delighted to see you. Come on in sir. Himself is in the kitchen, listening to the news from Radio Eireann."

"Thank you Mrs. Purcell. I am glad to see you looking so well."

Monsignor Dan O Driscoll was Parish Priest at the Church of the Immaculate Conception at Farm Street Berkeley Square London. He was in his sixties and had spent all of his priestly life working in London. He was a native of Bunclody, County Wexford and was proud of that county's contribution to the 1798 Rebellion.

The Monsignor was quick to point out that seventy five per cent of his parishioners were either Irish born or of Irish extraction. And he was often heard to say that; if his parishioners were ever to loose the faith he would not be able to keep it himself. "Indeed 'tis my firm belief that I would have lost the faith many times were it not for the steadfast trust of my people in the promises of Christ."

He sat now on a solid oak cushioned armchair, which Luke Brannigan had bought for him many years before. It was positioned in front of the old Pye radio with the magic eye in the top right hand corner. He sat staring at it until one might think that if he closed his eyes he would be no longer able to hear it. The old wireless was sat on top of an even older upright piano that had strung its last melody some twenty-five years earlier. The Monsignor listened with his eyes and his ears as the set stuttered out the Irish news. He looked up as his housekeeper came into the room.

"Mr Brannigan from Hayes Mews is here to see you."

"Tell him to come right in Nellie and see if there's a drop of Red Breast in the glass cabinet. One glass will do and a small jug of water."

Nellie ushered Luke in as the Monsignor stood up, and put out his hand. "It's always good to see you Luke. Take off your coat and make yourself at home. I was just listening to the Irish News. We are fully-fledged members of the EEC now Luke. The European Economic Community. It can only be a good thing for Ireland. The chances are it will help the Reunification of the country as well as boosting the economy."

"Whatever about the economy needing a boost, I'm beginning to wonder if the reunification of Ireland is worth all the bloodshed and torture of so many young men."

"It's a bloody sacrifice Luke, like it was in ninety eight, when Fr. Murphy called on the men of Wexford to take up arms. Being a member of the EEC will be nothing new for Ireland. Wasn't it the Irish monks who travelled throughout Europe during the Dark Ages and kept the light of the Faith and Learning alive. The land of Saints and Scholars they said. They owe us for that Luke."

"I'm not disputing that at all Monsignor what I am saying is this: when it comes down to a young Irish lad taking his own life in an English prison cell, one has to wonder how much is the reunification of Ireland worth? Its only when the tragedy strikes home, that we are brought to our senses. Monsignor Dan O Driscoll was looking at Luke Brannigan like a short sighted old lady would look intensely at the eye of a needle, trying to thread it." Concern and anxiety covered his face.

"There is something radically wrong Luke. What has happened, in the name of God?"

"As a matter of fact that's the very reason I came over to see you in the first place. I got the terrible news of young Billy McNeill's death less than an hour ago. I told you about him when he was first sentenced to five years in Wormwood Scrubs for possession of a loaded revolver."

"Yes of course I remember. I spoke with the prison Chaplain, who told me Billy hadn't accepted his imprisonment at all, said he was mentally immature."

"Just imagine how I felt when Jack Bolland phoned me to say young Billy Mc Neill had done away with himself in his cell. The prison guards found him hanging by the neck from a leather strap."

"O' Luke, I'm so sorry to hear it. He was your sister's son, wasn't he?"

"Aye, my sister's son, God help her, – poor Meg. Do you think you could meet his mother when she arrives from Galway to take his body home for burial, Monsignor?"

"Of course Luke. I'll do everything in my power to ease the terrible pain and suffering."

"All I'm hoping for now is that John won't arrive in London, after serving three years of torture in a Chinese Communist jail, at the same time as his sister Meg, arrives from Ireland to collect her dead son's body."

"With Gods help Luke, the authorities will have released the body before Fr. John arrives in London."

"Can you imagine what the news hounds would do with such a story. The headlines would be sensational: Irish Priest released after three years in Chinese jail, to take home his nephews hanged body from Wormwood Scrubs. News like that would circle the world, Monsignor. The repercussions would become unbearable, for those at home as well as those of us who are here."

"Don't torment yourself Luke, God is good. I'll say first Mass in the morning. Do you think you could come over for it?"

"Yes I will and thanks. But first I need you to hear my confession?"

PEGGY GIVES ALLEN A GUIDED TOUR DOWN THE VICTORIA EMBANKMENT

Allen Hunt and Peggy O'Shea, had made an impromptu itinerary of the many places of interest, after leaving 'The Poppy'. Peggy had insisted that the Victoria Embankment was a spectacular sight that stretched for more than a mile and a quarter from Westminster Bridge to Black Friars Bridge and was not to be missed. They travelled by Underground. On the way the train made a stop at Sloane Square. This prompted Allen to tell Peggy of the invitation he had received, to read with Patrick Kavanagh, at the Empress of Russia Pub in Sloane Square. To Allen's amazement, Peggy became emotional and cried. And the train ran on to Victoria, St. James' Park and Westminster which was their destination.

Peggy was absolutely right. It was a beautiful tree-lined thoroughfare that had been constructed by Sir Joseph Bazalgette between 1864 and 1870. It proved to be the shortest and most delightful way from Westminster to the centre City. Nearest the Bridge was a statue of Queen Boadicea in her chariot. She who routed the Roman invaders and later poisoned herself rather than be taken alive. The Victoria Embankment Gardens with the York Watergate.

Further down beyond the railway bridge was Cleopatraa's Needle. This Egyptian obelisk that stood in front of the Temple of the Sun at Heliopolis, 3,500 years ago. When it was being towed to England in 1877, this 'Needle', which is 68 feet high and weighing 180 tons, had to be abandoned in the Bay of Biscay during a storm.

"And there's more Allen, its sister column is now standing in Central Park, New York."

Allen felt like Ali Baba in the treasure cave of the Forty Thieves.

"How is it you're so well informed Peggy? There's more to you than meets the eye."

"You had better watch out. I'm a dark horse Allen."

After eating and drinking at the Savoy Hotel, off The Strand which was quite expensive, Peggy insisted on paying half the bill. It saved a big embarrassment as Allen found out later. He would have been short five shillings and sixpence.

When he told Peggy she laughed and said: "I forgot to tell you but I'm also a Seer. I've got a third eye."

"I'm beginning to believe you do."

"We'll go by bus to Covent Garden and from there we'll travel by Underground. Covent Garden to Kings Cross on the Piccadilly Line. You can get off at Baker Street and take the Circle Line to Edgware Road and I'll continue all the way to Watford Herts by my poor little self."

"When will I see you again?"

She searched his face for a full half minute before she spoke: "Did you enjoy the day Allen?"

"I really can't remember when I had such a great time. It was truly inspirational. You were fantastic Peggy. He smiled. And now I know for certain you are not just a pretty face."

She threw her arms around him.

"Give me a big hug. I've got an awful long way to go, Allen. I'll phone you at 'The Poppy' mid week. Again she studied his face: "Is that alright with you, Allen?"

"Yes of course. I'll be waiting for your call. Take care of yourself."

"You too."

KILKENNY'S
GREENVALE WOOLEN MILLS
BY SEAN KENNY

A CHANGE COMES TO 'THE POPPY'

On the first stairs landing at 'The Poppy' Allen saw the light on in the Staff dining room. Matt Ryan was waiting for him. Allen knocked before turning the knob and walked into the room.

There he was, as large as life, the big head- barman at 'The Poppy.' He was reading the 'Ireland's Own' which was sent to him every week without fail, by his old mother of seventy five years, still hail and hearty in West Cork. Matt read that homely magazine from cover to cover. The front cover was always a sketch by that famous artist Charles MacNeill with the title of the sketch at the bottom of the square. Beneath the sketch was the slogan: THE WEEK WOULDN'T BE THE SAME WITHOUT IT. Inside the front page what Cassidy says would warm the hearth of a frozen Eskimo. The ballad sheet gave the words of *McAlpine's Fusiliers*.

As down the glen came McAlpine's men,
With their shovels slung behind them
It was in the pub they drank their sub
And out on the spike you'll find them
They sweated blood and they washed down mud,
With pints and quarts of beer
And now we're on the road again
With McAlpine's Fusiliers.

I stripped to the skin with Darkie Finn
Way down upon the Isle of Grain;
With Horse – Face O' Toole we knew the rule
No money if you stopped for rain
McAlpine's God was a well filled hod
Your shoulders cut to bits and seared
And woe to he who looked for tea
With McApline's Fusiliers.

I remember the day when Bear O' Shea
Fell into a concrete stairs;
What Horse face said when he saw him dead,
It wasn't what the rich call prayers
"I'm a Navvy short; was the one retort
That reached unto my ears –
When the going's rough then you must be tough
With McAlpine's Fusiliers.

Now, there's a Ballad that Donall Mac Amhlaigh would appreciate. There isn't a man or woman in Kilkenny who doesn't read his article: 'The Irish Abroad', in the 'Ireland's Own.' This very year, the great man brought out his first book. Being a Gaelic scholar he wrote it in Irish. Dialann Deorai, se ainm ata ar: Diary of a Navvy, he named it. Although Donall was born in Galway, Kilkenny is his adopted home. And like myself, Allen thought, he too worked for a time in Greenvale Woolen Mills, before emigrating to England.

"You wanted to see me Matt?"

"Yes I did Allen. Did you have a nice day with that young woman from Callan?"

"We had a great time Matt."

"Sit down for a few minutes, there's some news about 'The Poppy' that you should know. I've already spoken to Ivor Davies about it and for what it's worth, he said he'd be happy to go along with it. The first thing is the former Governor and his wife Mike and Mary O' Hara will not be coming back to 'The Poppy.' To make a long story short, his father died and left Mike a substantial auctioneering business. A week ago Mike wrote to Whitbreads and recommended me for the job as Governor. Whitbreads agreed and so you see before you the new Governor of 'The Poppy.'

"I'm delighted for you Matt. It really couldn't happen to a nicer fellow."

"Thanks for that Allen. Now this is where you come into it. I am promoting you Head Barman at 'The Poppy'. You will have an increase of ten pounds per week in your pay packet. What do you say?"

"I don't know what to say Matt, except that I am over awed. Thank you Matt for having so much confidence in me. I only hope I can live up to your good opinion of me. First I was asked to read with the great Monaghan Poet Patrick Kavanagh. Next Peggy O' Shea reappeared as if from nowhere and now I'm to become Head Barman at 'The Poppy'. All I can say is 'wonders will never cease.' Thanks again Matt."

"You're the right man for the job, Allen."

EPISODE TWELVE

TO TRIP THE LIGHT-FANTASTIC DOWN TO 'DIRTY DICKS'
A GATEWAY TO NOWHERE
MRS. ROSIE TAYLOR NEE KEEGAN
A KITCHEN MECHANIC

TO TRIP THE LIGHT-FANTASTIC DOWN TO 'DIRTY DICKS.'

Pat Hunt sat in the Lounge bar at 'The Champion' on Bayswater Road, London. He was skimming over the pages of the Daily Mirror like a Kingfisher bird gliding back and forth across a fish infested water.

"Who made this coffee, – for God's sake, it's awful? Was it you Gwen? T'would poison that Russian monk Rasputin."

"I'm not saying. If you don't like it you don't have to drink it. You've probably got a sick head anyhow. You know what they say; the morning after the night before."

"Thanks for your diagnosis."

"You wha?" "Never mind Gwen just pour that rehashed beverage down the sink and try making some fresh coffee."

Pat was to meet his brother Allen at eleven o'clock this morning at the Marble Arch. Allen had phoned him the previous night saying: "It is of great importance that we should meet and talk. My guess is, you will be very surprised with what I have to tell you. The most important matters revolve around the lives of Mrs. Rosie Taylor and her daughter Patricia."

"Now why does that statement make me feel uncomfortable? I mean, how does Allen think that I am connected or could be involved in any way with their lives? And if that's not enough he said he had got the character of Nancy Blackmore under wraps. It's as if he had dug up her past and has compiled something of a dossier on her. How does he do it, – he's unbelievable.

Allen never liked her, – not from day one. He saw through her instantly. He's as sharp as a head-hunter's scalpel, that brother of mine. And then there is something else he wants to talk to me about. It concerns something that has come up at 'The Poppy.' I wouldn't be surprised if Mike O'Hara has called it 'A Day' as Governor.

He was due back at 'The Poppy' more than a week ago. Soon enough I'll get the lowdown on the whole shebang. He'll have it all off pat. And now that I think about it he will most likely want to know all about the Marble Arch. All the whys and wherefores of its erection and its' history. I wouldn't be one bit surprised if he should want to take notes. I shouldn't think he will stay in the bar trade for very long."

"Gwen, what do you know about the 'Marble Arch?'"

"Well Pat, its on Oxford Street."

"And – everyone knows that."

"Well, it's made of marble,"

"There's no mistaking it – you're a genius. Anything else?"

"Don't think so. Are you going sight-seeing Pat? Who's the lucky girl?"

"If I ever find her I'll let you know."

"You could tell that brother of yours, I'm free tomorrow night. He may call for me here at seven o'clock. I'll be ready and waiting with my glad rags on. Together we'll go tripping the light-fantastic down to 'Dirty Dicks', at Bishops Gate. The sky's the limit."

"I promise to tell him Gwen but don't hold your breath. I think you might have missed the boat."

A GATEWAY TO NOWHERE

"Then I'll have to make do with you, won't I?"

"It's my hard luck Gwen, but I'm working tomorrow night. Apart from all that excitement, is there anyone working in this establishment who knows anything of the history of the Marble Arch?"

"I think old Bert, the Potman was born down around there – on the Old Green Street off Park Lane. He's down in the cellar right now. Shall I ask him to come up?"

"Yes, please do Gwen. These old-timers often have handed-down knowledge from fathers to sons."

Old Bert was a typical Londoner, dressed in blue denim smock, canvas bootees and black beret. He had a pair of quizzical eyes above a Roman nose and a white goatee beard bristled under his chin.

"You wanted to see me Pat?"

"Yes I did Bert. Thanks for coming up. Would you like a cup of coffee and a ginger nut?"

"Yes please, - I'd like that."

"Take a seat Bert. Gwen will see to the coffee and biscuits. I am going to meet a brother of mine about a half hour from now at the Marble Arch. He has got a most inquisitive mind and wants to know all there is to know about anything and everything. Can you tell me anything about the Marble Arch?"

"I were born between Green Street and North Audley Street, an 'alf mile from 'Marble Arch.' T'were built for an triumphal Arch and were meant to be an entrance to Buckingham Palace. But wouldn't you know it, 'twere made too narrow for the State Coach and became a gateway into Hyde Park instead. That's a nice cup of coffee Gwen. Thanks for the treat Pat."

"You're welcome Bert, and you're earning the cuppa with your knowledge."

"There's a little more to it Pat. Later when the park boundary was moved back as far as Speakers Corner, the Marble Arch became a gateway to nowhere's."

"That's good stuff Bert: 'A Gateway to Nowhere.' Allen will enjoy that."

Bert was beaming. He never knew before, the value of what he knew. He was gaining confidence. "I know a little bout Tyburn Gallows too Pat, that stood across the road from Marble Arch where Edgware Road meets Oxford Street. That were the place of Public Executions. In the far off times when murderers and robbers were taken to Tyburn from Newgate to be publicly 'anged, the cart that carried them criminals were named 'the Ship of Fools. Nobody never seen a ship on wheels pulled by an 'orse. "

"Enough, enough Bert. There are nuggets of gold in what you have told me. I only hope I can remember it all."

Allen Hunt saw his brother Pat dismount from the 88 bus in front of the Odean Cinema on Oxford Street. Above the entrance to the cinema was the name of the latest blockbuster western then showing: The Magnificent Seven featuring Yule Brunner.

Must see that, one of these days. It got a great write up from the critics. Still a boy at heart. Cowboys and Indians. – Here he comes walking like a soldier on Parade, confident yet careful. All the time watching, always aware of his surroundings. He has seen me but made no sign of his recognition. At ten feet from me he smiles and speaks: "It's good to see you brother. This here is the Marble Arch, – a gateway to nowhere."

MRS. ROSIE TAYLOR NEE KEEGAN

"I like that: A gateway to nowhere. I just wonder then could Speakers Corner be an illusion – a place of the imagination, that doesn't exist in reality."

"You won't know that until you get up on your soap box."

"And if I don't feel the barbs and the arrows of critical dissent then I will know it is but a modern day Utopia."

"Now brother, tell me before you go off into a remote frame of mind, what is it that we need to speak about so urgently? Because I feel like a man about to be hanged, waiting for the drop."

"Certainly brother, that's why we are here. We'll take the least important question first: How things stand at 'The Poppy?' It only requires an explanation.

Mike O'Hara will not be returning as Governor. He recommended Matt Ryan for the job and Whitbread's Brewery accepted him. Matt came to me with the offer of Head Barman and a rise in my pay packet of ten pounds per week, – which I gladly accepted. So you are looking at the new Head Barman at 'The Poppy'. What do you think?"

"Congratulations brother. You understand you have been thrown in at the deep end. It won't be easy, but I reckon you can handle it. Matt is a great bloke, he will be there when and if you need him. That's put that problem to bed. Now tell me about you digging up the character of Nancy Blackmore. It wasn't a pick and shovel job, more than likely you poured over a police gazette with a magnifying glass."

"She has a criminal record alright and has done time in Pentonville Prison."

"Where did you get that information and how can you be sure it's true?"

"The answer to that brings us face to face with the most important question of all, namely, the lives of Mrs. Rosie Taylor and her daughter Patricia."

"Just ahead of us in the Park there is an underground restaurant. Let's go in and have some refreshments."

"Sure that's a good idea."

Once inside they sat down drinking coffee and tea with doughnuts and muffins, a little like characters from the Mad Hatters Tea Party.

"Aren't you becoming very Anglified brother, with your tea and muffins?" asked a wide grinning Pat.

"I wouldn't think so at all. I believe the Irish are bigger tea drinkers than the English. But to get back to answering your question: It was Mrs. Rosie Taylor nee Keegan, who as State Witness gave the evidence that helped convict Nancy Blackmore of fraud and embezzlement at Whighteleys of Bayswater. And saw her sentenced to six months imprisonment at Pentonville."

Pat Hunt's expression changed rapidly from the jovial altruistic to the sorrowful introvert. He looked at his brother narrowly and in near disbelief. But his intelligence was so quick witted that its electrical currents made contact with a whole series of events that had lain dormant for a long time. Once touched upon all these were recognised, engaged and understood.

"Of course," he said, partly to himself and partly to Allen. He laced his hands together as if in prayer and yes-nodded his head a half dozen times before he spoke. "What age is the child?"

"Patricia is three years old."

"Good God it's like something from the pen of Charles Dickens. Bill Taylor is not the child's father?"

"No. Her name is Patricia Keegan."

"How is Rosie? Is she well? It's so strange, – I've been thinking about her a lot lately. Did Rosie tell you the child was mine?"

"No. She didn't have to. Patricia is the moral of you. Everything fits into place. Bill Taylor is of the old school of gentlemen, but her marriage to him was a marriage of convenience. And the reason, Rosie told me all this was that she wanted me to warn you about Nancy Blackmore's criminal character. Rosie was afraid that Blackmore would destroy you. That's where it all stemmed from. Bill Taylor's health is not the best. I'm not at liberty to say any more, as I gave my word."

"And there was I all set to tell you about the history of the Marble Arch and Tyburn Gallows across the road from it, but you've driven it all out of my head, brother."

"Yes but what I've driven into your head is more than a gateway to nowhere. It's more likely the blueprint of a pathway to your future, brother."

"Ask Rosie if she'd write me a letter at 'The Champion, as soon as she can."

"As far as I am aware she'll be leaving 'The Poppy' this week and returning with Bill and Patricia to their home in Knightsbridge. But yes of course I'll tell her we discussed this matter and yes I'll ask her to write to you at 'The Champion.'"

"You are the best brother a man ever had, Allen."

A KITCHEN MECHANIC

"What's the matter with Ivor?" Matt Ryan asked Allen, in the Public bar at 'The Poppy.' "He's like a foal separated from its mother."

"I think he has got woman trouble Matt. When I asked him what was wrong he just shook his head and said, "it's Eileen. She's gone missing. I hope she hasn't had an accident."

"Look Allen, Ivor's got the afternoon off. Why don't you go along with him to her flat or place of work and see if you can find out what has happened. I don't think there will be any good news coming from that quarter. You could give him some support. He trusts you. I'll take over here."

Ivor Davies and Allen Hunt boarded the District Line train at the Edgware Road Underground station.

They would need to change at Paddington and take the Metropolitan line to Ladbroke Grove where Ivor's fiance Eileen Murphy had a flat.

"What does Eileen work at Ivor?"

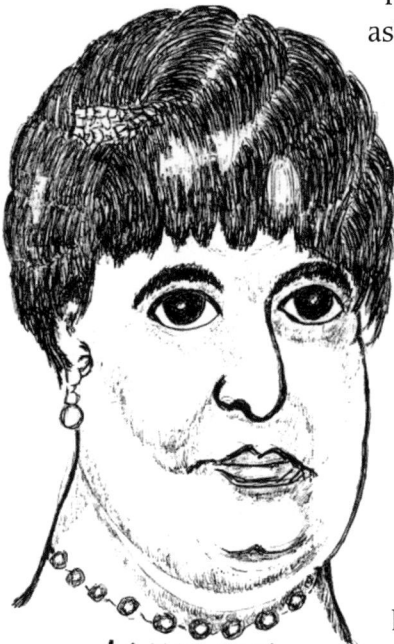

LANDLADY
HAD JOWLS ON HER LIKE A BULLDOG
BY SEAN KENNY

"She works in a 'Caff.,' called the 'Breakfast Dinner and Tea House' on the Harrow Road. She's a kitchen mechanic."

"That's a new one on me."

"It's London slang for anyone who works with pots, pans and plates."

"She's a cook then I expect:"

When they got to her basement flat at 56 Chesterton Road, they climbed the six steps and rang the bell at the main door.

"Does Eileen Murphy live here?"

"She did and left without paying her rent. She's a bad un, she is. Can't say I'm sorry she's gone – 'cept for the rent. Good riddance. I've set the Police on 'er."

The Landlady had jowls on her like a Bulldog: and was as fat as a Walrus in pup.

"Well she won't be coming back here Ivor, wherever she's gone to – and that's for sure."

"We'll try the 'Breakfast Dinner and Tea House' on the Harrow Road, Allen – maybe she's at work there today."

EPISODE THIRTEEN

I'VE GOT THE SPONDULICKS
A SUPTERFUGE
A SEARCH PARTY
THE POET, PATRICK KAVANAGH, ARRIVES IN LONDON

I'VE GOT THE SPONDULICKS

Eileen Murphy who was engaged to Ivor Davies, a Barman at 'The Poppy', was standing inside the front door of 'The George', Lounge bar and Restaurant, on the Hammersmith Broadway, London. She was looking for a certain man whom she had arranged to meet here, at this time. She looked searchingly around the large room which was already more than half full.

"Where the hell is he?" She patted her hand-bag with her right hand and smiled with satisfaction. It was a huge Lounge that could hold two hundred people comfortably. Some customers were sitting on high stools in front of a forty-foot English oak bar counter. The wall behind the counter was almost entirely covered with mirrors which made the large room look even larger. The shelves which were arranged in sections between the mirrors, were laden with every conceivable brand of bottled Spirits and Liqueurs. The multiplicity of shapes, colours and designs gave an air of artistic presentation to each section. The effect was not unlike an exhibition of Collage Art. All the usual and popular Spirits like: Brandy, Whisky, Gin, Vodka, Rum etc were turned upside down on 'optics'. The mirrors helped to promote the illusion that everything and everyone was in a state of flux. Large numbers of people sat in chairs at tables that were carved from the same wood as the long bar counter and high stools. These people were eating, drinking, talking, laughing, reading, smoking, smiling, sighing, scratching, staring, belching and some were coughing into serviettes while others were gesticulating with their hands and tapping their feet. And always there was a steady flow of people going towards the toilets and returning from them. All together it was a manifestation of the human condition and the herd instinct. "That's him over there. Who's that yob talking to him? Yew whoo, Winston." As she crossed the room the man who had been speaking to him suddenly disappeared.

She stopped at the table where a big black South African male in his early thirties sat. In front of him on the table were a glass of Spirits and a silver tankard of Lager beer. The very first words he said to her were: "Did you get the money?"

"That's a nice how do ya do, I must say. You might ask me how I was or tell me how nice I look. After all the trouble I went to and committed robbery into the bargain."

"Keep your voice down, will you, or you'll get the two of us lifted. Look I'ze sorry babe. Yo sure do look nice 'n pretty. I woz getting' a mite worried there fur a while. 'Cause ifn I don't come across wud the brass today, I'm a gonner fur sure."

"No yer not, my love. When I say I'll do id, it's as good as done." She opened her handbag and shoved it under his nose. "Smell that" she said and gave a screech of laughter like a surprised barn-owl and sat down facing him. "I've got the spondulicks right here. It's plain sailin' from here on in, for the two of us, Winston. By the way who was that you were talking to just then?"

"O him, – he was only lookin' fur directions. But I just knowed you'd come through, honey." Then he downed a large Gin and tonic faster than a Boa-Constrictor could swallow a duck egg.

"That was bloody quick. I mustn't have a mouth on me a-tall."

"Sorry babe, – what's yer poison? The usual is id, – vodker an' lime?"

A SUBTERFUGE

"I'd murder a large wan right now." He stood up and caught the attention of most of the occupants of the room except those whose backs were turned to him. Standing six feet four inches and weighing two hundred and thirty eight pounds, he looked like a contender for the heavyweight championship of Britain. Eileen Murphy exhaled loudly as her champion went towards the bar like a moving Pillar of the Acropolis. He was back in seconds with her large Gin and a dash of lime.

"Got to go to the wash room love. Be back in a minute." He walked through the signed, double oak doors leading to the Ladies and Gents toilets. Eileen fixed her handbag in front of her on the table.

"A cigarette would be just the job for this", she thought to herself. Opening her handbag cautiously, she foustered through it until she fished out a twenty packet of Marlborough cigarettes. Another probe and the plastic holder was out. "A match and I'm on fire." She scratched one against the side of the box that made a sispy sound and gave off a smell of brimstone. It lit in a little ball of pink and yellow flame. She brought the miniature torch to the tip of the cigarette and pulled on the plastic holder with a pop-pop of the lips. The smoking ritual was set in motion.

As she inhaled deeply and was about to relax a Drunk fell against her table and knocked over her drink. The lighting cigarette and holder fell from her lips onto her lap and she jumped up screaming, mille murder. When she turned to lambaste the stupid Drunk, he was nowhere evident. He was last seen running out the front door faster than Rodger Bannister on the day he broke the first four minute mile. She looked around the table – then under it. "Christ almighty where's me bloody bag with all the bloody money in id? The bastard has taken me money. The dirty rotten robber. I'm done for. I couldn't have luck. Now I've lost the two of 'em for certain. Poor old Ivor. What'll he think? Winston, where are ya? Jesus Christ, Winston I've been robbed and plundered entirely."

Winston came sauntering through the double oak doors back from the toilets. A group of people had gathered around Eileen's table. Some were trying to comfort her, others were merely curious and delighted with the fracas. She was in convulsions with crying. "Wha's up honey? Wha' happened?"

"I was robbed. Where the hell were you Winston when I was robbed?" and she went into another bout of bawling. One of the group who had gathered around Eileen's table gave Winston a running commentary on what had happened in his absence. But Winston didn't look overly surprised or concerned. He just kept nodding his head every now and then like a determined buyer chasing a bargain at an auction. When the hubbub had died down and the group disappeared, Winston looked at Eileen: "How much money was in the bag?"

"Three hundred and fifty quid. A friggin' fortune. Get the manager quick."

A SEARCH PARTY

Allen Hunt and Ivor Davies were out searching for Ivor's fiancé, Eileen Murphy. They called to the main door of the house above the dingy basement flat and rang the bell. "Does Eileen Murphy live here?"

"She did and left without paying her rent. She's a bad un, she is. Can't say I'm sorry she's gone – 'cept for the rent. Good riddance. I've set the Police on 'er."

The Landlady had jowls on her like a Bulldog: and was as fat as a Walrus in pup. "Well she won't be coming back here Ivor, wherever she's gone to – and that's for sure."

"We'll try the 'Breakfast Dinner and Tea House' on the Harrow Road, Allen – maybe she's at work there today." First we've got to get back to the Paddington area. The Harrow Road covers two sides of the Paddington parallelogram. The Caff (cafeteria) is located where Warwick Crescent intersects the Harrow Road. I'm not a very good Chapel person Allen but I'm praying she's not in big trouble." Allen didn't reply to this. It was common knowledge that Eileen Murphy was flying her kite over more than one mans territory and had gone to ground when the wind dropped in her favour. But, as is mostly the case; everybody knew except Ivor.

The Cafeteria was obviously a self service and so the two men collected their trays and walked along the selection counter. Allen chose a ham sandwich and Ivor picked an egg and mayonnaise one. At the end of the counter the only white person on the premises was serving tea, coffee, milk etc. "I'll have a cup of tea please. I wonder if you could help us. We are looking for a lady named Eileen Murphy. She works here," Allen said. The woman looked hard at Allen then at Ivor. She grimaced like Socrates did after drinking the Hemlock. "Are you from the Police?"

"No we're not. She is my fiance. Is there something wrong? Is she here?" Ivor looked very worried.

"She'll never come in that door again. She was caught with her hand in the 'till after she had got someone else sacked for it. I should have had her arrested." The middle aged woman looked at Ivor without a blink of sympathy. He turned to Allen: "I don't feel like eating."

"Me neither." They left down their trays and turned towards the door. All eyes were upon them. Ivor looked like he had been hit by a bus. He was in bits. As they neared the door she shouted after them in a sneering voice: If you two seriously want to find that one, you'll catch her doing the only thing she's good at, parading up and down the Bayswater Road after dark."

"Come on Ivor, let's get out of here – it's repressive. How about a drink?"

"Yes, I could use one now." As they walked down the Harrow Road there was a long pause. A pause that was pregnant with memories of better times, before the sweet and fresh had turned to sour and stale.

"What did I do wrong?"

"I don't think you did anything wrong."

"Then what happened? We were to be married next year, - in Kilkenny."

"Were you saving for it Ivor?"

"Yes we were. I scarcely spent a shilling in the past year."

"Who is holding the money, Ivor?"

"Eileen is." He looked at Allen, like a man who had just got a life sentence.

THE POET, PATRICK KAVANAGH, ARRIVES IN LONDON

Jack Boland, Construction Engineer, Building Contractor and partner of Luke Brannigan, was at Euston Station waiting for the Boat Train. The Monaghan born, Dublin based Poet, Patrick Kavanagh was coming to London to give a Poetry Reading at the Empress of Russia Pub Sloane Square. A small group of young Irish radicals had invited Patrick (not for the first time) to exhibit his Poetic genius.

Jack Boland had only met Patrick Kavanagh once before, but once met was well met where Patrick was concerned. And once seen and heard, was never to be forgotten.

If one was expecting to meet the popular conception of what a living Poet was one might expect to see a well honed, long haired, highly refined kind of person. Patrick Kavanagh was none of those things. He manifested none of those attributes. But he truly was a poet, first and last. Every inch and every word of him: in the Dantean depths of his soul, in the Olympian heights of his mind and in the Johsonian proportions of his body.

Jack spotted Patrick with his head and shoulders stuck out of a carriage window as the boat-train came to a stop on Euston Station. Ideally he was the picture of a big Irish countryman, – a west of Ireland Navvy perhaps. This nonchalant, awkward looking big man,

THE POET PATRICK KAVANAGH
BY SEAN KENNY

stepped down from the train and looked disdainfully all around him. Jack waved enthusiastically like a shipwrecked sailor trying to attract the notice of a searching aeroplane. Patrick began walking with the gait of a tired farmer following a deep-set plough pulled by two horses. He carried a small brown belted suitcase and had a pale cream coloured light-weight raincoat on his shoulder. Thick rimmed glasses rested upon his well shaped bigish nose and he was growling something aloud to himself while wagging an unlit cigarette north and south with his lips, when he came abreast of Jack Boland. "Those blasted lighters never work when you want them to. Have you a match my friend? It's good to see you again. Thanks. Does this place ever sleep?" His steel blue eyes were smiling faintly behind the slightly enlarged lenses. "Let us begone from this overcrowded meeting place." He spoke with authority like W.B. Yeats might have done in the Senate. "Is there a Pissary in this bloody place?

"Yes there is Patrick, over here." "I need to empty the bladder if I'm going to imbibe a naggin or two of Irish Whiskey that will bring me back to my old self."

"Right, that's that. As me poor mother used say: 'Tis better out than your eye." He gave a loud raucous laugh that sounded a bit like hailstones hopping on a galvanized roof. "Next stop Fleet Street if my memory serves me rightly, 'tis the home of British newspapers, and that exasperating but affectionate old rag called the Irish Times. After I've walked the land, because we are neighbours children, and made a phone call back to Dublin – no charge, you and I will adjourn to the nearby hostelry known as 'Mooney's Tavern and we'll talk in our cups for an hour or two. Then when I'm feeling me oats you can tell me something of this young Kilkenny poet that you have invited to read with me."

EPISODE FOURTEEN

WALKING THE LAND
THE LAST LAUGH
A NEW MAGAZINE SECTION
AN EXPLANATORY NOTE

WALKING THE LAND

Patrick Kavanagh the great Monaghan Poet had arrived in London. Jack Boland, Building Contractor was at Euston Station to welcome him on behalf of a group of young I.R.A. men. This group had paid Patrick's expenses. They also had organised a venue for a Poetry Recital at the Empress of Russia Pub, Sloane Square, on the following Saturday night. Patrick and Jack were now on their way to Fleet Street, the home of British newspapers.

"Whenever I'm in London Jack, I always call at the office of the 'Irish Times.' I regard these people as my neighbours and I'm just dropping in to walk the land. I can phone Dublin from there. There's no charge. 'Tis like when your car is broken you can borrow your neighbours. Then when we've turned over the sod of our communications we can adjourn to Mooney's Tavern, a few footsteps down the street and water our horses, to say nothing about ourselves of course. We can talk in our cups then for an hour or two. And when I'm feeling me oats we'll talk about the arrangements for the Poetry night and you can tell me something about this young Kilkenny poet whom you have invited to read with me."

Jack Boland felt a little like Thomas Carlyle must have done when he spoke about Thomas Macauley's unceasing flow of conversation which gave him little or no chance to get a word in: "Macauley was all very well for a while, but one couldn't live under Niagara." If Jack felt somewhat deafened by Niagara's roar he felt that its powerful flow fertilized everything before it. The nutrition compensated for the noise, you understand.

"Now how does that sit with you Jack?"

"That's first class with me Patrick."

"You're the master of ceremonies here. Like they say in America; you're the man."

Together they walked into the 'Irish Times' office on Fleet Street. Patrick went to the front to let Jack see he knew the lye of the land. He spoke to the young receptionist seated behind the counter: "Good day to you young woman. Is the manager of this old news rag on the premises?" His voice boomed like a large Chinese gong when struck with a hammer. He startled the receptionist who rose off her chair and flopped back down again like a plump young duck learning to fly.

"Is your boss accepting calls from fellow scribblers or newspaper hacks these days?"

As the plump young bird made another attempt to rise, an office door opened with a laugh and a middle-aged broadly smiling man stepped out with hand extended towards Patrick. "Patrick my old friend you are very welcome to the 'Irish Times' office in particular and to London town in general. 'Tis yourself that's looking well."

"Not too much of that old stuff now, but 'tis nice to see your smiling face and know they haven't given you the sack yet." This is my friend and connoisseur of the Arts, Jack Boland."

"I believe I've heard of Jack. You are a Building Contractor and partner of Luke Branningan. Have I the right man?"

"Indeed you have. You've got me down to a 't'."

"Trust a newspaper man to dig up who's who."

"Well that's our trade and calling Patrick. You're not a bad hand at it yourself. Listen, come on in here until I see if I can find a little holywater to bless yourselves with."

THE LAST LAUGH

"If you're going to go religious on us, maybe 'twould be best if you stuck to the miracle of the Marriage Feast of Kana." And you can kneel down yourself, and I'll give you the pledge for life."

The newspaper man found two tumblers in the bottom of a cupboard. These were half pint decorative drinking glasses, as heavy as a small earthenware flower pot but twenty times more expensive. "Waterford glass are they?"

"The same. They don't make them like that anywhere else in the world."

From the bottom drawer of a filing cabinet he lifted an unopened bottle of Powers Gold Label. The cork popped. "Say when? Do you want water?"

"No thanks. There's enough there already."

"How about you Jack?"

Yes please. I was born beside the sea."

He filled up his large whiskey to the brim with H2O. "Go ndeirig an bothar lib."

This was replied to with; "Slán," and "Slán go saoghal agib."

Patrick swallowed down half of the double whiskey and made a noise like a Winter wind worrying an empty tin can across a lonely street.

"That hit the spot, I dare say Patrick."

"Aye, like a nail on the head. You're not having one yourself?"

"No Patrick I have to put the paper to bed. But I'll join you if I may in Mooney's a little later?"

"We'll consider it a privilege, won't we Jack?"

"Yes indeed. I'm looking forward to it."

"Are you in London for pleasure Patrick or are you plying your trade?"

"I'm setting up my shop window now and I'll be selling my wares next Saturday night at the Empress of Russia Pub Sloane Square, at a Poetry Recital."

"Well Patrick, that was good timing. I'll give your Poetry Recital night, prominence in the Literary Review Column of the 'Irish Times' tomorrow."

"A thousand thanks for that. May you be the father of an Archbishop, the uncle of a Lord Mayor and discover some kinship between the two of us in the propagation of the Word, Amen." Patrick scoffed what whiskey was left in the glass and stood up. "I'd be much obliged now if I could use your telephone to make contact with Dublin about matters of a most compelling nature?"

"My house is your house and everything that's in it. Go right ahead."

"Thanks again. But I must tell you, that's what the spider said to the fly before he ate him."

"Now would I do a thing like that. In any case Patrick, I think I'd need to sharpen more than my wits if I were to chance taking a bite out of you. I'd bet you're as tough as a veteran two horned bull rhinocerous."

This seemed to please the poet no end and he guffawed like the long and wrongly accused victim, who had had the last laugh.

"There is a phone in the next room Patrick if you want a little privacy."

When Patrick had gone into the next room the newspaper man turned to Jack: "That was a tidy contract, Luke and yourself landed. I understand it's for five hundred, three bedroomed semi-detached dormer houses at Wimbledon."

"That's accuracy to the point of perfection – Sir. You are bang-on. I'll bet there is nothing flies over your head that isn't recorded and examined under the microscope!"

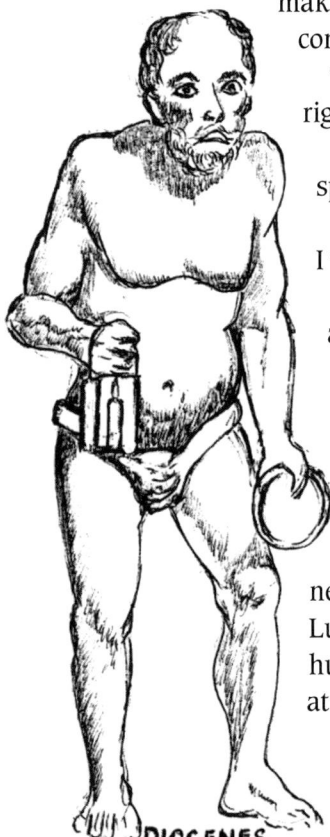

DIOGENES
SEARCHING FOR AN HONEST MAN
BY SEAN KENNY

"That's not completely true. There are some objects that fly at night and therefore escape detection."

"But, did not Diogenes walk about with a lighted candle at high noon and when asked what he was doing replied, I'm looking for an honest man?"

"Touché, Jack."

A NEW MAGAZINE SECTION

"Allen the phone is ringing in the hall. Do you think you could get it?"

"Yes I can. I'm all set here and there's ten minutes to opening time. It's probably Whitbread's Brewery calling about their delivery time today."

"If it is tell them to get here between two and three o'clock if possible, when there's a lull."

"Right Matt, I've got that." Allen Hunt went to answer the phone at 'The Poppy'. "Hello. Who's speaking please? Is this Whitbread's Brewery?"

"No 'tis not. This is your Irish newspaper correspondent, calling."

"'Tis you Pat. Something has come up. What's the good news? But first of all, how are you?"

"As your old friend Johnnie Dowling used to say: 'I couldn't bear to be better, because if I was I'd bust.'

"And there was another character who used to say: I wouldn't tell you a lie yousir. And the same fellah couldn't tell the truth if he was paid for it. So said the Red Grace."

"I'll tell you this Allen: Dad will never be dead while you're alive. It's not that but this: An old schoolpal of mine, Paddy Kelly, walked into The Champion last night with a copy of the 'Kilkenny People' in his fist. He told me it's on sale here in a Newsagent's shop on Tottenham Court Road, every week. Dunphy's Newsagents right beside the Underground Station. Make a note of that."

"It's done brother. Always have pen and paper ready. Now, what's this sensational piece of news from Kilkenny?"

"It's right up your alley, brother. Listen it's about a New Magazine Section for the 'People.' The heading reads: "I Wish This Venture The Greatest Success." So said Alderman Seamus Monahan, Mayor of Kilkenny (I'm reading this verbatim) when he visited the offices of the 'Kilkenny People,' to watch the first copies of the 'New Magazine Section rolling off the huge presses. Mr. Monahan said that he was very impressed with the production and expressed great interest in some of the specially written feature Articles. (It goes on)

The Mayor was quite intrigued with the principal heading in our feature; 'Looking Back On Long Ago." The headline reads: When Mayor Threw Champagne Luncheon, and it recalls the pomp and ceremony attached to the Mayoral Elections of the year 1861, just a century ago. Times have surely changed since those days."

"If I may interject brother, this is history in the making. I'll read on."

The introduction of a regular weekly Magazine Section, produced in entirely different format, is an historic milestone in the records of Irish Journalism. It is the first regular Magazine Section of its kind to be produced by Any Irish Newspaper and its introduction this week is a very proud occasion for the Editor and Staff of the 'Kilkenny People.'

This week also we publish the first article of a series on the life and times of the late Jim Landy – the Kilkennyman who travelled the world and experienced excitement and intrigue in China, in Russia, in the Argentine and in the U.S.A. In 1930 he returned to Ireland to manage the firm of Clover Meats (then the Irish Co-operative Meats Ltd.) in Waterford and later became Managing Director. The Kilkenny People has the copyright of this brilliant autobiography."

"What do you think?"

"I think it's superb. Can't wait to read it."

"And, at the end of the New Magazine Section there's a brilliant photograph of two men, – one of whom is a very good friend of yours. The caption read: Setting the New Magazine 1961 are Sean Kerwick and Sean Nevin."

"Don't let anyone have that newspaper Pat. I'll be over tomorrow to collect it."

"I thought you would. Watch how you go brother. Slán leat."

"Agus slán agat, Pat."

AN EXPLANATORY NOTE

Dear Pat,

It has been a long time since we saw each other and much has happened in both our lives that has probably changed us forever. I hope you are in good health and taking care of yourself. Your brother Allen is very like you in many ways. He is a lovely person and a good friend to Patricia, Bill and myself. He told me that you wished I would write to you. I presume you have questions that you want answers to, and so have I naturally enough.

I did write to you from Ireland at your old address in Notting Hill Gate several times. But my letters all came back unopened. I didn't know at that time that you were suspected of having links with 'you know who', and were constantly moving house. I had no way of knowing all this at that time. I also presumed you were no longer interested and that you must have found someone else. What I cannot understand though is why you never wrote to me, – that is supposing you were still interested?

In case you have not found out up to now; it was Nancy Blackmore who was at the back of my leaving London in the first place. It was she who stole the money from the Accounts Dept., at Whighteleys of the Queensway, Bayswater, where I worked.

I was called to give evidence against her at the trial in Marylebone Crown Court. She was quite belligerent during the trial and made several threatening remarks to me. When the magistrate eventually gave her a three-month sentence in Pentonville Prison she swore she would come looking for me as soon as she got out. Instantly the magistrate doubled her sentence to six months.

As the months went by my health deteriorated. To tell you the truth Pat, I feared for my life. I couldn't bring myself to tell you, believing you would think me a silly little woman. And I really did need to get away – to breathe the west of Ireland air, and avoid being confronted by that woman. I was so ill in fact, I was not sure if I was pregnant or not.

Our daughter (yours and mine) was born in Bantry on the 7th July 1958, and was Christened Patricia after yourself.

One year and a half later, I left Patricia in the care of my mother and returned to London, in the hope of finding out what happened to you.

It was through Matt Ryan, then Head-barman at The Poppy that I found out where you were. Matt is from Ballylicky Cross, about a mile from Bantry and is a good friend of the family. It would be hard to meet a finer man! I'm so happy he has been appointed Governor at The Poppy.

To get on with the story Pat: Try to imagine my horror when I discovered you were engaged to the woman who had caused me so much grief. The very person who had driven us apart.

I met Bill Taylor and we got married quietly in St. Patrick's Catholic Church Soho Square. I told Bill about Patricia and about you too, Pat. To my surprise Bill suggested we should bring Patricia to live with us in London. He is a man of great understanding and great kindness.

We are leaving The Poppy today and returning to our home in Knightsbridge. Take care of yourself Pat. I'll always remember you.

Love

Rosie.

EPISODE FIFTEEN

RENEWING OLD ACQUAINTANCES
THEY CAME TO CLAIM THE BODY
WHO WAS WATCHING WHOM

RENEWING OLD ACQUAINTANCES

The hubbub had died-down and the customers had returned to their normal behaviour patterns at The George Lounge bar and Restaurant on the Hammersmith Broadway, London. Most people who had witnessed the uproar and confusion were excited by it and elated, as well as being shocked and frightened.

"I mean, it could have been me dear," a comfortably well rounded, fifty year old woman was saying to her near emaciated, keen eyed husband. "I don't know that you would have been much help if that Drunk, had fallen across me."

"He wasn't a Drunk and he didn't fall. He ran against her. It was a set-up from start to finish. If you kept your eyes on your surroundings instead of in that Alice in Wonderland make-up mirror, you might see what's going on."

"I've never heard such rubbish. He was the drunkest man I ever saw in my life. Disgraceful that's what it was and in the middle of the day at that." Her skinny partner shook his head from side to side like a wagging pendulum clock.

"Are you not aware that he stole her handbag and went out the front door faster than Jesse Owens at the 1936 Berlin Olympics. But that's not the half of it: That supposed Drunk was deep in conversation with that man-mountain Negro before that misfortunate woman sat at that table."

"Christ Almighty, you have your eyes on everyone except me. Don't I count at all?" He made no answer but played a tattoo on the table while humming, "tiddley um, tiddley um, tiddley um tum tum." She looked at him like an exasperated fourteen year old sister would eye the nasty idiosyncrasies of her ten year old brother. "What exactly happened here?" The manager of "The George" was at the table where a distressed Eileen Murphy and her black South African partner sat. "I can't say boss. I wuz out in the toilets when she wuz robbed. You tell 'em babe."

"Do I know you Sir?" The manager was searching the face and person of the giant black South African who was almost as tall sitting as the manager was standing. "No Sir. I don't reckon you do boss."

"You certainly look familiar. What is your name Sir?" He asked while producing official company writing paper and pen.

"It wasn't me was robbed boss, 'twas her" and he jabbed a large index finger as big as the handle on a fireside shovel into Eileens shoulder.

"Hey Winston, that hurt for Christ's sake. I'm not a punch-bag, you know!"

"Winston what?" asked the manager who was showing greater signs of interest by the minute. "I asked you a question Sir."

"Winston Warbarton." Eileen blurted out the information without thinking.

"Would I be right in saying that our paths have crossed once before Sir?"

"I jus' don't know what yer talkin' about," and he began to fidget and scratch like a Doss-house dog with fleas.

"And can I have your name and address madam please?"

"Eileen Murphy from Chesterton Road, 58A Basement...a, – no. I've left there and, a – where are we staying now Winston?"

"Wha's that got to do with the robbery Mr?"

"The Police will need to call and take a statement, sir. I am required by Law to furnish the Police with the necessary information. If you are reluctant to give your addresses, please keep your seats while I go and ring Hammersmith Police Station. In the meantime you may have what you want to drink, with the compliments of "The George." He walked smartly towards the right end of the long bar counter and through the door with the gold lettering that spelt; "Managers Office. On his way he winked at one of the barmen who followed him into the office. "Is that him Mick?"

"That's him. He pulled the same stunt about three months ago over in the 'Clarendon.' He's a well-known Pimp, among other things. I'm told he's got three women working for him on the Bayswater Road."

"That's where this Eileen Murphy – if that's her real name, – is heading for now, – or my name is not Bobby Moore. Get the Police Station on the phone quick and I'll see if I can get them over here before this pair leave."

"I'd bet a pound to a penny he's taking her off the premises as we speak."

"Is the phone ringing?"

"Yes it is. There's someone on the line now. Here take the phone. I'll check if they are still on the premises."

"I'm not leaving here until I get my money, and that finishes it. I'll stay here 'till Doomsday."

"Then you'll be lifted an' brought fur a ride in the 'Paddy Wagon.' Where are you gonna tell 'em you got the money in the furst place, eh? – from yer Fairy Godmother? Lets git outa here while the goin's good. Do ya hear?"

WINSTON WARBARTON (THUG)
BY SEAN KENNY

Meanwhile Mick had poured a large Vodka and lime for Eileen and had pulled a pint of Larger beer for Winston. Winston was getting to his feet when Mick arrived at the table with the drinks. "Now folks, these drinks come with the compliments of the management. If there is anything further don't hesitate to ask." Winston put the pint of Larger on his head. It was like pouring a cup of water down a manhole. He lifted Eileen to her feet as easily as a child could stand a toy soldier. "Git that into you, an' lets go."

She tried to imitate the black man's cataract swallow and took a fit of coughing half-way through her drink. "Gimme that," he said, "afore ya drown," and he downed it. He marched her out of the Lounge by the arm like a burly Garda Sergeant would march an elusive young truant back to school. "They've gone Bobby. He knew we were onto him. She's got no cop-on at all. He led her out like a lamb to the slaughter."

"I don't think so Mick. She may not be the brightest but she's no angel. That one has been down more than one dark alley in her time. I reckon if she does take up a beat on the Bayswater Road she'll be but renewing old acquaintances."

THEY CAME TO CLAIM THE BODY

Meg McNeill and her one remaining son Sean were travelling light to London. Neither she nor he had ever been outside of Ireland before. She was a big woman with near masculine features and a fluency of expression. Approaching her forty seventh birthday, she had been a widow for almost ten years. To anyone familiar with the arts, she looked for all the world like 'Whistlers Mother.'

Her son Sean was a big angular, wide-eyed eighteen year old lad who looked like his mother, except in the communications department. He was more likely to do it than to talk about it. He carried a small dark brown suitcase in his boney red hand and had an old L.D.F. knapsack strapped to his slightly stooped back.

They were arriving at Euston Station hoping to meet Luke Brannigan who was Meg's brother and Sean's uncle. The underlying reason for their presence in London was a tragic one. They had come to claim the body of young Billy McNeill, who had hanged himself in his cell at Wormwood Scrubs Prison.

Luke and Monsignor Dan O'Driscoll who was Parish Priest of the Church of the Immaculate Conception at Farm Street, Berkeley Square, were waiting patiently for their arrival.

Meg wore a black Satin two piece suit with lapels on the jacket as big as a mans suit. On her feet she wore navy blue flat heeled size eight laced shoes and on her head a navy cake-tin shaped hat with a veil of black muslin gauze hanging before her face.

Sean's hair was standing erect like a tuft of brown grass. On his feet he carried a well polished pair of size ten brogues. He wore a grey tweed double-breasted jacket and a black corduroy pants.

"Here they are Monsignor. Poor Meg, – she looks terrible."

"Meg, how are you poor woman?" He put his arms around her. "This is Monsignor Dan O'Driscoll." They shook hands. "It's a sad state to meet you in Monsignor. This is my son Sean. He's the man of the house now."

"He will be your pride and joy Mrs. McNeill. It's good to meet you Sean." Sean made no answer but merely nodded his head.

"You must be weary Meg. A cup of tea would work wonders."

"I see a toilet over here. I'll be back in a few minutes."

"We will be in that restaurant over there." Monsignor O'Driscoll pointed at the neon lighted sign "Tea and Sandwiches." Sean nodded and was gone, leaving the small suitcase with his Uncle Luke.

Meg sat down with a sigh at a small one legged formica covered, round table. She sipped the tea and looked all around her in amazement. Her native intelligence told her that even though this gigantic place was overflowing with great masses of human kind it showed no signs of humanity. It was but a giant conveyor belt that continually transported people back and forth, in and out with marvelous monotony, untouched by human emotions like sorrow or pain. It was a cold calculating monster, a mechanical hub, that attracted and then dispatched the young with the old, the foolish with the wise and all with the same disinterested exactitude.

"How do you feel now Meg?" Luke asked his sister.

"I would just as soon the ground would open up and swallow me. I have Sean here with me and all he wants to do is kill someone for the death of his brother. And I haven't the courage to tell him Billy committed suicide, for fear he might be tempted to do the same himself in a fit of remorse. The poor lad believes Billy died for Ireland."

"Is there no God, Father? Will we ever get out of this black hole we've fallen into? All the good is torn out of me. I'm like a poor cripple in body and mind. If it wasn't for Sean, I'd give up the ghost. If his father were alive itself, I could turn to him for consolation. I know he'd carry the load. He was a gallant man but God took him too. What did I ever do to deserve this? Why didn't God take me and leave poor Billy his young life. Mine is over and done with now anyhow. If I can stay on my feet 'till we can get him back home, I won't care whether I'm buried along with him or not."

"Hush Meg, Sean is coming back. Don't be breaking your heart."

"No Luke, let her talk. It will be good for her to talk it out."

"Will I be able to see Billy or will the coffin be sealed?"

"You'll be able to see him, Meg."

"Did Fr. John contact you today Luke?"

"He did. He wired me from Ankara."

"Where's that place?"

It's in Turkey. He'll be in Rome this evening. Then on to Paris and London tomorrow with God's help."

WHO WAS WATCHING WHOM

Two young men strolled into 'The Poppy' Public Bar on the Edgware Road. They were talking in undertones and were obviously on good terms as they joked and smiled about things that they alone understood. One was a born Londoner and the other was from Cashel, Co. Tipperary. These were the two who had been in 'The Champion' on the night Pat Hunt had demolished the two thugs who had accompanied Nancy Blackmore, for the purpose of Pat's destruction.

"Good evening gentlemen. What can I do for you?"

"Good day to you sir. We'll have two pints of your Best Bitter, – in your own time."

"Am I right in thinking we have already met?" Allen asked.

"You are quite right. But could you tell us where it was that we met?" and he turned smiling to his south of Ireland friend saying; "I'll eat my hat, if he not only remembers where it was, but also when it was and with whom."

"You're on."

The two men looked quizzically at Allen Hunt, one pursing his lips and the other grinning like a punter who had just been given the winner of the Grand National, straight from the horse's mouth.

Allen answered "It was at the Savoy Hotel off the Strand, last week where I was having a meal with a lady friend, whom I am quite sure you also know all about her by now. Before that I spotted the two of you at Charing Cross Pier and later at Cleopatras Needle. Now, there is no need for you to eat your hat sir. But tell me what is it that you really came in here for?"

The two men who were the soul of secrecy moved closer to the bar counter. Again it was the Londoner who spoke "We have a proposition for you Allen Hunt, one we feel you will be proud to execute."

EPISODE SIXTEEN

YOU MUST KNOCK THEM DEAD
TO SHUN THE ENGLISH LYRICAL TRADITION
WHEN I AM OLD

YOU MUST KNOCK THEM DEAD

"Could I speak to a young man named Allen Hunt?"

"This is he. Who's speaking please?"

"Patrick Kavanagh. I was given your number by Jack Boland, who is your friend, I understand."

"That's right Mr. Kavanagh. He said you would phone me some time today, about your Poetry Reading on Saturday night at the Empress of Russia Pub."

"You will be reading too won't you?"

"Yes. I can't find the words to express my gratitude sir?"

"Don't bloody well call me sir. And in any case it's your business to find words for every and any occasion under the sun. You are a poet are you not?"

"A poor poet trying to learn his trade Mr. Kavanagh. Could I ask you where you are right now?"

The storm subsided and a warm breeze got up to replace it.

"I am in a pleasant little pub called 'The Hoop' at Notting Hill Gate."

The lumber jack is in the forest and the sailor is on the high seas, Allen thought to himself. "I'll be there in twenty minutes" he said.

Allen stuffed the few poems he had selected into a large used envelope and hurried out the door. He felt like James Clarence Mangan going to Kincora. He recited the poem Kincora on his way to the Underground tube station.

"O dear are the images my memory calls up
Of Brian Boru! – how he never would miss
To give me at the banquet the first bright cup!
Ah, why did he heap on me honours like this?
Why, O Kincora?"

He was just in time to board the District Line which was leaving for Earls Court and destinations outward like Ealing Broadway, Richomnd, Upminster and Wimbledon. Allen would be getting off three stops down the line. First stop Paddington, then Bayswater and Notting Hill Gate. The Hoop was within shouting distance of the Underground Station.

Patrick Kavanagh was sitting on his own in the upstairs Lounge on a cushioned armchair with a large Irish whiskey nudging a glass of beer that touched a twenty packet of Gold Flake cigarettes, in a fog of smoke to prove it. He looked like the enormous Gaekwar of Baroda being weighed after eating a sumptuous meal to ascertain how much gold he would be paid for his annual remuneration.

"I'm Allen Hunt Mr. Kavanagh."

"I thought as much seeing your pose and your portfolio. What are you having to drink?"

"A pint of Best Bitter please."

He took a ten shilling note from his pocket. "Here, I'll do the honours."

Allen bought his drink and left the change in front of Patrick. "Thank you."

"Don't mention. It's an ancient Irish custom. Now have I got your attention?"

"I'm all ears." Allen answered. "Then let us begin."

Patrick cleared his throat, then coughed and Allen thought the noises he made were like a horse with the whooping-cough. He took a mouthful of whiskey and began to speak: "A poet preparing to read his works in front of an audience is like a soldier going to war. One, has to have his gun cleaned and cocked, ready to fire. The other must have his poetry primed and ready to spit out, a rat-a-tat-tat. And don't ever be afraid to offend their sensibilities or make them feel outraged. Remember what Oliver Goldsmith said of Samuel Johnson's style in metaphor: "If his pistol missed fire, he would knock you down with the butt." "Wounding them is never enough Allen. You must knock them dead."

TO SHUN THE ENGLISH LYRICAL TRADITION

"A poet can never be one of the people. He may and indeed must live and socialize with the people, but he can never be part of their mundane togetherness. He must always be apart, pulling his cart up-hill and away from the crowd, on his lonesome. If you can understand that you are on the right road, Allen. I see you spell your name Allen and not Alan. That's an instant give away. It shows, if not yours, your family's political aspirations. Allen, Larkin and O'Brien – the Manchester Martyrs. Am I right, young man?"

"Yes you are right sir."

"I'm neither a knight nor a baronet and I would be obliged if you would call me by my Christian name or not at all."

"I'll address you as Patrick from here on in."

"Now I've read a few of your poems, given to me by Jack Boland and let me say, they are not without some merit. Largely speaking your poetry is written in the conventional form and language of the English lyrical tradition. In fairness you could scarcely have done otherwise. You had no Irish tradition in the English language to draw from. But now you have me. I am the first of the Irish born English speaking writing poets to shun the English lyrical tradition. I penned poems just like you are writing now, right up to six years ago."

"It was 1955 after coming out of hospital in Dublin while sitting on the banks of the Grand Canal between Baggot and Leeson Street Bridges, in that warm Summer of fifty five I wrote:

"Leafy-with-love banks and the green waters of the canal
Pouring redemption for me, that I do
The will of God, wallow in the habitual, the banal,
Grow with nature again as before I grew."

"And there and then in that moment of great daring I became a poet. I had broken free. You see Allen, poetry is a way of seeing and a way of saying."

"But Patrick, I thought 'A Soul for Sale' which you wrote for The Penguin Book of Irish Verse, was great stuff."

"Not a bit of it. It is loud, journalistic and worst of all untrue. That one was sought after by the English publishers mostly, along with another dreadful dirge called Mother Ireland:"

"It would never be Summer.
Always Autumn
After a harvest always lost."

Poetry is the expression of a personal point of view. In point of fact I would have to say that my poem, "The Great Hunger", is not strictly speaking, poetry. There are some queer and terrible things in "The Great Hunger", but it lacks the nobility and repose of true poetry." "The standing army of Irish poets never falls below 10,000 – and they all write out of the 'Golden Treasury.' But to tell the truth so did I, up to 1955, as I have just told you. Therefore it is the poets task to find, to invent that special language with which he alone will be capable of expressing his personal vision or point of view."

The heart of a song singing it
Or a poem writing it
Is not caring

Not caring is really a sense of values and a feeling of confidence. A man who cares is not the master. Avoid artificial diction Allen like the plague. Poetry should express itself in a personalised vernacular."

"Could I ask you Patrick, what do you think of Cyril Connellys statement on the creative writers role in society? He said that it was the true purpose of a writer to produce a masterpiece. How does that hang with you?"

"It hangs like Pierpoint, hanged the innocent, along with the guilty. How many masters do we have? Who is to say what a masterpiece is? Was Shakespeare: 'An upstart Crow as Robert Greene maintained in 1592 when he wrote "there is an upstart Crow beautified with our feathers with that his tigers heart wrapped in a players hide, supposes he is as well able to bombast out a blank verse as the rest of you." Was he then a plagiarist; or was he something tremendous: Not a man, but a whole continent; there lived in him great men, whole multitudes, whole landscapes. And then again what was it George III said of him according to Fanny Burneys Diary:

"Was there ever such terrible stuff as the greater part of Shakespeare? Only one must not say so."

Allens thoughts were spinning like the spindles spun on the old spinning machines called 'mules', back home in Greenvale Woolen Mills.

WILLIAM SHAKESPEARE
BY SEAN KENNY

"Now tell me about this great Literary Magazine that ye brought out in Kilkenny last year? What did ye call it?"

"The Kilkenny magazine. It was subtitled; An All-Ireland Literary Review. The Kilkenny Literary Society was formed in January of last year and they were the ones who had it published."

"I bought the first edition in Hodges Figgis and Company Dawson Street. James Delahunty from High Street Kilkenny is the Editor."

"That's right, – James and Frank McEvoy are responsible for putting it together. As well as writing for it they also did the donkey work – I couldn't be sure but I think the original idea to bring out a Literary Magazine was the brain-child of Frank McEvoy, who then went on to convince James Delahunty that it would be a worthwhile venture."

"Francis McManus threw a lot of cold water on the attempt, while at the same time praising the idea. Only what he said might yet prove to be correct."

"What do you think of W.B Yeats' poetry?"

"I read somewhere Patrick, that, and I quote: What Yeats and Kavanagh had in common was that it took them a considerable time to find their own voices, unquote."

"Yeats, until his old age worked a very precious but very narrow vein or ore. It was only towards the end that he saw the potentials of mass production, but did not have the raw material of experience to keep such a venture going. He was too restricted in his material. Shakespeare, Swift, Auden, Yeats, Thomas etc., all give the impression that they have found a formula and that they could employ ghosts to turn out their particular line of poetry. For part of genius is the discovery of rich veins of 'gold' in a world that we all thought exhausted or even bankrupt. You see Allen, there is something of the Prospectors luck about a great poet's success."

"What do you think of todays poets and their poetry, Patrick. Should we believe W.B. Yeats when he said:

"Poets of Ireland learn your trade
Sing of whatever is well made
Scorn the sort now growing up
All out of shape from toe to top."

"Great poets never teach us anything. They burn in the 'Smithy' of their souls the raw material of life and produce from it, this erotic creative essence which is an orgy of sensation and nothing more – when we say 'The poet is born not made,' – He is to this extent, that no one else by taking thought can produce in himself this synthesizing nature."

"Much of todays poetry is a sham. It's a scissors and paste job. Study it closely and you'll discover that a lot of today's so called poetry is only prose cut up into lines to make it look like poetry. Another thing I would say to young Irish poets: instead of trying to be more Irish, try being more human."

"You used an expression a while ago: 'I'm all ears: Now listen to this which was written by a truly great poet:

"Every evening the oddest collection
Of characters crowd this inn;
Here a face from the farm, its frankness yearning
For corruption and riches; there
A gaunt gospel whom grinning miners
Will stone to death by a dolmen;
Heroes confess to whores, detectives
Chat or play chess with thieves."

"Now that is the voice of a great poet W.H. Auden."

"Have you decided what poems you are going to read?"

"If I were to read three poems would that be too much?"

"Well now, if all three of them are longer than Bryan Merryman's, "The Midnight Court" as translated by Frank O'Connor, then I definitely would say you'd be pushing your luck. Have you read the "Midnight Court?"

"Yes. It's a bit risque isn't it, not to mention being a long distance runner? Long winded I mean. There must be seven or eight thousand words in it!"

"Well, for one thing you'd have the Irish Censorship Board after you and you'd be running the risk of excommunication from the Catholic Church, for good measure."

"I'll read it so, for the fun of it."

"Not on my podium. No you won't young man. I've got to go back to Dublin next week. I don't want to be met by a lynching mob on Kings Bridge Station. I'm talking in me cups Allen – take no notice. Right, I'll hear one of your latest poems."

WHEN I AM OLD
When I am old
I'll sit and watch the grass grow
And listen to the leaves blow.
And count dead years
on crippled fingers.
And daydream dead dreams again
And make images out of dreams
And talk and laugh and play with them
When I am old.

When I am old
When my back's bent like the bow.
And my arms like half sawn
boughs hang low.
And my feet are made of lead
With legs of straw.
When I but nod and wink my way
Through all the dream filled days.
And nevermore may wander
proudly free 'mid hill and sky.
That seeking I might chance to see
God's handy-work, in
some twisted elderberry tree or trace
His footprint sunk
into a stony pass.

When I am old
I'll know the bone in all things
man needs knowing.

From the maker to the breaker,
everyman, that struggles
from the belly of a woman
is made alive to puzzle out
God's plan.

When I am old
my young face will have grown
a wrinkled flesh.
The glad will be a sad smile
ear to ear, and
A white beard I will set
against the north wind.
Then my weary eyes won't sin to see
a flash of lace from
some feminine place.
The passions then in me
will be outdated
And all the while my heart run on
like a mad-fast watch
to its winding hour.
To beat its last in this clay tower
When I am old.

When I am old
I'll treat death with much respect
and call him by his Christian
name, of peace.
My soul and body I'll bleach well
And wear white linen next
the skin
For fear he might drop in,
to measure me dead accurately
against my bag of sins.

EPISODE SEVENTEEN

DON'T PAY NO P.A.Y.E.
LIKE A HUNTED ANIMAL
PAT HUNT COULD HANDLE HIM
IF IT KILLS ME

DON'T PAY NO P.A.Y.E.

"Can't you see it babe. That bloke was goin' to call in the 'fuz'. The first thing they'd wanna know is what you woz doin' carrying three and an 'alf 'undred nicker in your 'andbag. The next thing was, where did you git that kind of 'lolly'. And the 'Fuz' don't buy no fairy-godmother stories. Do you ketch what I'm sayin' Babe?" Winston Warbarton was pleading his case for not standing his ground and waiting for the Police to arrive at 'The George.' But he was doing so on the pretence of protecting Eileen Murphy, whom he would have discarded without a moments hesitation. He planned to use her and the ordained Robbery, to force her into another more infamous occupation, that of prostitution.

"Sure I know what you're saying, but Christ Almighty, what's to become of us now? I've lost my feckin' job at the Caff (cafeteria) and I'm stoney broke, not a nicker."

"There's other ways of makin dow besides workin fur it. I'll watch out fur you Babe. I'll see that nobody hurts you. It's easy money on the Bayswater Road Babe. Plenty of high rollers cruise along that patch after dark, all night every night. 'Tis like takin' gumdrops from a baby. With bankrolls in their backpockets they come all soused-up outa the Dean's Court, the Hyde Park Towers, The York, the Inverness, the Court Royal and the Post House, all lookin' fur a good time. An' you don't pay no P.A.Y.E. neither."

"No, but how much do you take? Besides I never said I'd walk the Bayswater Road. Do you still have that flat, back of the Florence Nightingale Hospital?"

"I sure do Babe. It's just five minutes, "ball of chalk" (walk) from Marylebone Underground Tube Station." Eileen Murphy and Winston Warbarton boarded the Metropolitan Line at Hammersmith Station and embarked on their journey, visiting Goldhawk Road, Shepherds Bush, Latimer Road, Ladbroke Grove, Westbourne Park, Royal Oak and Paddington.

There they crossed over the tracks to board the Bakerloo Line for Edgware Road and on to Marylebone, which was their destination. Here they got off and proceeded to walk across Lisson Grove Street in front of the Florence Nightingale Hospital, and into Bell Street. In an alleyway off that street, Warbarton had his 'flat.' It was a claustrophobic one room, partitioned to look like two with outside bathroom sharing.

If Eileen had thought her dingy basement 'flat' on Chesterton Road was cheap and mean, it was a mansion compared to this hovel. Not only was it cramped but it was dirty as well. The kitchen sink was filled up with unwashed delph and drinking glasses. Empty and half-full beer cans stood like bored sightseers on every stick of furniture waiting to be picked up. The stink smell of stale liquor hung over the place like a Shebeen. But what alarmed her most were articles of womens clothing strewn about. He caught her looking at these and hurriedly stuffed them into a disabled tallboy. He then took two cans of beer out of a battered 'dresser' and handed her one. Then with one of his bacchanalian swallows he emptied his can and stood it on the mantlepiece to correspond with two similar vessels.

"I've got ta vamoose now an' see if I can git them hustlers off my back an' git more time ta come up with the 'lolly.' You just take it easy an' make no mind about me. There's more where that came from:" He pointed a finger like a miniature blackthorn stick at the drawer of the 'Dresser'. "You just have yourself a sup an' a kip. I won't be long Babe," and he was gone before she realized it.

LIKE A HUNTED ANIMAL

She slumped into a rickety armchair and pondered over her latest and worst debacle. She had hit a new low. 'Murphy's Law' 'Anything that can go wrong will go wrong,' dominated all her affairs of late: There was no way she could go back now to her old fiancé Ivor Davies. It was his money and he had trusted her with it. She had put his savings into Barclay's Bank, in her own name. Ivor knew this and never questioned her motives. He was a bit of alright, but there was nothing exciting about him. No great shakes to look at, – just another 'Joe Soap.' He didn't make a woman proud to walk by his side. Nobody stopped to look after him. His conversation too was harmless and matter of fact. There wasn't a dashing bone in his body. Ivor Davies was an ordinary everyday kind of bloke. He made no waves.

Whereas Winston Warbarton was all man, – a man and a half. He made a woman feel like a woman. Full of fun and devilment he kept a woman at the top of her game. He never let her forget she was Eve enticing Adam in an eternal garden of Eden. Then she looked at the broken tallboy into which Winston had pelted the articles of womens' clothing and a shiver of fear and loathing came over her.

Where Harewood Avenue meets Marylebone Road Winston Warbarton walked into the Central Bar and Lounge. He stood inside the front door for a full minute until he was satisfied that no one on the premises posed a problem for him. Then he went towards a table at the top left hand corner of the room. Here an unwholesome squinty-eyed character was sitting slouched over a half empty pint glass of dark beer. His eyes never rested but were furtively darting from left to right and back again, like a hunted animal.

"What's that yer drinkin'?"

"A bottle of Stingo, with a Burton draught fill-up."

"Have ya got the money with you?"

"Sure I've got it." He patted his side pocket. The big black South African went up to the bar counter and got the drinks. All eyes turned towards him as he crossed the room. He moved like a Goliath at large, whom some admired but others feared.

"Did ya count the money mate?"

"Yea, 'twas more than I expected."

"How much more, man?"

"Three hundred quid, Winston."

"Pass it over to me now."

The squinty eyed one pushed a folded over newspaper packet towards the giant Negro. "What's my cut Winston?"

Winston grabbed the packet and shoved the bundle roughly into the inside pocket of his jacket. "You've had your cut mate."

He stood erect, looking down menacingly at his accomplice. The pint glass of Larger beer was smothered in his giant hand. "If'n I finds theres less than three big ones here," and he clapped his inside pocket, "I'll be comin' lookin' fur ya. You've ripped off fifty already an' that's yer lot." He poured the pint of Larger down his throat like a cha-woman would empty leftovers from a canteen teapot down a sink. "Do I make myself clear Paddy?" There was no answer from his accomplice. All eyes followed him as he shuffled towards the bar counter again. He ordered a pint of Larger beer, a large Whiskey, two large Gin and Tonics and a Bloody-Mary. He carried these on a discoloured dingy tray, to a table at the top right hand corner of the room. Three women sat there in gaudy attire and bawdy conversation.

EILEEN MURPHY (LIAR & CHEAT)
BY SEAN KENNY

Alison was the oldest hitting on forty. Chloe was the youngest at twenty nine and Stella was the in-between, pushing thirty five. All three were heavily painted. The whole paraphernalia of feminine allurement was put into effect. Mascara lassoed the eyes, rouge highlighted the cheeks, making them blush, eyebrows darkly pencilled like the arches of bridges, lips pouting like half eaten jam-tarts and a smattering of fake beauty spots to finish off the masquerade.

"Nobody given' you girls no trouble is there?"

"They wouldn't dare, Winston. They know what's good for 'em."

PAT HUNT COULD HANDLE HIM

Back at Warbarton's grubby flat Eileen Murphy was beside herself with remorse: "If only I had taken more care with my hand-bag. If only Winston hadn't gone to the toilet when he did. If only I had left the money in Barclay's Bank in the first place none of this would have happened." She tried to reason out her folly. What was it her old teacher, Sister Myra, used to say about the word 'if': "Remember girls, if is a very small word that can suppose an awful lot." Eileen was anxious and weary but she couldn't rest. An immense number of aggravating thoughts were shuttling in and out of her mind like trains through Clapham Junction: "Where has Warbarton gone to now? He wasn't very upset when I was robbed in 'The George'. I keep on thinking, the gammon Drunk that robbed me was the same bum I saw yapping with Warbarton when I first went into the Lounge. If so then the whole thing was a fix. I was friggen well set up. Wonder if Ivor Davies has found out his money is missing from the Bank? He's probably searching for me right now, – poor fecker. It's too late now. No use in crying over spilt milk. And this place is a dive. A bloody pig-sty – it stinks. I'm not staying here for too long. Definitely, the bloke who robbed me was the yob I saw yappin' to Warbarton. He'd murder me if he thought I suspected him. That's where he's gone now: to collect the money, from his 'fence' – as sure as there's down on a duck. Big an' all as he is I know Pat Hunt could handle him. That's if I could convince Pat that Warbarton is the real robber. Pat Hunt would want to get Ivor's money back. Supposing I said I had taken out the money to return it to Ivor and Warbartoon waylaid me. Would that work? He's a shrewd one, Pat is.

Still, Nancy Blackmore took him to the cleaners just the same. I wonder should I make contact with her and try doing a deal. Maybe I could play the two ends against the middle. I'll have to think it out. First thing tomorrow I have to write home and tell mother the wedding is off. She won't be bothered if I tell her Ivor was in a car crash and will be in a wheelchair for life. She wouldn't want me to marry a cripple. An' I'll tell her we had to spend all our savings on operations and hospital care. That should put paid to the coming home to get married, 'lark.' It should work anyhow.

Eileen Murphy looked around the room for the twentieth time. This place is like a tomb. Me head is busting. What time is it? Christ Almighty, it's 9.30 p.m. He's been gone for four hours. Maybe he aint comin' back. What was that? Someone was turning a key in the lock. "'Tis him." Warbarton stooped automatically as he came through the doorway into the kitchen cum sitting room. He was besotted with alcohol. She rounded on him immediately. "It took a pile of money to get you into such a drunken mess, or my name is not Eileen Murphy."

IF IT KILLS ME

"I knows damn well who you is. Yer a piece a white trash who's burned all er bridges behind 'er. Is ya satisfied now that ya got them all out lookin' fur ya; yer boyfriend, yer Landlady an' the long arm o the Law."

"Why you bastard," she said and sprung from the rickety old armchair. She took hold of an unopened can of beer and hit him with it on the jaw. It was as effective as an ageing flyweight boxer, throwing a punch at a champion Sumo wrestler. He merely shook his head and gave her a back handed slap that sent her to the floor unconscious. Nor did he trouble himself to look down to where she lay in a crumpled heap. Instead he went into the bedroom adjoining the kitchen and took off his jacket. He threw it on the bed and fell down upon it. In seconds he was dead to the world.

It was 10 p.m. when Eileen came to her senses. She felt like she had been in a stampede. Her face and neck pained her. Slowly it dawned on her how dangerous her predicament really was. Silently she got to her feet. The first sounds she heard were the snores of the giant black man stretched across the bed in the next room. It was like a snorting rhinoceros disputing with one of his peers for possession of the latest female acquisition at the Zoo. The bed shook with every guttural snore. She took off her six inch stiletto heeled shoes and tightly gripped one in her left hand as a weapon. She remembered reading in the newspapers how a woman had escaped from a rapist by driving the steel tipped heel of her stiletto shoe into his forehead and smashing his scull.

She moved closer to the bed. He was lying across it, with his feet touching the ground. He looked like a fallen tree. His jacket was under his trunk with the neck and part of the lapels sticking out. "If it kills me," she said to herself, "I'm goin' to find out if he set me up." She knew he never carried notes in his trouser pockets, only loose change But how was she going to get the jacket out from under him? He was out for the count now. But he wouldn't stay asleep forever.

EPISODE EIGHTEEN

A FOLLOWER OF IGNATIUS LOYOLA
BRAIN WASHING
AN OLD RUSSIAN ORTHODOX MONK
SCOTLAND YARD

A FOLLOWER OF IGNATIUS LOYOLA

He was pale, tired and anxious looking as he glanced for the tenth time at the big electric clock above the red Exit sign at Heathrow Airport. It was fifteen minutes after eleven o'clock. Luke was late. Held up in traffic no doubt. He had been sitting on a wooden bench since eleven o'clock and although he was very tired he was restless. He stood up and shuffled his feet, like a tap dancer. A grey all-wool jacket covered his upper body. The sleeves were short like a hand-me-down garment. Under it he wore a navy blue shirt with an off white necktie. His grey flannel trousers were well creased and fastened at the waist with a black leather belt. On his feet he wore size ten shoes, black and shinning like a pair of sunglasses in August. He had with him a lightweight dark overcoat thrown across a mahogany coloured suitcase which was sitting on the bench beside him. Locks of grey hair peeped out from under his black Tribly hat, like fledgling chicks from their nest and his slightly hooked nose gave to his appearance an aquiline alertness. He could be mistaken for a member of the Italian Mafia. But this notion would be instantly overthrown on reading the inscription on the travel label attached to the suitcase: Rev. John Brannigan Society of Jesus, Church of the Immaculate Conception, Farm Street, Berkeley Square London.

Fr. John Brannigan had spent a lifetime in China. The last three years he had spent in a Communist Jail. In his time he had met people like Agnes Smedley, Rewi Alley, Max Granich, Edgar Snow who had written "Redstar Over China", Ma Haide otherwise George Hatem. Madame Sun Yat-sen and many many others. George Hatem was probably the most remarkable of them all: Born in America to a Lebanese family. He was described as, "the only American who had seen and been part of the whole Chinese story, from Chiang Kai-shek to the International Settlements, life in the Communist-held areas, the Japanese invasion, Civil War and the Communist take-over.

But Fr. John Brannigan had seen as much and more. On one side in the earlier years he had literally seen young men marched out and executed. Many of these were not Communists at all. Some were just workers who had said something against the Local Authority. They went to their death shouting, "Down with the Kuomintang. The Kuomintang party of Shiang Kai-shek were an inefficient gang of crooked politicians.Where Shanghai Hongqiao Airport stands to day, – that was the execution grounds, the original Killing Fields. It was a tourist sight.

People were taken there off their Round the World tours to see the place, and some actually witnessed executions.

But later John saw the other side of the coin which was equally as savage and even worse. For three terrible years he endured torture and deprivation that almost destroyed him in a Communist jail.

"O it's you Luke I was beginning to think you couldn't make it. It's good to see you. Thanks for coming. I've been waiting for you like a lost child for its mother."

"You are welcome home John. I'm only sorry I'm not meeting you under better circumstances." The two brothers shook hands and then embraced.

"Did you come on your own or is Meg and Sean with you?"

"I came on my own. They are back at my place in Hayes Mews. I thought it would be better if I came alone and I could fill you in on all that's happened, before you meet them."

BRAIN WASHING

"How is Meg bearing up?"

"Surprisingly well, all things considered. I haven't seen her cry even once."

"She would be better if she could cry. It would help to relieve the tension. It's good she has Sean. He is her saving grace"

"The car is around the back of the airport. Here give me that suitcase. You look tired." Luke led the way into the carpark.

"This is my car," Luke said as he opened up the boot of a highly polished span new Austin Cambridge and deposited the suitcase inside.

"It looks like you have done well for yourself, Luke."

"I can't complain. God has been good to me. He opened the door on the passenger side. "Sit in John and tell me a little of what you have had to suffer in that Communist Jail." As he started the car he turned to his brother with a look of concern. "You have lost a lot of weight John."

"That's not all I've lost. I damn near lost my mind as well."

"We only heard rumours of how Mao's peasant army meeted out torture and pain to all foreigners and especially to Catholic priests. You, who had tried to do so much to relieve their poverty and suffering."

"Wasn't it the same with Jesus Christ. They murdered Him because He tried to show them a better way to live. "Love one another," was what He told them. Not content to do that, they killed Him."

"Is Mao Tse-Tung still in control?"

"Yes he is. In 1949 he formed the communist People's Republic of China and set himself up as Chairman. Although Mao retired from this position two years ago in 1959, he never-the-less remained in control of the entire country. China is presently suffering a severe economic set back. It has been like that for the past two and a half years. The Soviet Union who is supposed to be her ally refuses to allow a single days' reprieve on China's debt. China has become Russia's arrogant step-child. In fact only last year in 1960 the Soviet Union suddenly pulled out all its experts and cancelled contracts on 156 projects involving scientific and technological co-operation. Now the Soviet Union has sent many divisions to patrol the borders along China's Inner Mongolia and along the northeastern Provinces. Also it has sent large numbers of troops to occupy Afghanistan and has established military bases in Vietnam, both of which are China's neighbours. If a war ever erupts between the Soviet Union and China it could bring about the end of civilization as we know it."

"You are well up on international affairs John but tell me about your three years in the Communist jail, if it's not too painful for you."

"Have you ever heard the expression Brain Washing?"

"I have heard of it but I don't know exactly what it means?"

"To put it simply it is a method Chinese Communist jailers have perfected, to get the likes of me to recant all the beliefs, ideals and opinions that I hold dear. I was subjected to a systematic indoctrination that little by little sought to uproot my faith in God, my hope for the future and my love for my fellow man. When I say me here, I mean all those like me. My jailers ultimate goal was to make me confess that I had committed a dastardly crime against the Chinese people. They claimed that by teaching the Divine message of Christ I had offended their culture and sought to tear down the Peoples Republic. The weapon they use to weaken one's resolve is lack of sleep. And all the while their relentless method of indoctrination, which is full of hate and lies goes on and on, until one is no longer certain what is right and what is wrong.

"How in God's name did you hold out and keep your sanity?"

"There is a strange and wonderful story attached to that part of my incarceration. You will be the first to hear it, Luke."

MAO ZEDONG
BY SEAN KENNY

AN OLD RUSSIAN ORTHODOX MONK

In Xiangtan City in Hunan Province we ran a small Hospital and we dispensed some medicines as well. Of late an officer of the Red Army had called on a weekly basis and was asking a lot of pertinent questions. He hoped we weren't teaching a foreign culture to the Chinese people. And then one day he got so worked up that he smashed his cane by bringing it down on the Dispensary table, breaking some phials of medicine in the act. He left instantly without an apology. An old Russian Orthodox Monk who had been coming to help out everyday at the Dispensary had witnessed the Officers display of anger. He came to talk with me that night when we closed our doors." That officer dislikes you and if he fails to intimidate you he will throw you into prison. He will not lose face. You must pack up and go to another Province. Will you do that?" he asked.

"No," I said "I can't do that."

"Then he will send you to jail the next time he sees you."

"So be it" I said. "I must do as my conscience directs me."

"You have a long hard road ahead of you. But I will give you a prayer with my blessing. If you remain faithful to it you will be saved by the mercy of Christ."

The origin of this prayer, he went on, is to be found in the early Greek Church. A simple Russian peasant lost his family and his home in a fire. It was the culmination of a long series of Job-like calamities and so he decided to become a pilgrim. He started off with knapsack and Bible looking for a teacher who would teach him the secret of continual prayer, being mindful of Saint Paul's warning in his First Letter to the Thessalonians, "Never cease praying." (V:17).

This old Russian peasant met many monks and holy men, but none could teach him the secret of constant prayer. Almost worn out with his travels and ready to quit he chanced to meet a very old monk at prayer on the roadside. When the pilgrim greeted him and told him of his quest the old monk said: "Give thanks to God. I'll teach you what you are searching for." He brought the pilgrim to his monastery which was near at hand and put him in a completely bare room. Kneel down where you are now and repeat this prayer 500 times, "Lord Jesus, Son of the living God, have mercy on me, a sinner."

At the end of the day the pilgrim told the monk that he had fulfilled his command. "That's very good," he answered him, tomorrow you will repeat the prayer 1,000 times. The following day the monk told the pilgrim to repeat the prayer 2,000 times and on the third day 3,000 times and so to increase every day. Soon after this the old monk died, and with sorrow in his heart the pilgrim took his knapsack and Bible and resumed his pilgrimage. He took the prayer and teaching of the old monk to the Greek doctors and theologians.

They advised him to link this prayer with his breathing, rhythmically breathing in and breathing out.

Later an Indian Jesuit priest said that Saint Ignatius Loyola, the Founder of the Jesuits, picked it up and incorporated it into the Exercises. Later still this prayer was linked with the heart-beat and so could be prayed continuously.

And here was this old Russian Orthodox Monk telling me a Jesuit, that the Founder of my Order Saint Ignatius Loyola had incorporated this Jesus Prayer into the Exercises. Now you know Luke how I was able to survive their systematic indoctrination, known as Brain Washing."

"It's a marvelous story John. I've never heard anything like it before. Would you recite that prayer for me once more?"

"Lord Jesus, Son of the living God, have mercy on me, a sinner."

SCOTLAND YARD

"That's enough out of me for the present anyhow. Tell me Luke what really happened to young Billy McNeill?"

"It should never have happened. The whole sorry mess was a terrible mistake, from the start to finish. He may have had patriotic feelings but most of the young Irish lads do. They seem to think anything else would be a betrayed of their country."

"Was he a member of the I.R.A.?"

"Not at all. He had absolutely nothing to do with them. What happened was a total stranger passed a loaded revolver to him to escape detection at the Galtymore Dance Hall. The fellow was a marked man and when he saw the Police seal off the doors he knew he would be arrested and so he got rid of the gun. Weeks later Billy still had the gun and he was carrying it around with him. He showed the gun to a few of his friends and word got around that Billy McNeill was an I.R.A. activist. I only heard all this afterwards when the damage was done." As you well know the greatest Police force on earth operates here. Scotland Yard has its undercover men, – plain clothes detectives who infiltrate every level of society. Billy was arrested early one morning before he was out of bed. They found the loaded revolver under his pillow. The poor misfortunate foolish lad. And after all that he took his own life."

"Monsignor Dan O'Driscoll, the man you will be staying with, spoke to the prison Chaplain. He told Dan that Billy never accepted his prison sentence and that Billy was mentally immature."

"What became of the fellow who passed the gun to Billy in the first place?"

"He wasn't with the I.R.A. either. They got him for armed robbery of a Jewellers shop in Piccadilly. All of this information came out afterwards when it was too late to help Billy."

EPISODE NINETEEN

THE BEAU BRUMMELL OF LATTER-DAY LONDON
THE SQUARE ON THE HYPOTENUSE
HE WOULDN'T BE A GO-BETWEEN
AN URGENT PHONE CALL
ANGINA PECTORIS

THE BEAU BRUMMELL OF LATTER-DAY LONDON

Allen Hunt, walked soldier-like, straight as a dye, up the Bayswater Road. He was on the broad footpath just outside of Kensington Gardens. He passed the Colburg Hotel which was on the other side of the road. Seeing it, his thoughts took him back to a wedding reception he had attended there a month earlier. It was a strange and perverse kind of event, in a droll sort of way. "It could never happen in Kilkenny. Over here anything goes. In London, life is the sum of all possible thoughts and actions of conscious existence," Allen thought to himself. "And human attractions here are often weird and inexplicable: the absurd can become conventional by repetition."

Two nights previous to that bizarre wedding reception, a twenty six year old Kilkenny man swaggered into 'The Poppy' on Edgware Road. "I'll have a large 'Old Tom' with a slice of lemon and a tonic water, Mate, and whatever you're having yourself." He blinked twice in an attempt to brush away the fog of inebriation that seemed to be settling over his eyes.

"Are you sure you can handle a large Gin?" Allen observed him closely. He shook his head as if to unseat any uncertainty that had climbed on board and returned Allen's gaze.

"Don't I know you from somewhere Mate? I never forget a face."

"I suppose you could be like the fellow who said: I'll never forget what-you-may-call-him," Allen said with a grin. "But to answer your question; you don't know me from Adam." Allen gave him the drink but resolved to see how he behaved after he had drunk it. Still sizing him up Allen saw that he had a great head of well groomed hair, black and glossy like a shovel-full of anthracite coal. His double-breasted, pin-striped, navy blue suit was Saville Row vintage. Black Doc Martins shoes fitted his feet like gloves and a lily white shirt, fit for a Carmelite Monk was fastened at the neck by a sky-blue cravat.

In all his life Allen had seen only one other person dressed with such penchant. It was John Kerwick from Greens Hill, owner of the Wheatsheaf Inn on Kilkenny's Parade.

He took a roll of notes from his pocket that would choke a crocodile and peeled off one. "Where's your drink?" he asked Allen.

"I never drink behind the bar."

"Then I'll have to celebrate on my own. I'm having a one man 'stag party.'" He threw a five pound note on the counter and lifted the large 'Old Tom.' Wish me luck Pat. I'm getting married the day after tomorrow."

Allen felt he detected a note of melancholy in his voice. There is something extraordinary going on here, he thought.

THE SQUARE ON THE HYPOTENUSE

The exceptionally well dressed man hit the counter a loud thump with the heel of his fist. "That's it, – it just dawned to me: You're Pat Hunt. We went to school together in the good old C.B.S. in James's Street. Remember old Goll Coffey, Broko, Mick Bolger and Dynamite Joe Mullally? Those were the days my friend, we thought they'd never end. Like the song says."

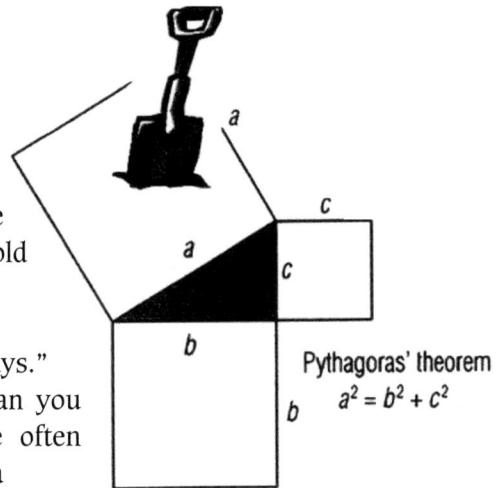

Pythagoras' theorem
$$a^2 = b^2 + c^2$$

THE SQUARE ON THE HYPOTENUSE
BY SEAN KENNY

"I have to tell you friend, I'm not the man you think I am. But I am his brother. We are often mistaken for each other." Allen extended a hand, "I'm Allen Hunt, Pat's younger brother. And who are you may I ask?"

"I'm Larry Holden from Muckalee near Mount Margie."

"I wish you and your blushing young bride every good luck, good health and happiness. And like they say in the best Irish tradition; May all your troubles be little ones."

"That's right kind of you, but that can never be. It would be nothing short of a miracle." So saying he finished off the large 'Old Tom' and pushed the empty glass under Allen's nose. "I'll have what made the Manxman mad."

"What was that?"

"The same again."

Allen wanted to ask him why he was having a stag party on his own and why it would take a miracle to have his good wishes come true. But instead he asked him: "What line of business are you in Larry?"

"I'm with Brannigan and Boland building contractors, working on a site down in Wimbledon."

"O, I see, you are a construction engineer or works manager, or such like".

Larry laughed and laughed until the tears came streaming down his face. "Not a bit of it," he said, "I have worked it out on real estate instead of paper, that the square on the hypotenuse takes longer to dig out with a shovel than the squares on the other two sides. I should know. I'm a first class pick and shovel Paddy, better known as an Irish Navvie. And before I say any more I'm giving you an invite to the wedding reception at the Colburg Hotel off the Bayswater Road." "Isn't it a bit late to be giving out invitations at this stage?"

"It's never too late to learn. And if you want the answers to all the questions you are asking yourself concerning me, you'll have to turn up at the Colburg, at 3.00 p.m. day after tomorrow and bring Pat if he is available. I'll have that drink now. Then you can call me a taxi."

Either he hadn't as much drink taken as Allen had previously thought, or he was well able to wear it. In any case he couldn't go too far wrong if he was going home in a taxi."

Allen put the empty glass under the optic, once, twice and pulled the cap off a tonic water. "That's on me," he said. He had already resolved to attend the wedding reception at the Colberg Hotel, and discover the mystery behind the machinations and lifestyle of the intriguing Kilkenny man, Larry Holden.

HE WOULDN'T BE A GO-BETWEEN

There were as many pedestrians going up the Bayswater Road as there were coming down, or so it seemed. Although it was choc-a-bloc, it was far from chaotic. In fact it was rarely that people bumped into each other. But when they did, it was only the green-horns who apologised, – the Johnny-come-latelys. If someone said 'sorry', he, she, was looked at with something akin to suspicion or even fear. Londoners, when they hit the streets put on their dead-pan faces, as one would don a raincoat in wet weather.

Allen came to a stand still at the traffic lights and waited along with about fifteen people for the lights to change. The green walk signal came on and he went with the others across the pedestrian walk, through the densely packed traffic left and right, like the Israelites crossed over between the separated waters of the Red Sea. Then before the next wave of pursuers could follow, the lights changed to red don't walk once more and the groaning traffic flowed on like a great river to the sea. On the other side of the Bayswater Road Allen continued to walk in the same direction for a hundred yards or more until he arrived at The Champion. The main doors were opened wide and fixed to the walls with steel clasps. He pushed the Lounge swing doors in front of him and went inside.

In a flash two pairs of look alike eyes made contact and Allen gravitated towards his bigger brother Pat, in accordance with the principle of magnetics, one could say.

"Thanks for coming over Allen."

"You are welcome brother. What can I do for you?"

"There's something I need to ask your opinion about. But first, what are you having to drink?"

"I'll have a pint of Best Bitter Pat."

"I suppose you have figured out what it is I need you to do."

"I could make a stab at it. Has it got something to do with Rosie Taylor nee Keegan?"

"You are spot on brother. Sharp as a hounds tooth after chewing on a shinbone, as father used to say."

"So she wrote to you like she said she would, – right?"

"Yes she did and explained a lot of things that were a puzzle to me."

"And now you have written a reply and you need me to find a way of getting the letter to her without posting it. You don't want to cause friction between herself and Bill Taylor. Is that more or less the gist of it?"

"That's just about the whole kit and caboodle. Listen take those two pints with you over to the table beside the window. I'll be with you in a moment as soon as I serve these customers. Gwen seems to have done a disappearing trick."

Allen did as he was asked and sat waiting for Pat. He wondered what Rosie had written in her letter to him and if she had told her husband Bill Taylor that she was writing to Pat? He was not going to be a middle man or go between if there were any suggestions of an extramarital nature. Unless Bill Taylor was fully aware of what was going on he would decline to have any hand, act or part in the affair.

AN URGENT PHONE CALL

The public phone rang inside the swing doors and Gwen the barmaid appeared out of nowhere and was sprinting towards it. It was closer to Pat than to her but she beat him to it hands down. He went back behind the bar counter smiling like a clown. Obviously she had been waiting with bated breath for a call from some male admirer, Allen thought. Nothing else would put the skids under her as fast as that. No sooner had she lifted the phone than her face shed its state of expectancy.

"It's for you Pat. It's urgent," Gwen called out.

A frown replaced the clown's grin and Pat looked hard in Allen's direction. On hearing the word urgent, both men's thinking automatically turned to the family home in Kilkenny. Did mother or father have an accident or was there worse news?

"Hello, yes, - this is he." Without thinking Allen was straining to catch any word or phrase that would indicate the source of the urgent phone call. And then, he heard his brother say; "O I'm sorry to hear that. When did it happen?"

Then there was another listening interlude after which Pat spoke again: "As a matter of fact, Allen is here with me now." Another pause followed. "I will of course. Where are you ringing from?" The caller obviously answered that request and Pat answered saying: "Right Rosie, I'll tell him. I'm sure he will. By the way, thanks for your letter. It was great to hear about Patricia. Take care, – I'll talk to you later. Don't worry. Bye for now." He put down the phone and stroked his chin thoughtfully.

Pat went over to Allen's table and sat to the front of him beside the window.

"Well brother, as far as it went, your dead reckoning about why I wished to speak with you was pretty accurate. But what has happened now gives the situation a new dimension. Bill Taylor had another heart attack early this morning. He is presently in Saint George's Hospital Knightsbridge. That was Rosie on the phone. She rang to tell you at 'The Poppy', but you had just left. She did speak to Matt Ryan."

"I guessed as much after I heard you say you were sorry to hear it. Where exactly is Saint George's Hospital in Knightsbridge?"

"It's beside Hyde Park Corner Underground station. It's on the Piccadilly Line. If you took the Circle Line from Bayswater to Gloucester Road and changed to the Piccadilly Line bound for Cockfosters, you could get off three stops down the line. Rosie and Patricia are at the hospital now. She is waiting to see a doctor. Apparently Bill has had a bad attack. She doesn't think he's going to make it this time."

Allen's thoughts flashed back to the evening he had found Bill on the upstairs floor of the managers living quarters, at The Poppy. Bill asked Allen not to tell anybody about his heart attack. Allen advised him then to tell Rosie about his state of ill-health. "Wouldn't it be better to let her know, rather than to have her find you, as I did now? It could frighten the life out of her", he advised Bill.

ANGINA PECTORIS

As Allen, was about to leave 'The Champion' for Saint George's Hospital, the phone rang again. Again the barmaid Gwen came out of the stocks in an Olympic dash to pick it up, but was forced to hand it over like the baton in a relay race. "It's for you Pat," she said begrudgingly.

"Don't go Allen until I take this call it could be Rosie again."

But it wasn't Rosie, it was Matt Ryan Manager at "The Poppy" enquiring if Allen was on the premises and if so could he speak with him? He spoke with Pat for a few minutes and then Pat beckoned for Allen to come to the phone.

"I understand you've heard the news about Bill Taylor's heart attack and Pat told me you are ready to leave for the hospital now. I have been thinking about Rosie and the child being left on their own while Bill is in hospital. It might not be safe for them."

"You are absolutely right Matt. If that venomous shrew Blackmore, got wind of how things stand, she would be likely to do them harm."

"Rosie and the child can stay at 'The Poppy' until we see how things turn out. Tell her I will not take no for an answer. Hire a taxi Allen and I'll foot the bill."

At the hospital Allen told Rosie of Matt Ryan's invitation to stay at 'The Poppy'. With tears in her eyes she put her arms around Allen. "You have been so good to us, Allen. All of you have."

He waited with Patricia when Rosie was summoned to the Chief Medical Officers room for a consultation.

"Please be seated Mrs. Taylor. Would you like a cup of tea?"

Rosie shook her head. "No thanks I'm fine."

"Do you have relatives in London?"

She hesitated while twisting the wedding ring on her finger. "No, – but I do have good friends."

"Your husband is a very ill man. Angina pectoris is marked by paroxysms of intense pain, a pain that radiates from the breast bone mainly towards the left shoulder and arm. Since he was admitted this morning he has had several of these. I'm sorry to tell you it is unlikely that his heart could survive another one."

At approximately 3.15 p.m. Bill Taylor died in the presence of his wife Rosie, her daughter Patricia and their good friend Allen Hunt.

EPISODE TWENTY

A FRANKENSTEIN CONCEPTION
WORMWOOD SCRUBS
ONE OF IRELAND'S GREATEST LIVING POETS

A FRANKENSTEIN CONCEPTION

Luke Brannigan, (Building Contractor) had less than half an hour earlier collected his brother Fr. John Brannigan, (Society of Jesus) at Heathrow Airport. John had been released from a Communist jail in China after being incarcerated for three terrible years. During his detention he was subjected to torture by a systematic indoctrination known as 'Brain Washing.' It was a Frankenstein conception. The brothers were now on their way in Luke's luxuriant new Austin Cambridge to Hayes Mews, Berkeley Square. There, their sister Meg and her son Sean were waiting for them. You will remember that Meg's older son, Billy McNeill, had committed suicide in his cell in Wormwood Scrubs Prison, where he was serving a five year sentence for possession of a loaded revolver.

While on their way, Fr. John had at Luke's request described how he had survived the ordeal of torture and finished by saying:

"And here was this old Russian Orthodox Monk telling me a Jesuit, that the Founder of my Order, Saint Ignatius Loyola had incorporated this 'Jesus Prayer' into the Exercises. Now you know Luke, how I was able to survive their systematic indoctrination, known as Brain Washing."

"It's a marvelous story John. I've never heard anything like it before. Would you recite that prayer for me one more time?"

"Lord Jesus, Son of the Living God, have mercy on me, a sinner."

Meg McNeill was standing at the front door of her brother Luke's impressive residence at Hayes Mews when the Austin Cambridge came to a stop. As John stepped from the car she opened her arms to welcome him. Looking tired and gaunt he went to her instantly and each were locked in a common embrace. The sight of him and the circumstances under which they were meeting now was too much for her. The sluice gates opened on the flood of her sorrows and flowed into the hearts of John, Luke and Sean and welled up in their eyes.

"Surely it is a valley of tears," John thought to himself as his sister cried and sobbed helplessly. "What's happening to us at all John?" Has the Good Lord turned his back on us?"

"Not at all Meg. He only gives the burden of hardship to those who are able to carry it for Him. Your reward will be all the greater in heaven."

"You look tired and worn John. What have they been doing to you, poor man?"

"I'm better than I've been for a long time Meg. Now we can help each other to cope on life's pilgrimage."

WORMWOOD SCRUBS

Next morning saw Meg, Sean, Luke and John on their way to Wormwood Scrubs Prison to take home the body of young Billy McNeill for burial in County Galway. Following them like a recurring nightmare was a hearse with two undertaker's helpers. Luke Brannigan rang the bell at the main gate once, twice, three times before a spy-hole shutter was opened in the wicket door. Only the eyes and nose of the prison guard were visible. "Yes, – what is it?"

"We have come to claim the body of young Billy McNeill."

"Let me see your identification and letter of approval from the Ministry for Justice." Luke pushed the papers through the spy-hole. "How many of you are there?"

"The dead man's mother, his brother and two uncles, counting me."

"You must park the car outside and walk in in single file. I will return your papers to you on the way out. You may be searched"

Luke did as he was told and the wicket door was opened after no less than two bolts and two locks were released. Luke walked in front, followed by Meg, then Sean and John brought up the rear. Once inside they were met by the Chief Prison Officer, who asked them if they had any concealed weapons before taking them to the Wardens Office.

A big sixty year old Derry man with a red face and a full head of white hair was standing erect behind a cluttered desk. Like a friendly father figure he moved to meet them the moment they entered the room.

"'Tis sorry I am for your troubles Mrs. McNeill." He went from one to the other shaking each hand, until he came to Sean who was hanging back and refused to accept his condolence. The Warden took no offence but still offered Sean his sympathy. "Would you like a cup of tea or perhaps something stronger?"

"I'd like to see my son please." Meg spoke softly but firmly.

"I'll take you to the mortuary so." On opening the office door two guards stood to attention. Both of them were armed, and as the Warden led the four visitors, the prison guards followed at arms length.

"I'll leave you now to your commiseration's," he said at the mortuary door. "We have a Chaplain here, should you require him." He said this while looking at John. "That will not be necessary thank you," John said as he donned a Stole.

"I understand perfectly." The Warden bowed and turned on his heel. Right behind him the two armed guards kept pace until he arrived at the office complex and then they turned away.

"Thy Spirit shall open my lips O Lord."

"And my tongue shall announce Thy praise."

"Brethren: Behold, I tell you a mystery: We shall all indeed rise again. In a moment, in the twinkling of an eye, at the last trumpet: for the trumpet shall sound, and the dead shall rise again incorruptible and we shall be changed. And when this mortal hath put on immortality, then shall come to pass the saying that is written: death is swallowed up in victory. O death where is thy victory? O death where is thy sting?

To these O Lord and to all that rest in Christ, grant we beseech thee, a place of refreshment, light and peace: through the same Christ our Lord. Amen."

Meg wrapped her Rosary beads round the clasped waxen hands of her dead son and kissed him on the mouth. "It won't be long until I'll be with you Billy,"

When the four came out of the mortuary, the two armed prison guards moved in to close the lead coffin and escort it to the main gate. Outside the hearse stood waiting, with rear door open wide, like the yawning grave waited in Connemara.

Before the bereaved party left the prison yard the Warden came to speak to Meg a last time: "If it's any consolation to you Mrs. McNeill, your son was never treated as a terrorist in here. From the start it was obvious to us he had no such characteristics."

"Then why was he convicted and sent to prison like a criminal?"

"Because he carried a loaded revolver about with him and foolishly assumed the role of an I.R.A. activist to impress his so-called friends. I had made contact with the Ministry for Justice and asked that your son's mental maturity be assessed with a view to a remission of sentence."

"But it's a bit late now, isn't it?"

"Yes it is, I'm sorry to say. Only we did try and might have succeeded except, for what happened."

"He should never have been convicted in the first place. He was only a softie."

"We have no say in who should or should not be sent to prison. Ours is not to reason why, etc. Sorry again. Goodbye and safe home."

Luke followed the hearse with Sean silent as a dumb beast beside him. In the back, Meg and John spoke in undertones. They were on their way to Hollyhead to meet the Boat.

A long sad journey lay ahead of them: from Hollyhead to Dun Laoghaire and from Dublin on the east coast across the width of Ireland to Galway on the far west coast. It was the McNeills and the Brannigans Via Dolorosa.

ONE OF IRELAND'S GREATEST LIVING POETS
Friday night is my delight
And so is Saturday morning
But Sunday night gives me a fright
To think of Monday morning.

So says the old piece of doggerel describing the delight and dilemma of the long–ago schoolboy.

The much waited for Saturday night had arrived at last. It was the Poetry recital night at the Empress of Russia pub, Sloane Square, London. The great Monaghan poet Patrick Kavanagh would read his own works and give a talk with each poem to explain the theme and the history behind it.

The Auditorium could accommodate almost two hundred people and the entrance fee was ten shillings. A podium had been erected and a microphone installed on the readers' table. And there were two chairs instead of one; an armchair and a kitchen chair.

The second chair was for a young Kilkenny man who had been asked to read some of his own poems. This was by way of giving the established poet a break when he needed it on the night. And this prodigious event had been high-lighted by the influential 'Irish Times.' Also it was advertised on posters exhibited in 'The Poppy', 'The Champion', 'The Hoop,' 'The George,' and many other symposiums and watering holes where the poetry loving Irish frequented. "Patrick Kavanagh, is one of Ireland's greatest living poets", was the headline in the Irish Times.

Allen Hunt felt butterflies in his stomach. He wasn't too worried about it though, because he read in a boxing magazine that the irrefutable heavyweight champion Joe Louis always suffered from butterflies before a fight. And when some lightweight reporter asked Louis did that mean he was scared, the 'Brown Bomber' smiled and said: 'On the contrary mister, a boxer wouldn't be any good if he didn't have them butterflies." It is the same with a poet Allen reckoned. Without butterflies there could be no sensitivity. Without the sensitivity there can be no poet. Allen knew this instinctively.

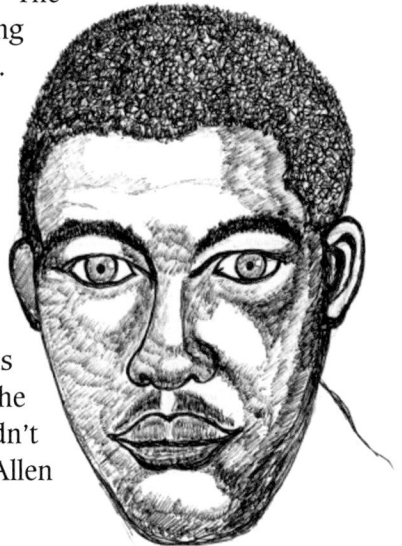

JOE LOUIS   THE BROWN BOMBER
BY SEAN KENNY

The Auditorium was filling up slowly. Jack Boland was Master of Ceremonies. He would introduce the poet, no the poets. Allen noticed that some members of the audience came in carrying drinks with them. It was not a good idea he felt but then he had no say. He was only a guest. The great man himself was imbibing a ball of malt with a glass of beer to wash it down. He was turning the pages of his robust poetic itinerary, inside a cloud of blue and white smoke. Allen knew he was champing on the bit, ready to run in the literary stakes of Calliope.

Did he have his gun cleaned and ready to fire with the hammer cocked? Would he knock them dead as he had told Allen a poet must do? And still they came in dribs and drabs now, with the odd one half jarred or under the weather. "Don't let anyone else in who has drink on him," Jack Boland said to the two men on the door. These were the two who had been in 'The Champion' on the night Pat Hunt had demolished the two thugs who had come in with Nancy Blackmore looking for his blood. The same two Volunteers who made a proposition to Allen at 'The Poppy.' A proposition they believed, he would dearly want to fulfill. Now one of them signalled Allen and he went over to them. "What time is this Reading due to begin?"

"Eight o'clock Irish time," Allen said with a grin. It was already fifteen minutes past eight.

"O well, that's all right then. I thought for a minute they were adhering to Greenwich meantime."

Jack Boland climbed on to the podium and briefly spoke with Patrick Kavanagh. Patrick was sitting back in the armchair, surveying the extraordinary assembly of hearers.

His hat had been given a holiday and his jacket hung loose on the back of the chair. His yellow and green necktie was pulled open and his shirt collar unbuttoned. The sleeves of his white cotton shirt were turned up to the elbows and were just the job for the unpretentious down to earth gathering. Quickly Allen made his way to the podium.

Jack Boland was peaking: "Good evening ladies and gentlemen. Thank you for coming. Most of you no doubt will recognise the Monaghan born, Dublin based poet Patrick Kavanagh. Indeed I suspect many of you will have heard Patrick read his own works here in London on other occasions. That newspaper of excellence The Irish Times has described Patrick as; ""one of Ireland's greatest living poets."" Ladies and gentlemen please give a warm welcome to the poet Patrick Kavanagh."

Patrick waved his arm frantically like a drover hunting cattle into a field, to get rid of the pall of smoke, that hid him. He stood up and briefly bowed. Before sitting down he turned to Allen. "Remember what I told you now: Shoot to kill. Knock them dead."

"Also this evening I have the pleasure of introducing for the very first time to read some of his own poetry in London, a young Kilkenny man, named Allen Hunt. Give him a big hand. But first and foremost I give you Patrick Kavanagh."

Patrick cleared his throat with a sound resembling a lorry load of shingle being heeled-up on a bed of stones to make a road.

"For me, poetry is primarily an expression of the personality. And poets can be compared to torch-holders who briefly illuminate the dark road we travel upon or kindle whatever material we chance to find. Poetry is personal speech in its purest form. To do this properly I believe that it is fundamental for the poet to find his own true self, – his deepest and truest self."

Commemorate me where there is water
Canal water preferably, so stilly
Greeny at the heart of Summer.   Brother
Commemorate me thus beautifully
Where by a lock naigarously roars
The falls for those who sit in the tremendous silence
Of mid July. No one will speak in prose
Who finds his way to these Parnassian islands.
A swan goes by, head low with many apologies,
The bending light peeps through the eyes of bridges
And here! A barge comes bringing from Athy
And other far-flung towns mythologies
O memorial me with no hero-courageous
Tomb but just a canal-bank seat for the passer-by."

EPISODE TWENTY-ONE

ODYSSEAN WANDERINGS
PRELUDE
SHANCODUFF
"THANK YOU FOR LISTENING"
WHEN I AM OLD

ODYSSEAN WANDERINGS

It was Saturday night at the Empress of Russia pub, Sloane Square London. The long waited for occasion had come at last. The Poetry recital night featuring the great Monaghan born poet Patrick Kavanagh and an unknown young Kilkenny poet named Allen Hunt was about to kick off. A group of young I.R.A. men were responsible for inviting Patrick to London, and not for the first time either. As was usual, they would pay his expenses as well as providing payment for his poetic outpourings. It was Patrick's third time to read in London, but his first at the Empress of Russia pub.

It was to be expected that ninety percent of his audience would be the Irish in London and the London born Irish. The other ten percent would consist of poetry loving Londoners, newspaper columnists and patrons of the Establishment. The latter being delighted with the novelty of attending such a singular and distinct type of entertainment, – like a child with a new toy.

Patrick was sitting at the reading table, on the podium, with the microphone in front of him and his Odyssean wanderings well documented at his fingertips. He began his Parnassian disclosure with these words: "No man can be happy who is not in sympathy with the poetic spirit. No society can prosper without the poets spirit of adventure and courage. The only thing new under the sun is the personality. And if a statement is new it is not true. A man is original when he speaks the truth that has always been known to all good men everywhere. There is no merit in trying to impress people with bogus accounts. Learn a lesson from life: Never pretend or exaggerate, as the simple truth is plenty. You can be sure that the truth is sometimes dangerous, but it is always the hallmark of a man, all be it, a man of Letters".

"We, the Irish, are a nation of hypocrites, Christ help us. I have first hand knowledge of this, for I have been hated for telling the truth at home in Ireland.

Like when I castigated the gammons in a poem which I will read for you in a moment. It is called – Prelude. As all of you well know a prelude is an event or passage preceding and leading up to an even greater event." Patrick was in his element like Apollo at the pinnacle of Parnassus. He turned towards Allen Hunt and said listen:

PRELUDE

Give us another poem he said
Or they will think your muse is dead;
Another middle-age departure
Of Apollo from the trade of archer.
Bring out a book as soon as you can
To let them see you're a living man.
Then link your laughter out of doors
In sunlight past the sick faced whores
Who chant and praise of love that isn't
And bring their bastards to be Christened
At phoney founts by bogus priests
With rites mugged up by journalists.
Walk past professors looking serious
Fondling an unpublished thesis-
A child! My child! My darling son
Some Poets of Nineteen Hundred and One.
Note well the face profoundly grave
An empty mind can house a knave.
Be careful to show no defiance
They've made pretence into a science
Card-sharpers of the Art Committees
Working all the Provincial cities.
They cry 'Eccentric,' if they hear
A voice that seems at all sincere
Fold up their table and their gear
And with the money disappear.
So now my gentle tiger burning
In the forest of no-yearning
Walk on serenely, do not mind
That Promised Land you though to find
Where the worldly-wise and rich take over
The mundane problems of the lover
Ignore Power's schismatic sect
Lovers alone lovers protect.

Patrick Kavanagh paused like Aristotle might have done after delivering his ideal 'Republic,' where artistic evaluation is closely connected to social and ethical criteria.

He leaned over to Allen Hunt: "Well young fellow, did I knock them dead?" Allen had to strain to hear the normally earsplitting voice, but having caught the evocative words; knock and dead, he knew instantly what was said. "The answer to your question is ringing in my ears, loud and clear," he shouted.

Not only were the listeners clapping their hands but were stamping their feet too. And there were shouts of 'bravo' and 'good on you Patrick.'

Patrick downed the glass of beer and lit up a Gold Flake cigarette. Standing close by him, Jack Boland was jubilant. "Your glass is empty Patrick, – same again is it?"

"Something similar will do, Jack." But what about Allen? His glass too is less then half-full." Patrick got back between the shafts of his own vernacular, prose carrying cart.

"To revert to tragedy for a while, I do not feel that a wise man expects any favours from his fellow man. For the most part it's every man for himself. Any one who believes anything else needs to have his head examined. Especially in a place like Ireland, I am sorry to say. There are people who actually hate any man who is exceptional and they take a wicked delight in any misfortunes that might befall him. Like that time when I lay on the broad of my back in a Dublin hospital in 1954. A few Dublin, not so civil 'Civil Servants; came to visit me and to gloat over the calamity, that saw me looking death in the face. They said they had got together and come up with a marvellous idea. "We'll have you dead body laid out in State and draped in the flags of the United Nations above in City Hall along with all the statues. They might just as well have told me they'd dance on my grave. In those days my weekly remuneration came mostly from short articles on sporting matters, written anonymously for 'Sporting Prints,' at three guineas apiece."

Again he changed carts.

This one was pure poetry and as a result was swifter, surer, and more beautiful too.

ARISTOTLE
BY SEAN KENNY

SHANCODUFF

My black hills have never seen the sun rising
Eternally they look north towards Armagh
Lot's wife would not be salt if she had been
Incurious as my black hills that are happy
When dawn whitens Glassdrummond chapel.
My hills hoard the bright shillings of March
'Till the sun searches the last pocket.
They are my Alps and I have climbed the Matterhorn
With bundles of hay for three shivering calves
Under the Big Forth of Rocksavage.
The sleety winds rustle the rushy beards of Shancoduff
While the cattle smugglers sheltering near Fetherna Bush,
Look up and say: Who owns them hungry hills
That the waterhen and snipe must have forsaken?
A poet! then by heavens he must be lean
I hear and is my faith not somewhat shaken.

Again there erupted a crescendo of hand clapping, feet stamping and shouts of eloquent praise. And when the tumult subsided, a beaming Patrick Kavanagh confidently told his enthusiastic audience: "All that experience can teach us is the way from simplicity back to simplicity. That poem is one of my earliest attempts to compose. But what I didn't know then was, it was also one of my best."

Allen Hunt was searching through the faces in the audience for Peggy O'Shea. She had not arrived.

What had happened? She was so enthusiastic about the Poetry Night when he spoke with her over the phone during the week. But then she had expressed some anxiety about getting off on time. He knew she would be disappointed if she wasn't in time to hear him read his poetry and he reckoned Patrick would need to take a break shortly.

It looked like most of the audience were smoking and the windows were shut tight. Maintaining a proper tone of voice would not be easy in that atmosphere. It was already getting to Patrick who was giving the occasional cough like a cranking noise in a worn back axle. Nor was he helping himself with his twenty box of Gold Flakes left open at the ready.

There was a teeming pause then, and people could almost be seen to collect their thoughts like luscious black-berries from a gorgeous green bush, to make delicious pots of jam and sweeten the bread of life.

A coarse and passionate woman's voice rang out: "Any chance of a piece from The Great Hunger, Patrick?"

"Like I said to my young friend and poet Allen Hunt, sitting here beside me; strictly speaking, 'The Great Hunger' is not poetry. There are some queer and terrible things in it, but it lacks the nobility and repose of poetry. At your request though I will read a dozen lines from it and then we must all give pride of place to this young Kilkenny man who has been so patient. Here now are a few verses from chapter eleven of 'The Great Hunger.'

A year passed and another hurried after it
And Patrick Maguire was still six months behind life,-
His mother six months ahead of it;
His sister straddle-legged across it:-
One leg in hell and the other in heaven
And between the purgatory of middle-aged virginity
She prayed for release to heaven or hell.
His mothers voice grew thinner like a rust-worn knife
But it cut more venomously as it thinned,
It cut him up the middle till he became more woman than man
And it cut through to his mind before the end.

"THANK YOU FOR LISTENING"

It seemed as if Patrick's physical proportions had grown in stature to equal Rabelais's hero Gargantua. Everywhere one looked one could see his massive image. And strange to tell even when one closed one's eyes this vision of him persisted. This poet certainly had the powers of projection. His verse filled the live ether, even after he had done.

Jack Boland who was M.C. for the night stepped up onto the podium: "What can I say about this man's work, – this man's genius. We owe him our profound thanks, – and our profound admiration." The hand clapping, the foot stamping and the plaudits began all over again. Jack raised his hands for calm and having got it, he began speaking once more.

Allen Hunt did not hear a word of what Jack Boland was saying. His thinking had become introspective and superseded everything else around him.

He was beginning to doubt the wisdom of the greatest heavy weight boxing champion the world had ever known, about butterflies before a fight. Allen's confidence was under fire and he felt his butterflies had had another metamorphosis and were now falcons attacking his resolve. But he understood what had happened: The genius of Patrick Kavanagh had temporarily undermined his confidence.

"I will be the captain of my emotions," he told himself. "Self possession is the key to self reliance. It's all in the head. What was it Emile Coué said? "Every day in every respect I am getting better and better." Self-mastery through conscious autosuggestion."

Allen had confronted his fears and was gaining the upper hand when he heard Jack Boland say: "Ladies and gentlemen it is my pleasure to give you for the very first time in London, reading some of his own poetry, the young Kilkenny man Allen Hunt. Give him a big hand." By this time about half the audience had got to their feet and were leaving.

"That was a magnificent display of poetry and prose by Patrick Kavanagh, – truly inspirational. How can I follow such genius. I have one consolation however; at least not all of those who heard him can be disappointed with me, seeing as how half have already left." This brought on a burst of laughter.

"I have always been captivated by the passage of time. Even as a boy going to school I use to wonder where yesterday had gone to, that it could never be called back? These thoughts arose mostly on Sunday nights and Monday mornings, when school loomed large on the horizon."

The poet tells us: "Times change and fashions alter, But old friendships never falter. I hope that's true. That's how it was with the Past. The Present is always with us, like a constant companion. But the future can never be embraced. No matter how swiftly a love inflamed Present gallops after fulfillment, it may never overtake the future."

"I'll read for you now a poem called. 'When I Am Old.'"

Patrick growled something under his breath like "Jaysus, you're starting young enough." Out loud he said "Silence now for a young poet."

WHEN I AM OLD
  When I am old
  I'll sit and watch the grass grow
  And listen to the leaves blow.
  And count dead years on crippled fingers
  And daydream dead dreams again
  And make images out of dreams
  And talk and laugh and play with them
  When I am old.

  When I am old
  When my back's bent like the bow.
  And my arms like half sawn boughs hang low
  And my feet are made of lead with legs of straw
  When I but nod and wink my way
  Through all the dream filled days.
  And nevermore may wander proudly free
  Mid hill and sky, while seeking
  I might chance to see God's handy-work

In some twisted elderberry tree, or trace
His footprint sunk into a stony pass.
When I am old
I'll know the bone in all things man needs knowing
From the maker to the breaker, everyman
That struggles from the belly of a woman
Is made alive to puzzle out God's plan.

When I am old
My young face will have grown a wrinkled flesh
The glad will be a sad smile ear to ear and
A white beard I will set against the north wind
Then my weary eyes won't sin to see
A flash of lace from some feminine place
The passions then in me will be outdated
And all the while my heart run on
Like a mad-fast watch to it's winding hour
To beat its last in this clay tower
When I am old.

When I am old
I'll treat death with much respect
And call him by his Christian name of Peace
My soul and body I'll bleach well
And wear white linen next the skin
For fear He might drop in,
To measure me dead accurately
Against my bag of sins.

EPISODE TWENTY-TWO

THE CONTAGION OF EXAMPLE
THE IRON CURTAIN
MY TALKATIVE FOOT
A BREAK-IN OR A BURGLARY

THE CONTAGION OF EXAMPLE

It was Poetry Night at the Empress of Russia pub, Sloane Square London. Patrick Kavanagh had just finished reading. He had been given a hand clapping, feet stamping and verbal acclamation. His prose was loaded with poetry and his poetry came down from Mount Olympus. So prolonged was the din of applause that Jack Boland had to ask for silence over the microphone. Scarcely had he got it when a large number of the audience were on their feet and seemed to be leaving. Jack persisted: "Ladies and gentlemen, it is my pleasure to introduce a young Kilkenny man named Allen Hunt. Allen will now read his own poetry for the very first time in London. Please give him a warm welcome."

There was a sizeable clap from those who were leaving as well as from those who remained seated. This surprised Allen, especially when more of the audience began to leave. It reminded him of the old story called the 'Contagion of Example': An honest and upright citizen named Panurge, had engaged in a large financial transaction with a wealthy but deceitful merchant who had literally fleeced him. A year later as Panurge was sailing on the Garonne from Agen to Montauban he discovered that the infamous merchant was on board and was bringing one hundred pedigree sheep for sale at the market in Montauban. Panurge bought the vile merchants biggest sheep and proceeded to throw it into the Garonne, being certain that the entire flock would follow, which indeed they did, due to the contagion of example. People are like sheep in this respect, Allen told himself. They imitate their peers for better or for worse.

The two Volunteers now fastened the doors back to the wall, to allow freedom of movement. Immediately there was a surge of fresh air as the smoke was sucked into the vacuum of the combined bar and lounge with nobody in it. Apparently the previous occupants who were regulars had drifted into the Auditorium.

When word went around that a highly controversial and foremost Irish poet, was about to read his risqué poetry, wild horses couldn't keep them away. They just had to hear it. This blabbing of information was let slip by the two Volunteers. Had Aesop been present he would have invented his treatise on the tongue, there and then: "It is at the same time, the best and the worst thing in the world."

What Allen didn't know was that those who had left had merely gone into the next room which contained the bar and lounge, to replenish their drinks. Imagine his surprise then after finishing his poem; When I Am Old, there was a resounding clap from outside as well as inside the Auditorium. Allen could hardly believe his ears and later his eyes, as the supposed deserters came back in slowly to fill their vacated seats.

The first to come through the open doors was Peggy O'Shea, accompanied by Allen's brother Pat. She was clapping like mad. Waving and clapping and laughing, she looked radiant, like a bride after the wedding breakfast. Pat didn't wave but was clapping discreetly. He knew Allen had spotted them the moment Peggy and he had arrived. Allen beckoned for them to come up closer to the podium where Jack Boland was conversing with Patrick Kavanagh. Jack climbed onto the podium and took hold of the microphone once again. "Ladies and gentlemen I believe it would be in everybody's interest if we were to take a fifteen minute break for those who wish to refill their glasses and those who wish to use the washroom. Thank you."

THE IRON CURTAIN

"You did well there, young man. There is merit in that poem, considering the distance of your projected vision. You fired your thoughts on your present state into the future on board the high powered rocket of your imagination and brought them back fifty years on. You came up trumps. It was a credible piece of imagining."

"And all the while my heart run on
Like mad-fast watch to it's winding hour
To beat it's last in this clay tower
When I am old."

"I like that."

"Did you know that on the 12th of April this year a Russian Cosmonaut named Yuri Gagarin rocketed into space and circled the Earth. But at the same time the Russian Hierarchy were building the Berlin Wall or Iron Curtain as Churchill has christened it, cutting off the freedom of movement from East to West. Poetry is the sign of freedom. With it you have dared to venture into the future like Jules Verne."

"That's very kind of you Patrick. I didn't see it like that at all. You have made me look at it in a new light."

"Poetry can also be an enigma though better when easily understood."

"Is this your ladyfriend?"

Allen was so engrossed in what Patrick was saying he hadn't noticed Peggy O'Shea steal up beside him. "Patrick would like to know if you are my girlfriend," he asked Peggy. "Oh by the way this is the poet Patrick Kavanagh, Peggy. Patrick, this is my very good friend Peggy O'Shea who has travelled all the way from Watford in Hertfordshire to hear this Poetry Recital."

"Then she either likes you or your poetry, because she doesn't know me or mine." Neither Allen nor Peggy knew how to respond to this but Peggy made an attempt: "Well, I've not heard any of your poetry Mr. Kavanagh, but Allen assures me that you are Ireland's greatest poet."

Allen was surprised when Patrick was taken aback at this. He looked in great earnest from Peggy to Allen and said very slowly: "That's one of the nicest things anyone ever said to me." But had not the Irish Times said as much in it's Poetry Review, Allen thought. Perhaps it was because that was on paper but this was from the heart. Patrick gave a cough like a train going through a tunnel, into a very large handkerchief that smothered his face. Allen suspected there might have been a tear of joyful appreciation concealed in the spacious nose-wipe. Then in an attempt to throw off the limelight he said; "Look, it seems all those who left are coming back and bringing their brothers and sisters with them. You are going to have more people listening to you than I did, Allen."

"But surely you'll read another few poems, Patrick?"

"We'll see, we'll see."

Allen left the podium and went to speak with his brother Pat and his girlfriend Peggy O'Shea, who had gone back to her seat. He gave Pat the money to buy three drinks and then sat in Pat's seat to have a chat with Peggy.

"Sorry I was late Allen, but I did hear you reading; "When I am Old" from outside the door. There was a dreadful hold up at Baker Street, waiting for the Circle Line. Your poem was marvellous."

"Well I hope the audience liked it even half as much. Thanks for the vote of confidence Peggy. I wouldn't doubt you."

Pat arrived back with the three drinks and Allen resumed his seat on the podium. As soon as Allen sat down, Jack Bolland took up the microphone and asked for quiet. Patrick Kavanagh gave Allen the thumbs up sign. "Allen Hunt will now continue with the reading of his own poetry. Allen!"

"Thank you Jack and thanks for returning ladies and gentlemen. This time I will attempt to hold you with words that promote laughter. There is an old saying, Laughter is the Best Medicine. Looking at you looking at me and none of us knowing what's in store for us, I am reminded of what the small town

Grocer said to Mark Twain, after Mark had asked him if there was anything happening in town that night?"
"Mark had been commissioned to give a lecture." "I reckon sir," said the Grocer, "somebody's giving a talk or a reading or something like that, at the Town Hall."

"And what makes you think that my good man?" asked Mark Twain.

"Well sir, I've been selling eggs all day," came the glib reply. (A peel of laughter rang out.)

"But I don't suppose I need have any worries on that score, – eggs are far too expensive nowadays to pelt them at people."

MARK TWAIN
BY SEAN KENNY

MY TALKATIVE FOOT

"This then is the story of a foot. The personification of a foot to be exact. I have found that although I am attached to it, it and I do not share common opinions. Morally and ideally we are at opposite poles, I had a sudden urge to remove my shoe and stocking. Then to my flabbergasted disbelief, I heard a voice coming from my foot. Hoping that my imagination had not eclipsed my reasoning, I listened and felt as if thunderstruck.

My big toe was wagging
and wriggling up and down,
Circling and fencing around and about.
"Listen to me," it said,
"I am the foot that feels.
Let me gaze awhile on the countenance
of your serrated physiog.
That valleyed and mountainous orb of flesh,
that great cave that is your gob.
At that bulbous elongated smeller,
wide nostrilled triangular nose.
Tell me chum, is it the work of a Pharoh,
Or just a pyramidal pose."

I lament that your reason is shadowed
and by competition confused.
That you haven't found yourself as yet.
That your intellect is ill-used by bad opinion.
Let me broaden that narrow noodle nook

that you erroneously call a brain.
Drive out conceit, open your eyes
And tell your friends the same.
Tell them that your foot knows more
Than the grand total of their knowledge,
For all their books and bachelorhoods
Of arts, parts and college.

There must be an end to the abuse of feet
torture of toes and absence of heat.
An end to barbarous broken boots,
Water-logged boots and shoes too narrow.
Oh how I fret for feet cut to the marrow
with great leather lumps of the crudest hide.
And for poverty's feet ever cold and wet-wise.
For feet that were severed because of the gout
By some Sawbones with hacksaw clout.
Murdered and buried in pine wood chest.
No coffin it is called, but a final foot rest.

I say away with the tyrant maker of clogs
Hobnailed boots and stiletto jobs.
Off with Wellington and his rubbery breed,
There will be no rest until feet are freed.
This is the slogan of my invent
That from heel to toe by foot was sent.
A gawk behind a bawk, eyes stalk, squint talk.
A wriggle and a giggle a size six for kicks.
What's the time, 'sgetting late retreat attack retreat.
A ride beside the slide a clout about the snout.
Toe's red, do as I said
Take off your boots and fly in bed.

Attention all you feet
from instep to ankle street,
The time of liberation is at foot.
Stir yourselves when the feet of the clock shows eight.
When the big foot counts the hours
and the little foot is in debate with minutes
Mark you time. Mush, mush. Away you go,
Scuffle, shuffle, clip clop into the street

Feet feet in thousands meet. Hurry Harry ho!
Helter Skelter High street high heels and low.
Look up, look down the shoed and booted town.
The population is on its feet.
Black and brown and white all meet
On clatter patter natter street."

A BREAK-IN OR A BURGLARY

Outside the Lounge and bar there was something of a commotion on foot. A policeman briefly appeared in the doorway and after pausing to hear what was going on quickly pulled back. He was satisfied there was nothing seditious about the meeting. One of the Volunteers went and spoke with him and discovered there was a plain clothes detective there also. The Volunteer returned after a short conversation and with an imperceptible signal to Jack Boland he indicated that his presence was required. Quickly he filled Jack in on why the police were on the premises. "There has been a break-in at your Offices in Spitalfields. A plain clothes detective and a policeman want to talk to you about it outside." Jack Boland's expression turned grim as he went into the Lounge and bar to meet them.

"I understand you want to speak with me!"

"Is your name Jack Boland, sir?" Yes it is, as you are well aware."

"Are you the same Jack Boland of Brannigan and Boland Building Contractors with Offices at 9 and 10 Lamb Street, Spitalfields London?"

"You know that I am. What has happened?"

"Apparently there has been a break-in, – a burglary to be more precise. A concealed wall safe has been forced open and some items strewn around the office. Did you have money or other valuables in it?"

"Not much by the way of money. A few hundred pounds at most. There were a few items of value. Has the safe been emptied?"

"Yes, I'm afraid so. I would be obliged if you would accompany us to the station for the purpose of making an inventory of the missing objects belonging to yourself and Mr. Luke Brannigan. I understand that Mr. Brannigan is presently over in Ireland at his nephew's funeral in Connemara."

"You are well informed sergeant." "Thank you sir, that's my job."

"Would it inconvenience you too much if I were to call to the police station tomorrow morning for the purpose of making this list? As I see it, it would be impolite of me to walk out on my friends and especially the renowned Irish poet, Patrick Kavanagh."

"As you wish sir. Tomorrow will be fine. You're offices are now secure. There is no need to worry about that. See you tomorrow then."

"Thank you officer, good night."

EPISODE TWENTY-THREE

THEY WERE IN CAHOOTS
THE LAMBEG DRUM
A LADY'S SIZE EIGHT LETHAL WEAPON
A VULTURE

THEY WERE IN CAHOOTS

It was five minutes after ten o'clock p.m. when Eileen Murphy regained consciousness. For more than an hour she had been out of it. She felt like she had been in a stampede. Her head ached with a throbbing intensity. Fearfully she investigated the source of the pain. A large lump as big as a golf ball had risen at the back of her head and her hair was matted with blood. With every second it became more clear to her how dangerous her predicament really was. Slowly and silently she got to her feet and almost fell over again. One of her shoes was missing. It must have fallen off when she was sent crashing to the floor with a back handed blow from the huge right hand of the giant South African, Winston Warbarton. What had happened was: Eileen Murphy had withdrawn three hundred and fifty pounds from Barclays Bank which was her fiancé's entire savings. Being one of natures gentlemen, Ivor Davies had allowed her to lodge the money in her own name. This money was to pay for their wedding in Kilkenny City on the following first week in September. Eileen had other ideas. She was on her way to The George on the Hammersmith Broadway to rendezvous with this giant black South African named above. There she was robbed of the £350. She knew that Warbarton was no good, but it didn't seem to bother her. He was a thug and a pimp. Inevitably and invariably, people are like water in that they always find their own level. Later when Warbarton had left her alone in his flat, while he went to seek out his accomplice and retrieve the stolen money, she had begun to piece together the many parts of the rip-off jigsaw. The sham Drunk who had snatched her bag was the same man she had seen speaking to Warbarton, when first she entered 'The George'. They were in cahoots. She had no doubt about it, – she was set up good.

The first sounds she heard now were the snores and snorts of the giant blackman as he lay in a drunken stupor on the bed in the next room.

It was like being outside the monkey cage in the zoo. The flat was a dingy and dirty little claustrophobic hovel, situated in a near derelict alleyway off Bell Street. This was a no-go area, where a body could be murdered and not found for a month. Slowly and silently she got to her feet after removing her remaining shoe, and examined the steel-tipped heel. "This was the lethal weapon," was the headline on the "News of the World" story, that told how a young woman had escaped from a convicted rapist. A photograph of the blood stained shoe showed how she had driven the stiletto heel into the forehead of the rapist, smashing his skull.

THE LAMBEG DRUM

Cautiously she crept into the room. Her knuckles showed milk white as she gripped the shoe with deadly earnest. Her heart was up in her throat and was pounding like the Lambeg drum on the Twelfth of July. She knew that if Warbarton had set her up, he would have the money on him, – in the inside pocket of his jacket. He would have no truck with banks or saving institutions. But he was lying on his jacket and how was she going to get it out from under him? "I'll do it if it kills me," she told herself while looking hard at the steel tipped stiletto heel. All the while she was cogitating with herself over the pros and cons of her search. The neck of the jacket was sticking out about three inches from under him. She was about to catch this by the loop hanger but changed her mind. "First things first," she thought; "I should make the road clear for a quick getaway like the gangsters in a Sherlock Holmes film. I'll open wide the hall door and the front door too." There wasn't a sinner on the street. A mangy old alley cat scampered into a derelict building chased by a caterwauling tom. The bawling gave Eileen the creeps. Back inside she studied the situation again. She knew in her heart that if Warbarton woke while she was attempting to search him, he would surely throttle her. If that happened, her only chance would be to lash out while he was in a lying down position. To lash out with the lethal weapon. "This is it," she said to herself in silence, as she gave him a push away from the neck of the jacket. He gave out a groan like an old oak tree being felled but he was still lying on part of the jacket. The left front and left inside pockets could not be searched and she could tell by looking at the right hand side pockets, there was no wad of money in either of them.

THE LAMBEG DRUM
BY SEAN KENNY

Nevertheless she went through them in a hurry, without letting go of her only protection against the sleeping Apocalypse. Two pound notes and some change were all she found in the front pocket. A dipped silver, half-full cigarette case with lighter attached, was in the other. She took the lot and left them on a chair beside the bed. Then she stuck her free index finger through the loop hanger inside the neck of the jacket and was about to give him another push when he turned back to his original position and was now partly lying on her hand with her index finger caught in the loop. She was like a live rabbit in a snare. The giant Negro then began to shake his enormous head rapidly from side to side like a punch-ball in the hands of a boxing champion. He was trying hard to shake off his drunken stupor. Somehow he knew he was being invaded.

A LADY'S SIZE EIGHT LETHAL WEAPON

Eileen Murphy began to panic as his eyes opened and closed and his lips began to move. Winston Warbarton was on the verge of rejoining the alert and conscious human race. She would have to act quickly or she was a gonner. Inside the flicker of a coal black eyelid, a powerful arm as big as the shaft on a horse's cart shot up and a hand as large as a tennis racket caught her by the throat with a grip as tight as a bear trap. She thought her wind pipe was caught in a vice and was slowly collapsing. Her eyes looked like they would pop out of her head any minute. Eileen Murphy knew that if she did not act immediately it would be too late. With all the strength she could muster she brought the six-inch steel tipped stiletto heel down with a vengeance that buried it in the black giants right temple. A warm spout of blood shot up like a geyser hitting her on the face.

Winston Warbarton was actually on his feet with the shoe sticking out of his head. And he was still holding her by the throat but his grip had loosened. In an other second he had let her go and she fell to the floor gasping for breath. He was aiming a kick at her while trying to pull the lethal weapon out of his head. There was absolutely nothing she could do to save herself except cradle her head in her hands. She tried to say an Act of Contrition but couldn't remember the words. She braced herself for the blow that would undoubtedly send her to meet her Maker. But it never came.

Instead he let out a hideous curse that brought a shower of blood with it, as he haemorrhaged from the mouth. Then with a roar like a goaded bull he fell back onto the bed with a crash like thunder.

She waited for another minute before she attempted to get to her feet. Eileen was shaking like a shirt on a clothes line on the Cliffs of Mohar when the west wind blows. She looked at him fearfully and saw that his eyes were wide open, with the pupils turned up. They were rapidly filling up with blood and overflowing at the corners like over-ripe, bursting tomatoes.

A great black bluebottle flew about the room in circles, making a droning sound as loud as a helicopter. It was the only noise around, but it was deafening. The snorting and the snoring had finished. She couldn't tell if he was breathing or not and she wasn't about to feel his pulse either. His jacket was no longer beneath him. She made a grab at it and ran out of the bedroom. There was a bulk in the left inside pocket. It had a safety flap that was buttoned down. Frantically she tore it open. The button sped across the pockmarked floor like a runaway wheel from a race-car at Le Mons. A pocket full of five pound notes, all new and crispy and straight from Barclays' Bank.

"The dirty rotten robber" she thought to herself, never thinking for one minute that she had stolen the same hard earned money from Ivor Davies. But Ivor Davies, wedding bells and living happily ever after, were all water under the bridge now.

With a broken scissors she ripped open a soiled cushion and threw the stuffing on the ground. She would carry the money in the cushion cover. The bluebottle flew noisily into the bedroom and was hovering over the enormous trunk of Winston Warbarton. Eileen Murphy cautiously went to the bedroom door and looked in.

The bluebottle had landed on his nose and was preening itself in a shaft of sunlight that had found it's way in through a broken window pane that otherwise scarcely let any light through. The bluebottle rose vertical, then dived into a pool of blood that had formed in the indented area above the cheekbone. There it floated with wings spread wide like a Hooker.

Suddenly the enormity of what had happened hit her, and she began to talk gibberish. With the illogical reasoning of her shattered nerves, she somehow thought that by holding a lively conversation with herself she could halt the onset of madness that was overpowering her already crumbling state of mind.

"Poor Winston, poor Ivor, poor Eileen and poor me. Everything is going to be alright. It was all a mistake. There's no need to panic, to panic, to panic. Disinfectant, soap and boiling hot water with a glass of brandy and a 'Bloody Mary' and clothes off the bed and the blood off his head." She caught sight of herself then in the cracked mirror above the dirty wash-hand basin. "Who is that 'effin bitch looking at? How did she get in here? 'Tis me poor mother come over from Ireland to see me, and take me home. O my God I am heartily sorry for having offended Thee. And I, and I."

Eileen Murphy ran out the door in her stocking feet still clutching the cushion cover with the wad of five-pound notes in it. Her face, her hands and blouse were covered in blood. A Policeman stopped her near the Florence Nightingale Hospital and brought her by Taxi to Marylebone Police Station. She kept saying over and over again: "Look Ivor, Eileen got your money back, your money back. Eileen got your money back. Now we can get married."

A VULTURE

Rosie Taylor nee Keegan was sitting with her daughter Patricia in the front room window on the second floor of 'The Poppy' on the Edgware Road. It was the managers living quarters. Matt Ryan had temporarily vacated it to allow Rosie and her daughter the security and the time to come to terms with the death of her husband Bill Taylor. Matt felt it would not be safe for them to be left on their own in Knightsbridge. His head barman, Allen Hunt had agreed with him. There was always the danger that the infamous Nancy Blackmore might pay them an uninvited visit. She was as deadly as a plague.

Rosie put down a pair of socks she was darning for Matt Ryan. A Police car had pulled up across the street in front of the 'Red Lion', which was a Scrumpy house. It was the scene of many a 'punch-up'. Scrumpy being a very potent Cider, was apt to set tempers flaring and fists flying. A plain-clothes detective got out of the squad car. Rosie knew they were not there because of some fracas or free-for-all. Had that been the case there would be a 'Black Maria' present, which was colloquially known as the 'Paddy Wagon.' Instead of entering the 'Red Lion' the detective crossed the road and was heading for 'The Poppy.'

Allen Hunt turned his head as a tallish, middle aged man entered the Public bar. "Good day to you. Does a Mr. Ivor Davies work here?"

"Who wants to know?"

The detective flashed his badge of office. Allen exchanged his stare for a smile. "Yes he does. He's on duty in the Lounge right now. You can go through here," and he indicated the door joining the two bars.

Matt Ryan was in the Lounge bar with Ivor, lending a hand to serve a group of men and women who were on their way to an antique furniture exhibition at Earls Court.

"Are you with the group?" Ivor asked the detective. He shook his head and flashed his badge once again. "I'm looking for Ivor Davies."

"That's me. Is it in connection with a woman named Eileen Murphy?"

"Yes it is. Could I have a word with you in private sir?"

The two men went to the far end of the Lounge and sat at a table to talk. Matt Ryan cottoned on instantly. He looked around the group to see that everyone had a drink and then went into the Public bar to see Allen.

"They must have found Eileen Murphy. I wonder what condition she was in?"

"More to the point Matt, – did she still have Ivor's £350 on her? That's the burning question." Matt, who was renowned for his turn of phrase answered: "Not a pigeon's chance in a falconry. Not that she was a pigeon mind you. She was more of a vulture if you ask me. But even vultures are preyed upon by bigger vultures. How come Ivor never copped on?"

"Love is blind" Allen said dryly.

EPISODE TWENTY-FOUR

THE COMIC MUSE
THE NOBEL PRIZE FOR HOPING
A POOR POET

THE COMIC MUSE

Allen Hunt, just finished reading his amusing poem 'My Talkative Foot', at the Empress of Russia pub Sloane Square, London. The last lines were:

"Look up look down the shoed and booted town
The population is on its feet
Black and brown and white all meet
On clatter, patter, natter street."

There was an awkward silence and Allen wasn't sure how the audience had taken it. Their reactions during the reading were positive. Indeed, there had been outbursts of laughter which were just what the doctor ordered. Like Allen had said at the introduction to the poem: "Laughter is the best medicine." But this turn-up was a horse of a different colour in that there seemed to be no reaction at all. Were they struck dumb or had he finally shot them all dead, as Patrick had told him he must do, from the start? Whether or which Patrick for one wasn't waiting any longer. In double quick time he jumped to his feet and for a moment seemed to be defying the law of gravity, as was claimed, Nijinsky often did. And he began to clap and shout "Well done young fellow." At which intervention the audience likewise got to their feet and clapped until Patrick stopped and resumed his seat.

Patrick looked at Allen with eyes beaming. "When I said knock them dead, I didn't mean you were to strike them speechless as well." Then he put up his hands showing his palms. They understood he wanted to speak. "Thank you ladies and gentlemen. There is only one true Muse, the Comic Muse. In tragedy there is always something of a lie. The best poetry is always comic in the profound sense. Comedy is abundance of life. All true poets are gay, fantastically humorous.

It is not true to say that; Our sweetest songs are those that tell of saddest thought, as is written in the foreword of that mediocre Anthology of poetry named, 'Flowers from many Gardens'. No, our sweetest songs are those that derive from that gay abandon which is the keynote of the authentic Parnassian voice. This abandon is not the riotous braggadocio which is often associated with the poet. True gaiety of heart springs from the sense of authority, confidence and courage of the man who is on the sacred mountain.

Thank you Allen Hunt. (A loud clapping) In speaking about Flowers from many Gardens just now, it strikes me that perhaps I was a little too harsh, because there are at least a few poems in it that have merit. There is a little poem again in the foreword entitled "To the Student" and was written by a poet named J. Byrom.

Now I'm not sure if Byrom is a misspelling and was meant to be Byron, who was born George Gordon, the British poet. Whether he was or wasn't I'll give you, whom I consider to be excellent students of Poetry, his poetic piece of advice.

To the Student
In reading Authors when you find
Bright passages that strike your mind,
And which, perhaps, you may have reason
To think of at another season;
Be not content with the sight,
But take them down in black and white;
Such a respect is wisely shown,
And makes another's sense one's own.

And now one little piece of prose poetry by John Ruskin, eminent British essayist.

Make
Yourselves
Nests of pleasant
thoughts - houses built
without hands for your souls
to
live
in
Soul Is More Than Syntax

A man at the back of the auditorium stood up: "We had Flowers from many Gardens" in third year C.B.S. in Letterkenny." "And so had I, in Cork" another said. "And me too in Wexford" came a third.

Allen turned to Patrick: "So you see Patrick when you wrote "No one will speak in prose who finds his way to these Parnassian islands," you were speaking the absolute truth. And maybe the standing army of Ireland's ten thousand poets which is also one of your pet observations, is not all together a figment of your imagination, either."

"Allen, the public at large don't care who invented the metaphor or the wise-crack; they are only interested in the interpretation. Beware of those who see you as a colourful character, – a kind of Don Juan. When someone dislikes you he refuses, or is unable to see beneath your mannerisms, and peculiarities. But love sees into the unique wonders of the loved one's heart."

"Patrick that's pure gold."

"I believe it was the Chinese Lin Yutang who said, 'the highest criterion is not whether the artist /writer shows good technique, but whether he has or has not a 'high personality'. The bottom line is Allen, soul is more than syntax. If your readers dislike you, they will dislike what you write no matter how good it is. Human nature is so influenced by personal likes and dislikes that if they dislike the writer they will more than likely deny him even justice. But if the spark is there, it will find a way out. It will explode and burst out a road that will lead to full expression. And finally, Allen, as a man is, so too are his words. You cannot separate the poet from his poem."

Jack Boland was back on the podium. He had a few words with Patrick, then took the microphone in his hand. "Thank you ladies and gentleman." Silence descended almost immediately. "Patrick Kavanagh, Ireland's greatest living poet will read for us a few more of his short poems and perhaps give us a little talk on their genesis." Patrick cleared his throat. It was a bit like a first attempt by a greenhorn to play the Didgeridoo.

"I arrived in Dublin in 1939. I know now it was the greatest mistake of my life. Britain had just declared war on Germany. I could never see my own interest. What was called the Irish Literary affair was being brandished around Dublin like the legend of Excalibur in ancient Somerset. Dublin was said to be the literary metropolis, and was crowded with writers and poets. Especially the Poet's Pubs. These were full of writers who thought their work had the Irish quality or character. It was all bunkum. And they thought so much of poetry they didn't believe the poor poet had a mouth on him. I blame myself for putting up with it.

G.K. CHESTERTON
BY SEAN KENNY

Another thing that mattered those days in Dublin was the peasant quality. Everybody wanted to be of peasant stock. In no time at all I was installed as the authentic peasant. The peasant was said to be the real thing whose songs were of the soil, – the hands-on condition.

But I, trained in the slum pubs of Dublin
Among the most offensive class of all
The Artisans – am equal to the problem;
I let it ride and there is nothing over.
I understand through all these years
That my difference in their company is an intrusion
That tears at the sentimental cliches
They can see my heart squirm when their star rendites
The topmost twenty in the lowered lights.
No sir, I did not come unprepared

I'm ashamed sometimes when I remember the bad verse I wrote as a very young man. There was one such poem that I wrote for the 'Dundalk Democrat." I called it:

Lines on an Old Wooden Gate
Battered by time and weather, scarcely fit
For firewood; there's not a single bit
Of paint to hide those wrinkles and such scringes
Tear hoarsely down the silence - rusty hinges.
A barbed wire clasp around one withered arm
Replaced the old latch with wanton charm
This gap ere long must find another sentry,
If the cows are not to roam the open country.

Patrick guffawed and ha-haed a bit like the great Australian Kingfisher called the Laughing Jackass. "Imagine a whole column of that stuff. Was it any wonder I wasn't paid for it." (More laughter).

"A few words now about the newspaper 'Kavanagh's Weekly'. Our trouble was twofold: There was a lack of writers and an absence of audience. We needed a £1000 gift if we were to continue to publish, but it wasn't forthcoming, so we were forced to close down. In Ireland nothing seems to matter but the momentary sensation, whether that sensation be wine, women or song. And so it is that we are one of the most drunken nations on the face of the earth. There is a lot of despair about and it fills the pubs like a mind eating monster that drives men mad – anything to forget the futility of life in Ireland. There is a conspiracy of mediocrity at large. But the only things that matter are people thinking good thoughts, dreaming, hoping, loving, living.

God is good and he gave us our lives that we should live them. It is usually taken for granted that there has been a great literary Renaissance in Ireland over the past fifty years. Poor and all as most of it was, it was an attempt at imaginative activity along the right lines.   But without a doubt it was a movement of mediocrities and has now arrived at its logical conclusion: a counterfeit Academy. Now and then we did discover some faint flickering of the light of genius, but there was nobody to encourage it into full life as we would have done had we been able to continue with 'Kavanagh's Weekly.' And the so-called Cultural relations Committee that was founded by the Irish Government, they were our nastiest opponents. And there was a 'Cultural' set who were willing to "do all in their power" to help the Editor (yours truly) so long as he would guarantee to remain poor and ineffectual and never to enter into competition with the world on any serious level. How right Oscar Wilde was when he remarked that anybody can sympathise with failure, but that only a great saint can sympathise with success. The only power that has any real value is knowledge. To know ones self and to know others in relation to that self.

G.K. Chesterton said: "To the pagan the small things are as sweet as the small brooks running out of the mountain, but the broad things are as bitter as the sea."

Patrick threw up his hands, palms turned towards the audience. They clapped, whistled and gave a few cat-calls. Someone shouted more, then another and there were many mores. Patrick took off his spectacles. His face looked strangely naked and lifeless. "You have been a great audience. It was my pleasure. My sincere thanks but I've said too much already. In time to come I hope you will remember some of the issues I raised here tonight. Please give your attention now to our young Kilkenny poet, Allen Hunt."

"Thank you Patrick. Once again I've got to run in order to keep up with you standing still, Patrick. Thank you ladies and gentlemen.

"There is Faith, Hope and Charity" Christ said, "and the greatest of these is Charity." But when the very Reverend Charlie Kavanagh PP VG Dean of Ossory back home in Kilkenny City asked one of his better off parishioners if she would contribute to the Christmas fund for the Poor, she quickly told him the philosophers all agreed that "Charity begins at home."

As regards faith, – my own belief is; it is a case of hope and hang on. Of course I know it is a confidence and a trust in God, properly speaking. And now we come to Hope. The poet tells us that: Hope springs eternal in the human breast. Which seems to presuppose that even if we lost our Faith and our Charity we would still have hope. Now I am well aware that there are such international awards as The Nobel Prize for Peace, – for Science, – for Literature etc. But if ever the Powers that Be, decide to give a Nobel Prize for Hoping then I feel I will win that honour hands down.

To prove my point I took time out to pen this poem which I have called:
THE NOBEL PRIZE FOR HOPING

Aye, I say to myself
Why not now at twenty three
My clip clop feet complaining
About the implacable track
Of my fameless years
Without respite, and the hope
That was hammered by hope
To the shape of a capital D
For despair, when out of fear
I raced from that dead image
On the cross tree, bearing its terrible truth
I'd repent, to good day meet
My genesis.

But what I have done with my days
Hopping about like the sparrow
Water henning in and out of the swim
And being consistently narrow
Mea culpa beating the belly from sin
And from drunken debate
And what have you
Where now do I aim
My treadmill feet
Used in the past
Only to meet
Myself on the way coming back
Crossly like Christ I'm fastened
To an evergreen tree my mediocrity
But with hope I'll go on
From past hopeless decades
Reciting myriads of Our Fathers
Forever and never amen
My sin body flabbergasted
Forever imbibing the acid cup
In an urban Gethseame
Being certain that I must win
The Nobel Prize for Hoping.

There was clapping and calls for another. "I'll give you a very short one then, called "A Poor Poet." In this I may have been influenced by the amazing fact, that Christ never wrote down anything, but did all his teaching by word of mouth. Also there was the time when his enemies tried to contradict his teaching and He answered them by making symbols in the soil with a twig.

A POOR POET
A penless paperless poet
A vagabond scribbler I
Would trace in the clay
With my fingers
Symbols and signs for joy
By lovingly rearranging
A fistful of fertile dust
Discover some common wonder
Of myself at the paps of earth.
With dust for page
With finger for pen
And with no art that's my own
I write on clay
As a simple man
To prolong the living poem."

EPISODE TWENTY-FIVE

REFLECTED GLORY
TRAVELLING INCOGNITO
A POLICE INFORMER – A RAT
NOT A PIGEON'S CHANCE IN A FALCONRY

REFLECTED GLORY

The Poetry Night at the Empress of Russia pub had come to a close. For Patrick Kavanagh it was like a champion taking the Laurels at a minor Stadium. For Allen Hunt it was like crossing the line at the end of a fast Four Forty (440 yards) race, or hearing the bell at the end of a grueling amateur boxing match. No pain no poem, Allen thought to himself. For him there was neither the winning nor the loosing but to have played ones part to the best of ones ability. It was an experience he wouldn't have missed for diamonds.

Patrick and Allen were still sitting at the table while about twenty people queued to talk to, and shake the hand of Patrick Kavanagh before leaving: It was a case of reflected glory. Hadn't Tasso said only God and the poet can create. Everyone wants a piece of the winner, Allen knew this. He also knew it would be impolite to leave the podium without taking lief of Patrick. After all he was only there on Patrick's sufferance.

He is a poet truly whose insight pocket of knowledge is outside of learning. And so the poet can see without looking and understand without being told. As a consequence of this, Patrick said to the second person in the queue: "Indeed it's kind of you to say so but why don't you tell Allen that yourself." The amazed admirer could only nod in obedient disbelief as she was handed over to an even more amazed Allen, to congratulate him. Every other person after that felt obliged to converse briefly with Allen. And so the spoils of literary fame were shared between them, albeit unfairly in Patrick's case. Allen told Patrick as much and was answered like so: "One must redden the iron and the other hammer it into shape. It matters not who does which, just as long as the horse is properly shod and returned to carry its daily load." Still sitting in the auditorium Pat Hunt and Peggy O'Shea were waiting for Allen. "You won't make it back to Watford tonight Peggy, so where are you staying?"

"At the nurses quarters in Hammersmith General Hospital with a friend."

"Would that be male or female?"

"Why you cheeky so and so!"

"You can stay with me if you like," Pat said with a grin.

"And have Allen beat you into mince meat and dispatch me to Timbuktu. Besides what makes you think I'd do such a thing?"

"Just checking, to make sure you don't lead that young brother of mine astray. He still believes women are all sugar and spice and as quiet as mice. Whereas you and I know most of them are craftier than a jig-maker and bolder than brass."

"I don't know who she was but she certainly gave you a right roasting" Peggy said rather scornfully. But it didn't ruffle Pat's feather's one bit. On the contrary he stood up and roared with laughter. It caused something of a stir and a tall blonde haired young woman came to the doorway of the auditorium and stood looking in. She was looking daggers at Pat.

The two Volunteers spotted her instantly and nodded to each other discreetly. Pat sat down still gurgling with subdued laughter, a bit like water caught in the neck of a bottle. Peggy looked like she was fuming but it was a counterfeit fume.

On the podium Allen was standing and shaking hands with Patrick and thanking him with obvious sincerity. "A thousand thanks Patrick for giving me the privilege of reading at your side."

"I tell you this truly Allen, the people of the world should be satisfied to love God and to praise His works and one of the greatest of God's works, on this earth is the dancing flame of the poet's imagination."

TRAVELLING INCOGNITO

Allen left the podium and went down to Peggy and Pat. "There is something I meant to tell you brother earlier but the pressures of reading pushed it right out of my head. As Rosie Taylor and Patricia are now staying at 'The Poppy' don't you think it might be a good idea if you were to answer that letter she wrote to you prior to Bill Taylor's death?"

Pat looked at Peggy. "This fellow is something else. He doesn't miss a trick, does he?"

Peggy was all smiles then. "Look at it this way Pat; someone has got to tell you how to behave where women are concerned."

Pat wore a grin like the keel on a boat and Allen was looking from one to the other wondering what had sailed between them.

"I'll have to think about that brother. I may need your help concerning the lye of the land though. In one way it is a bizarre development that could go wrong but I can sympathise with it in another way. In any case I've got to go now. I'll be in touch."

Pat began walking towards the two Volunteers. The three of them went out into the bar and Lounge in the next room where Pat bought three drinks. "Have you seen who is here, Pat?" the London born one asked.

"Is it a he or a she?" "It's a vicious and dangerous she, and she is travelling incognito with a man who calls himself Larry Holden."

"Is this she, Nancy Blackmore?"

"She is."

"What in Christ's name is going on here? Have you any idea how those two got together?"

"Yes, but first things first Pat. You cannot be aware that the Brannigan and Boland Offices at Spitalfields were broken into some time tonight. A plain-clothes detective and a Policeman arrived here some time ago to tell Jack Boland about the break-in. We think that Blackmore is responsible for passing information to the Police. Otherwise what is she doing here? She is here to gloat or I'm the new Don Quixote."

"What information could she have to pass on to the Police?"

"That Jack Boland was a member of the I.R.A."

"Where could she have got such information?"

"We believe she got it from you," the Irish-born one said.

Pat stiffened and the hands went up. He was about to let fly but the other one quickly got between them. "Hold it Pat. He's not saying you deliberately gave her the information. You let her get too close to you and she was able to dig up scraps and put them together like the cunning bitch that she undoubtedly is. We also believe it was the Police who engineered the break-in at Spitalfields, but we can't be sure of this until we have had a chance to examine the premises. We will do that at first light in the morning."

"Do you need me to come with you?"

"I don't think it would be a good idea for you to come. You would be tipping off your hand and making it all too easy for them."

The other Volunteer spoke then: "We don't know exactly how much they know about us until we have inspected the break-in and Jack Boland has spoken to them tomorrow at the Police Station."

A POLICE INFORMER – A RAT

Pat took a deep breath. "Where does Larry Holden fit into all this? That's if it's the same man who called to 'The Poppy' and spoke with Allen. He obviously thought Allen was me. Then he gave Allen an invitation to his wedding reception and told him to bring me along. But I couldn't get off on such short notice. Allen bowed out after half an hour. It was a morbid affair, with only a handful of guests and not very friendly. The bride was said to be wealthy but was in a wheelchair."

"My guess is, the whole affair was staged. There was no wedding and no wheelchair bride either."

"But why go to all that trouble, – such an elaborate hoax?"

"It was you they were after Pat. Larry Holden is a Police informer, – a rat."

"And so the money, clothes and lavish lifestyle, all comes from…?"

"From M.I.5 He had the loan of them, though I expect he is well paid for what he does. Gets more than thirty pieces of silver for the Judas job."

"He was always a deceiver. Once a betrayer always a betrayer. And Nancy Blackmore didn't pick him up then?"

"No, he picked her up but made it look like she had manipulated him. He gave her a good time and then pumped her for whatever information she had on you and your friends, Pat. Whatever she knew or thought she knew, Holden has got it out of her by now. The problem for us is how much did she know about us."

"To my mind this woman knows little or nothing. I'd be more worried about what the Police found when they broke-in to the Offices at Spitalfields."

The London born Volunteer replied cheerfully: "I believe we have good news on that score.The two of us removed a sizeable amount of controvertible materials from those offices after Billy McNeill hanged himself at Wormwood Scrubs Prison.They will have been bitterly disappointed with their elaborate piece of deception. They found nothing more explosive that a bottle of Poitín".

"Are Holden and Blackmore still on the premises?"

"Yes they are and they are sitting only twenty feet away from us. Blackmore is wearing a blonde wig with spectacles and Holden a two week beard and moustache with bifocals."

"How on earth did you spot them?" "We have had them under observation for quite some time now. And they obviously don't know because when you let out a peel of laughter in the auditorium, Blackmore came to the open doorway and stood there watching you. But I'll tell you this, I wouldn't care to be in her shoes right now. As I see it, she has reached the end of her usefulness and in American movie-land lingo: her life aint worth a plugged nickel."

NOT A PIGEON'S CHANCE IN A FALCONRY

As the Police car pulled up across the road close by the Red Lion which is a Scrumpy house, Rosie Taylor nee Keegan and her daughter Patricia were sitting in the upstairs window of 'The Poppy'. A plainclothes detective got out, crossed the road and entered 'The Poppy.' He flashed his badge of office at Allen Hunt and told him he wanted to speak to Ivor Davies. Allen let him into the Lounge where Ivor and Matt Ryan were serving a group of men and women who were going on a tour to Earls Court to see an antique furniture exhibition. "Are you with the group travelling to Earls Court, sir?" Ivor asked the detective.

"I'm looking for Ivor Davies" and he flashed his badge again.

"I am he. Are you here in connection with a woman named Eileen Murphy?"

"Yes that is why I am here. Could I have a word with you in private?"

The two men went to the other end of the Lounge and sat at a table. Matt Ryan checked to see if any of the group needed attention and then went into the Public bar to have a word with Allen.

"They must have found Eileen Murphy. I wonder what condition she was in?"

"More to the point Matt, – did she still have Ivor's £350 on her?"

Matt who was renowned for his turn of phrase answered: "Not a pigeons chance in a Falconry. What I can't understand is how Ivor never copped on?"

"Love is blind," Allen said dryly.

After their talk in private the detective asked Ivor to accompany him to the Marylebone Police Station.

"I'll need to tell the Governor I'm leaving with you." Allen went into the Public bar and spoke with Matt and Allen. "They have found Eileen Murphy and are holding her at Marylebone Police Station. She's in big trouble. Some black man she was seen with yesterday has been found dead. "

"Did he charge you with anything?" Matt asked.

"No, he said it was just routine as I may be able to help them with their enquiries. I had better go. See you later."

Ivor was taken into the Dayroom at Marylebone Police Station.

"Please take a seat sir. You are Ivor Davies, barman at 'The Poppy' on Edgware Road, are you not?"

"Yes I am."

"Do you know a woman named Eileen Murphy?"

"Yes I do, – she is my fiancée, – or was"

"When did you last see Eileen Murphy?"

"Ten days ago. She came to see me at 'The Poppy.'"

"What was the purpose of that visit?"

"She told me she had written home to make arrangements for our Wedding in Kilkenny City."

"Did she say anything else? Was there any mention of money?"

"She said she would need to withdraw forty or fifty pounds from the bank to send home to book the Club House Hotel for the reception."

"And did she withdraw the money?"

"Apparently she withdrew all of it, – the whole £350 from Barclays Bank."

A stenographer was busy taking down the two-way conversation.

"Did Eileen Murphy have many friends?"

"She had lots of friends."

"Was she friendly with a black man named Winston Warbarton?"

There was a big fellow who used to come into 'The Poppy' quite a lot about a year ago. I didn't know his surname, just his Christian name; Winston."

"Were you friendly with Eileen Murphy at that time?"

"Yes, we were going out together."

"Did Eileen Murphy, used to come into 'The Poppy' when you were on duty there?" "Yes she did, – lots of times."

"Was Eileen Murphy and this Winston fellow ever in the bar at the same time?"

"I don't know. I suppose they must have been."

"Please think, and take your time before answering the next question. Don't get upset now. Could Eileen Murphy have had a sexual relationship with the black man Winston Warbarton?"

Ivor jumped to his feet. The veins stood out on his forehead. "Christ Almighty man, what are you trying to do to me? Isn't it enough that my future has been hijacked and my savings robbed? What more do you want from me?"

"Take it easy Mr. Davies. I am bound to ask these questions, personal though they are. This is not a case of petty larceny. This is a murder investigation, sir."

Saint Mary's Cathedral, Kilkenny City

EPISODE TWENTY-SIX

THIS IS A MURDER INVESTIGATION SIR ABANDON ALL HOPE YE WHO ENTER HERE AN AL CAPONE, A MATT DILLENGER OR A BABYFACE NELSON

THIS IS A MURDER INVESTIGATION SIR

Ivor Davies who was a barman at 'The Poppy' on the Edgware Road was being questioned by the Chief of Police in the Dayroom at Marylebone Police Station. "Please take your time before answering the next question Mr. Davies. Could Eileen Murphy have had a sexual relationship with the blackman named Winston Warbarton?"

Ivor jumped to his feet. The veins stood out on his forehead like railway tracks from a central station. "Christ Almighty man, what are you trying to do to me? Isn't it enough that my future has been hijacked and every penny I had in the world robbed from me?" Ivor felt more destitute than a witless old pauper.

"Take it easy Mr. Davies. I am bound to ask these questions, personal though they may be. This is not a case of larceny – far from it. This is a murder investigation sir."

"Murder? But as I understood it, this man had been found dead. No one said he had been murdered.Who murdered him?" "We have established beyond doubt that Winston Warbarton was murdered between ten and twelve o'clock last Saturday night. Now where were you between those hours?"

"Me? Is this a ready-up or a joke? From seven to eleven I was serving behind the bar and from eleven to twelve cleaning up and restocking the shelves. I have a half hundred witnesses." "I see. I am not accusing you of anything Mr. Davies but I must warn you that if there is anything that you know and are not telling us you will be charged with withholding evidence. But, you may innocently have some vital information and not be aware of its importance. For instance, in the days prior to her disappearance and the withdrawal of money, did you notice any change in Eileen Murphy's behaviour? Did her affections towards you change in any way? Did she give any indication that she was leaving you? Did she change her address or her job or perhaps both?"

"That's an awful lot of questions, but she did in fact change her address and she was fired from her job after being caught with her hand in the till at the Caffeteria."

"Do you remember the name of the Caffeteria?"

"It was the Breakfast, Dinner and Tea House on the Harrow Road."

"And where did she live then?"

"Fifty-six Chesterton Road, the basement flat."

"Right Mr. Davies. Now one more question: If the savings were not in your name how were you able to establish that they were withdrawn?"

"The manager at Barclays Bank wouldn't give any specifics, but he did say that if ever there had been an account there in the name of Eileen Murphy, there was no such account now. And now that I've answered all your questions would it be possible for me to see Eileen Murphy? I understand you are holding her here!"

"What will it benefit you at this stage to see her?"

"I'd very much like to know what she did with my money."

"She did have a rather large amount of money concealed in a cushion cover when she was apprehended near the Florence Nightingale Hospital. I am not saying the money belongs to you but there is a distinct possibility that it does. Of course that will have to be proven. Would you have any idea where she was coming from or going to when she was picked up near the Florence Nightingale Hospital?"

"No. I have never been in that part of London. I would like to see her now if you wouldn't mind."

ABANDON ALL HOPE YE WHO ENTER HERE

"I have to tell you Mr. Davies, when Eileen Murphy was apprehended she was in a very distressed state of mind. She has been seen by a Medical Practitioner and a Psychoanalyst. Seeing you might push her over the edge completely. But there is also the possibility it might bring her back to reality."

"Are you telling me she has gone mad?"

"The Psychoanalyst believes she is only temporarily insane."

"What caused her to go mad?"

"He said it was the trauma brought about by the fight and the death of Winston Warbarton. I will let you see her for two minutes, that is all. First I will observe how she is, then if she is reasonably coherent you may speak to her. Do you understand Mr. Davies?"

"I understand." "Right then, come with me."

The Police Chief brought Ivor along a narrow corridor that led to two padded cells at the rear of the station. Two solid steel doors were inset in opposite walls in an eight-foot square passage that was finished in blue and gold terrazzo.

Each door had a peephole and was numbered one and two. The Chief nodded to a Police woman who was sitting there on guard. She left down her book and silently slid back the shutter to check if everything was in order. It was and she indicated as much by returning a nod to the Chief. In undertones the Chief told Ivor he could look in. Ivor hesitantly peered through the peephole. The Policewoman watched Ivor's expression take on a look of horror as he saw and heard Eileen Murphy rehearsing her madness. She was combing her hair, then plaiting it and combing it out again, while saying aloud to herself over and over: "Poor Winston, poor Ivor, poor Eileen and poor me. There's no need to panic, to panic, to panic. Look Ivor, Eileen got your money back, your money back. Eileen got your money back, now we can get married."

Ivor looked at Eileen Murphy like Dante did at the inscription over the Gates of Hell: "Abandon all hope ye who enter here." The dismal prospect of what awaited her assaulted Ivor's sensibilities and he burst into tears. He put his hands over his eyes and turned away. Not even Virgil, had be been there could have taken him by the hand and led him in. His memory was turning over poignant thoughts faster than a boulder speeding downhill in a landslide. What had brought about this terrible transformation? Are all of us susceptible to this unholy deterioration under certain circumstances? If so, how true the premise: 'Only a hair's breath separates the sane from the insane'. The Police woman looked Ivor in the right eye, then in the left and then fore square full in the face as he shook his head like he had contracted the palsy. Then she sat back down and resumed her reading. She was as hard as the bole of a bastard teak tree. It takes all kinds and they are all here with us, Ivor told himself.

AN AL CAPONE, A MATT DILLENGER OR A BABYFACE NELSON

At five o'clock on the following Saturday morning, Jack Boland and the two Volunteers alighted from a black, near new Rover at the front of 9 and 10 Lamb Street, Spitalfields. Except for an old tomcat rifling through an overflowing dustbin left out of doors, there wasn't a cricket to be seen or heard.

The three men made a thorough search of the two Offices. They went over the premises inch by inch and item by item. In the wastepaper basket half-full of shredded letters, the London born Volunteer found a broken toothpick. "Rather careless of them don't you think?"

"Very much so," Jack replied and put the two pieces into an envelope. Five minutes later the Irish born one discovered a 'bug' in the telephone. It was a tiny transmitter inside the speaking end of the phone that was held in place by a magnet. "They don't seem to think too highly of our intelligence."

"That's a mistake they continue to make. It is the result of an inordinate assumption of race-superiority."

"Wouldn't you think they'd cop on?"

"I sincerely hope not."

At 10.30a.m. same day, Jack Boland walked into Marylebone Police Station and asked to see Detective Inspector Garry Knowlsworth.

"Do you have an appointment sir?"

"Yes I do."

"Could I have your name please?"

"Jack Boland of Brannigan and Boland Building Contractors."

The reception officer made a phonecall. "He will be with you shortly. Please take a seat." Jack Boland sat on a wooden bench and looked around the walls. Posters showed photographs of wanted men and women both young and not so young.

A large well-defined photo of what looked like a classical American type gangster held centre-stage. He might have been an Al Capone, a Matt Dillinger or a Babyface Nelson. 'Have you seen this man. Reward for information leading to his arrest. If sighted do not approach. He is armed and dangerous.' Detective Inspector Garry Knowlsworth was standing beside Jack but not without Jack's knowledge, through he thought otherwise. "You look like you might know that bloke," he said by way of poking fun at Jack. "I bloody well know I know him," Jack replied intent on stirring things up.

"O yeah, – from where exactly?"

"He robbed the out bound mail train while it was stationed at Paddington. He was disguised as a Mailman and made off with a barrowful of money sacks without being detected. In fact one of the Paddington Barrow-boys helped him to load the sacks onto his barrow."

"So you do know the bastard."

"Sure I do and so do all the wide-awake Londoners who can read."

"What do you mean?" the Inspector asks derisively.

"It was you who said I looked like I might know the bloke. It was all in the papers. The front page news and very appropriately too in the Daily Mail," Jack laughed, "three weeks ago."

"You're some smart-arse, you are. Enough then, lets get on with this inventory of missing objects from the break-in at your offices in Spitalfields."

HAVE YOU SEEN THIS MAN?
BY SEAN KENNY

Jack followed the detective to his office and was stopped in his tracks when he saw one of the barmen from 'The Poppy' coming from the rear of the station with the Chief of Police.

It was Ivor Davies, a good friend of Allen Hunt. He looked distressed and was holding one hand up to his face. Jack wasn't about to pass by him without enquiring what was the matter.

"Is that you Ivor? What in God's name is the matter man? Has there been an accident?"

The Chief of Police looked at Jack Boland with menace. "Excuse me sir. We do the questioning in here. This is a Police Station not a public highway."

"I meant no disrespect. It's just that I know the man and wondered if he had had an accident."

THE TOOTHPICK SNAPPED IN THE INSPECTOR'S MOUTH

This seemed to take the acrimony out of the confrontation and the Chief's tone softened. "I wasn't aware that you two were friends."

"I suppose I would be assuming too much if I were to say we were friends. It would be fairer to say we are acquaintances who have the same people for friends."

Ivor Davies had a hang-dog expression and looked like a school-boy caught out playing truant.

"Hello Mr. Boland. It's good to see you sir. I was thinking the same thing just then: What is Mr. Boland doing in a Police Station I was asking myself."

"We all have to suffer for our sins I suppose."

This observation seemed to please Inspector Knowlsworth and he flashed a smile at everyone before saying, "Let's get on with it then, crime waits for no man." He obviously thought himself to be an inventor of wise-cracks.

"Once I've seen Mr. Davies on his way I'd like to have a word with you Mr. Boland."

"Of course" Jack said and went with the maker of fake aphorisms.

"As I understand it Mr. Boland these Offices at Spitalfields are owned and shared by yourself and Mr. Luke Brannigan. Correct me if I'm wrong."

"That is so."

"I understand that you and two others paid an early visit there this morning. I take it therefore that you are now aware of what has been taken from your premises." The Police Chief knocked and entered and the Inspector repeated every thing he had said for his benefit. "So what did you discover was missing?" With that he took a toothpick from a pack on his desk and held it between his teeth at the corner of his mouth.

"Well did you take anything away with you from the Office as evidence Inspector?"

"I wasn't in your offices. The break-in was discovered by two Policemen on the beat who phoned in the burglary and then secured the premises. You said something last night about there being £200 or more in the concealed wall safe. Was that money there when you checked it this morning?"

"No it wasn't, but that doesn't surprise me. The safe was burst open, – a very amateur job."

"It would be highly unlikely then that someone who had gone to the trouble of breaking in, would leave behind such easy pickings, don't you think?"

"Indeed I do, Inspector. Especially if those who broke-in wanted to make it look like a burglary, as you called it."

"Do you have information that contradicts the burglary theory, Mr. Boland?"

The Police Chief hadn't said a word, but sat there looking from one to the other as the conversation changed characters. However, when Jack Boland replied "I most certainly do Inspector" the Chief stood up and making a face like one fit for murder, glared at the Inspector.

There was an ominous pause during which the toothpick snapped in the Inspector's mouth and caught the attention of Jack Boland and the Chief. Jack jumped to his feet saying "You distinctly said a moment ago, Inspector, that you were nowhere near our Offices at Spitalfields last night and yet we found your after dinner pick which is identical to the one in your mouth, in our wastepaper basket at Spitalfields." As he was speaking he took the envelope from his pocket and let the broken parts of the toothpick, fall onto the Inspectors desk. "That and the fact that our telephone was bugged. Would you recognise this?" he said and he took the tiny magnetic transmitter from his pocket and left it pointedly beside the broken toothpick on the desk.

EPISODE TWENTY-SEVEN

THE FRUIT OF THEIR AFFAIR WAS THEIR FOUR YEAR OLD DAUGHTER PATRICA
SOUNDED LIKE MAN TROUBLE
MATT RYAN'S PROPOSAL
HEAD BARMAN AT THE LOAD OF HAY

THE FRUIT OF THEIR AFFAIR WAS THEIR FOUR YEAR OLD DAUGHTER PATRICA

Pat Hunt, head barman at 'The Champion' on the Bayswater Road was in an unusual frame of mind. He was taking stock of his life. For him, these were unchartered waters. In the normal course of events Pat paid no heed to the passage of time, nor the Jekyll and Hyde cycles visited upon the very best of men and women. He took whatever good and bad the world saw fit to send him. Without thinking about it he saw both the rose and the thorn as parts of his inheritance from the brotherhood of all mankind. In the past, all obstacles were there to be overcome. He saw no need to question where they came from or why. Whether these hardships were of his own making or were mere accidents of fate never bothered him. As he saw it, yesterday, today and tomorrow were all in the here and now. They were welded together with a nervous energy that was unaware of time. But time is a great reformer that sharpens the perception by removing the scales from the eyes. It's one thing to be alive to the requirements for self-preservation, i.e. a strong body and a steadfast will. But it's quite a different thing to be able to appreciate another's point of view even at the expense of ones own. Pat was now deliberating with himself on the pros and cons of asking a certain young lady to accompany him for a night out on the town. He had been thinking about her since the night of the Poetry reading at the Empress of Russia pub, Sloane Square. It seemed to him that the man who was supposed to be her suitor was neglectful of her romantic disposition. On the face of it at least his brother Allen was taking Peggy O'Shea's affections for granted. One didn't have to be a genius to notice that it was she who was left to do all the running, and to make all the advances. As Pat saw it, Peggy must be wondering if Allen was really and truly interested in her? He thought he saw this in her body-language on the night of the Poetry reading.

Especially after he made the crack, that she could stay the night with him. And although her objection was confident, he felt it was not conclusive. However, be that as it may, one thing was certain, he would never interfere between Allen and Peggy if they were committed to each other. And there was only one way to find that out: He would have to confront Allen and talk it over with him, face to face and man to man. He knew no other way. Whatever the outcome Allen and he must always remain friends. Nothing else would be acceptable. He would need to speak to Allen on the phone and set up a meeting. It would not be easy. But that wasn't Pat Hunt's only problem. There was the problem of his association with his former lover Rosie Taylor nee Keegan and the fruit of their affair, their four-year-old daughter Patricia.

Pat hadn't got around to answering the letter Rosie had written to him. She wrote it at Pat's request, when Bill Taylor was still alive. That letter was without feeling, – clinical almost. It had a philosophical che sará, sará about it that seemed to need no reply. Allen had advised him to answer it after Bill Taylor's death. But there was nothing in it that held out any hope of revisiting the heights of togetherness and sharing that had once been theirs. Whatever there had been in the past had since sickened and died. The old verse about lost-love came into his mind then. That in itself was weird, because it was Rosie who had taught it to him all those years ago. Now he found himself reciting it aloud: "Lost between sunrise and sunset two golden hours, each minute studded with sixty diamond seconds. There is no use searching as they are lost and gone forever."

SOUNDED LIKE MAN TROUBLE

It was nine o'clock a.m. when the alarm clock rang in dead awaking earnest. Like a firebrigade ding-a-linging down a midnight street in helter skelter search for a reported conflagration, the career of Peggy O'Shea's slumber came to an abrupt end. She shot out her hand automatically to silence the din. It wasn't there Half awake she tried again but it went on clanging and reverberating this time like a Cathedral bell up close, calling the community to prayer. She opened her eyes and sat up in fright. "O God where am I?" She looked around her. "O yes, I'm in the nurses quarters at Hammersmith General. She found the alarm clock and guzzled it. There was a scribbled note on the locker beside the bed: "Gone to the kitchen for a cup of tea and a roll. You were talking in your sleep all night long. Sounded like man trouble. Who is Pat? Hadn't the nerve to wake you. See you later when you can tell me all about it. Stella."

"Not on your life, Stella. The truth is I couldn't even if I wanted to, and I don't. I don't even know myself. But there is one thing I do bloody well know: there isn't a whole lot going on between Allen Hunt and myself. His last salute when saying goodbye last night was something like two boozing pals after a session arranging to meet at a later date, to continue with the bender.

He said; "Safe home Peggy. I'll give you a call mid-week." "It's not exactly a lovers farewell, is it? For a poet he can be very pedestrian. He is a nice person but he's not very daring. Now on the other hand, his brother Pat is much more fun. If he should ever ask me out on a date and I suspect her will, I just don't know what I'd do. I'll have to think about it. In the meantime I'll have to get my skates on. I don't want to be here and get the third degree when Stella comes back. Besides, it's a long way to Watford in Hertfordshire. It will give me a chance to put things into perspective: Allen or Pat, Pat or Allen? He loves me, he loves me not."

Rosie Taylor nee Keegan was sitting in her favourite position in the upstairs window of the managers apartment in 'The Poppy' on the Edgware Road. Her four year old daughter Patricia was engrossed in a colourful story book called 'Snow White and the Seven Dwarfs'. Patricia would be starting school in the autumn. Rosie's husband Bill Taylor had died earlier in the year but he had left them financially secure. She had no worries in that department. But there were other considerations. She was still a young woman in her late twenties. Nor did she consider herself to be the stuff that widows are made of. She knew she could still attract a young enough man, with a view to marriage. She could still dream of having a loving relationship with a handsome virile man. Her prince charming could arrive at any time on his white charger and kiss her back into life. She would definitely not entertain any fly-by-night arrangement with any of the so-called jet-set. If she was ever going to take the plunge again it would have to be with a decent, sensible sort of man. Those with delusions of grandeur or madcap idealists she would avoid like the road to hell. Her long-ago lover Pat Hunt, had disgraced himself with the notorious Nancy Blackmore. Worse still, his membership of an outlawed organisation that condoned violence to achieve its objectives had to her mind, debased him. His brother Allen was more like what she wanted to see in a man. He was sensitive intelligent and responsible. There was none of the bravado and couldn't care less attitude that Pat exhibited whenever he felt himself disapproved of. That kind of reaction might have been admired years ago in the eyes of an innocent west of Ireland maiden, – but not anymore. Pat needed to grow up before he thought about settling down. Look at him at 28 years of age, the father of a four year old girl and he is still behaving like a maverick.

PRINCE CHARMING
BY SEAN KENNY

MATT RYAN'S PROPOSAL

And there was something else that had raised its head in the recent past. It was something she would never have anticipated. Her best friend, her father figure, Matt Ryan whose apartment she and her daughter were living in, had made romantic overtures to her. It was inconceivable. She felt sick to the stomach. There were no doubts in her mind but that she would have to move and in a hurry too. How had Matt put the question?

"Rosie my dear, I hope yourself and little Patricia are making yourselves at home in 'The Poppy'. You need not be in any hurry to leave. The truth is Rosie I'm hoping you'll consider staying for good. You know I'll look after the two of you better than any man alive. I know you were happy with poor Bill Taylor and its not even a year yet since he passed away. But I'll not be rushing you or asking you to make any promises one way or the other. Please don't think me insulting or take it the wrong way when I tell you that I am nearly twenty years younger than Bill was when he died. Given time Rosie I'm hoping you might consider settling down with me. As you well know I have an excellent job here as Governor. The money is great and the accommodation is free. I was never a drinking man, a gambler nor a big spender, so I have a sizeable nest-egg put aside. The two of you will never see a poor day as long as you live. I've said me piece and thanks for listening."

Rosie was so distressed that she choked up and cried and gulped and gulped and cried in spasms. She couldn't answer him, but rolled her head like a spinning wheel.

From that moment on, Rosie knew that she and Patricia, would have to leave 'The Poppy' as quietly and as quickly as they could.

Next day during Allen's lunch break Rosie spoke briefly with him: "Something extraordinary has come up, Allen. I really need to discuss it with you. I cannot continue to stay on here any longer. It has become impossible."

Allen was flabbergasted: "What's up, for God's sake? Did somebody say something?"

"I can't go into it now and I'd rather we spoke about it outside of here."

Allen looked at his watch. It was 2.25 p.m. He wasn't due back on duty until 7.00 p.m. "Do you know 'The Load of Hay' outside Paddington station?"

"Yes of course I do."

"Can you be there at 4.00 p.m. approximately?"

"I'll be there. I'll have Patricia with me. Thanks Allen."

At 3.30 p.m. Rosie and Patricia arrived at Edgware Road Underground station. Within minutes the Circle Line train arrived from Baker Street. Paddington was just one stop down the line. Like Baker Street, Paddington caters for three Underground lines. The only other stations in all of London's Underground system to do so are, Hammersmith and Kings Cross St. Pancras.

HEAD BARMAN AT THE LOAD OF HAY

It was 3.45 p.m. when Rosie and Patricia entered the Lounge bar of 'The Load Of Hay' at the top of the road outside Paddington main line station. They stood at the door, barely inside the Lounge as Rosie searched the faces of the many men and women on the premises. Children were not allowed inside. There was no gainsaying this rule. A barman had come from behind the bar counter and was walking towards them, shaking his head from east to west. Rosie began shaking her head from north to south in acknowledgement. Just as the two of them turned to leave, Rosie felt a hand on her shoulder. It was the timely welcome hand of Allen Hunt, "Sorry I'm late"

"You are not as it happens. We were early, Allen."

The barman was beaming like one who had just got news of a win in the 'Pools'. "It's great to see you again Allen. How is that big brother of yours these times? I heard you played a blinder in the Empress of Russia pub some time ago."

"Who told you about that?"

"Nothing escapes the pub gossiping grapevine. You should know that. Listen, you people obviously want to have a little palaver. We have a small private room here for V.I.P.'s only. I do believe you fit that description admirably."

"That's very kind of you Seamus. I didn't know you were in this neck of the woods. When last I heard of you you were in 'The Redan' down on Queensway."

"Would that be when it was called the Sean Hayes and Seamus Shortall shack?"

Allen burst out laughing. "The pair of you are some operators. Your likes will never be seen again and that's for sure. Sometime in the future I intend to write you all into history."

"I have no doubts but that you will, old son. But be sure to flavour it with merriment."

"How could it be otherwise old friend?"

"I'm obliged to keep a record of the unique and eminent persons who condescend to linger here awhile." So saying, Seamus bowed, pressing palms together like a Chinese Mandarin. Then in his less oriental tongue he said: "What are you having. The drinks are on me. Come on now, chop, chop."

"Could we have a mineral water with a few biscuits for Patricia please. And a Brandy and Port for Rosie. And I'll have a pint of your Best Bitter, if you please Seamus."

"And you're no way shy about ordering either" Seamus said and went away to fulfil the order, roaring with laughter.

EPISODE TWENTY-EIGHT

LIKE A VOLCANIC ERUPTION
LIKE A VENDETTA
A CITY SINCE 1609
BACK AT THE CHAMPION

LIKE A VOLCANIC ERUPTION

Jack Boland was being questioned at Marylebone Police Station in connection with the break-in at the Offices of Brannigan and Boland Building Contractors Spitalfields. He was being interrogated by Detective Inspector Knowlsworth with the Chief of Police sitting in on the session. Jack quickly defined that Knowlsworth wasn't happy with the Chief's intervention. So he decided to use the circumstance to his own advantage.

"You distinctly said a moment ago, Inspector, you were nowhere near our Offices at Spitalfields last night. And yet we found one of your after dinner toothpicks, identical to the broken one in your mouth, in our wastepaper basket at 'Spitalfields'. As he was speaking Jack took the envelope with the broken toothpick from his pocket and emptied it out onto the Inspector's desk. Then he pointed to the plastic package of toothpicks standing upright beside it. "You seem to have a penchant for them. And that's not all," he said, "our telephone was bugged. Would you recognise this Inspector?"

It is a well-known Police instrument. I wonder if there was a license issued for it. And he produced a tiny magnetic transmitter and pointedly left it down close to the broken toothpick. The Inspector was gob-smacked, while the Chief of Police sat there with flushed face and seething with rage. He was growling to himself like a volcano on the brink of eruption. Suddenly he shot up out of his chair. The red-hot magma in the crater of his emotions burst forth like lava from his pipe shaped mouth: "Why you blithering idiot Knowlsworth. You stupid assinine amateur. His instant wrath had momentarily got the better of his discretion. "I apologise for the Inspector's inexplicable handling of the investigation. It was unauthorised. Would you excuse us now for a moment Mr. Boland?".

"Certainly Chief Inspector."

The Chief jerked his head towards the door with such violence that he might well have caused himself an instant dose of whiplash. Knowlsworth sprang at the door faster than a half-starved cat after a boiled fish. He held it open and turned briefly to stare at Jack Boland before following the Chief into the hallway. The look he gave Jack was like the look the stupid young crow gave the clever old fox after it was fooled into opening its mouth to sing thereby letting fall its delicious tidbit at the feet of the fox. Jack gobbled up the honours, knowing full well he'd have to watch how he went henceforth where Knowlsworth was concerned. The comparison crossed his mind of M. Madeleine being hounded down the years by the notorious Policeman, Javert, in Victor Hugo's "Les Miserables".

The barrage of hostility went on in the hallway unabated. The Chief didn't seem to care who heard it. "This isn't the first time you have dropped me in it, Mister. You have proved yourself to be the biggest bungler Marylebone Station has ever had to suffer under its roof. As of now you are suspended from all outside active duties. You will report here tomorrow morning for office duties only. Now get out of my sight." And he shouted after him "I'm done carrying the can for you, Knowlsworth."

The Chief of Police returned to Jack Boland. He seemed completely unaware that his verbal assault had been witnessed by the accused and accusers alike. "I hope I haven't kept you for too long. I thank you for your co-operation in this matter. Please don't hesitate to call on me should you deem it necessary at any time in the future Mr. Boland. God day to you sir."

"Thank you Chief Inspector and good day to you too."

Jack Boland walked with a spring in his step and a thrush in his throat as he went whistling from Marylebone Police Station. He knew he had won the first round under the Marquis of Queensbury Rules, but the gloves would be off in round two. It would be a brutal barefisted battle from here on. The last man standing would take the laurels and who would that be?

LIKE A VENDETTA

The Marylebone Underground tube station is quite close to the Police Station, so Jack walked to it. Only one train line runs through here, i.e. the Bakerloo line. It runs from the Elephant and Castle in the South to Harrow and Wealdstone in the North and back again. Jack boarded the first train bound for Harrow. He got off two stops down the track at Paddington. Here he boarded a district line train to Bayswater. He came up out of the Underground at the junction of Bayswater Road and the Queensway. Then he turned right and walked for less than a quarter mile to 'The Champion'. Jack knew that Pat Hunt would be anxious to learn what he and the two Volunteers had discovered about the break-in at Spitalfields.

Also how he had been treated by Detective Inspector Knowlsworth at the Police Station. Pat breathed a sigh of relief when he saw Jack coming through the open door of the Public bar at 'The Champion'. Pat thought he looked like Standish O'Grady's Cuchulain coming through the "Gates of the North".

"They found nothing, then?"

"The only contraband there was a bottle of 'Poitin'. We found a few things ourselves though. They dropped a clangour." Jack went on to tell Pat about the toothpick penchant and the tiny transmitter planted in the telephone. "How could they be so careless? "

"Apparently, Knowlsworth is noted for his lack of finesse. The Chief gave him a dressing-down and within ear shot of all and sundry at that."

"The Chief has been at Knowlsworth's throat since a young Pakistani choked on his own vomit while being interrogated by Knowlsworth in the station at Marylebone six months ago. The Chief was suspended and damn near lost his job."

"So that's what it was all about. It's like a vendetta." Jack then told Pat of his meeting with Ivor Davies at the Station and how near demented he had looked. "Did Ivor say if the £350 – which Eileen Murphy had stolen from him had been returned?"

"He didn't say. I wasn't allowed to speak with him for very long.

"You are going to have to watch yourself from here on in Jack, where Knowlsworth is concerned. He'll do everything in his power to destroy you, within or without the Law. He attacks both the innocence and the guilty. He is a Herod."

"I reckoned as much, but it had to be done nevertheless."

"By the way Jack, your two Volunteers told me that Nancy Blackmore and that Informer, Larry Holden, had teamed up together. You know, it bloody well breaks my heart to think that a Kilkenny man could be an Informer."

"What do you mean Pat, – what Kilkenny man?"

"That bastard Larry Holden."

"Holden is not a Kilkenny man."

"Yes he is. I went to school with him. He came from Johnswell, Muckalee, near Mount Margie." "He may have done when you knew him at school. Larry Holden was born in the Shankhill area of Belfast. His father worked at Harland and Wolffs shipyard. He was one of the very few Roman Catholics employed there. Because of his affiliation to a Loyalist group of subversives, he was kept on the payroll. As a Catholic he was able to infiltrate the clubs and parties that championed 'Civic Rights'. But he was caught in the act passing on information to a leading Loyalist who had returned to the North after spending three years in Germany as a British commando. Holden was given a punishment beating and given forty-eight hours to get out of Belfast and Northern Ireland".

"He got out and went to live at Roundwood near the Vartry Reservoir in Wicklow. His wife drowned in a boating accident off Brides Head and he and his only child a lad of thirteen years left Roundwood and went to live in Kilkenny, near the Johnswell Hills, also known as Mount Margie. It was about that time the young Larry Holden was enrolled at the C.B.S. in Kilkenny City. Two years later the father and son pulled up stakes again like wandering Nomads and came to London. The old man continued to do the same dirty work here as he had done in Ireland. For a front he worked as a lift-hop in the Russell Square. Last year he walked into an empty shaft seven stories up and went down roaring like many a man's wife roared after he had fingered their husbands. And now his son has stepped into his father's shoes. There's nothing truer on this earth than the old wisdom; Like father like son."

A CITY SINCE 1609

"Well, you are a many-sided man, Jack. As they say in Kilkenny; there's more in your head than a comb could take out. And you have certainly taken a load off my mind. The thought that we had another 'MacMurrough', – the Irish Traitor amongst us, and that he was a Kilkenny man was going between me and my nights sleep. If I didn't know better I could almost feel sorry for that Jezebel Nancy Blackmore. But they are well matched and will no doubt kill each other off when the dust settles between them."

"I don't think so. If it comes down to it, it will be a very unequal contest. He has got an army of trained CID men and women to brief him and watch his back. Whereas she has got a handful of ignorant thugs as you well know, to watch out for her."

"Will she be eliminated, Jack?"

"More than likely, if she becomes a threat to their field of operations by exposing their cover. They won't hesitate to dispose of her."

Every time the lounge door was pushed open at "The Poppy" on the Edgware Road, Matt Ryan looked towards it. He was expecting his assistant head barman, Ivor Davies to walk through.

It was more than two and a half-hours earlier that he had left with a Detective Sergeant for Marylebone Police station. Matt was getting worried. He called across the partition: "Are you busy there Allen?" "Not particularly Matt, – What is it?"

I'll come into you for a moment. Allen shot back the bolt on the connecting door in the partition. "Ivor has been gone for quite a long time. It's getting close to three hours now since he left. I wonder if they are holding him?"

"They would have to charge him with some offence before they could hold him, Matt. And what in God's name could they charge Ivor with except gross negligence with his own hard earned savings?"

"I suppose you are right, but it's hard to know what to expect where the Law is concerned." Many a man swung in the wrong Allen".

"Certainly many an Irish man did.
"Remember Ireland in famed '98 when,
England was busy with Gallows and Yeomen
Propounding the 'Laws of the State'
They were hanging a young lad, - a Rebel
On a Gibbet before the old Jail.

And that was in Kilkenny, Matt, in 1798. It's from the poem in the 'Old Marble Town of Kilkenny'.

"But I always though that Kilkenny was a City?"

It is and has been a City since 1609, when James the 1st made it a City by Charter

In any event Matt, a town is often the nucleus of a City. "Even here in this Great metropolis people speak of London town, which is the heart of the City."

"Don't start reciting that sort of stuff out in the open or you'll be arrested."

I'll be doing better than that soon Matt. Wait and see. But let's get back to Ivor.

There is always the possibility that he has gone over to "The Champion" to ask Pat's opinion on what has happened. Ivor believes Pat can solve every problem under the sun. I'll phone the Champion later and see if he is there?"

BACK AT THE CHAMPION

Pat Hunt and Jack Boland continued to iron-out some imponderables. "The first I heard of Larry Holden being in London was when Allen told me that he had visited 'the Poppy' thinking that Allen was me. Then, when he found out that Allen was my brother, he invited him and me to his gammon wedding reception at the Colburg Hotel. We now know it was an elaborate hoax and that it was me they wanted to investigate".

"That night at 'the Poppy', Holden told Allen he was working for Brannigan and Boland on a housing construction site in Wimbledon, as a Navvy. Now here is my question: If you knew so much about him why did you employ him?"

"I didn't employ him. It was the general foreman who gave him the 'start'. And it was later-on, the foreman came to me and said this bloke is asking an awful lot of questions that don't concern him or what he is working at. He asked other workers how long Mr. Brannigan and yourself were working as partners. Where you were living. Were you married. Did you have families etc, etc."

I knew then this fellow was no ordinary Navvy. He obviously had a hidden agenda. Without he knowing it I had him photographed and had his voice taped. Within days I was given all the information that I have told you now."

"We made sure to let him think his cover was good and then we set about letting slip misinformation. It was this misinformation that provoked the Police break-in at Spitalfields, and you know what befell them there".

I'll bet Knowlsworth is not the only one who got wrapped across the knuckles. Mr. Holden must have got a kick in the teeth too. But the down side of all this is that they now know you are on to them Jack".

"Yes Pat, that's a problem, but it was inevitable. It was on the cards".

"One more question, Jack, – if I may?"

"Right Pat, lets have it". "Does your partner Luke Brannigan, still refuse to associate himself with the 'cause'?"

"Yes he does and I respect his stance and point of view. He is a very religious and sincere person who refuses to condone violence for whatever reason. That's his opinion and he is perfectly entitled to it". "When is he to return from Ireland?"

"Tomorrow I do believe".

"Thank you for that Jack, but we had better leave all that for now. Look who has just arrived on the premises!, your friend of this morning. Ivor Davies walked in off the Bayswater road having arrived by Taxi. The phone rang as he walked in.

"Excuse me Jack. I must answer that". Ivor waved at Pat as he picked up the phone. Hello, this is "The Champion". O it's you Allen. There was a pause. Well you won't believe this: Ivor Davies has arrived here this very minute brother. I know you were always a disciple of Mental Telepathy. You must have mastered it. The voice on the phone asked; "How does he look?"

He looks O.K. Jack Boland who is here also met Ivor this morning at Marylebone Police Station. Ivor saw Eileen Murphy but wasn't speaking to her."

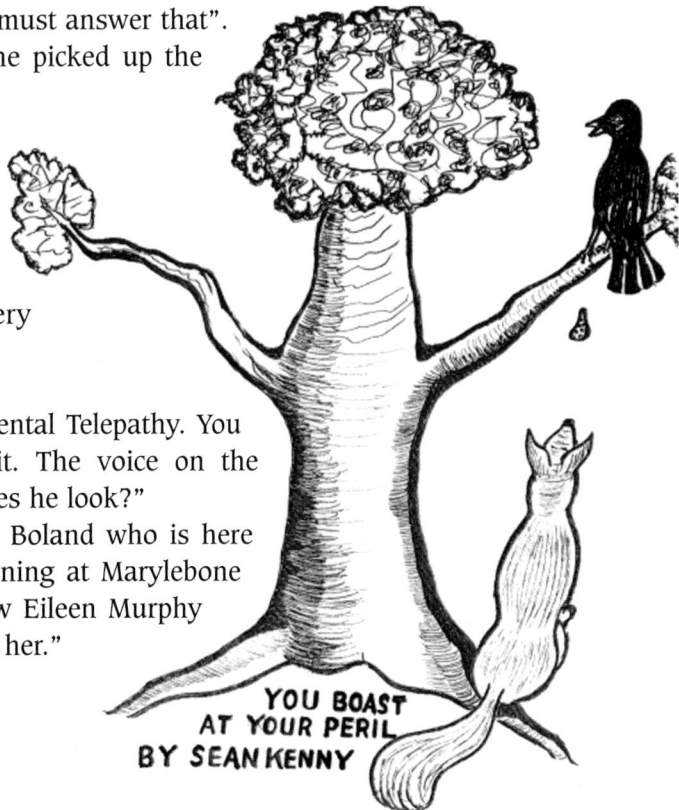

YOU BOAST
AT YOUR PERIL
BY SEAN KENNY

EPISODE TWENTY-NINE

NEVER A PRINCE CHARMING
A BLESSING INSTEAD OF A CURSE
LIKE THE BOOM OF DOOM

NEVER A PRINCE CHARMING

Rosie Taylor nee Keegan and her daughter Patricia had been staying in the governor's apartment at 'The Poppy', since the death of her husband Bill Taylor. She had known Matt Ryan, (governor) all her life. He was a friend of the family. The Keegans and the Ryan's came from West Cork, their family homes being less than a mile apart.

A situation had now arisen that was totally unexpected. Matt Ryan had dropped a bombshell on the pleasant and peaceful terrain that had always existed between Rosie and himself. Without making any definite proposals Matt had suggested that Rosie and her daughter might stay-on at 'The Poppy' indefinitely. Were they to do so, he would see to their personal safety and would guarantee Rosie that she and Patricia would never want for anything for as long as they lived. In due course he said she might consider becoming his wife. Rosie was so taken aback she was unable to make a reply. She had never for one moment entertained any thoughts of Matt Ryan other than as a Friend of the family.

If she thought of him at all otherwise it was as a 'Little John' type of person from Sherwood Forest, who might save her from the hoofs of a runaway horse or the horns of a mad bull. But as a Prince Charming who would one day sweep her off her feet and onto the broad back of his white-charger, he never figured. To Rosie's way of thinking he was a thistledown in a high wind. And as far as providing for them for the rest of their lives, there was no need of it.

Bill Taylor had left her a wealthy woman. When she married Bill in 1959 he owned his own public house on Streatham Common called 'The Greyhound'. Three years later he sold it to Charlington's Brewery and made a huge profit. He also had an Officer's army pension that transferred to his wife at his death. This substantial pension would remain with her for life unless she remarried.

All that and more: She now owned the family home at Knightsbridge which was a four bedroomed house on its own two acre site within walking distance of the Underground Station on the Piccadilly Line. Rosie Taylor née Keegan was a woman of substance. She knew that Matt Ryan wasn't interested in her for her money and she doubted he would be aware of her financial well being. Whether or which his intentions were utterly futile, and that was that. As a result it would no longer be possible for herself and Patricia to live at 'The Poppy'.

Rosie had asked Allen Hunt, who was the head barman at 'The Poppy' to meet her in an out of the way place and discuss her problem with him. She valued his opinions on all matters. But there was another motive behind her wanting to meet him away from 'The Poppy'. She knew she would be able to gague from his answers if he was interested in her, and if so, to what extent? She was now convinced she would have to move back to the family home at Knightsbridge. The idea of doing so alone was daunting. What if the harlot Nancy Blackmore got wind of the move and paid them an uninvited visit? Even if Allen was really interested in her he might be morally reluctant to stay with them, when they weren't even engaged never mind married.

A BLESSING INSTEAD OF A CURSE

Was she taking too much for granted? After all he did have a girlfriend of sorts who lived out in Watford in Hertfordshire. But it couldn't really be a very serious affair because they only met twice monthly or thereabouts. Allen seemed to prefer reading books and writing poetry to the company of women. But perhaps he hadn't met the right woman. Maybe she could help him make up his mind. "This is it, she said to herself. "It's now or never". It came to her in a vision like a poet's subconscious knowledge. What had happened had been a blessing instead of a curse. Matt Ryan's approach had driven her on to determine if Allen had any real interest in her. "This is it", she said to herself once again. Allen was so fond of telling the story about the Taj Mahal in India, which is one of the Seven wonders of the World: It was built by the Shay Jehan, in honour of his favourite wife, 'Later after she had died he had the main hall inscribed with this poignant message written in gold: "If there ever was a heaven here on earth: This is it. This is it. This is it".

Rosie looked around the walls of the V.I.Ps room at 'The Load of Hay". Heavily embossed scarlet and gold paper covered the room and black and white photographs of horse drawn cabs and drays stared back at her. Men in white overalls with handlebar moustaches served prim and proper gents in serge suits with hard white collars, black ties and bowler hats. She looked back at Allen. He looked splendid in his pepper and salt wool jacket and dark grey leather belted pants. His all leather black Irish Brogues shone like polished ebony keys beside their counterpart ivories on a grand piano.

"A symphony of sights and sounds" was how he had once described her. And rendered speechless with emotion, she was unable to ask what had moved him to pay her such a compliment. It wasn't the first time she had let the magical moment slip past her. But she hadn't forgotten it. She never would. The memory of it sustained her like an oasis of hope in a desert of dull monotonous days.

"Thanks for coming Allen. It was good of you at such short notice" "You are welcome Rosie. I know you wouldn't ask unless there was something worrying you. But I suspect you might just be needing someone to confide in". He turned to Patricia. "How is my favourite girl? I'm told you will be going to school next September". Patricia smiled up at him and offered a biscuit. "Thanks but no thanks Patricia", and he stroked her long flowing fair hair. She was Pat's daughter all right, just as sure as fish swim, birds fly and race horses run. "So Rosie, what happened that gave you such a fright? Was it something someone said. "Yes it was".

"But do you remember the day Bill died, Allen? You came to the hospital. I was feeling very lonely then but when you arrived I knew I could face any hardship, – even Bill's death".

Rosie was watching Allen closely as she said this and thought she saw a flicker of anxiety cross his face. Was she being too daring, too bold? Would this very personal kind of exposition only serve to scare him off or embarrass him. She changed her tune. "When I saw you I realised I had good friends that I could rely on, – like yourself and Pat and Matt Ryan. And later when you told me that Matt wished that Patricia and I would come and stay at 'The Poppy', I was relieved. I knew I was amongst friends and didn't have to worry any more for our personal safety. And Patricia became more fond of you with every passing day". Both of them looked at Patricia then and she smiled up at them happy in her childish knowledge that she was part of the equasion. Rosie knew that what she was going to say next wasn't strictly speaking, the Gospel truth, but she felt she had to make Allen sit up and take notice of her. "We were all so happy together and then two days ago Matt Ryan broke the spell. He asked me to marry him". Her eyes swam in pools filled with tears and as they moved rapidly from right to left, watching for any display of emotion, from Allen, the tears burst their banks and flowed down the contours of her face. Allen was momentarily overwhelmed. Was it Talleyrand who said: "These are the two weapons God gave woman to combat against stubborn man: Crying and Spinning?"

"What?" Allen jumped to his feet.

"Has he lost his senses? What in God's name is the man thinking about? It's not like him". Allen went silent then, puckering his lips and scratching the back of this head. Rosie looked at him uneasily. What was he contemplating? He gave her his handkerchief. Don't distress yourself Rosie, it's not a life-threatening situation afterall and his face broke into a broad grin.

She looked at him in puzzled disbelief.

"You have known Matt all your life Rosie. What age is he?"

Fiftyish", she said rather dismally.

And what age was Bill Taylor when he died?"

"Seventy", she said testily.

"There you are," Allen said, "a man is as young as he feels".

"I don't see the point. What does that mean?"

"It's not because a man is rich in years that he should consider himself to be old. Old age is a condition of the mind. Some men feel old at fifty, while others don't feel old at seventy. It's all in the head". This conversation wasn't going down the road that Rosie had routed. Allen had sabotaged her trip to the land of roses. Maybe not with malice, but his reasoning as she saw it, had spiked her highway which was signposted for romance.

LIKE THE BOOM OF DOOM

Pat Hunt and Jack Boland were engrossed in deep discussion in the 'The Champion' on the Bayswater Road. They were attempting to dissect the many dangerous problems that had arisen from their involvement with a proscribed and illegal organisation called the IRA. As they spoke Ivor Davies walked into the bar, having arrived by taxi. Pat told Jack of Ivors presence and said: "We had better leave this conversation for now". The phone rang as Ivor approached them. Pat took leave of Jack to answer the phone and Ivor waved as Pat picked it up. "Hello this is Pat Hunt at 'The Champion' O, it's you Allen". There was a pause as Allen spoke and then Pat spoke again.

"You won't believe what has happened. Ivor Davies walked in the door as you were ringing to see if he was here. Now I know that you have been a disciple of Mental Telepathy for many years but I reckon you must have mastered it brother". The voice on the other end of the phone asked,

"How does he look?"

"He looks O.K., Jack Boland, who is also here met Ivor this morning at Marylebone Police Station. Ivor saw Eileen Murphy but wasn't speaking to her".

"Tell Ivor it was I who was on the phone. Tell him also Matt Ryan is very concerned about him. Is he under the weather?"

"He's not what you'd call stone cold sober, but he's standing up straight."

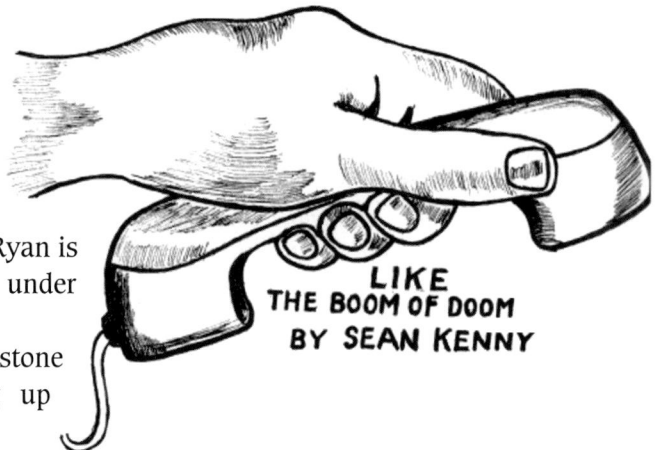

LIKE
THE BOOM OF DOOM
BY SEAN KENNY

"Don't let him get drunk if you can help it and send him home by Taxi. Matt Ryan will foot the bill. You can tell Jack Boland I am putting everything into place for that attack on Imperialism. Take care brother and watch your back".

"Hold it there for a moment. What's this attack on Imperialism you're talking about?"

"I can't be too specific over the phone but Jack Boland knows all about it. He will fill you in".

"There is something else I'd like to discuss with you Allen".

"What's that brother?"

"It's a rather personal matter and could not be realistically resolved without we meeting face to face brother".

"This sounds very intriguing. My first question is; Is there a woman at the bottom of it?"

"I can hardly believe my ears. Are you becoming clairvoyant? Seeing as how you are so sharp, who am I speaking about?"

"You are speaking about Peggy O'Shea. You want to know if we are lovers. If not you are going to ask her out."

There was a lengthy momentous pause, which caused Allen to believe he was right.

"Am I right", he asked Pat?

Pat, confounded by Allen's directness could only answer "Yes".

"Then there is no need for us to meet to discuss it further. You go right ahead and ask her and if she says yes, don't worry about me. Slán brother."

Pat heard the click of the phone being put back in its cradle. Somehow it was like the boom of doom. He was still holding the phone to his ear and looking vacantly into space when Gwen tipped him on the shoulder. She had been calling his name for next to a minute.

"Is there something wrong Pat? I hope it wasn't bad news from Ireland".

"No Gwen, but it just may have been bad news from London".

"Has someone close to you been hurt, Pat?"

"I think so, – someone very close has been very badly hurt."

It took Pat a while to rediscover his composure.

Prior to Allen's wounded reaction to Pat's interest in Peggy O'Shea, Pat had suggested to Jack Boland that he should make an anonymous phone call to the Chief of Police. Tell him that Knowlsworth authorisied the partnership of Larry Holden and Nancy Blackmore, into a criminal alliance to do Police dirty work. Then leave down the phone without another word.

EPISODE THIRTY

THE SUNDAY MIRROR
HOLLYWOOD KISSING TIME
THE ORATORY
TUB-THUMPING PUBLIC ORATORS
HYDE PARK
A LETTER TO THE CHIEF

THE SUNDAY MIRROR

It was going to be another glorious day. The weatherman on B.B.C 1 had said the temperature would reach twenty-seven degrees centigrade in London and over most of south east England. No rain for the foreseeable future. London was in the throes of an August heatwave. Hotter than a spoon full of mustard on a slice of salty bacon. It was Sunday morning, 8:15 am in the year of Our Lord 1962. Allen Hunt was about to fulfil the proposition the two Volunteers had put to him all those months ago at 'The Poppy'. Like the poet Robert Servise once said in his much loved poem: "Sam McGee" –' A promise made is a debt unpaid.' Allen bought the 'Sunday Mirror' at Noonan's Newspapers, stall, outside the Edgware Road Underground Station, before boarding the Circle Line train for South Kensington. The Mirror headline boldly prophesied: 'Blistering Heatwave to Continue'. Allen thumbed the pages and stopped where another headline caught his eye: 'The Sad Moral State of Our People', and in an obvious attempt to substantiate the caption the Columnist gave the following statistics: "The records show there were five divorces for every thousand married couples in England and Wales during the past twelve months. Have we now begun to go down the road that the United States of America has gone?

Their marital breakdown figures show a staggering Fifty-five divorces per thousand married couples. Even when one allows for the higher life style and lesser religious influence the difference seems extraordinary. I understand there is to be a debate in the American Senate next September on the whole issue of Marital Status. The article went on:

Sodomy

Sodom was one of the 'cities of the plain': In the evening the two angels reached Sodom. Lot was sitting at the gate, and when he saw them he rose to meet them. "

Please come to your servants' house and let me wash your feet and prepare
a meal for you". They had not gone to bed when the house was surrounded by
many men from the town both young and old. These called out to Lot saying
"Where are the men who came to your house this night? Send them out to us so
that we may abuse them". The angels struck blind all those without and told Lot
to gather his sons and daughters along with his wife and all good people from
the town and to flee from it. "We are about to destroy this place and everyone
in it, for there is a great outcry against them, and it has reached up to Yahweh.
Now run for your lives. Neither stop nor look behind you at this great calamity".
And Yahweh rained on Sodom and Gomorrah brimstone and fire. He overthrew
the two towns and all their inhabitants and everything that grew there. But
Lot's wife, not satisfied to escape looked back and was turned into a pillar of
salt.

Last year Illinois was the first state in the U.S.A., to make the act of Sodomy
legal. However, it must be said we beat them to it. Here in Great Britain we made
Sodomy Legal some years ago. The Wolfenden Report stated it was permissible
for consenting adults of any or either sex to copulate behind closed doors. This
is now U.K. Law.

At least some historians have claimed it was this malfunction in the natural
practice of sex i.e., male with female, that largely contributed to 'The Fall of the
Roman Empire'.

HOLLYWOOD KISSING TIME

All the major Hollywood film Studios including Paramount, Universal,
Columbia and Warner Brother, have agreed that Kissing on Screen will hence
forth be limited to 30 seconds with mouths shut tight. At least that will put an
end to the Kiss and Tell movie star brigade.

Allen Hunt, closed the newspaper while thinking to himself. "Why is it that
we fall for the sensational sex stories every time? He had asked himself the very
same question many times before and had arrived at this conclusion: It is only
natural that we should, because we are the sexual act made flesh. It makes sense
doesn't it? The river always runs to the sea."

Having closed the paper, Allen opened his briefcase. He took out a large blue
folder with many pages of handwritten notes. He could rattle these off by heart.
But would he be able to deliver the message in front of a very large mixed
audience? One that delighted in heckling and hurling abuses. What was it Asquit
had said? "Wait and see. Time will tell".

The train had slowed down and was coming to a stop at Gloucester Road
Station. Allen would be getting off next stop at South Kensington. He looked at
his watch. It was now 8.35am.

The doors of the train closed with a hissing noise like an old fashioned hand propelled bellows in a blacksmiths shop. A shower of sparks flew up from the tracks, like they do when the red-hot iron is hammered on the anvil.

Five minutes later Allen emerged from the Underground up unto Thurloe Street. He quickly crossed over on to Brompton Road. Again he glanced at his watch. He would be in good time for the 9 o'clock Mass at 'The Oratory'.

THE ORATORY

This beautiful old church was built in the Italian Renaissance style during the 19th century. It is renowned for its grand musical services. Cardinal Newman served here as priest after his conversion from the Anglican to the Roman Catholic faith. As good luck had it, the old Dublin born priest who was saying the Mass was a visitor to the parish and was something of an historian. He cleared his throat. It was like coal been shovelled into a stainless steel wheelbarrow. He began. – "I feel privileged to be saying Mass here in the church where Cardinal Newman once served as a priest. John Henry Newman was ordained an Anglican priest, and in 1827 was appointed Vicar of St. Mary's at Oxford. With other members of the University he started the 'Tractarian' movement in 1833. It attempted to revive Catholic traditions in the Church of England, and took its name from 'Tracts for the Times', which were a series of articles on that subject. In 1845 Vicar Newman became a Roman Catholic. He was appointed parish priest here at 'The Oratory' and later in 1854 was appointed Rector of Dublin University and was created a Cardinal in 1879. His best-known written works are The Idea of a University (1854), his autobiography Apologia pro vita Sua (1864) and the hymn 'Lead kindly Light'. Cardinal Newman has himself been a leading light to all Christians who would walk in the path of Christ. In the name of the Father and of the Son and of the Holy Ghost Amen.

The mass concluded at 'The Oratory' at 9.35am. Outside on Brompton Road, Allen looked down into Cromwell Road to where the Victoria and Albert Museum dominates the thoroughfare. It is one of the greatest museums of fine and applied arts in the world. It has on exhibition artistic achievement throughout the centuries and these are arranged into two groups. (A) Primary Collections of style, period or Nationality. (B) Consists of Departmental Collections – sculptures, textiles, woodworks, etc. And the Museum incorporates the National Art Library and to top it all there are free lectures every weekend. Allen had been to two of them and had notes to prove it.

Allen then walked South down Brompton Road, across into Thurloe street and turned left into the South Kensington Underground Station once again. He would have to wait for the Piccadilly Line from the northern Rayner's Lane or the southern Heathrow Terminals. The Rayner's Lane train came first.

His destination was but two stops up the line. Knightsbridge was first and Hyde Park Corner was next. Allen had arranged to meet with Jack Boland at the Marble Arch.

TUB-THUMPING PUBLIC ORATORS

Some student of psychology once observed: 'A man is only as good as his word.' Jack Boland always was. He was there like Stanley waiting for Livingstone near Lake Tanganyika. And the two Volunteers were with him, as constant as Castor and Pollux.

They were carrying a sturdy, folded wooden frame between them. Allen indicated the frame, saying "I hope that's not a bier for burial."

"Not a bit of it", Jack replied, smiling.

"That's your pedestal to raise you up and give your voice more substance. Let us walk into the Park and hear whether Mark Anthony came to bury Caesar or to raise him".

ILLUSTRATED   BY   SEAN KENNY

HYDE PARK

This is known as a Royal Park and covers 341 acres. On the south side from Hyde Park Corner westwards, many of London's wealthy merchants take an early morning ride down Rotten Row before going to business. This is the famous 'Rotten Row' in song and story of the 'Easter Parade' and other glamorous extravaganzas.

Every Sunday morning and afternoon the park is more crowded than an emigrant ship leaving Ireland in the late thirties. And this Sunday morning was no exception. Especially around Speakers Corner, 'near Marble Arch where Tub thumping Public Orators on rostrums, and soap boxes were loudly airing their opinions on every kind of argument under the sun. It looked like every race of people on earth were represented here, Black, Brown, Yellow and White mixed and mingled with carefree abandon. These were the fruit of empire. The chickens had come home to roost.

And the setting was magnificent. Acres of grassland with noble oaks and silver barked beeches crowned in verdant glory and the clear still – water Lake called The Serpentine. This beautiful stretch of water is one of London's Lidos where from May to middle October mixed bathing is allowed and boating is also provided for, especially on its south-eastern waters. And the cobweb like walks criss crossing and spotlessly clean and straight as the flight of an arrow. All in all, Hyde Park is a piece of heaven in the otherwise rip-roaring, break-neck, super city of London. The two Volunteers set down the sturdy, folded, wooden apparatus. With deft hands they converted it into a podium, the centre part of which had a raised stand with a pulpit. Allen felt a tightening in his gut. The butterflies were winging back and the adrenaline was pumping. He would have to remain focused if he was to carry the day.

A LETTER TO THE CHIEF

Jack Boland finished his drink at 'The Champion' before saying goodbye to Pat Hunt and Ivor Davies. He did not take lightly what Pat Hunt had said about letting the Chief of Police know what Detective Inspector Knowlsworth was up to. But phoning the Chief was not the best way to get the message across. The written word was always more persuasive and the cold black print from the typewriter left an indelible mark on the mind as well as on the page.

Never one to procrastinate, Jack Boland sat at his typewriter in his Office at 9 Lamb Street, Spitalfields.

To Mr. Walter Pearson, Chief of Police Marylebone Police station, London.

Sir, as a concerned citizen with no axe to grind, I wish to point out that there is an illegal force operating within your own branch of the Metropolitan Police. Your second in command, Detective Inspector Knowlsworth has recruited a well known hoodlum named Larry Holden. Formerly from the Shankill area of Belfast, Holden has now teamed up with an ex jail-bird named Nancy Blackmore who was originally from Dublin. Together these two ingrates have sought to disrupt the course of Justice and in some instances at least, have succeeded in doing so. Were you to investigate this matter I have no doubt but that you would soon discover the truth of these allegations.

Fear for my life prevents me from signing this complaint.

In the normal course of events a letter like that would be destroyed there and then. Dozens of 'crank letters' are shredded every week especially those without signatures. But because of the hatred and rivalry between the Chief and his second in command, he not only read it but did so with relish, thinking: 'It's a pity it's not signed. Yet it has the ring of truth about it. I'll get to the bottom of this and nail that bastard if it's the last thing I do.

EPISODE THIRTY-ONE

DISGUISED AS A LADY'S MAID
THE SLATE HOUSE AT BALLINGARRY
THE WIDOW MCCORMACK'S HOUSE
JAMES STEPHENS' PRISON ESCAPE

DISGUISED AS A LADY'S MAID

Allen Hunt mounted the sturdy wooden podium that had been constructed in the Carpenters shop on the building site of Brannigan and Boland at Wimbledon. The apparatus was four feet square with a central stand two feet square and thirty inches high. Inserted in a slot that touched the ground was a five-foot pole with a one-foot square pedestal at its top to rest the speakers' notes upon.

"How does one attract attention?" Allen asked Jack Boland.

"Can you do an Irish jig?" Jack asked jokingly. Then the three of them began cheering and clapping loudly, as the Three Musketeers must have done when they discovered that D'Artanion was the son of their brave dead comrade. Allen knew that the podium and their moral support was all he was going to get – all he could expect in fact. He took a deep breath and held it while saying to himself: "Every day in every respect, I am getting better and better." It was the catchphrase of Emil Coué, that extraordinary French psychologist, who perfected a do-it-yourself form of healing. (Physician heal thyself). He exhaled slowly and then took a moderate breath. In a raised voice eight feet above the ground he began: "I call your attention ladies and gentlemen to bear witness to an historical, unique and courageous episode in Irelands' fight for freedom. Gather 'round and if you would be wise, listen well. The episode about which I am going to speak happened in the lifetime of Kilkenny's James Stephens, otherwise known as the 'Fenian Chief'. Please feel free to question my narration. Indeed if it so pleases you, I invite you to criticize my story ... On the 19th August 1848 the 'Kilkenny Moderator', gave the following account in its obituary column."

A small crowd had gathered one of whom jeeringly shouted up "As dead as a stuffed duck, like you're going to stuff us, – I don't think." The heckler was rotund. Allen had him sized up in a second: "You've got absolutely nothing to worry about mister. You couldn't take another spoonful of stuffing if you tried."

Those around the heckler having taken stock of him burst into laughter. That shut him up. "To continue; the account in the obituary column of the 'Kilkenny Moderator' read as follows: "Poor James Stephens, who followed Smith O'Brien to the field, has died of a wound which he received at Ballingarry whilst acting as aide-de-camp to the insurgent leader. Mr. Stephens was a very amiable, and apart from Politics, most inoffensive young man, possessed of a great talent, and we believe he was a most excellent son and brother. His untimely and melancholy fate will be much regretted by a numerous circle of friends."

"James Stephens father, ladies and gentlemen (a goodish crowd, had gathered) was a clerk with a well-known and much respected establishment of Auctioneers and Booksellers in Kilkenny City. He gave his family a decent living and a good education and enrolled his son James in a Catholic seminary for the purpose of making him a priest. But James thought he could best serve his God, by fighting for his country.

And as the Stephens family went into mourning for their loving son, so too did the people of Kilkenny grieve for their Rebel hero. And a multitude followed his coffin through the streets of Kilkenny, amid scenes of sadness and anger. But at that same hour the very much alive and well Fenian Chief, James Stephens was boarding a ship that would soon sail for France. He was disguised as a lady's maid. Truly he was the Pimpernel of Irish politics. This was the first of many deceptions that the cool, calculating James Stephens was to perpetrate on the British forces of occupation in Ireland."

"Go home you bloody Shinners," was the angry reply from one of the now large crowd. "What the hell are you doing over here anyway?" "Why didn't the Tommies go home to Britain and stop interfering with Irish affairs?" Allen asked. "We were there to keep you from murdering one another. You blasted savages."

"Was that what you were doing in Gibraltar, keeping the peace and in Malta, Cypress and Ceylon and the Straits Settlements, and in South Africa, Rhodesia, East, Central and West Africa, in Canada, Newfoundland and Labrador, Guyana, The West Indies, the Bermudas, Honduras and the Falklands, Australia and New Zealand. You were in all of those countries out of the goodness of your hearts you say, – the saviour of the world. Is that a fair assessment sir? It wasn't for nothing that the Welsh Wizard boasted "The sun never sets on the British Empire." The negatively bitter reply said it all: "Piss off mate."

"To get on with the story of James Stephens, known as the Fenian Chief. John O'Mahony escaped to France with Stephens, where they joined the Paris Republican body. The influence of that body would later be seen in the Fenian movement, which they founded in America. This was named the Fenian Brotherhood. The leaders of that great organisation were James Stephens, John O'Mahony, John O'Leary, Thomas Clarke Luby, Michael Doheny and Charles J. Kickham".

"They adopted their own flag, which was orange and green stripes, with thirty-two stars representing the thirty-two counties of the Irish Republic. But all of that came years after the attempted rising at Ballingarry."

THE SLATE HOUSE AT BALLINGARRY

"The three hundred men who gathered around Smith O'Brien at Ballingarry were a motley throng. They had courage and resolution in plenty but many were famished and half-naked. O'Brien looked at them with an uneasy mind. Less than twenty had arms and about forty had pikes and pitchforks. The remainder gathered sticks and stones to fight against a well-armed and well-trained Constabulary. With Smith O'Brien was the young James Stephens, McManus and O'Donoghue. Maher, Dillon and Doheny had taken different paths to raise the flag of insurrection in other parts of the country.

THE WIDOW McCORMACK'S HOUSE

Sub-Inspector Trant marched out from Callan at the head of forty-six fully armed and well-trained policemen, going in the direction of Ballingarry. He thought he would capture the leaders of the Rising and win for himself a deathless fame. When they reached Farrenrory, which is about two miles from Ballingarry, they found the road barricaded. Someone behind the barricade fired a shot before the order was given and Trant and his men took to their heels across the fields. They didn't stop until they reached a slate house on the brow of a hill, known locally as the Widow McCormack's House. The rebels gave chase but the police force reached the two-story house unscathed.

The Widow McCormack and her six children were in the house when the police broke in. The insurgents quickly surrounded the slate house and it looked like all the occupants were doomed. The Widow called out to Smith O'Brien to spare the lives of her children. With the courage of a lion, O'Brien walked up to the house alone and told the police to lay down their arms, and to march in single file out of the house. Just then some stupid and irresponsible rake pelted a stone through one of the windows and the police began firing in all directions. Smith O'Brien was forced to withdraw and returned to his comrades on the double. The firing went on for about two hours without pause. The police fired 220 rounds, killing two men and wounding many others. James Stephens was shot in the thigh and was forced to retire to a ditch, bleeding profusely. The insurgents ammunition was all but exhausted and they were forced to reply to the bullets with stones. McManus consulted with O'Brien and Stephens and then took six Colliers with him into a field close by. They returned with a cartload of hay and pushed it right up to the house, placing it against the kitchen door. He fired into the hay several times but it failed to light. The previous days rain had robbed them of certain victory.

Soon after that the parish priest of Ballingarry, the Rev. Fitzgerald and his curate Fr. Maher went among the rebels, begging them to stop fighting and go home to their wives and families. A little later when a large force of the Constabulary was sighted marching from Cashel towards Ballingarry, the rebels scattered and fled to the hills.

Nine months later on the 29th July 1849, the Brig 'Swift' sailed from Kingstown with Smith O'Brien, Meagher, McManus and O'Donoghue, bound for Van Diemans Land. As already stated James Stephens had escaped to France, disguised as a lady's maid. It has been truly written that with the exception of Napoleon Bonaparte, and Adolf Hitler, no other individual caused as much worry and torment to the masters of the then mighty British Empire as the bold James Stephens from the 'Marble City' of Kilkenny, did.

Stephens studied the mistakes of the gallant but Military unwise 'Young Ireland' leaders. Through a new approach to military strategy he organised an underground movement, whose members were bound by oath to the establishment of a Republic and to secrecy. He was a master organiser. When he began to organise the Irish Republican Brotherhood in the 1850's the National spirit was all-but dead. Another outstanding quality in Stephens make-up was his ability to gather around him the ablest literary people and the bravest men in the country. Some of those whom he chose to run his newspaper: the 'Irish People' were, Charles Kickham, Thomas Clarke, Luby who was a 'Protestant and O'Donovan Rossa. In the uppermost branches of the I.R.B. were men like John Devoy and John o'Leary.

Down through the centuries Irelands' downfall has been that we always had informers. There were always those who would sell out their country, and abandon the land of their birth for positions of power and reward from the British Crown. Stephens wasn't ruthless enough in dealing with informers within his ranks. Probably one of the most treacherous of the informers among the Fenians was Pierce Nagle. Nagle who was a heavy whiskey drinker wormed his way into the highest echelons of the I.R.B. He was able to do this through his work on the 'Irish People' newspaper. O'Donovan Rossa disliked Nagle and tried to convince Stephens to get rid of him. But the good natured Kickham, with the support of Clarke, Luby used their influence to hold on to the very popular Mr. Nagle.

Because of this the R.I.C. were made a present of the information that led to the arrest of James Stephens. He was found to be at Fairview House in Sandymount and was arrested and lodged in Richmond jail. There were great celebrations in Dublin Castle and Whitehall when he was jailed. Their celebrations were scarcely over when the Fenian Chief made a daring escape with the help of two brave men from the Fenian ranks, J.J. Breslin and Dan Byrne. They had infiltrated the British Regime and were on the prison staff.

All hell broke loose throughout Britain and Ireland. There was consternation among the R.I.C. and in Dublin Castle. To add salt to the wound the Ballad makers set to work on one of the cleverest ballads of that era:

JAMES STEPHENS' PRISON ESCAPE
Perhaps you'd like to know,
Says the Shan Van Vocht,
Which way did James Stephens go, Says-
When from Richmond snug and tight
He walked off out of sight
And never said 'good night'/ Says-

They thought it very hard, Says-
That he'd only leave his card Says-
At Mr. Lawson's gate
Who'd much rather he would wait,
To see him in full state, Says-

The Queen had kindly fixed, Says-
For a party nicely mixed, Says-
To give him honour due
Thro' her judges staunch and true
And her Peelers all in blue, Says-

When the Marquis found him 'out,' Says-
His warders tall and stout, Says-
He roused them from their rest,
And says he, 'May I be blessed;
But my bird's not in the nest! Says-

Lord Woodhouse went to spend, Says-
Some bright days with a friend, Says-
'Twas there he heard the news.
Says he, 'You will excuse
But I must homeward cruise,' Says-

When he reached the Castle steps, Says-
He scaled them with three leps, Says-
Most loudly he did roar,
Would he never see him more,
And I am afraid he swore, Says-

His council kindly tried, Says-
Could he be pacified, Says-
Said they'd give to any man
A thousand spic and span
For catch-him-if-you-can, Says-

You may catch old birds with chaff, Says-
You may coax a cow to laugh, Says-
You may teach a pig to sing,
Or dance a Heiland fling,
Or whistle anything, Says-

You may wash a blackman white, Says-
Set Whig and Tory right, Says-
But one thing you'll never do,
That is get from 'Parley-voo'
The bird that thither flew, Says-

And the illusive Kilkenny rebel had broken out of Richmond Prison, to the unspeakable horror and humiliation of the British Government and the unfettered delight of the Irish nation.

James Stephens has never been fully recognised for the enormity of his Political achievements. The I.R.B. which he established survived to pass on the torch that ignited the flame of the 1916 Easter Rising. How strange it is that in his own country nay, in his own city, James Stephens has never been given the full appreciation and honours due to him who laid the foundation stone for the Ireland we live in today.

"We may have brave men but we'll never have better.
Glory O, Glory O to the bold Fenian men."

The Fenian Chief James Stephens was born in Kilkenny City in the year 1825, and died in Dublin in 1901. cx

Police Gazette,

OR

'HUE-AND-CRY.

Published for Ireland on every Tuesday and Friday.

DUBLIN, TUESDAY, OCTOBER 23, 1866.

By the Lord Lieutenant-General and General Governor of Ireland.

A PROCLAMATION.

WODEHOUSE.

WHEREAS, *James Stephens* has been an active Member of a Treasonable Conspiracy against the Queen's authority in *Ireland*, and escaped from the *Richmond Prison* on the *Twenty-fourth* day of *November* last.

NOW WE, being determined to bring the said *James Stephens* to Justice, Do hereby offer a Reward of

ONE THOUSAND POUNDS

to any person or persons who shall **give such Information as shall lead to the Arrest** of the said *James Stephens*; and a further Reward of

One Thousand Pounds

to any person or persons **WHO SHALL ARREST** the said *James Stephens*.

AND WE do hereby offer a further Reward of

THREE HUNDRED POUNDS

to any Person or Persons who shall give such information as shall lead to the Arrest of any one whomsoever who has knowingly harboured or received, or concealed, or assisted or aided in any way whatsoever in his Escape from Arrest, the said *James Stephens*.

And We do also hereby offer a FREE PARDON, in addition to the above-mentioned REWARD, to any Person or Persons concerned in the Escape of the said JAMES STEPHENS who shall give such Information as shall lead to his Arrest as aforesaid.

Given at Her Majesty's Castle of *Dublin*, this *Twenty-sixth* day of *January*, 1866.

By His Excellency's Command,

THOS. A. LARCOM.

Reward Notice for James Stephens, 1866.

EPISODE THIRTY-TWO

SHE LOVED THE NORTH, SOUTH, EAST AND WEST OF HIM
CRIED OUT FOR HER ANCIENT SEXUAL INHERITANCE
THE END OF AN ERA
A GOLD CROSS AND CHAIN FOR ROSIE AND A CABBAGE PATCH DOLL FOR PATRICIA

SHE LOVED THE NORTH, SOUTH, EAST AND WEST OF HIM

Rosie Taylor nee Keegan and her daughter Patricia were in the company of Allen Hunt in the V.I.P Room at The Load of Hay public house outside of Paddington, main line station. Patricia was there because she was only four years of age and went almost everywhere with her mother. Allen was there because Rosie had asked him to meet her and discuss her problem with Matt Ryan's proposal. And Rosie was there principally to resolve once and for all if Allen had designs on her. Since they had come to live at 'The Poppy; she had grown to like him more and more. He had been like a father to Patricia, – taking her for walks and into Kensington Gardens to feed the ducks. Rosie knew that Patricia idolised him. As for herself she loved the North, South, East and West of him and all his territory within. Only things weren't shaping up too well at this juncture. It seemed Allen had found something funny in Matt Ryan's sudden romantic interest in her.

"Don't distress yourself about it Rosie, it's not a life-threatening situation after all," Allen said and his face broke into a broad grin. Rosie looked at him in puzzled disbelief.

"You have known Matt all your life Rosie. What age is he?"

Fiftyish," she said rather dismally.

And Allen went on: "And what age was Bill Taylor when he died?"

"Seventy," she said testily.

"There you are," Allen said, "a man is as young as he feels."

"I don't see the point Allen. What do you mean?"

"It's not because a man is rich in years that he should consider himself to be old. Old age is a condition of the mind. Some men feel old at fifty, while others don't feel old at seventy. It's all in the head."

"Maybe I'm stupid," Rosie said with sarcasm, "but I still can't see the point."

"The point I am trying to make is that Matt Ryan is only a man after all. Who could blame him for making an attempt to marry a beautiful woman even if she is twenty years younger than he?" He has got good taste and I salute his integrity."

Rosie smiled while thinking to herself: "This is more like it." And then before the door closed on that thought she asked him trembling: "Do you think I'm beautiful, Allen?" Rosie put down her glass because she was trembling. She held the top of the mahogany table to steady herself. She was shaking enough to churn butter, and was studying Allen closer than Einstein studied the figures that substantiated his Theory of Relativity. Allen went silent pursing his lips tight. His manly look made contact with Rosie's affectionate gaze, beaming Lighthouse like on the twin sailing ships of her deep blue eyes, lest they might founder upon the rocks of hopelessness. And for no reason that he could fathom the iron words fashioned on the Metalman Lighthouse at Tramore flowed into his thinking like a tidal wave:

"Keep far far away from me,
For I am a man of misery"

CRIED OUT FOR HER ANCIENT SEXUAL INHERITANCE

"I don't think you are beautiful Rosie, I know that you are, as sure as apples grow on apple trees and sailors go in ships down to the seas."

"O Allen," Rosie said in a voice that quaked like a quagmire, "no one ever said such wonderful things to me before now, except yourself. It is so beautiful it makes me want to cry." She reached over and rested her hand on his. "I love you Allen and can only hope that you love me, – half as much as I love you."

"Of course I love you and Patricia and not just a little bit but a lot." There was an ominous pause. "You are aware Rosie that I have been seeing Peggy O'Shea, for quite some time now. I wouldn't wish to do anything that would betray the trust that she has in me, and I have in her. And I know that a fine person like yourself will appreciate such feelings."

She felt like saying to him: "That's a load of old rubbish." But she did not, and instead she played the part of the wronged but still virtuous woman. While every fibre in her female composition cried out Eve-like for her ancient sexual inheritance, though long cast out of Eden. What she said was: "I understand perfectly Allen, and I hope the two of you will be happy together. I'm really sorry for wasting your afternoon off. Patricia and I will be leaving 'The Poppy' tomorrow and returning to our fine home in Knightsbridge." Patricia looked up. "Will Allen be coming with us Mammy?" She must have sensed that all was not well.

She ran to Allen and hugged him like a child who discovers its parents after having been lost in a crowd for a longish time.

"Allen has to work love, he can't come with us."

"But I'll make sure to come and visit you as often as I can. By the way Rosie, have you made arrangements to remove your belongings to Knightsbridge? Can I be of any help?"

"Thank you Allen, but it won't be necessary. Jack Boland phoned me yesterday and said he would send a van whenever it was needed to transport whatever there was and take Patricia and me in his new Red Rover motorcar."

"I wasn't aware that you were on such friendly terms with Jack."

"I have known Jack Boland since the old days when your brother Pat and I were going out together. Lately he has asked me several times to eat out with him, – to see a film, to have a drink. He even bought tickets for the three of us to take a Thames River trip on a Catamaran Cruiser from Westminster Pier to Greenwich." "And did you go on any of them?"

"No. Something else blinded me, but my eyes have been prized wide open now. Let's get out of here. This place gives me the colly-wobbles."

Allen went silent then as with his highly imaginative minds-eye he saw a glorious Rosie, in brilliant beachwear gamboling with a fine physiqued Jack Boland and Patricia all smiles behind a giant icecream cone and the warm breeze caressing their near-naked bodies, sailing out to sea on a surging, exhilarating Catamaran.

Like Rosie had said the van called and collected the clothing and little pieces of furniture and Patricia's games and story books on the following day. And true to his word Jack Boland brought them back in his new Red Rover motorcar to their elegant four bedroomed house on its own grounds in Knightsbridge.

THE END OF AN ERA

From the day that Rosie Taylor nee Keegan and her four year old daughter, Patricia departed 'The Poppy,' Matt Ryan never mentioned Rosies' or Patricia's name again. It was almost as if they had never existed. It is hard to understand how a few moments conversation that failed to see eye to eye could obliterate a lifetime of friendship. There is no doubt about it but life really is stranger than fiction. Rosie felt that her sense of propriety had been usurped and Matt felt his self-esteem and gallant gesture had been thrown back in his face. It was a no win situation. Not in their wildest dreams could either one of them have imagined such a bizarre ending to their entente acquaintance. Like they say when someone or something dies: 'it was the end of an era.'

Peggy O'Shea vacated the nurse's quarters at Hammersmith General Hospital faster than Archimedes did his bath, having discovered the principles of buoyancy. She did not run shouting Eureka (I have found it) nor was she naked. But she ran fully clothed carrying a small suitcase to Hammersmith Underground station and boarded the Metropolitan line train for Baker Street.

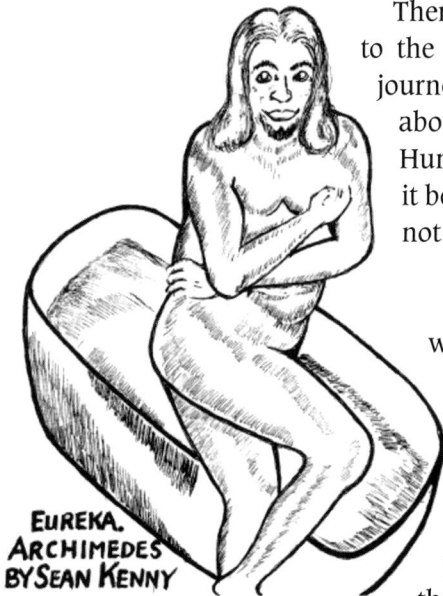

There she would wait for the Whitechapel train going to the end of the line at Watford. It would be a long journey but she didn't mind. She had plenty to think about: The lookalike Irish brothers Pat and Allen Hunt were the source of her romantic enquiry. "Might it be Allen or could it be Pat. He loves me, he loves me not. One facing east, the other west, like Gemini the two-faced god of the Romans." The midweek phonecall that Allen had promised to make would determine the end or a new beginning for their present dispassionate affair. But he didn't phone all day Wednesday, though she went running every time it rang. And he didn't phone Thursday morning. Neither did he phone in the afternoon. It looked as if the absence of a phonecall might be an even greater cause to end their unsatisfactory 'affaire d'amour.'

EUREKA.
ARCHIMEDES
BY SEAN KENNY

Peggy O'Shea went to bed with 'A Man For All Seasons' at eleven o'clock Thursday night and didn't put Thomas A. Becket down until Henry II had him elected Archbishop of Centerbury in 1162. Before she went to sleep she told herself she was glad he hadn't phoned.

A GOLD CROSS AND CHAIN FOR ROSIE AND A CABBAGE PATCH DOLL FOR PATRICIA

Five days after the disastrous discussion between himself and Rosie at the Load of Hay public house, Allen decided it was about time that he fulfilled his promise to visit Rosie and Patricia at their home in Knightsbridge. With hindsight he could see that he had made a shambles of Rosie's problem with Matt Ryan's proposal. In fact his handling of it had troubled him all week. So much so that he wondered if he had fallen in love with her. He was so preoccupied with his dilemma that it had just occurred to him that he had forgotten to phone Peggy O'Shea midweek. That oversight in itself spoke volumes. On the Wednesday when he should have phoned Peggy he went into a Jewellers shop on the Edgware Road and bought a gold Cross and chain for Rosie. He felt it in the pocket of his best sports coat as he walked out of Knightsbridge Underground station. The 'Cabbage Patch' doll was for Patricia. As he neared their home his pace quickened. He wondered how they had got on, on their own in such a large house. Perhaps he could suggest to Rosie that he would be willing to come and stay with herself and Patricia for their safety. He knew she loved him. Hadn't she freely admitted it at the Load of Hay public house? As he came within fifty yards of their home, the front door opened.

"That's a piece of good luck," he thought to himself. "Another minute and I'd have missed them. I wonder where they can be going at nine o'clock on a Saturday morning?"

But it wasn't Rosie and Patricia who walked out the door. It was a man, carrying a briefcase. Allen stopped dead. It was Jack Boland who closed the front door behind him and walked to the garage at the side of the house. Any fool could see he had stayed the night. Allen was crushed as he turned his back to the street. He was looking into a Jewellers shop when the beautiful red Rover motorcar drove past. His eyes fell on a gold Cross and chain which was a carbon copy of the one in his pocket. Slowly and with downtrodden step he walked back to the Underground station and boarded the Piccadilly line train for Earls Court. From there he would change to the District line train for Edgware Road which was the end of the line. Allen knew in his heart, it was the end of the line too for himself and Rosie. He had done too much toing and froing with Rosie's affections and he saw now that his conversation with her in the V.I.P room at the Load of Hay left a lot to be desired. Why is it that we are always wise after the event? Wasn't it Plato who had said "The words must always be cousin to the deeds."

Pat Hunt had been troubled all week. The last thing in the world he wanted to happen was that he and his brother Allen, would fall-out. He was sorry he had ever brought up the name of Peggy O'Shea. He had no right to interfere. That last phonecall from Allen ended on a note of severance, Pat thought: "Go right ahead and ask Peggy O'Shea out on a date if you want to. And if she says yes don't worry about me. There will be no need for us to meet to discuss it." The sound of the phone being replaced in its cradle was like the boom of doom.

Nurse Peggy O'Shea was sitting beside the phone in the Canteen in Leaviston Hospital Abbots Langley Watford Herts. She took the phone in her hand several times and left it down again. "I will I wont. What will he think of me? Will he think I'm a tart?" Again she lifted the phone but this time she dialled his number. It was ringing: buzz, buzz, buzz. "There's no one there" she said to herself with relief. But there was someone on the other end "Hello, whose speaking?" She caught her breath and asked "could I speak to Allen Hunt please?" "I'm afraid you've got your numbers crossed. This is Pat Hunt, Allen's brother. Who is calling please?" "O hello Pat. This is Peggy O'Shea. Sorry about that. I see now I've got the phone numbers confused." "That's O.K. Peggy. As a matter of fact I'm delighted you called. There is something very important I want to speak to you about. Do you think we could meet soon? I expect you'll be as concerned about this as I am." "It sounds like a great mystery. What is it?" "It concerns yourself, Allen and me. There is something that needs to be clarified." "But of course Pat – I'd be delighted. I've got three days coming to me starting tomorrow. Just tell me where we can meet and when."

EPISODE THIRTY-THREE

HOLY ORDERS
BREAKING THE GOOD NEWS
THE HOOP AT NOTTING HILL GATE
THE LEGENDARY JACK DOYLE

HOLY ORDERS

Luke Brannigan, of Brannigan and Boland Builders with his brother Fr John, Society of Jesus, arrived at Heathrow Airport. Both men were tired but contented, like the proverbial ploughman after ploughing from dawn 'til dusk. They had come back from Ireland where they had gone to bury their nephew, young Billy McNeill, in Galway. Some weeks earlier Billy had hanged himself at Wormwood Scrubs Prison where he was serving a five year sentence for possession of a loaded revolver with intent to commit a felony. His uncle Fr John had officiated at the funeral mass and at the burial service.

"And did it take young Billy's death to bring about this change of heart in me John?" Luke asked his brother.

"Not at all Luke. God works in mysterious ways, but I don't believe it is all down to a loss of life. Neither do I think this will come as a great surprise to anyone who really knows you. As I see it this is your destiny. So there was no change of heart per sé. I distinctly recall what mother said the day I told her I wanted to give my life to God."

"Indeed it is great news entirely John," she said. "and isn't it marvelous how we can loose sight of the miracle under our feet while watching the heavens for a sign. Your father and I always thought it would be your brother Luke who was most likely to study for 'Holy Orders'. But that is not to say we are in any way disappointed. The fact is John, we could not be happier for both of you, and God has been good to us."

"John, I have to tell you that's the first I've heard about that," confided Luke.

"It was a well kept secret. No one ever mentioned it for fear of putting you under any pressure to study for the priesthood. You know what is often said about failed priests: "Sure he never had the vocation in the first place. It was his mother had it.""

They both laughed then, aware of the validity as often as not of that summing-up. Jack Boland kissed Rosie Taylor nee Keegan where she stood on the last step of the stairs, in her dressing-gown. He was carrying a brief-case. "Hello and goodbye Rosie." He looked at his watch. It was exactly 8.59 a.m. "Will you be coming back for lunch, Jack?"

"I've got to collect Luke and his brother Fr John Brannigan at Heathrow Airport about an hour from now and drive them back to Hayes Mews near Berkeley Place. I expect Luke will want to know what has been happening on the construction site at Wimbledon. So I'll need to fill him in." And he tapped on the briefcase. "It's all in here, signed sealed and accounted for, – the proof of my stewardship."

"I would have thought at this stage you two trust each other."

"Of course we do. Only it's never enough in business to be honest. One must be seen to be so."

Rosie smiled. "My sentiments entirely."

Jack pulled the front door out behind him and walked jauntily to the garage. His new red Rover motor car still gave him a thrill of excitement just to look at it. It was the old story: He was like a child with a new toy. He opened the door at the driver's side. The smell of new leather, fresh paint, and new rubber filled his senses. Life was good and getting better all the time. Ever since the day he first met Luke Brannigan, he had never looked back. There was something extraordinary about the man. An aura of unworldliness went hand in hand with a simple straightforward manner that made everyone respect him. Luke had been like a father figure to Jack, – like a favourite brother and a best friend rolled into one. And much more than that, Luke had saved his life, many years earlier while risking his own to do so.

Jack threw the briefcase onto the passenger seat and got in. He switched on the engine. It purred softly and smoothly like Dick Whittington's cat after the ship's captain returned his pet to Dick, with gold from the King.

Jack Boland backed the car out onto Montpelier Street. And as he was driving past Bonhan and Sons Auctioneers he thought he recognised the man looking into Rochdales Jewellers shop beside it. "Could it have been Allen Hunt?" he asked himself. "It certainly looked like him. O but it couldn't be. Not at nine o'clock on a Saturday morning."

BREAKING THE GOOD NEWS

At the junction of Montpelier Street and Brompton Road Jack made a right turn and drove west in the general direction of Heathrow Airport.

As Luke and John Brannigan came out of the Luggage Dept., at the airport Jack spotted them and jumped out of his car. After handshakes and greetings all three men were soon careering towards Luke's home.

"You'll be happy to know Luke that we are right on target with the five hundred houses at Wimbledon. We might even be ahead with the plumbing and the tiling." "That's great news Jack. Have you had engineers from the Government department doing inspections?" "Yes, several of them. They found fault with nothing. In fact they have been complimentary about the materials we are using. Our floors, windows and doors have been singled out as first class."

"Great stuff Jack. Good timber makes good carpentry every time, as you and I well know." Luke paused for a moment. "So therefore if there are no major disruptions we should finish six weeks from now."

"Give or take a week. That should be it."

"Good. As soon as we reach Hayes Mews, I want you to come inside with us. There is something very important I must tell you. I want you to hear it first hand and be the first outside of the family to be told."

"That's a bit scary Luke. I'm not even sure that I want to hear it. Or if I do that I'll be happy about it."

"Whether or which Jack there is no way of avoiding it. I'm like Paul on the road to Damascus my mind is made up for me. I had been deliberating upon it for far too long any how."

Jack Boland brought the red Rover to a halt outside Luke's residence. "You two go on in, I'll take care of the luggage."

"No Jack, we'll carry our own load. Come on in with us."

Inside Luke played the part of the perfect host. "Make yourselves at home, gentlemen while I get a little 'Irish' to wet out whistles." He returned with a large bottle of Irish Whiskey and three crystal glasses sparkling on a silver tray. Jack Boland watched bemused as Luke poured the whiskey to within a sip of the rim of the three glasses. Then he raised his glass and addressed his words to Jack: "Wish me God-speed and good luck Jack. Once the five hundred houses are completed at Wimbledon, I'll be selling up and going immediately into a seminary with what is called a 'late vocation' to study for the priesthood."

Nurse Peggy O'Shea had her diary in front of her as she sat by the staff phone in the Canteen at Leaveston Hospital Abbot's Langley Watford Herts. She was looking at the entry with the phone number under the name of Pat Hunt at 'The Champion' on the Bayswater Road. She lifted the phone, dialled the first and second numbers but left it down while expelling air like a pin-pricked balloon. She did this several times. "What will Pat think of me?" Will he think I'm a tart?" Again she lifted the phone and dialled all the numbers. She waited, full of tension. It was ringing, ringing only there was no one answering. Strangely she was relieved, and just as she was about to hang-up a mans voice answered: "Hello, who is calling please?" Peggy caught her breath with a gasp and in a broken voice asked: "Could I speak to Allen Hunt please? This is Peggy O'Shea."

"O Peggy how are you? I'm afraid you've got your numbers crossed. This is Pat, Allen's brother."

"Sorry about that Pat."

"That's all right Peggy. As a matter of fact I'm delighted you rang. There is something very important I have to speak to you about. Something that needs to be clarified. It concerns yourself, Allen and yours truly."

"I've got three days off staring tomorrow Pat. You have only to say where and when you want to meet me."

"If I said 'The Hoop' in Notting Hill Gate about 4.00 p.m. tomorrow. How would that suit?"

"Down to the ground Pat. I'll be looking forward to it, – bye Pat."

THE HOOP AT NOTTING HILL GATE

The attractive young woman who was in charge of the Back Bar at 'The Hoop' in Notting Hill Gate was a Kildare woman.

When Peggy O'Shea arrived there were only six people on the premises in the Back Bar. She had been there once before with Allen Hunt and she knew that Allen had been there often. It could be his local. "Wouldn't it be awful if he were to walk in while Pat and I were here," Peggy said to herself. "It would look like a doublecross. At least it wasn't I who requested the meeting. That was a bit of good fortune. I hope he means business."

"Nora could I have the same again love?" The huge man standing at the top of the counter wore a stained pin striped Saville Row suit that had a shine on it. The crumpled pink carnation in his left lapel was three days dying. His once spotless white shirt showed beer stains and the collar tips had turned up to escape scrutiny or so it seemed to Peggy. His extravagant and flamboyant tie portrayed a gaudy representation of a floosie. And he smoked a cheap obnoxious smelling cigar. One could tell he had once been a handsome virile man and the twinkle in his eye had never faded. He was obviously in the twilight of his physical powers and yet he had a commanding presence.

Pat Hunt came into the Back Bar cautiously, looking all around him. He seemed to move like a cat as he took in everyone and everything around him. When his eyes rested on Peggy a smile broke across his otherwise serious face. The big man at the top of the bar spoke then: "Pat Hunt it is. How are you doing Pat?"

"Not too bad Jack. Haven't seen you in a whale of a time. How is the health?"

"I've seen better days, physically and financially," and he gave a hollow spiritless laugh.

"And how are you Peggy?"

"Very well thank you Pat, and yourself?"

"Tip top. I could run ten miles across country with John Joe Barry. What would you like to drink?"

"A light ale Pat, if you please."

"Nora, could I have a light ale, a pint of Best Bitter and whatever Jack is having and he put a pound note on the counter. "Let's sit over here Peggy. Nora will bring the drinks over when ready."

THE LEGENDARY JACK DOYLE

"Who is that big man you were speaking with Pat?"

"That's the famous Jack Doyle, otherwise known as the 'Gorgeous Gael'. He lives across the way from here in Pembridge Gardens. He used to come into 'The Champion' quite a lot."

"How is Nancy Blackmore doing these days, Pat?" The big man hurled the question at Pat.

"I couldn't tell you Jack. She took off with a blackman and never looked back."

Jack was highly amused. He made a raucous gurgling noise down in his throat. It was a near perfect imitation of the call of the great Australian Kingfisher known as the Laughing-Jackass.

"She didn't break your heart then." "No, not the heart Jack, just the pocket."

Jack was shaking his head from side to side like a child opening and shutting a door over and over again.

"He is down on his uppers now", Pat whispered to Peggy. But he had other days. The man you see before you was once a living legend. He truly had the world at his feet. During his boxing career he used to pack the Albert Hall or the White City Stadium here in London. The Irish alone used to fill every venue. Most of them it was said were women who would go a few rounds with the 6ft 5ins Gorgeous Gael at the drop of a hat, if he would only have them."

Peggy was enjoying the story about the handsome womanising colossus who was standing not more than twenty feet from her and exchanging jokes with Pat.

"Is he married Pat?"

"Well when he went to Hollywood he stole Carole Lombard from under Clarke Gables nose. Later he met and married Judith Allen who had just been discovered by Cecil B de Mille. Later still he married Movita his Mexican girlfriend. After bringing her home to Ireland, they were married in Westland Row Church in Dublin. They put together a song and dance act that packed the Theatre Royal to the rafters for months on end. He had a marvelous tenor voice and Count John McCormack gave him lessons to improve it.

"So he was a champion boxer, a film star and a great tenor. What age is he Pat?"

"He was born in Cork in 1913."

"That makes him 48 years of age. He's still a youngish man."

"Ah will you have a lick of sense, he's burned out like an ash tree caught in a forest fire. Listen I'll tell you a funny little anecdote that Jack once told me about himself. He told me this story against himself: "In 1935 I was brought out to America to box, and I flattened three American heavyweights (pros) inside six weeks. Three nights a week I had a singing part in a Broadway Show. The public dubbed me "The Irish Nightingale And even if I do say so myself I was a sensation.

At the same time, in my boxing career I was set up to meet Buddy Baer in a world title elimination. The great Jack Dempsey who was my idol came along to my training camp. Dempsey said: "I came to see the man who claims he can sing like John McCormack and fight like Jack Dempsey." After watching me scrapping for a few rounds with a couple of pros, he turned to my manager and said: "That guy has got it all wrong, – he sings like Jack Dempsey and fights like John McCormack."

Peggy had only one word for it "Brilliant."

Pat was having a double think on what he intended saying to Peggy concerning herself and Allen.

"Can I ask you a pertinent question Peggy?"

"Of course you can, Pat."

"Are you and Allen serious about each other?"

She looked at him like Isolde looked at Tristan when he vowed to love her forever.

"I'm afraid not," she said, "it is merely a platonic friendship, nothing more."

EPISODE THIRTY-FOUR

A PRE-TRIAL HEARING
WHEN ROMMEL'S AFRIKA KORPS WAS ROUTED
A JUDAS GOAT

A PRE-TRIAL HEARING

Eileen Murphy had been held in custody at Marylebone Police Station in Hammersmith for two weeks when the Department of Health and Welfare intervened. She was examined by two Psychiatrists, male and female in the company of Mr. Walter Pearson Chief of Police. Their report confirmed that Eileen was non compos mentis (of unsound mind) and could not be detained by the Police any longer but should be confined to a Mental institution for treatment, to help relieve her psychosis. At that stage she was still ranting and raving in her then familiar role which exhibited a duel personality syndrome: "Poor Winston, poor Ivor, poor Eileen and poor me. There's no need to panic, to panic. Look Ivor, Eileen got your money back, your money back. Eileen got your money back, – now we can get married."

Disconcerting though this was to the average human being, her doctors' all agreed this commitment to marriage was a healthy sign for her rehabilitation. Her expression they said is the universal woman's response to the coming together of man and woman with a wish to co-habit and procreate.

Two days later an ambulance called to collect Eileen. In the company of a male and female nurse and a uniformed member of the Police, Eileen Murphy was driven to the Psychiatric Unit at the back of Hammersmith General Hospital where she was detained as a patient. Almost immediately she was allowed to mix and mingle with other patients.

On her third day at the hospital, crazed and all as she was, she literally got the fright of her life. The shock gave her a jolt like a hundred volts of electricity, when she witnessed a beautiful young woman standing erect on a table barking and howling like a dog. Always at the cutting-edge of medicine, the British doctors discovered the cause of Eileen's psychosis and prescribed the appropriate drugs for her eventual rehabilitation.

Her mental state and capabilities were assessed on a monthly basis and inside six months she was deemed to be of sound mind once again.

The Dept. of Justice that had been monitoring her mental state of health moved in, once the doctors gave Eileen a clean bill of health. Once again the Police took her into custody with the intention of bringing her to stand trial for the murder of the giant blackman named Winston Warbarton.

There was a pre-trial hearing headed by a Judge of the High Court, a senior Barrister of the Inner Bar and a senior detective Inspector or Chief of Police. The Police Chief also summoned three detectives who had a working knowledge of the criminal records of the victim Warbarton and the accused Eileen Murphy. As a result of this preliminary hearing the charge of murder was dropped and one of manslaughter was preferred. Eileen was more relieved by the news than Stella (Ester Johnson) was when Swift eventually asked her to marry him in secret after a lifetime of waiting.

The circumstances that brought about this change were varied and many. The main one being that, when Eileen Murphy was taken into custody in the first place, it was obvious from her appearance and her manner, that she was mentally unstable. She was carrying a cushion cover case stuffed with five-pound notes and her clothes and hands and face were covered with blood and she was ranting and raving. Also during her stay in the mental hospital it was discovered she had a brother living in Manchester who could not be contacted by letter, as he was unable to read or write. He was Eileen's older brother Edward Murphy, called Ned. A plain-clothes detective went to Manchester and found him working on a building site. Pretending he was a relative of Ned's, to the foreman and to Ned's fellow workers, the Detective was able to talk to him in private for a few hours. During that time he convinced Ned of the gravity of the charges being brought against his sister.

WHEN ROMMEL'S AFRIKA KORPS WAS ROUTED

"What you have to say regarding your sister could be of benefit to her case. There could be extenuating circumstances brought forward that might reduce the charge of murder to a lesser one. The man who was killed was known to the police as a dangerous criminal."

Ned told the detective he was born in Kilkenny City, Ireland in 1922. Along with his older brother Peter he joined the British army in 1941. Both of them were sent to Aldershot where they got six months training with rifle and bayonet practise and hand to hand fighting. Afterwards they were posted to different regiments and they lost contact because neither could read nor write. But in the last days of the war in 1945 his Captain sent for him one day after mess. At that time his regiment was stationed at Turin in Northern Italy. "At ease Corporal Murphy. Do you take a drink?"

"Indeed I do sir" Ned answered in amazement.

"Do you smoke corporal?"

"Yes sir, that too."

The Captain opened a ten packet of Players and handed over the packet. "Hold on to those corporal, and he lit a match. When did you join the army yourself corporal?" the captain asked while pouring whiskey into a large tumbler.

"Me and my brother joined up in 1941, sir."

"Have you seen action corporal?"

"I was at Alamein in 1942, sir with the 8th Army, led by Field Marshall Montgomery."

"Were you, by God. You were there when Rommel's Afrika Korps was routed."

"I was there, sir in the front lines."

"When was the last time you heard from your brother?"

"I haven't heard from him since Aldershot sir."

"Take a good mouthful of that whiskey, corporal. I'm afraid I have bad news for you. Your brother Peter, who was also a corporal has been shot and killed in house to house and hand to hand fighting in Berlin. He died where he stood. I'm sorry to be the bearer of bad news, but as your captain it falls to me to do so."

"I understand sir. Thank you. When did Peter die?"

"Your brother died three days ago, corporal. I am reliably informed also that your brother Corporal Murphy had been mentioned in Dispatches on more than one occasion, for bravery under fire."

"He was a tough one alright. sir. When can I see my brother sir?

"I don't know for sure corporal but I'll tell you the minute I find out I guarantee you that."

"Thanks again. Can I go now sir? We're pulling out this evening, under orders, and I have to pack my kit. The Sergeant will be looking for me sir."

"Yes of course. Good luck to you Corporal Murphy. I'll talk to you again. Dismissed."

All of the aforementioned came to light during the pre-trial. The history of Eileen's two brothers in the British Army cast another light on the case of the Commonwealth versus Eileen Murphy. Her trial was set for the 10th September 1962. It would be held at the Central Criminal Court at Newgate Street, London. This building was completed in 1907 and was built on the site of the Old Newgate Prison. The Central Criminal Court, is more widely known as 'The Old Bailey.' Mounted at the top of its' famous tower stands a huge figure of justice covered in bronze guilt. As the vibrant news of the murder trial went around the pubs and clubs frequented by the Irish, (there was no mention of manslaughter) the stories grew more horrific and alarming with every telling.

As a result a large crowd had gathered outside 'The Old Bailey' early on the morning of the trial.A few hundred people were hoping to gain admission to the Public Gallery, which seats only 28 persons, in Court Number One. It would be like pouring the Serpentine Lake into a bowler hat. There are five other Courts that seat 32 persons each.

Eileen Murphy was given free Legal Aid. The barrister who headed her defence was an ex-British Army Major General who had served under Field Marshall Bernard, Viscount Montgomery at the Battle of Alamein in 1942.

He proved conclusively that not only was Eileen Murphy innocent and could not be held responsible for the manslaughter of Winston Warbarton, but that neither could she be accused of acquiring monies under false pretences. "All monies were lodged in her name with the knowledge and approval of the said Ivor Davies." He went on, "if she could be held guilty of anything it was for her stupidity in her choice of friends i.e. Winston Warbarton, a known criminal, and her lack of common sense due no doubt to a poor education." So said her Barrister.

Allen Hunt, Ivor Davies and Matt Ryan were part of the 28 persons in the Public Gallery at 'The Old Bailey' who saw her walk free that day.

Matt Ryan, gave his considered opinion "She couldn't be all bad as she killed the thug in self-defence and as regards to your money Ivor, she obviously regretted what she had done and was intent on returning it to you. And she risked her life to do so."

Ivor nodded his head sadly but said nothing. Allen spoke, "As I see it now she was a victim of circumstances all her life."

STELLA HESTER JOHNSON BY SEAN KENNY

A JUDAS GOAT

The Chief of Police Mr. Walter Pearson had set in motion an undercover internal investigation into the allegations in the unsigned letter made against his second in command Detective Inspector Knowlsworth by Jack Boland. It wasn't too difficult to mount this secret inquiry because Knowlsworth was hated by just about every policeman and woman working in and out of Marylebone Police Station. After a months witch-hunt it was finally established beyond all doubt that Knowlsworth had in fact succeeded in setting up an alternative force that was answerable to him alone. It was a small but deadly gang of four malpracticers who operated behind a badge of good intent.

They were like a lawless Trojan Horse inside the precincts of the Police Station. One policewoman and three policemen were found to be acting under Knowlsworth's instructions. The woman was one of Knowlsworth's whores and all three men had been verbally disciplined and suspended from duty on more than one occasion by the Chief of Police. It was further discovered that Knowlsworth had set up a liaison with M.I.5 without the knowledge and approval of the Chief of Police. It was the M.I.5 agents who had installed Larry Holden's father as a collector of information, an infiltrator, an informer and spy more than a year earlier. He had been found at the bottom of a lift-shaft, in Russell Square, dead as a door-nail. Now Holden's son Larry had stepped into his father's shoes and had recruited Nancy Blackmore to help incriminate her former lover Pat Hunt, and his "Young I.R.A." associate Jack Boland.

The Chief of Police was outraged on the one hand and highly delighted on the other. Now at last he would have his revenge. Once and for all he would be able to remove the terrible thorn that was Knowlsworth, from his side.

Knowlsworth and Larry Holden met in an out of the way pub called 'The Glue Pot' in Camden town. They were like Fagan and Bill Sykes in their relentless pursuit of money, even if it meant murder to acquire it. There they hatched a deadly scheme to assassinate Nancy Blackmore. She was of no further use to them and had of late become a liability, drinking and whoring and robbing, but worst of all mouthing all over London town. She would be the death of the two of them if left to her own devices. "What do you propose we do with her?" Knowlsworth asked Holden.

"Eliminate her as quickly as possible."

"And how do you propose to do that?"

"Drown her with her feet encased in cement. That's one way. Arrange for a car crash that bursts into flames. OR make it look like a suicide after a drunken lovers quarrel."

"Get on with it then and keep it within the jurisdiction of the Burough of Hammersmith. I'll make sure to head the investigation into her death, be it seen as accident or murder. When do you see it being done?"

"I'll need two days to rig it up." "You had better be sure it's foolproof. I'm not going down for a drunken Irish slut no more than I'm going down for a Judas-goat like yourself, if you're caught." That said it all. It had become a case of self-preservation. It was now every man for himself. Knowlsworth had got wind of the Chief's secret internal investigation. Only a whiff mind you but it was enough to put the fear of God in him. He wasn't aware that it was mostly himself who was under the microscope but being as clever as a grain-store rat, he hid every time he heard the rattle of a bucket and shovel. "I don't want to see you again" he told the vicious Larry Holden. "Don't phone, don't write and keep your mouth shut or I'll shut it for you for good."

EPISODE THIRTY-FIVE

THEY DO LOOK AFTER THEIR OWN
EILEEN RETURNS THE STOLEN MONEY
TO YOU JACK, HALF A MILLION POUNDS
ON BENDED KNEE
EDUCATION A LA CARTE

THEY DO LOOK AFTER THEIR OWN

This is by way of adding detail to the story of the Murphy brothers from Kilkenny City who joined the British Army back in 1941. Peter who was the oldest member of the family was killed in house to house fighting, in the last days of World War II, in Berlin. His parents were brought over from Kilkenny for the funeral services. They had with them their youngest, a thirteen-year-old girl named Eileen. Peter was interred with two of his companions from the same regiment. They were buried with full military honours in Highgate cemetery London. Captain Owen O'Sullivan who was himself a poet, gave the graveside oration and stood to attention in salute as the bugler played the final farewell – the 'Last Post.' The Captain nodded his recognition of Ned who smiled back at him in appreciation.

"Ladies and gentlemen," the Captain said: "With your permission I'd like to recite a little poem by a poet named Beatrice Redpath. This is a poem of true loveliness and one that to my mind is very appropriate. The title she gave it was:

"To One Lying Dead
What has gone out from thee this hour
That leaveth thee, unstirred by word from me
Low lying, like a fallen scentless flower?
Hadst thou a soul which through the drifting years,
My earth bound vision was too dull to see?
And didst thou know the weight of unshed tears?
Hadst thou a spirit straining to be free?"

The parents were given a 'Lump-Sum' and a pension for life. "They do look after their own," a parent of one of the dead remarked. That happened on the 5th day of September 1945.

Corporal Peter Murphy was buried with his comrades less than a stones throw away from the grave of one of the foremost revolutionary thinkers of the 19th Century. Born in Germany in 1818, Karl Marx was a political theorist and economist. He was the founder of Marxist Communism. He collaborated with Friedrich Engels in 1845, and wrote the Communist Manifesto in 1848. This piece of political propaganda was commissioned by the London Communist League. He wrote what is said to be his greatest political work in 1867 'Das Kapital.' None of his writings were financially profitable and he and his family were forced to live on the generosity of Engels, whose father owned a Cotton Mill in

**KARL MARX
BY SEAN KENNY**

Manchester. Such industries were notorious for the employment of child labour. Wasn't it ironic then, that it was these very conditions in his father's mills that Friedrich studied that led to his first major political work, which was The Condition of the Working Class in England (1845.)

I think it was Marx who said that Jesus Christ was the only true Communist that ever lived!

As a result of the Old Bailey court case verdict that saw Eileen Murphy walk free in 1962, the cushion cover full of five-pound notes, had to be handed back to her. Like Daniel O'Connell, was reputed to have done many times in Ireland's defence, Eileen's Barrister drove a Coach and Four through the Law to vindicate her.

And so the princely sum of £285 was brought into Court No.1 in a plastic bag and after signing for it was handed over to Eileen without a word by the court clerk. The original amount of Ivor Davies savings was £350. Warbarton's accomplice had siphoned off fifty pounds and Warbarton himself had squandered fifteen pounds on booze.

EILEEN RETURNS THE STOLEN MONEY

When Allen Hunt, Ivor Davies and Matt Ryan came out of the court-room into the main hall, they stood under the magnificent cupola.Ivor wanted to 'light-up' and blow away some tension, in the smoke of a cigarette. On a long wooden bench near the door, Eileen Murphy sat with her brother Ned. For an instant all five sets of eyes met and quickly disengaged. It seemed like their contact was too painful to endure.

Too much hurt had caused the windows of the soul to close the curtains against the glare of disgrace.

Imagine Allen's amazement then when Eileen Murphy walked into the public bar at 'The Poppy' on the Edgware Road that same night. She took from her handbag a well parcelled bundle and placed it on the counter in front of Allen. "That belongs to Ivor

Davies, Allen. It's the £350 I stole from him. Would you be good enough to give it back to him? I'm too ashamed to look him in the face myself." She caught her breath convulsively and turned to leave.

"Wait. Wait Eileen. This can't be the right way to go about saying sorry and goodbye. Ivor is in the Lounge bar and Matt Ryan is there with him. It's really none of my business but I think you should give it to him yourself. He may want to say thanks. And if he does I think you should be there to hear it. Shall I call him in here, Eileen?"

She was crying too much to speak and only nodded her consent.

TO YOU JACK, HALF A MILLION POUNDS

"There was a break-in at our offices in Lamb Street when you were over in Ireland burying your nephew, Luke."

"What was that about? Was there anything of value taken, Jack?"

"It was the police. But it wasn't an official search. It was master-minded by Detective Inspector Knowlsworth without the authority of the Chief of Police. They took about two hundred pounds to make it look like a burglary. The money was returned. Pushed through the letterbox. No explanation, no name."

"Did they find anything?"

"No. The fact is, they dropped a clangour."

"They can afford to do that. You can't.God knows, I told you often enough to get out of that organisation."

"Well I've taken your advice. I'm planning to get married in the near future."

"Thanks be to God for that. I only hope you haven't left it too late, Jack. I mean, will they let you out now?"

"I'm going one way or another."

"Who is the woman you are planning to marry? That's if you don't mind me asking."

"Her name is Rosie Keegan."

"Is that the woman who was married to Bill Taylor?" "The same."

"Well, for fear you are not aware of it, she has been seen all over London with Allen Hunt, even when Bill Taylor was alive. And she has a daughter for Pat Hunt, his brother. I just hope you know what you are getting into."

"I had no idea you were so well informed. And I thought you were more charitable, Luke"

"I'm not attempting to take the woman's character, Jack. I wouldn't do that, as you should well know. I am merely stating a fact. There might be the possibility that one day she could turn back to the father of her child. I wouldn't want to see you left high and dry."

"I appreciate that Luke. Sorry for the sarcasm. I know you mean well. It's just that I feel good about her."

"I'm happy for you Jack and hope things turn out the way you want them to."

"Thanks Luke. There is something else I wanted to speak to you about. Do you have anyone in mind to whom you intend selling your half of the company?"

"Yes I do, – yourself Jack. "

"That's decent of you Luke. Next big question what price tag is attached?"

"To you Jack – half a million pounds."

ON BENDED KNEE

"Luke Brannigan is selling up and going into a seminary to study for the priesthood," Jack Boland told Rosie Taylor nee Keegan, "there's a turn-up for you."

"I'm not surprised. He's half a priest already. Who is he selling to?"

"He wants me to buy it and at a knock-down price at that."

"What's the knock-down price, Jack?"

"A half million pounds. What do you think Rosie?"

"And do you have that kind of money to free-up?"

"Of course not. I'd have to go to the bank. It wouldn't be easy."

"What if I was to buy Luke's half?" She said it as casual as a woman talking about buying a pair of shoes to match her handbag. "Do you reckon it would be a good investment Jack?"

"It most certainly would. But I wasn't aware you had that kind of money, Rosie."

"You weren't after me for my money then," she said and laughed.

"If you are serious about it Rosie, we had better see our solicitors. Why don't we do the job right anyhow," and he got down on one knee. He looked up at her in deadly earnest. "Will you marry me Rosie?"

A flash of pain crossed her face and she gripped his shoulder with digging fingers. Patricia ran into the room just then and burst into laughter when she saw Jack Boland on bended knee.

"When is Allen coming to visit us, Mammy?" She was hugging a Cabbage Patch doll.

"Not right now Jack. I can't. I need more time. But I thank you for asking. I really do." Tightly in her hand she held a gold Cross and chain that hung about her neck.

Jack was visibly shaken. He went upstairs to his room and sat on his single bed contemplating the ceiling. He felt sure she would have accepted his proposal, seeing as how she was willing to invest half a million pounds in his company. Women are unpredictable he thought to himself. Just when you think you've got the race in the bag, the mare throws a shoe.

Eileen Murphy's brother Ned, the one who had survived the war was anxious to meet Allen Hunt. He wanted to thank him for the moral support he gave to his sister before he returned to Manchester. He called at "The Poppy" the day before he was to leave London. "Am I right in thinking that you're Allen Hunt, the Kilkenny man?"

"That I am. And you are Ned Murphy. What can I do for you?"

"I just wanted to say thanks for the way you treated Eileen. It wasn't all her fault you know. She didn't have much of a chance growing up. None of us did. If it hadn't been for the British army we'd have all gone hungry. It's said that life is a mystery. I surely believe that. I have seen strange and terrible sights. Things that no man should have to look at – death and destruction dealt out to the innocent more often than the guilty. The women and children are always made scapegoats."

"Eileen was the only one of our family who got any schooling and she wouldn't have without the British army paymaster sending a part of Peters and my own wages home every month. And strange as it seems she was the only one of us to go astray."

EDUCATION A LA CARTE

"I'll tell you a little story about our childhood, – especially Peter's and mine, if I may. But first I must tell you that Peter and I joined the British army in 1941 and Peter was killed in Berlin in the last days of the war in 1945. Neither he nor I ever learned to read or write. Peter was two years older than me but we were in the same class at school, – third book.

My father had a chronic illness all his life. He suffered from Tuberculosis of the lungs. Our only source of income was a few shillings paid out each week by the Department of Health at the Dispensary in, Kilkenny City. And you were made to feel like dirt, standing in a queue for hours. This is not a sob story Allen, – this is history."

"In any event when my mother heard there was a job going for a messenger boy at Smithwicks of High Street, she went immediately to the Headmaster of our school. He was one of the 'curl of the lip brigade' with plus-fours which was a knickerbocker suit. He wore a tartan beret and smoked a chestwarmer pipe. And for one who was supposed to be an educated man, he was as ignorant about people as a Manchurian monkey is about St. Patrick's Day. My poor mother who was waiting to talk to the Master was in for the shock of her life."

"She knocked and knocked on the classroom door. There was pandemonium within. The racket was louder than fifty soldiers bombarding targets on a 'Firing Range.' The Headmaster was out in the yard smoking his pipe. Eventually a pale faced boy came in answer to her knocking. He ran to the Headmasters favourite haunt and told him he was wanted at the front door".

Not in any hurry he sauntered to meet her. "Yes, – what is it you want?"

"I'm looking for a reference for my son, Peter Murphy, sir. There's a Runner's job going in Smithwicks of High Street. We need the money badly, sir."

"What did you say his name was? Did I hear you say Peter Murphy?"

"That's right sir."

"Is that the fellow they call Geronimo?"

"It's just a nickname sir."

"By God, that fellow has been a thorn in my side and no mistake about it. I'd give him a reference alright if I thought it would get him into Mountjoy." He opened back the classroom door. "Look in there" he said. "'Tis like 'Fiddlers Green." There was near chaos inside. About fifty boys were sitting and standing, and some were writing with chalk on the bare wooden floor, which was the only copy some of them had. "Take a good look at that lot," said the Principal Educator. "There won't be one of them but will help fill the jails and asylums of Ireland."

EPISODE THIRTY-SIX

EFF OFF QUASIMODO
A RENDEZVOUS WITH FATE
A FOOTBALL UP THE CHIMNEY
PAGING NANCY BLACKMORE

EFF OFF QUASIMODO

There can be little doubt but that 'The George Pub and Restaurant' on the Broadway in Hammersmith is one of the most popular drinking and eating establishments frequented by the Irish in London. At any given time as many as one quarter of its customers could be from the 'Land of Saints and Scholars.' In an earlier episode I tried to describe for you the ambience and the grandeur of that great place. On Bank Holiday weekends Bacchus leaves Mount Olympus and comes to sample the wine at 'The George.'

Nancy Blackmore who was the goddess of wickedness was not aware that she was under close observation. She was being watched more closely than a hungry hawk would watch a grazing rabbit. Nancy was well known to the management and staff at 'The George' and for all the wrong reasons I might add. Since she and Pat Hunt had broken up a long time ago, she had been working as a barmaid manageress in a Darkies Club on the Harrow Road. This notorious establishment was called 'Othello the Hun' and was said to be one of the roughest joints outside of Soho.

Nancy had now consumed six Gin and Tonics and was becoming intoxicated. She sloshed down the very potent dregs of the sixth drink and beckoned to the bar man to draw near. "I'll have the same again sonny, or something similar, haw, haw, haw. And I don't want to wait all day for it either." "You won't have to wait at all Madam, because I am asking you to leave right now."

"Why you cheeky little jumped-up lavatory cleaner. Got your hair cut for the first time in your life after crossing the 'herring pond,' – you stupid little Culchie." A big security man arrived at her table. He had positioned himself within earshot of her scurrilous tongue. The big man was an ex-Mayo All Ireland footballer, who knew the score. In his summation, she had just kicked an own goal. "Walk Mrs. or I'll carry you to the door, now."

She knew strength and determination when it looked at her straight in the face. There was nothing for it but to retire under protest. She knocked her empty glass to the floor with a broadside from her handbag as she turned for the door. With a swagger of the hips and a welter of abuse she gauched towards the street. The Mayo man walked at her side determined to see her out, like a referee would accompany a many times fouling footballer to the sideline. She stopped at the door and turned towards him. "I'll be back, you bloody Balooba."

BACCHUS AT THE GEORGE
BY SEAN KENNY

"Don't even think about it. You are barred for life." "Eff off Quasimodo," she said while making a kick at him that would have launched one of Hitlers Doodlebugs during the '39 War. But the half dozen G and T's had got the better of her. Instead of landing the kick her shoe went flying back into 'The George.' She lost her balance and fell outside the door. Sitting in a most unladylike fashion, she cursed and swore like a sore-headed sergeant major at a bunch of raw recruits. The big Mayo man retrieved the shoe and fired it back at her, hitting an unmentionable part of her anatomy. Now, both of them were speaking in diverse tongues like those who tried to build the Tower of Babel. Nothing constructive came from either. After an innocent passer-by helped her to her feet and was thanked with a vulgar four-letter word, Blackmore abandoned the scene.

A RENDEZVOUS WITH FATE

She wobbled into Hammersmith Underground station and boarded a Metropolitan Line train for Paddington. There she changed to the Bakerloo Line, heading for Harrow and Wealdstone. One stop down the line she got off at Warwick Avenue. She walked across Clifton Gardens and into Warrington Crescent. As she entered the Colonnade Hotel she looked at her watch. It was 2.35 p.m. She was due to meet Larry Holden at 3.30 p.m.

Nancy Blackmore saw herself as the apple of Larry Holden's eye. She firmly believed they got on together like earth and sky at the fairest horizon. Further, she felt she had him in the palm of her hand. For quite some time now she had been hinting at him that they should move in and live together. It must have paid off. "What's the point of paying out good money for two flats when one would suffice?" she told him many a time.

'Twas true he was never short of cash. He seemed to have it coming out of his ears, and he dressed like Lord Haw Haw. He'd be a good catch for any woman. She was getting her claws into him, a nail at a time. That way there would be no need to pounce. And today everything was coming to a head.

They were going to look at a couple of flats. One was at Amberley Road, which was within walking distance of the Colonnade Hotel. "The other is in Leinster Gardens," Larry told her. And, there was never a dull moment in his company. And he was afraid of nothing, – not even Pat Hunt, he told her and she said she believed him, but the thought sent a shiver down her spine. For had he known Pat Hunt, as well as she did he might think otherwise. Anyone who had seen what he did to the black and white street fighters that accompanied her to 'The Champion' on the night she sought her revenge, would tell him to beware. "But enough about Pat Hunt and his fisticuff competence. Once we settle down together everything will be fine and dandy," she told herself. "We'll be like Bonny and Clyde on a rip-roaring money-go-round."

She looked at her watch again. There was nearly an hour to kill before Larry Holden would arrive at the Hotel. She enquired from a bellboy where the Lounge bar was situated. "Hey boy, where's the watering hole in this here hacienda?"

"Excuse me madam, are you looking for the bar?" "How clever of you sonny. I can see you're going places in a hurry. Now if you were working for me I'd advise you to hang your coat next the door, for a quick get-away."

Larry Holden might well have been doing a written examination for 'Murder Incorporated.' In great detail on a page of foolscap he was setting out his plan of action. Nothing could be left to chance. And the timing would be all-important. "B is for Blackmore, M is for me and A is for alibi. So, when B is eliminated M must be at A. That's the nub of the plan," he told himself once again.

Holden was sitting at a woodworm infested table in the back room of a vacated house. It was located in a laneway at the back of Amberley Road. He scrutinized the plot for murder. There could be no loose ends. Every thread of thought had to be tied into the warp of the day's movements. And the weft must needs be well spun from counterfeit facts and fastened into steel shutters of resolution. Only then would the loom of fate weave the macabre shroud of death. Like all professional killers, Holden was as cold as Cocytus at the last and final circle of Hell.

A FOOTBALL UP THE CHIMNEY

He stood up and went to the old-fashioned fireplace. It had an open grate with a hob on both sides and was painted in the time honoured red brick style. He took off his jacket and turned up his sleeves. Lifting two old newspapers from the floor, he crumpled them into a football and stuffed them up the chimney with a balding kitchen broom.

Satisfied that these blocked any exit or entry of air, he went to the crude ironclad gas stove and turned on the main ring. Gas gushed out like the subdued whistle of a tired train having reached its distant destination. A devilish giggle escaped his lips as he turned off the lethal, unlit jet of gas. He put on his jacket and looked at his watch. It was 3.10 p.m. Blackmore would be at the Colonnade Hotel and no doubt scoffing down Gin and Tonics. That's all she was good for. She was a waste of space and energy and it would give him pleasure to dispatch her. He felt he was merely doing the world a favour by getting rid of her.

He took an unopened bottle of Gordons Dry Gin from a brown cardboard box along with two half-pint glasses and half a dozen bottles of Tonic. He looked all around him, satisfied that the stage was set for a flawless murder.

This was the Informers third trip to the vacant house in the cul-de-sac laneway, in as many days. He may have assumed he was working incognito, because of the remoteness and forbidding aspect of the place. The fact was however, he was followed there the very first time he went. He needed to size up all his options for committing murder on site. One of the two Volunteers was on to him from the start. He had had him in his sights since the night Patrick Kavanagh had given the 'Poetry Reading' at the 'Empress of Russia' pub in Sloane Square. It was he who had rigged the elevator in Russell Square that caused Holden's father to step into an empty shaft and fall seven stories to his death. This man was the London born Volunteer of Irish parents that originally came from Oranmore in County Galway. This day he had tailed Larry Holden in his 1960 black Peugeot from Lisson Grove where he lived, to Amberley Road. And when Holden took a slow left turn into a dreary and decrepit cul-de-sac laneway, the Volunteer sped past in his nondescript maintenance van and pulled up near a Minimarket. In well-worn boiler suit, wearing cap and glasses he emerged from the van.

As a born Londoner in working gear he had no problem melting into the locality. Pretending he was looking for directions from an old-timer resident in the area, he got all the information he required. "There are six pokey 'oles that passed for 'ouses in that cul-de-sac. Six Pakistani families had 'em. The Council condemned the lot and gave new 'ouses to the Pakistanis over at Westbeourne Terrace. These lot 'ill be bulldozed just as soon as the Council get 'round to turning off the water, the gas and the electricity. Meantime 'tis off limits for they don't want no squatters setting up 'ouse. Vagabonds and layabouts soon cotton-on an' take possession, for a week, a month or even a year. It all depends on how soon the Council moves in with the wrecking crew."

"I'll bet you'll be 'appy when those blokes move-in" You don't need no aggravation from that other lot of bums."

"You said it mate. It 'ain't safe in bed no more, – never mind coming 'ome after dark from the boozer."

PAGING NANCY BLACKMORE

Larry Holden came out of the vacant house numbered one and got into his black Peugeot. He drove to the top of Amberley Road and stopped beside a public phone box. "Would you page Miss Nancy Blackmore to come to the phone please, it's urgent? She should be in the loungebar."

"Yes. Who the hell is this?" She was rotten drunk.

"It's me love, – Larry. Listen I need you to meet me outside the hotel in a hurry. Stand under the awning at the Main door."

"Where the hell are you? You were supposed to be here half an hour ago."

"Never mind about that now, – just do what I ask you now love."

"Oh all right anything for you love."

Nancy Blackmore was spifflicated. The air must have hit her hard when she came out of the hotel. She was literally hanging on to one of the steel uprights that supported the grandiose awning. Holden pulled in close to the kerb and shot the passenger door open. Immediately she began to harangue him. "Don't you know you were supposed to step out and hold the car door open for a lady?" He was livid when she toppled into the car and fell across him letting out a gaseous Gin-pickled belch. Had it been dark he would have strangled her there and then. But he would soon be rid of her. "Where's this 'effin flat anyway?"

"Five minutes from here, love. Once you see it you won't ever want to leave it and that's a promise."

He drove her back to the vacant house in the cul-de-sac laneway and had to lift her out of the car. She was about to begin another tirade when her bleary eyes fastened on the Gin and Tonic.

"Now that's what I call a well decorated flat. I'll have a large G and T as a house-warmer before I inspect the cutlery and the linen." She laughed like a broken Wellington boot squelching through a muddy wet field.

"I'll have the same again with knobs on," Blackmore said half way down in the bottle of Gordon's. As Holden poured her third G and T and his second tonic water he thought he heard a noise outside. He went to a front window and looked out cautiously. A bent over old man wearing a boiled-suit and cap was carrying a dirty tin can as he shuffled out of the cul-de-sac onto Amberley Road. When Holden returned to Blackmore she was slumped in the sunken divan, smoking like a chip-pan caught fire. She had taken more drink on board than a camel preparing to cross the Sahara. She was out of it.

He turned on the gas and tightly closed the room door. Within seconds he was speeding from the scene. "Good riddance to bad rubbish," Holden said when he heard the explosion. That was only twenty seconds before he crashed into a petrol truck at 75 m.p.h.The bent-over old man in boiler suit and cap, straightened up after putting the tin can into the back of his maintenance van. It was half full of brake fluid.

EPISODE THIRTY-SEVEN

IVOR & EILEEN WERE ALL WASHED UP
LIKE LOADING UP A CART THAT DIDN'T HAVE WHEELS
OUT OF THE MOUTHS OF BABES
LOVE IS LIKE A VIOLIN

IVOR & EILEEN WERE ALL WASHED UP

Eileen Murphy walked a free woman from 'The Old Bailey' Courthouse in London. She was found not guilty of the manslaughter of the giant black man Winston Warbarton. Not only that, but she was awarded the £285 which was all that was left from Ivor Davies savings of £350, which she had taken. Although it must be said, the entire amount was in her name. What was it the loud-mouthed Mr. Bumble said in Charles Dickens immortal novel 'Oliver Twist:' 'If the Law says that The Law is an ass.'

Allen Hunt was working behind the bar in 'The Poppy' when Eileen walked hesitantly into the Public bar and went towards Allen. She took a neatly parcelled bundle from a large shoulder bag and placed it on the counter in front of Allen. "That's Ivor's £350 that I stole from him. Would you please give it back to him? I'm too ashamed to give it to him myself, Allen."

"It is really none of my business, Eileen, but I think you should give it to him yourself. He may want to say thanks. He is inside now in the Lounge working with Matt Ryan. Shall I call him in here Eileen?" She was crying too much to speak and only nodded her consent.

Allen shouted over the partition: "Ivor, there is someone here who would like to see you for a few moments. Can you come in?"

When Ivor discovered it was Eileen who wanted to see him, he almost had a seizure. The look on his face corresponded to the look on Edmond Dante's face when he saw for the first time Abbe Faria and his illustrations on the walls of his cell, in the Dungeons of the Chateau d'If. (From the classic, Count of Monte Cristo, brain-child of Alexandre Dumas.)

"I'm so sorry Ivor to have let you down so badly." She handed him the bundle. "There's all your money back. The full £350 – is there. I'll say goodbye now and sorry again for causing you so much trouble."

OLIVER TWIST
BY SEAN KENNY

Ivor was struck dumb, so Allen walked on his foot and gave him a look that would start a stopping horse. "Thanks for returning the money, Eileen. There's no hard feelings." He put out his hand. – "Goodbye and good luck." She shook his hand without enthusiasm. "Thanks Ivor, and you too Allen." She hesitated and was about to say something further but changed her mind when Ivor tore open the parcel. It looked like he was going to count it there and then. The blood rushed into her cheeks until she looked like a painted harlequin. She turned aside quickly, then slowly walked away. After taking three steps she stopped and turned again, "It's all there Ivor, honest," and she walked out into the hall. "Surely you don't think she has short changed you this late in the day?" Allen asked him.

"Considering what has happened, if it was your money would you be so trusting?"

Allen couldn't truly answer that so he kept his mouth shut.

On the other side of the partition that separated the Public bar from the Lounge, Matt Ryan had been earwigging as much as he could between orders. He was nobody's fool and he quickly put two and two together. Ivor and Eileen were all washed-up.

LIKE LOADING UP A CART THAT DIDN'T HAVE WHEELS

As had been the case for quite some time now the Whitbread Brewery that owned 'The Poppy' had been encouraging Matt to get married. It was company policy and easily understood. Also it was both reasonable and practical. According to the company's convictions, a married man was a happy man and there would always be someone to mind the shop. And more than that the Governor would be less likely to loose his way chasing after a bit of skirt if he had his own mannequin to model the garment.

Matt followed Eileen into the hallway that led to the Edgware Road. She was surprised when he came up behind her and put his hand on her shoulder. "Please don't be frightened Eileen. I couldn't help but overhear some of the conversation. I just want to say what you did was both brave and honest. Do you mind me asking you, what are you going to do with yourself?" She jumped when he put his hand on her shoulder.

"Oh it's you Matt. I thought for a minute that it was Ivor coming after me. I'm not completely over the fright of that awful attack yet. What am I going to do with myself, you ask? The truth is Matt, I haven't the faintest idea."

The Police and the fire brigade arrived almost simultaneously at the cul-de-sac laneway off Amberley Road. It reminded the old timers of the sights that were seen after the German Blitzkrieg in '39. The woman they found in one of the back rooms was burned beyond recognition. She had first degree burns to her face, hands and legs and her life was hanging in the balance. A scorched letter in her handbag was apparently from a former lover named Bat Hart or it could be Pat Hart or even Bat Hunt. The date of the writing was June 22nd 1960.

"Just as well for 'er she were gone," one of the firemen observed. "Too true mate, she ain't goin' to like lookin' at 'erself in the mirror no more."

"That's if she makes it, poor sod."

"It'll be 'er bad luck if she does. 'Cause if she does pull through, she'll most likely end up in the 'Looney Bin' an' I'll bet she were a bit of a beauty an' all, in her day."

Nancy Blackmore was never seen or heard of again by any of those who frequented the old haunts around Edgware Road and 'The Poppy,' Paddington and 'The Load Of Hay,' Notting Hill Gate and 'The Hoop', Hammersmith Broadway and 'The George' and a dozen other havens where the Irish in London hang out.

Larry Holden the Informer was speeding down past Little Venice on Bloomfield Road when he heard the explosion behind him. "Good riddance," he said, "to bad rubbish." He was approaching the junction at Warwick Avenue when the traffic lights changed to red. He slammed his foot down hard on the brakes and braced himself. Nothing happened. The brakes didn't work. His high powered black Peugeot doing 75 m.p.h ploughed into a moving Petrol truck. The truck was going south to deliver its cargo on the Harrow Road. It was nothing short of a miracle that the truck did not burst into flames. The driver would never have survived if it had. But the driver of the black Peugeot wasn't so lucky. He had to be cut out of the wreckage. In the hospital an hour later it was found necessary to amputate both legs above the knees.

And if that wasn't bad enough, three days later it was discovered that his back was broken. Originally the surgeons thought they would be able to fit artificial limbs sometime in the not too distant future, but with the spinal cord severed there would be no point. It would be like loading up a cart that didn't have wheels.

OUT OF THE MOUTHS OF BABES

On the Saturday morning that Jack Boland left Rosie Taylor nee Keegan's house in Knightsbridge he was going to Heathrow. Allen Hunt was about to call but when he saw Jack coming out of the house at 9.00 a.m. he presumed the worst and turned away. Back now in 'The Poppy' he went into the dining room to make a cup of tea and read the daily 'Mirror' and 'Star'.

He left the gold Cross and chain in an embroidered sachet on the table along with the Cabbage Patch doll. Deep in thought he boiled the water in the whistling kettle until it blew off the spout and hit the floor like an unarmed missile. "I yi, what's going on here?" Ivor Davies came into the room.

"Is there a bazaar in town?" Allen gave him a look that would freeze molten lava and Ivor changed his tune: 'That's a beautiful old fashioned doll. I'll bet Patricia will love it. Are you going over to Knightsbridge to see them today, Allen?"

"As a matter of fact I have been there already."

"So they have gone shopping for the day. Or maybe you just missed them?"

"It's worse than that," Allen paused and looked at Ivor, like Sherlock Holmes used to look at Dr. Watson before letting him in on the hidden cause and effect behind the pertinent mystery.

"Jack Boland is staying there with them. It looks as if that it how it has been since they left here."

"It doesn't necessarily mean anything untoward has happened," Ivor said, "they are both honorable people."

Allen saw instantly that his wounded ego had blinkered his sense of propriety. "Good man Ivor, you are absolutely right."

"At least phone her, Allen and ask her where you stand. If you miss this opportunity you may regret it for the rest of your life."

Back at her home in Knightsbridge Rosie Taylor nee Keegan, got Patricia out of bed. They both slept in the master bedroom for companionship and security at the top of the stairs. With the sleep still in her eyes Patricia's first words were: "Will Allen call to see us today Mammy? He said he would."

"He didn't say what day he would come, love. Allen has to work dear."

"Then can we go to see him, at 'The Poppy'. If we don't go to see him, he'll think we don't like him anymore."

Rosie was brushing her hair while looking at herself in the dressing-table mirror. Patricia's last words struck a tender chord: "he'll think we don't love him anymore," Rosie said to herself aloud, and let the hairbrush fall from her hand.

"What's wrong mammy?"

Before Rosie could answer the phone rang. She ran downstairs and picked up the phone. "Yes, who is it. Oh it's you Allen. You know that's amazing – Patricia was talking about you just now. She was asking me when would you be calling to see us?"

"To be hoonest with your Rosie I was within fifty yards of your front door about an hour ago when I saw Jack Boland coming out, so I took off lest I might cause any embarrassment."

There was no reply, just a stoney silence.

"Are you there Rosie? Is there something wrong?"

"Sorry Allen, – yes I'm here. No there's nothing wrong. It's just that Patricia is tugging at my dress since she heard me say your name. And, I can explain about Jack Boland and its not what you may think. It gets a bit scary these times for us living here alone in a big house without a man. Jack has a small room at the." "Listen Rosie, you don't have to explain anything to me. What you do is your own business."

LOVE IS LIKE A VIOLIN

"But that's just it Allen, I haven't done anything, honestly."

"Ivor was dead right. I was about to make a mistake I would regret for the rest of my life," Allen told himself. "Rosie would you please put the phone to Patricia's ear?"

"Yes I will Allen. She will be delighted." "Hello sweetheart, how are you?"

"Hello Allen, – are you coming to see us?" "Yes love, – tell Mammy I'm coming over today. I'm coming as soon as I've had a cup of tea. I have presents for the two of you." "Oh good, Allen has presents for us Mammy. We'll make him stay won't we?" Allen left the phone down softly and sat back in his chair with a cup of tea in his hand and a song in his heart. He turned up the radio. Helen Shapiro was singing: "Love is Like A Violin."

When Rosie and Patricia were out shopping two days later Jack Boland packed his bag and left. He left a letter saying thanks and goodbye, which he left on the kitchen table. He made no mention of Rosie's earlier offer to buy Luke's half of the Brannigan and Boland Construction Company.

"I'm very sorry Mr. Boland but a half million pounds is an awful lot of money. The real trouble here is that Mr. Luke Brannigan is leaving the company. You will agree that he has always been the anchor and front-man in the partnership. And the old saying that two heads are better than one is not empty rhetoric as you well know. What you need right now is someone with a proven record in the construction industry and with enough funds to buy himself that half share. It's not in my power to do as you ask. It would be more than my job here in the bank is worth, Mr. Boland." That was that. The bank wouldn't oblige and there was no point in speaking to Rosie about buying the half share since the prospects of marriage had retreated. One was dependent on the other. "it looks like Luke will have to sell his share of the business himself, if he wants out," Jack told the bank manager. To Rosie's and Patricia's delight, Allen moved in and occupied the room vacated by Jack Boland. And for the second time in one month, Patricia laughed but this time Rosie exulted when Allen Hunt went down on one knee and asked her to be his wife: "Will you marry me Rosie? I'll take care of you and Patricia for as long as I live, so help me God." "I thought you'd never ask. Of course I will Allen. I'm the happiest woman in London, today." Patricia sat on Allen's knee holding hands with the two of them.

EPISODE THIRTY-EIGHT

IF ANYONE SQUEALS WE'RE ALL FOR THE HIGH JUMP
THE VIRGIN OF THE ROCKS
SHE WAS A WHORE IN HER HEART
EGG ON HIS WRITTEN SUBMISSIONS

IF ANYONE SQUEALS WE'RE ALL FOR THE HIGH JUMP

Inspector Knowlsworth who was Deputy Chief of Police arrived on the scene of the explosion in the cul-de-sac laneway off Amberley Road. Inside he found two paramedics working feverishly to keep the victim alive and prepare her for removal to the hospital as soon, as was humanly possible. "Is she alive?" he asked rather brashly with a scowl like Attila the Hun must have exhibited before being assassinated in bed on the night of his marriage. The paramedics looked at each other. "Only just," one answered sourly. They paid him no further heed, but went on working as if he wasn't there. "What happened here?" he persisted. Visibly annoyed one answered, "we thought that question was self-evident. Our only concern here is with the preservation of life." That did it.

"Huh," he grunted while picking up what was left of a ladies handbag. Some commodities were scattered around the floor and a few remained in the tattered bag: a shattered mirror and powder compact, a tube of scarlet red lipstick that had bled in the bag, a nail-file and tweezers and a pulverized twenty packet of tipped cigarettes and a plastic cigarette holder that was twisted like a corkscrew by the explosive heat. And there were about five pounds in burnt notes, and loose change. In an envelope yellowed with age there was a letter from her former lover, whose name was partly obliterated. Knowlsworth put the lot into a plastic bag and was about to leave the paramedics when he asked abruptly: "What hospital are you taking her to?"

"Maida Vale Hospital for Nervous Diseases. It's the nearest."

A squad car screeched to a halt outside and a uniformed policeman quickly entered the wrecked building. He went straight to Knowlsworth and called him aside. "Larry Holden has had an horrific accident. He crashed into a Petrol Truck and had to be cut out of the car. He looks like he's a gonner, – more like dead mutton than a man."

"Where did it happen and at what time?"

"Around five p.m. at the junction of Warwick Ave and Bloomfield Road."

"Where is he now?"

"He's in Saint Mary's Hospital, South Warf Road."

"How much does the Chief know?"

"Plenty if you ask me."

"How come? What's happened?"

"There were two senior detectives from another jurisdiction in great consultation in the Chief's office early this morning."

"How early this morning? Did you know any of them?"

"Around eight a.m. the two of them were sitting, waiting for him in his office. And no I didn't recognise either of them. But they're top brass and no mistake about it. You could smell the polish of their presence."

"You had best keep your ear to the ground then. Your life may depend upon it, not to mention your job. And if you are brought in for questioning, – you know nothing, – not an effin thing. If anyone breaks now we're all for the high jump. If anyone squeals I'll see to it that his or her mouth is shut permanently. Now get out of here and tell the others to cover their tracks. And remember, Blackmore and Holden only got what was coming to them."

THE VIRGIN OF THE ROCKS

As Eileen Murphy was leaving 'The Poppy' on the Edgware Road after returning the £350 that she had stolen from Ivor Davies, Matt Ryan went out into the hall after her.

"Don't be frightened Eileen. I just wanted to say that I admire your bravery and your decency in doing what you did."

"Thanks Matt my only fear was that I might breakdown and run away before the job was done."

"But you did well and I'm proud of you – that's the truth. Could I ask you something, Eileen? What are you going to do with yourself now? Do you have any plans?"

"To be honest with you Matt, I haven't the faintest idea. I'm like a tinker without a tent as my poor father used say"

"Would you care for a cup of tea Eileen or perhaps a little drop of something stronger?"

"A cup of tea would be fine Matt."

"Then you won't mind coming upstairs to the staff dining room."

Sitting together upstairs with a cup of tea, Matt said exactly what was on his mind: "I'm sure you remember when Mike O'Hara was Governor here at 'The Poppy'?"

"Indeed I do, Matt."

"And you will remember Mary, his wife. To cut a long story short, a woman's touch is missing around the place. And there is a job vacant here now for a part-time barmaid and part-time housekeeper. The two jobs could be rolled into one. The money is good and it's live-in and all-found. I don't want to rush you, Eileen, but would you think about it?"

When Matt looked at her for an answer, she was crying, but they were tears of happiness.

"I don't have to think about it even for a second, I'd be delighted Matt. The truth is I didn't know where I was going to turn. But how do you think Ivor will take it? Will the sight of me from morn' 'till night be too much for him?"

"Let me worry about Ivor. Now when can you move in? Do you have somewhere to stay tonight?"

"I was going to look in the evening papers."

"You need look no further. Do you have a case or boxes that need to be collected?"

"I have a large suitcase in the cloakroom at Paddington Mainline Station."

"Do you have the cloakroom ticket?"

She gave it to him and kissed his hand as she gave it. Matt felt like he had been struck by a thunderbolt and only found his speech after a little while.

"You stay where you are, Eileen, and make yourself at home. I'll be back with your suitcase in two shakes of a lambs tail."

Matt Ryan went out the door like a man inspired. There was a picture of the Virgin of the Rocks over the mantlepiece which Matt's mother had given him to keep him safe from harm, many years before. Eileen looked at it and fell to the floor on her knees. For the first time in a long time a little prayer flooded into the ocean of her thinking "O Mary conceived without sin, pray for us who have recourse to thee."

SHE WAS A WHORE IN HER HEART

Chief of Police, Pearson, had had investigations going forward since Jack Boland sent him that unsigned letter. A letter, which indicated that his second in command Inspector Knowlsworth, was operating an illegal force of three Policemen and one woman inside the legal, Government constituted Marylebone Police Force. And he aptly likened this development to a 'Trojan Horse." The allegations had proved to be well founded.

Undercover detectives were brought in and no effort or money was spared to establish the extent of criminal conspiracy that had been perpetrated. Well might one of the gang of four have answered Knowlsworth's question: "How much does the Chief know?" with, "Plenty if you ask me." The fact was, at this stage there was nothing the Chief of Police didn't know, and he had concrete evidence to prove it into the bargain.

On the night that the renegade Knowlsworth met with the informer Holden they were both seen and heard. They erroneously supposed that because they were meeting in an out of the way public house called 'The Gluepot' in Camden Town, they were safe from eagle eyes and asses ears. An undercover agent in the guise of an Irish Navvy followed Knowlsworth to the pub and was sitting within earshot when Holden told Knowlsworth how he hoped to dispose of Nancy Blackmore.

And when Knowlsworth finally told Holden that if he didn't keep his mouth shut after the event that he would personally shut it for him for good, Knowlsworth's fate was sealed.

From then on it was only a matter of time before the Chief arrested him and his dastardly crew.

As stated previously, that ignominious gang consisted of three men and one woman. And strange though it may seem Jack Boland knew this very dangerous woman well. Her name was Linda Lovelace and her forte was the number of men she had known intimately.

She was a whore in her heart. Notwithstanding all that Jack Boland was on first name terms with Linda Lovelace, he had even been seen to buy her a drink and once or twice was seen in conversation with her.

This rather out of character connection could perhaps be explained by reading part of W.H. Auden's poem:

Every evening the oddest collection
Of characters crowd this Inn:
Here a face from the farm, it's frankness yearning
For corruption and riches; there
A gaunt gospel whom grinning miners
Will stone to death by a dolmen;
Heroes confess to whores, detectives,
Chat or play chess with thieves.

People will court danger for the thrill of it. Some psychoanalysts even claim that many sportsmen who engage in dangerous sports such as speed car racing, deep sea diving, lion taming, highwire trapeze without a net, etc, etc, all have a death wish. We are what we say and do, in the final analysis.

Linda Lovelace knew that Jack Boland had links with the I.R.A.

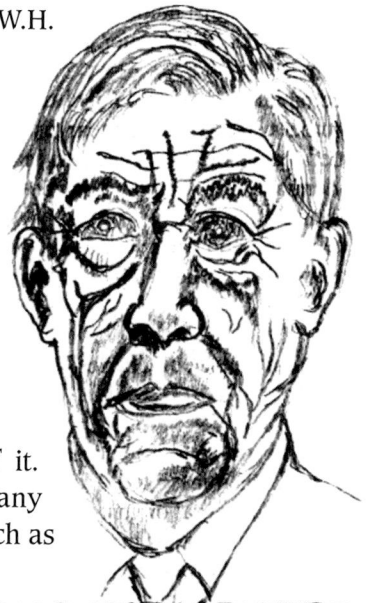

GONG TORMENTED FAC
OF W.H.AUDEN
BY SEAN KENNY

So did Knowlsworth and likewise the Chief of Police. And Boland knew that they knew. From spirited pillow talk that needless to say did not surface from Boland's bed, Linda Lovelace discovered that it was Boland who tipped off the Chief of Police about Knowlsworth's dissident gang of four, of which she herself was one.

This vital information she conveyed to Knowlsworth post haste. He roared like a castrated horse. "I'll get that bastard Boland if it is the last thing I do." She also extracted by courtesy of her 'boudoir' that Boland wanted out of the I.R.A. because he was planning to get married to the wealthy young widow, Rosie Taylor nee Keegan.

But what she didn't know was that the proposal had broken down and it was Allen Hunt who would be her next husband.

EGG ON HIS WRITTEN SUBMISSIONS

Early on the morning after the explosion at the old house in the cul-de-sac laneway off Amberley Road, Detective Inspector Knowlsworth, arose early. He had completed two written statements on the 'Explosion' and the 'Car Crash' before going to bed.

He glanced over them now as he ate his soft-boiled egg and well-buttered toast. But this morning in his anxiety to exhibit his expertise in handling the written as well as the oral submissions, he under boiled his egg and over buttered his toast.

As he brought a spoonful of trembling egg towards his savage mouth, three earsplitting knocks on his front door rang out. Knowlsworth nearly jumped out of his skin. He let fall the shivering spoonful of egg onto his written submissions. In an effort to prevent the drop he knocked over his cup of tea. Three more thunder claps were visited upon the door in rapid succession.

Like a mad bull Knowlsworth ran at the door. "What the effin hell do you think you're doing?" he asked the one of the gang of four, that he had spoken with the previous day after the explosion.

"Lovelace is being questioned by the 'Top Brass' at Headquarters. The other two have disappeared."

"What do you mean disappeared? They're not two effin Houdinis are they?"

"I've searched all over for them. I'm wondering have they been arrested and held under lock and key at another station, – like pigeons caught in a cat house."

"They have got nothing tangible on any of us. Any evidence they might produce would be circumstantial at best. They have nothing that would stand up in a court of Law. Now get to hell out of here and remember to hold your tongue, or I will cut it out of your head."

"I think it would be best if you were to tell Pat we are getting married, Allen – don't you?"

"Yes I do, Rosie and I think we should invite him along to our little engagement party."

"I think that's a splendid idea."

"And wouldn't it be nice Rosie if you, Patricia and I were to have a day out on the town by way of celebration?"

"Oh I'd love that Allen, and I know that Patricia would be beside herself with happiness. Where do you suggest we go?"

"Well we could visit places of historical interest. But especially I was thinking of Madam Tussauds."

"And we could have a meal at the Savoy afterwards."

"I think it might be a little rich for my blood, though Peggy O'Shea and I did have a meal there once.

"That will be my treat Allen, if you wouldn't mind."

"That would be fine Rosie."

"There's only one thing Allen, we couldn't take Patricia to see the 'Chamber of Horrors,' It would give her nightmares. I'm told it is gruesome."

"Yes it is Rosie though I would like to see it myself."

"That doesn't pose a problem. I can take her to see a less robust part of the exhibition, Allen. When can we go?"

"Wednesday next. I've got Wednesday off and a half day Thursday. In the meantime I'll tell Pat our good news and invite him to our private engagement party."

"Things are beginning to take shape at last," Rosie thought to herself; "Nothing can go wrong now."

EPISODE THIRTY-NINE

AS WELCOME AS THE FAIR DAY TO THE PUBS IN FRIARY STEET
AN ENGAGEMENT PARTY
ONE OF THE TWO VOLUNTEERS
THE LODGER

AS WELCOME AS THE FAIR DAY TO THE PUBS IN FRIARY STREET

Allen Hunt was serving behind the counter in The Poppy on the Edgware Road when his brother Pat, entered the Public Bar. "And how are you brother? Thanks for coming over. You are as welcome as the flowers in May."

"I'm very well brother, thank you. You know there was an old saying in Kilkenny years ago that went like this, "you're as welcome as the Fair Day to the pubs in Friary Street."

"But surely it wasn't only the pubs in Friary Street that made hay on the Fair Day? There was Sean Byrnes of the Green, Jack O'Connells and Larry Dowlings of Blackmill Street, Pat Gleeson's of Walkin Street, Brennan and Woodcock's of Walkin Street and New Street, Morrisseys Groceries and Provisions Friary Street and Denis Dohertys Public House at the top of Friary Street and Parnell Street."

"And in Dohertys Yard at the back of the Dublin and Kilkenny Road Service they had stallions standing to serve the mares for an agreed fee."

"The Fair Green was never big enough to contain the entire Fair. It always spilled over onto the streets all around the Green. Especially onto the Jail Road, Walkin Street and Friary Street. With the horses and cattle covering every inch of asphalt."

"And the pubs packed tighter than a sixpenny piece caught in the fist of a schoolboy going to the fourpenny matinee on a Sunday with twopence left over for sweets. With all the streets thronged till you'd think they were all going to the railway station to welcome home yet another victorious, Kilkenny All Ireland Hurling Team." "And Tom Ryans Newsagency, selling cigarettes, confectionery and sweets as well as Dinners and Teas."

"And who was it owned the Central Stores down past the Friary Chapel, and if my memory serves me right the same family owned the Bridge House at Johns Bridge."

223

"Those two houses were owned by a man named William Tynan. Both had a grocery and bar. And next door to Tynan's at 3 Friary Street was Andrew Ryan's public house. They also sold Teas and Dinners."

"It seems that George Bernard Shaw was right then."

"Why, what was it he said?"

"He said the further an Irishman travels from Ireland the more Irish he becomes. That is to say, the further he goes from home the more his roots dig into Irish soil."

"I'd believe that all right. Father used to say an Irishman's biggest cross was that he suffered from a long memory. That would seem to suggest the Irish had painful memories."

"They had hard times that's for sure. But they never lost heart, even after the famine."

"How long has it been since you went home to see Mam and Dad, Pat?"

"Well, it's been a long time I know, but I am definitely going home before the end of this year. But I hope you didn't invite me over here to give me a lecture."

"No, not at all Pat, just asking by the way." And then in an attempt to get away from Allen's probing questions, Pat quickly asked: "So what's the good news brother? You did phone when I was out yesterday, saying, you wanted to see me about something very important – didn't you?"

"Yes I did Pat, and thanks again for coming over. Before you die of thirst though what are you having to drink?"

"That depends on what you are going to tell me. If it's good news I'll have a ball of malt and if it's bad news I'll have a double."

"Then it's a ball of malt and a chaser, because the news is great. I hope you will be pleased Pat."

Allen looked at Pat like Socrates looked at Plato after asking him: "What is friendship?"

"Right then," Pat said, "hit me with it."

Allen swallowed hard, like he had consumed an Albatross and was finding it difficult to keep down.

AN ENGAGEMENT PARTY

"I asked Rosie to marry me, Pat. Happily she said yes and we are getting engaged on Wednesday next. Now tell me brother how does all this lye with you?" Without hesitation Pat answered Allen's anxious question. "I couldn't be happier for the two of you, brother. Good luck and full speed ahead."

"That's decent of you Pat. You know I'll take good care of Rosie and Patricia!"

"Of course I do. Things couldn't have worked out better as far as I am concerned." He paused for a moment. "You may or may not be aware but Peggy O'Shea and I have been going out together on and off for some time now."

"Yes I heard and I can only hope that the two of you will be as happy as Rosie and I are. Bar staff are better than Barbers when it comes to news or gossip. Nothing escapes that lives and breaths. And a little guzzling always helps to loosen the tongue. But like I said Pat we are getting engaged on Wednesday and the three of us are going out for the day on the town. I'm taking them to Madame Tussaud's and the London Planetarium and later to the Savoy for lunch."

"O brother that will cost you. You didn't win the Irish Hospitals Sweepstakes by any chance?"

"As a matter of fact, Rosie insists the meal at the Savoy will be on her. But this is the main reason for asking you to come over today. We will be having a little party to celebrate our engagement at Rosie's house in Knightsbridge on Wednesday night, starting about 8 p.m. It will be for family only. Will you come and bring Peggy with you. Rosie and I have spoken about it and we would be delighted to have you both. What do you think, Pat?"

"I'd consider it a privilege, Allen."

"Then that's settled. Rosie wants to keep the whole affair private. There will be just the four of us and Patricia of course. I don't suppose you are aware that Jack Boland, asked Rosie to marry him?"

"She could have done worse. He's a fine fellow you know. But I'm glad that it's you she's marrying, for everybody's sake and that includes Patricia."

ONE OF THE TWO VOLUNTEERS

A few day after the operation to amputate both legs, the Chief Surgeon was obliged to tell Larry Holden that his spinal cord had been severed in the accident. Holden rendered half crazy by this horrific news, screamed like a stuck pig. Later after being injected with morphine to calm him down his mind wandered back to what Knowlsworth had said to him the last time they met at 'The Gluepot' in Camden town. "Keep your mouth shut or I will shut it for you for good." "He didn't manage to shut my mouth but as sure as sin 'twas he cut off my legs and he slashed my spinal cord. I feel like Lucifer cast out of heaven and will now annihilate him with the only weapon left to me to destroy him; my tongue." He sent for Detective Inspector Pearson, Chief of Police at Marylebone Station. With all the evidence of corruption and treason committed by Knowlsworth and his infamous gang of four on the desk in front of him, the Chief went to question Larry Holden. Knowing full well that Holden was about to rat on Knowlsworth and company, he brought with him a stenographer. The Chief knew that the evidence he would extract from Holden would copperfasten the fate of his arch-rival. The evidence would in the first place warrant the Court-martial of Knowlsworth and his despicable crew and later would reinforce the case against them for aiding and abetting in the attempted murder of Nancy Blackmore and Larry Holden himself.

And Linda Lovelace had been singing like a canary since she was arrested, and detained for her own good, they told her. In the hope of making a deal and securing for herself a reduced sentence, she would give the Chief of Police a sensational piece of information.

"Will you give me a guarantee of immunity if I give you information that will rock the foundations of justice emanating from your subversive intelligence?" she asked.

"I cannot now give you immunity. Not after officers from an outside jurisdiction have been brought into the investigation. I can however, give you a guarantee of a reduced sentence, depending on how valuable your information turns out to be." It was the best she could hope for now. She told him "The Irish born one of the two Volunteers is acting as a double agent."

In a siren screaming ambulance the near dead Nancy Blackmore was taken at break-neck speed to Maida Vale Hospital for Nervous Diseases. The two paramedics never stopped for a second with their devoted efforts, to ensure that her heart continued to beat and make her as comfortable as was in their power. They cared not whether the victim was a Mary Magdalene or a Florence Nightingale kind of woman. Their only concern was to preserve the life that God had given her and they would move heaven and earth to accomplish that.

Because she was young, physically strong and loved life Nancy Blackmore's health improved rapidly. It was only when she was able to take stock of herself that her world fell in on her. The first degree burns to her hands and legs were unbearable. But when she eventually got hold of a mirror and saw for the first time the awful disfigurement of her face, her mind disintegrated. Like a plate glass shop window bombarded with sticks and stones by looters during a riot, first it cracked, then shattered and fell to the ground in pieces. Like Humpty Dumpty it could never be fixed again. It was beyond all repair. The observation made earlier by one of the Firemen, had sadly proved to be prophetic. He had said, 'If she lives poor sod she will spend the rest of her life in the 'Looney Bin.'" And so she did.

THE LODGER

The tall thirty five-year-old man walked slowly down Montpellier Street, in Knightsbridge. He wore a light brown trench coat and oatenmeal coloured cap. A dark brown pants with a crease that would peel potatoes showed beneath the overcoat, and rust brown shoes shone like mirrors. He carried a smallish suitcase in one hand and a banjo or guitar case in the other. In front of garden No. 33 a discreet wooden sign revealed there were "Rooms to Let. Apply within. No dogs or cats permitted. For respectable persons only, at moderate rates."

The tall well dressed stranger rang the bell. "Good day to you sir. Have you come about the rooms?"

A small elderly woman with a long nose and glasses confronted him. She spoke with a voice like a length of loose galvanise rattling with the wind on the roof of a garden shed.

"Yes I have. And good day to you madam." She noted he spoke with an Irish accent. "Won't you step inside please," and she looked disdainfully at the banjo case. "We do not permit music playing on the premises."

"You can put your mind at ease madam, the fact is I don't even play the instrument myself. It belongs to a friend of mine. I am to deliver it to him a few days from now before he leaves London for foreign parts."

"Oh that's alright then. There are two upstairs rooms available one to the front and one to the back. Won't you come and see which one you prefer."

"I rather like to see the world in motion and hear it's hussle and bussle. I'm neither a great reader nor a writer but like to look at people and things in flux. So without looking at either I can tell you right now I would much prefer the front room."

"If that's your choice it's fine by me. That will be five pounds in advance please. I'll show you to your room. He took a bulging wallet from an inside pocket and slid a mint fresh five-pound note from it. On the landing he stopped and looked out on the back garden. There was a concrete scullery roof about three feet beneath the landing window. At the end of the garden there was a car-road that ran between both rows of houses and out on to another

REV. CHARLES CAVANAGH   PP. VG. DD.
ST. CANICES BY SEÁN KENNY

street. "This is your room" she said. No visitors allowed after 11 p.m. He nodded and smiled as she went back downstairs. He went to the front window and drew back the latch. The upper portion of the window slipped down without too much pressure or noise. Directly in front of No. 33 there was a beautiful four-bedroomed house with a garage. It was standing on a three-acre site and must be worth a small fortune he thought. He knew or thought he knew the people who lived there. He couldn't have been better positioned to accomplish the task ahead.

EPISODE FORTY

VIRGIL NEVER GAVE DANTE BETTER ADVICE
THE RING
MADAME TUSSAUD'S
YOUR LIFE IS IN GREAT DANGER
DEATH BY MISADVENTURE

VIRGIL NEVER GAVE DANTE BETTER ADVICE

Allen Hunt couldn't sleep. A thousand thoughts raced into and out of his ever busy brain. The frenzied activity at Grand Central Station had nothing on him. Neither did the Bradford Weaving Shed with it's thousand automatic Dobcross Looms firing their six thousand shuttles per second, hither and thither. In a thunderous lightning quick clamour they make miles and miles of cloth for millions of people. Allen lay in bed in the upstairs front room of Rosie Taylor nee Keegan's house in Knightsbridge. It was Tuesday night, – the night before Rosie and he were due to become engaged. An over active imagination kept him busy most of the time anyway, but tonight he was busier than an October wind wailing and worrying around the near leafless trees in Blunden's Blackwood. "You guard it by day, and I will guard it by night." The story goes that Sir William said this to his son before he died.

Yet, Allen felt euphoric. His thoughts did battle with each other to come before him and plead their case for an audience. And to think he had almost let it all slip away from him. He would have too, had it not been for Ivor Davies, good advice: "At least phone her, Allen, and ask her where you stand. If you don't you may regret it for the rest of your life." Virgil never gave Dante better advice. How right he had been!

A false sense of pride can cause people to make terrible blunders. Fortune and her false wheel can often confound us. Sins committed from the neck up, make up ninety nine percent of the population of hell. And the tongue can be a terrible tyrant.

But all is well now, thanks to Ivor and his timely intervention. It was all the stranger too because of late Allen was beginning to turn against Ivor because of his persistent and hateful attitude towards Eileen Murphy. She didn't have to return the £350, according to the Court Ruling, but she did.

And she had only retrieved £285. Her brother must have given her the £65 to make up the original amount. She could have done a disappearing act and set herself up elsewhere with all that money. It was this inherent act of decency that had influenced Matt Ryan's decision to offer her a job. And isn't life stranger than fiction? Now, see how things have turned out: "Can I talk to you for a moment Allen?" Eileen had said to him during the day. "Matt Ryan has asked me to marry him and I said yes. What do you think?"

"I think your are absolutely right. You have to grab an opportunity like that with both hands Eileen. The truth is you are made for each other."

"Thanks for that vote of confidence Allen. My brother said from the start that you were a decent man. Did you hear that Ivor is going to Chelsea. He got the job as Governor at the King's Arms, on Matt's recommendation. Matt got the news by phone just a few minutes ago and told Ivor. He's over the moon."

"That's marvelous. We all seem to be panning out well. There must be someone praying for the lot of us."

"It must be our parents, Allen. I don't mean to pry but will you be staying on here after Rosie and yourself get married? I can only tell you that Matt thinks you're the greatest. He said it's a shame to see such talent wasted, serving drink."

"It's nice of him to say so, but there are far better men than me performing lesser duties. I don't think it matters too much what a man does, provided he does the best he can with what he's got."

Eileen looked at him with a glazed eye like an old mother seeing her son return from war without as much as a bruise or a black eye on him.

"Will I ever sleep tonight" Allen asked himself, as the old woman carrying her cardboard house on her back came and stood before him. She who used to erect her house every night in the blind alley at the back of Whighteleys of Bayswater. Why was she coming to present herself now? Once she said to him after he had given her a ten-shilling note: "I wasn't always like this you know. My mother loved me dearly and told me songs and stories. And with the best imagination in the world, one could never dream how strange and how sad things can turn out in the end. Take care sir, and watch your back." Was this a portend of good or evil?

Allen jumped out of bed. He was furious with himself because he couldn't sleep. He went to the window and drew back the curtains. It was a beautiful moonlit night. He glanced at his watch. It was 12.25 a.m. A blood red August moon hung high up in the sky like a Chinese lantern. It was so peaceful. He went closer to the window. There was very little traffic travelling along Mountpellier Street. The street lighting cast a ghostly shade of pale yellow over everything. He looked at his hands they seemed bloodless. In the house directly opposite there was someone sitting in the upstairs front room window.

The red, glow of a cigarette could be seen as it waxed and waned in the mouth of the smoker. Was he a poet perhaps, putting words together in the solitude of the night? Or maybe he was still watching and waiting for the return of a loved one with whom he had quarreled years before. Who could tell?

THE RING

At seven o'clock a.m. on that memorable Wednesday morning the alarm clock rang out louder than Saint Mary's Cathedral bell, as it called the people to first mass in Kilkenny City. Allen couldn't remember when he had been so happy. He felt like a child jumping out of bed on a Christmas morning. Today was the day he would remember for the rest of his life. He knew that Rosie loved him and he loved her more than life itself. And like an angel of hope Patricia forged a link of gold between them. Allen asked himself if anyone had a right to so much happiness? Then a voice called out: "Are you out of bed Allen? Do you know the day that's in it, love? I'm going downstairs to get the breakfast ready. Show a leg man."

"Yes, I'm out of bed love and coming down right now." As he descended the stairs another voice rose up from the deepest part of the red pond in his heart. "It is every good man's right to hope and love and glory. Length of days is of no consequence." Was this the poet's subconscious knowledge in advance?

After the three of them had eaten breakfast they sat looking at each other all smiles. Allen took from his pocket a tiny black box. It measured about two by two cubic inches and was covered with black satin. He put it on the table in front of Rosie. She opened the stiff hard lid slowly. Her eyes glowed when she looked inside. It was a solitaire diamond Engagement ring. Tears of happiness glistened in Rosie's eyes: "O Allen, my love, it's beautiful. Thank you, thank you."

"You are welcome love. I'm glad you like it."

"Can I see it Mammy, please?" Patricia pleaded.

"Of course you can dear and Rosie deftly slipped her own rings off while giving Patricia her new Engagement Ring. She got up from the table and went to the dresser where she deposited her old rings in an old-fashioned beer-mug shaped like a man with a three cornered hat and known as a Toby-jug. The old consigned to the past, – the new erected into the present. From the moment she put the ring back on Rosie kept turning it like a water-wheel turning in a Mill-Race.

Patricia skipped between her Mother Rosie and her uncle Allen holding hands as they walked to Knightsbridge Underground Station on the Piccadilly Line. Hyde Park Corner came first and Green Park next where they changed to the Jubilee Line going north. The first stop was Bond Street and the second was their destination, Baker Street. In fact Baker Street Station is next door to Madame Tussaud's Wax Museum.

MADAME TUSSAUD'S

This world famous Museum is at the Bazaar, a building near Portman Square in Baker Street, London. It was at the age of 74 years that Marie Tussaud decided to permanently settle her travelling exhibition of wax figures. Previous to that she had spent thirty-three years touring all the cities of England, Scotland and Wales. She did likewise in Ireland, after surviving a shipwreck in 1822.

Madam Tussaud was born Marie Grosholtz in 1761 in Strasbourg, France. Her father who was a German soldier, died before she was born. Financial difficulties forced her widowed mother to move with her baby girl, to Berne in Switzerland. There she got work as a housekeeper for a German doctor named Philippe Curtius. This man was a very talented modeller in wax and soon after moving to Paris he became famous when he opened an exhibition of life-size wax figures. The eager young Marie became his pupil and

at the age of sixteen years she was competent enough to model the genius Francois Marie Arouet whose pseudonym was Voltaire. This philosophical writer, playwright, poet and satirist was one of the most famous men of his day. He was banished three times from Paris and was imprisoned twice between 1716 and 1726 in the Bastille. He became famous or some would say infamous because of his satirical attacks on political and religious leaders. There is a funny story told about Voltaire as he lay on his deathbed. He was asked if at that juncture he would at last renounce the devil? Like lightning he replied: "It's a bit late in the day for that. This is no time to be making new enemies." A few sympathetic priests performed a hasty funeral service before the authorities could refuse him a Christian burial. He was a sceptic to the last.

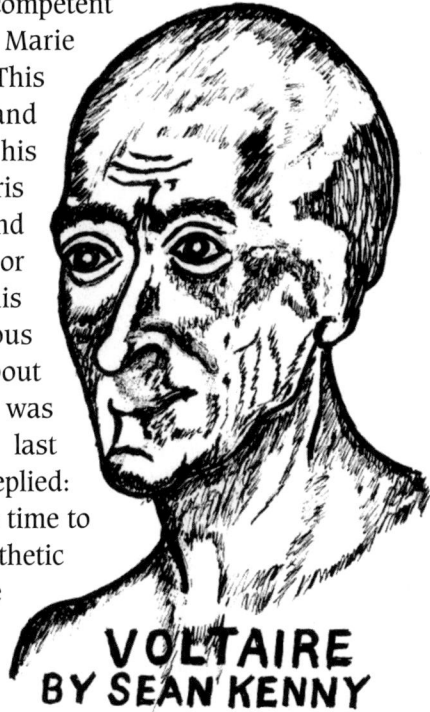

VOLTAIRE BY SEAN KENNY

It is said that Marie Tussaud's model of Voltaire was so life-like that an old friend of his forgot himself while looking at the wax model and began speaking to it: "And what was it that you said to Frederick the Great (King of Prussia) that he told you to go home and never to return, Francois?"

When no answer was forthcoming his friend told the wax effigy "You are as stubborn as pig iron, and I have no doubt but that you will be banished from here next."

YOUR LIFE IS IN GREAT DANGER

"Is that Brannigan and Boland Building Contractors?"

"Yes it is sir. How can I help you?"

"Is Mr. Jack Boland in a position to come to the phone?"

"Who will I say is calling sir?"

"A Mr. Pearson. We are old friends."

"I'll see if he is available sir. Would you hold the line while I check?"

"I will indeed. Thank you."

Jack Boland's secretary left the phone down off the hook and went next door to number nine Lamb Street.

Jack was beaming: "I've just had news from our works manager at Wimbledon that the five hundred houses have been passed as fit for human habitation as of now, by Government inspectors."

"That's marvelous news Mr. Boland. There's a gentleman who wishes to speak to you on the phone. Says he is an old friend of yours, – a Mr. Pearson. What shall I tell him?"

"I'll speak to him right away. Put the call through to here, Mary."

"Thanks for taking the call Mr. Boland. I would not normally conduct business of this nature over the phone but when needs must as they say: the devil drives."

Jack Boland sensed a great urgency in his voice. More than that there was an element of fear lurking beneath the less than casual call.

"Thank you Chief of Police. You are welcome and what can I do for you?"

"Would you be kind enough to come and see me at my office here at Marylebone Police Station as soon as possible. News of the utmost importance has just come into my possession. If it is true and I fear that it is, you had better watch how you go. I am sending a squad car out to bring you in. Your life is in great danger."

Detective Inspector Knowlsworth arrived early next morning at Marylebone Police Station with his soiled written submissions under his arm. He was immediately told by the Officer of the Day that his presence was required in the Interview Room by Detective Inspectors Stanley and Bell, in the presence of the Chief of Police.

He was asked to hand over his weapon and his badge of Office and to remain standing.

The Chief then read out to him a list of the charges which would be brought against him including treason, for the setting up of a subversive force within the legitimate Police Force and the attempted murder of Larry Holden, and Nancy Blackmore.

At these charges Knowlsworth snarled like a cornered and wounded wild animal, about to spring. Instead he put out his tongue like a cow licking its nose.

"You Sir, are a disgrace to the Metropolitan Police Force," said Detective Inspector Stanley. "Your treacherous gang of four have all turned informers against you." Detective Inspector Bell got to his feet, his face redder than a boiler ready to burst, and spoke with fiery admonition:

"Firstly, you shall be Court-martialed and then taken to stand trial at The Old Bailey for Treason and Attempted Murder."

DEATH BY MISADVENTURE

"I never told anyone this before; but when I first met Pat, I actually thought he was Allen. And when he didn't seem to recognise me as I walked into 'The Champion' I thought he must be a snob after all. It was only as I was leaving and feeling like a fool that I found out he was Allen's look-a-like brother," Peggy O'Shea told them during the Engagement Party.

"Weren't you the lucky woman," Pat quipped, giving everyone a laugh. And Patricia joined in the fun of laughter for laughter's sake. And to be sure Rosie proudly showed them her ring.

As Rosie and Peggy turned their conversation towards the female point of view, helped by the aspiring feminist Patricia, Allen and Pat went out onto the front porch for a manly chat.

The thirty-five year old Irish man sitting in the upstairs window directly opposite got out of his chair. He pulled his guitar case from under the bed and opened it. It didn't contain an instrument that one could compose music upon. Far from it – it was a breaker not a maker.

The instrument inside was lethal. He quickly assembled the two-part high velocity telescopic rifle.

"Wouldn't it be nice if we could all go home to Kilkenny City before Christmas and see Mam and Dad," Allen said. That was the last thing he said before a shot rang out. The thump of the bullet against his chest caused him to gulp in air and then he fell to the ground. "O Christ I have been shot, Pat." Pat fell to his knees beside him. "O Jesus Christ Allen where have you been hit?"

He couldn't tell if Allen had answered him or not because Rosie and Peggy and Patricia came running out onto the porch screaming their heads off. "Jesus Mary and Joseph what happened Pat?" Rosie screamed as she too fell to her knees beside him. "He has been shot. As best as I can tell it came from the house across the road. Phone for an ambulance and a priest, quick Rosie. And get the police." Rosie ran back into the house. Patricia was hysterical. "Take Patricia inside, Peggy," Pat pleaded.

Blood and tears flooded Allen's eyes until Pat knew he must be near sightless. His own stinging tears, flowing like acid rain were blinding him too.

And then Pat thought he saw their mother and father standing nearby as he heard Allen say in a gurgling far off voice: "Look Pat, it's mam and dad".

And there they were, smiling as he had always remembered them. He could see they were talking to Allen, only he couldn't hear what they were saying. But Allen was listening intently and briefly nodded his head before another spurt of blood escaped from the wound in his chest. Pat's lap was soaking with thick warm blood, some of which flowed down into his shoes. Allen was trying to focus on Pat and to say something to him.

His mouth was wide open and he was gasping for breath. Pat was afraid to touch his face for fear he might halt his breathing. Then with a super-human effort, Allen lifted his right hand. His lips quivered in an attempt to speak. Pat took hold of Allen's raised hand as he spoke his last words: "Goodbye Pat. Take care of Rosie, Patricia and Peggy. Tell mam and dad I love them too". Pat felt Allen's grasp tighten: "Stop the war, Pat, – enough killing. Make peace Pat". And as his jaw relaxed and his mouth closed tight, his grip let go. He smiled faintly just before the deadly tattoo struck up in his throat. Pat knew it was the rattle of death. The great goodness that had lived inside him all his life now flowed out from him like a shining ray of hope. Even in death, Allen was magnanimous.

"O, Merciful Jesus, is he gone Pat?," asked a distraught Rosie. "Allen has left us," Pat said, not having the heart to say another word.

⧼⧽

THE END

⧼⧽

City Status

PROLOGUE

MY ears have grown long with listening, long as an ass's ears. I have heard all the sounds that sadness breaks upon the gong smitten world and from day-break to night-fall commemorate lifes mystery of suffering. From the moaning worlds' despair to its running sore of pain, I have adhered faithfully. Never once I ran to hide. Nor did I turn aside, to escape the blows.

Time has taught me to be patient. To cast my net and wait, the length of the longest day – without winning. To be silent even in the company of buffoons, to be all ears and lipless. Not to follow fame but to seek the consolation of the common place. To shun the bright lights and record the shadows that cross the world's evening. At every day's end count those cast down and afflicted, those chastised and broken and those carried off in coffins, count the pebbles on the sea shore, 'tis all the same. Yet never despair nor give up the chase, but be fixed in the hope that one day your caterpillar form will turn butterfly and soar, – if only when you die.

Some one asked if I would attempt to make a poem, saying, "I read something belonging to you somewhere, once upon a time. Why don't you write a new vital verse. A string of whole words and stretch them across the gap of a dozen years. Then we might come to know your kidney. Use words that have human shapes and feelings. Words that work and play and love. That put on skirt and trousers to trespass on the busy street. Words that left right and centre the gamut of life's events. That tell how a little effort merits much reward. Showing man's thoughts with their bee-hive goings and comings. His wingless diablements. His little flowers of knowledge side by side with the piss-a-beds of ignorance. The sunny tasks, the heavy burdens, the minute parts of accomplishment and the recurring defeats. From the utterance of a fart to the high talk of kings."

But I must settle for less and not aim my dull and unwieldy arrow at the moon. For our desires are the corner stones of our existance and to temper them to the measure that best fits our skill is the only hope of contentment. At birth, the nymphs of fate may hew at the future with wood chisel in craftful carvings or hack with blunt axe the woods of mere existence. And there are some fools like me who go with billhook in hand against the forest.

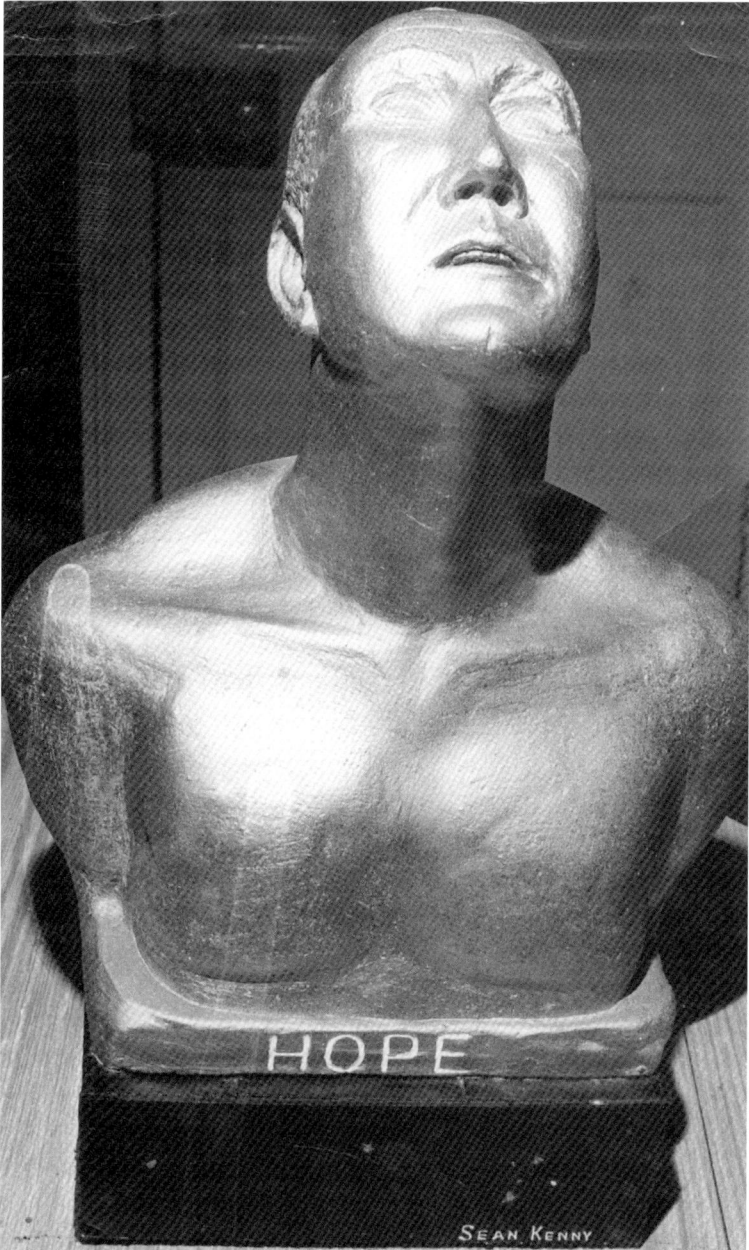

"CITY STATUS": WHAT WE THINK

HAVING read Minister Dempsey's letter to Deputy Aylward, I take it that he doesn't like it when we stand up and fight. Obviously he would much prefer that we would lie down like sheep and silently swallow his dose of Local Government Medicine even if it chokes us. We are not sick but we are thoroughly disgusted with his double talk. On the one hand he freely admits that Kilkenny, is known as a city at home and abroad. "Everyone calls it a city. I call it a city myself." Then on the other hand he says, "But strictly speaking, it never was, and never will be a city." A little later he thinks he might soften his last statement with this piece of gratuity; "but the people can call it a city if they want to". Please don't insult us with your condescending, alternatives, Minister.

In another observation he said the people of Kilkenny were behaving in a 'childish' manner concerning the dismissal of their city status. Believe me Minister there is nothing 'childish' about our concern for our cities status. It is a subject of great importance to every man, woman and child that lives and breathes in the Marble City.

"When I was a child, I thought like a child, and spoke like a child. But now I'm a man and I think like a man and I speak like a man". And I'll vote like a man also. The people of Kilkenny demand their rightful positive place amongst the cities of Ireland. Not content with that, the Minister then goes on to complain about out letters to the Newspaper Media with this unrealistic observation; "this is not the best way of doing business". What would he have us do-take up arms? One would have thought that seeking to right ones wrongs through the medium of the "Press" was by far the best way to achieve success. It has been the method adopted by civilized people throughout the ages. In any event this is not simply 'business'. Kilkenny city status is a deadly serious matter for the people of Kilkenny. It is a case of justice being done. The recognition and awarding of what is due.

The definition of "Justice" goes hand in hand with Plato's ideal city. I believe it was he who said that "justice" is done when every one minds his own affairs. No man should be put in a position to effect major social changes with complete disregard for the suffering inflicted. The State should be the Servant of the citizens, rather than the reverse.

When I wrote to the papers recently concerning the Charter of James 1st, I pointed out that Kilkenny had as a result, been a CITY for 290 years before that notorious Local Government Bill of 1898 had been enacted. A Bill which seems to me in Kilkenny's case at least, to be a classical example of Reductio ad Absurdum. Nevertheless, that Bill did not extirpate Kilkenny's status. It would have taken a PLEBISCITE to accomplish that. That's the first part. The second part is this; in the same letter I pointed out the irrefutable maxim, "Custom is Law". I ask you, does it take more than 290 years usage to become a custom? It was Herodotus, a Greek Historian (c485-c431) who quoted Pindar a Greek Poet (c518-c438). Saying: "Custom is King of all". This is a fundamental truth and is upheld in Universal Law.

Remember also that by the majority agreement of our people, Ireland in its wisdom declared that Kilkenny City should be the seat of the Confederate Parliament of all Ireland in 1642. That was only 33 years after the Charter. Previous to that Seventeen Parliaments were held here. Why do you think that was? Was it because we were a backward and uncivilized people – a grotty little TOWN? I think not.

History has proven otherwise. We were the Capital of Ireland from 1642 to 1649. Consult your History of Ireland book.

It was once said of George Bernard Shaw that, "he did not know his Ireland". Perhaps it could be said that Minister Dempsey does not know his Kilkenny.

The people of Kilkenny know their rights. They know where they came from and where they are going to. They also know they are free to exercise their right as an ancient and historical city, to extol their past, to protect their present, and to safeguard their future.

JUSTICE SHALL BE DONE

Kilkenny City by the Silvery Nore, Once capital of our Land.
We will fight for your status like Owen Roe
The Ballot-Box too we have planned
We will sweep out all who would plan our fall
From Dail Eireann down to the sea.
They'll be welcome no more to knock on our door
They'll be beggared, believe you me.
And truth will conquer the lie at last, As 'round in circles they will run,
When 'right' meets the light of Destiny, Then 'justice' shall be done.

IT WAS, IT IS AND ALWAYS WILL BE, KILKENNY CITY BY THE NORE

PERHAPS the best way to begin is to point out Kilkenny's antiquity and the role it played in the many developments of the Irish Nation. One thing is certain, Kilkenny's involvement with the onward March of our nation has been written with indelible ink across the pages of History.

Kilkenny's antiquity goes back to a time before St. Patrick came to Ireland in 432AD. Our own St. Kieran preached the Gospel of Christ to his own people, the Ossorians, twenty years before St. Patrick arrived. Kieran was the "First Born of the Irish Saints" and founded the first Apostolic see in Ireland, here in Ossory. The first Christian Temple raised in Ireland was Kieran's Church at the back of Kytelers Inn, in St. Kierans Street.

After St. Kieran, came the holyman who gave his name to Kilkenny, St. Canice or Kenny. He was born in Glengiven in Derry in the year 514AD. Kilkenny, simply translated means Church of Kenny or Canice. At first, Canice worshipped at Aghaboe and later came to Kilkenny where he built his wooden church on the hill above Irishtown. Today St. Canices beautiful Cathedral stands in Gothic splendour there. Prior to the Anglo-Norman invasion there were four parochial churches in Kilkenny; St. Kenny's, St. Patrick's, St. Mel's and St. Rioc's. St. Kenny's was the Cathedral church of the diocese of Ossory.

CHARTER BY JAMES I

In the fateful year of 1609, James I gave to Kilkenny, a Charter that conferred upon it the status of CITY. James I was the only son of Mary Queen of Scots and Henry Stuart who was Lord Darnley. When he (James I) succeeded Eliz. I as King of England, he had already ruled upon the throne of Scotland for 36 years. He was a man of many humours and firmly believed in the "Divine Right of Kings". At one time some of his staunch supporters claimed that a Coven of witches had provoked a storm in the Firth of Forth, designed to drown the King and his bride, Princess Ann of Denmark. Nevertheless the Charter stands and no Legislation was ever enacted to extirpate it.

Since Kilkenny was erected to the status of city, de jure, it has long since grown into a city, de facto.

But what are the requirements to become a city? The old definition used to be; a large town with a Cathedral. Well, Kilkenny has certainly grown into a very large town and it has two Cathedrals, no less and a magnificent Castle high above Spencer's Stubborn Nore, a royal charter and more, much more. Kilkenny has the AIR of a city – the character of a city.

It has been recognized for centuries at home and abroad as the Marble City. This is precisely because of the beautiful stone buildings, built with Kilkenny Limestone, mostly in Parliament Street, High Street, the Parade, Patrick Street and John Street. Proportionally, no other city in Ireland had as many examples of early stone buildings.

Still speaking about the air and character of a city, Kilkenny is rich in its ancient records and documents, dating back half a millennium. From the Ormond Deeds to the Histories of Dr, David Rothe (Bishop of Ossory) and from the writings of Richard Stanihurst which are part of the Holinshed Chronicles. Raphael Holinshed was an English Historian whose Chronicles we are told were a source for reading by the Bard of Avon; Wm. Shakespeare.

CITY OF THE CONFEDERATION

On 10th May 1642, one of the greatest events in the history of Ireland was set in motion here in Kilkenny City. Under the direction of Dr. David Rothe, Bishop of Ossory, a General Assembly was formed and this city became the seat of the Confederate Parliament of all Ireland. A Supreme Council was elected that consisted of twenty four members, six from each province. Lord Mount Garret was elected President. Patrick Darcy became Lord Chancellor of the House of Peers and Nicholas Plunkett was elected as Speaker for the General Assembly.

Four armies were raised, one for each province. Owen Roe O'Neill having arrived from Spain with one hundred officers was made commander in chief, of the four, but took command of the Ulster Army. The Leinster Army was given to Preston, Munster went to Barry and Connaught went to Burke.

A munitions' factory was built to provide weapons and powder for the four armies. A mint was established to coin money.

A Printing Works was set up to publish the Parliamentary Manifestoes. These were sent to Mallin and Mizen Head to Dublin and Galway Bay, and all destinations within.

At that time Kilkenny was recognized not only as a city but as the Capital of Ireland, by France, Spain, the Netherlands and Italy.

There was an exchange of "Intelligence's" and Ministers of State and Ambassadors visited and sat in Parliament here.

And now Minister Dempsey tells us we are no longer a city. With one stroke of his magic pen he will return us all to townies. I don't think so. He quotes a Local Government act of 1898, but that act did not dispute or extirpate the 1609 Charter. At that time Kilkenny had been a city for exactly 290 years. Neither did the act dissolve the ancient principle, "Custom is law", which is a fundamental truth and is upheld internationally. Coupled with that is our status as Capital and Seat of the Confederate Parliament of Ireland.

Finally, I'd like to tell all the Politicians of Ireland, that; any government that attempts to preside over the abolition of Kilkeny's City Status will be committing nothing short of political suicide.

P.S. I wonder if Minister Dempsey is aware what the founder of the Fianna Fail party, Eamon de Valera, said after he had been given the freedom of the City of Kilkenny? He said he was proud and honoured to be given the freedom of such an Ancient and Historical city. You flung that back in his face, mister.

I'LL SING YOU A KILKENNY BALLAD

I'LL SING YOU A KILKENNY BALLAD
by Sean Kenny

I'll sing you a Kilkenny Ballad
of our fame and fortunes of old.
When the sons and daughters of Ossory
Were true and wise and bold.
In this ancient Kingdom of Aengus
Founded, One hundred and eighty A.D.
He ruled with the might of an Emperor
Over all that the eye could see.
Later came Diarmuid Mac Carroll,
That proud and passionate King
Held Court in Kilkenny Castle
He made plowshares and swordblades ring.
Another was Donnchad Mac Kellach
Distinguished Chieftain of our Race
The King of culture, they called him
And the greatest of the great.

I'll sing you a Kilkenny Ballad
Of a Charter in 1609,
When James 1st, House of Stewart,
Made a City of our town.
Proudly we carried that honour,

Down through the centuries four.
Only inland City in Ireland,
Splendid Kilkenny, by the Nore.
Where Castles, Cathedrals and Colleges,
Still stand as in days of old,
When matchless harps made music.
And peerless Poets well told,
Of brave deeds done in battle
About feats of strength and of speed
Legends of Love, Hope and Glory,
Trusting in God, for our needs.
I'll sing you a Kilkenny Ballad
Sixteen hundred and forty two
In this City, the pride of all Ireland
In Government sat, to pursue.
For its people, Rights of Conscience,
Civil Liberties for big and small,
For Catholic, Protestant and Dissenter
Freedom, of expression for all.

In Kilkenny the Capital City,
Our Houses of Parliament made
The Laws for the island of Ireland
And four fierce armies were raised.
That gallant warrior, Owen Roe O'Neill.
Commanded the Ulster Brigade,
Burke took charge of the Connaught men
And Barry led the Munster braves
Preston with an army of 5,000 foot
And 1,000 Horse to the rear
Never an invader in Leinster stood
But perished by sword and in fear
Here we published Manifesto's true
And we minted the Nations coin,
We made deadly arms and ammunition,
And we fought with the heart of the Lion.

It was at Benburb on the 5th June
Our hero Commander Owen Roe
Destroyed fierce Cunninghams Horse and Foot
And annihilated – the – coward , Munro.

It was, the Confederation of Kilkenny
That set Ireland to take her place
Amongst, the great Nations of Europe
Where she stands proudly now, face to face
Oh don't ever forget true Kilkenny men
It's the Marble City forever
Let no man steal what's rightfully ours
We'll let go of our City: Never

Dedicated to the memory of my Father, Bob Kenny, who fought for his Country and respected his peers. Bob was a great Kilkenny man and had a marvellous saying about it: "I love every stick and stone that stands Kilkenny."

Jim Hudson

CHAPTER ONE

JIM HUDSON AT FOX AND GREENHAUGHS

HOW well we all love to recall stories of times long past and tell again colourful tales of characters and places, local as well as national. It is in this manner that 'legends' are born. The Video Shop, which is beside the Horse Slip at John's Bridge, was owned by Jimmy Bateman, one of Kilkenny's most popular sons. This building is scenically situated, with its right side to the bridge across the Nore and its front facing down the quaint old Canal Walk.

Incidentally, by an Act of George II, in 1751, the Commissioners were made into a Corporation for promoting and carrying on an "Inland Navigation in Ireland", and in 1755 the sum of £10,000 was granted by the House of Commons for making the Nore navigable from the City of Kilkenny to the town of Inistioge. There were two further grants of £4,000 each, making a total of £18,000. However that money was never fully accounted for and the scheme was abandoned.

Back to the Video Shop at John's Bridge. Before Jimmy Bateman purchased the premises it was owned by a Miss Mulrooney, who ran it as a fruit, sweet and paper shop for many years.

SNAPSHOT HOUSE

Once upon a time, though, this premises was a 'posh' shop and was known as 'Snapshot House'. During that period it was owned by Fox, Greenhaugh and Co. But after being hammered for a time on the anvil of common communications and gossip, the name was converted into the more colourful and memorable title of 'Fox and Greenhawks'. The proprietors declared themselves to be Specialists in photographic and cinematographic chemistry and composition" – a mouthful, you will agree, and long before the invention: "Say Cheese". And one would be 'taken' sitting or standing, in ornamental attire of homespun clobber.

LEFT FRONT WINDOW

The shop front had two fine windows of plate glass which were rounded at both ends, giving them a mirror-like quality. But the images they threw back were bloated and exaggerated in one position, slim and elongated in another.

In the left front window there was a large hooded studio camera, mounted upon a tripod. At its base a long white cardboard sign boasted of the photographers' near magical powers of portraiture, with these words:

Get a permanent souvenir
of a royal time spent in Kilkenny
Get your photograph taken here
We'll make you look nattier than any.

Nattier, mind you, and not nuttier. Nattier was a French portrait painter after whom the soft azure pigment known as Nattier Blue was named.

All of which made me afterwards see that the photographer at Fox and Greenhawk's was widely awake to the fact that most of us are not photogenic and need more than a little touching-up around the gills, if we are to turn out even half human.

Of course, this does not include those who read me.

RIGHT FRONT WINDOW

Slightly off-centre in the right front window stood a dark-stained oak easel. A large golden-framed portrait of a very good-looking woman was held in its jaws. She was dressed in a black satin dress and wore a diamond choker.

Sitting erect in a sturdy cane armchair, she gazed across John's Bridge towards Dr. Mitchell's house with sustained interest, or so it seemed to me.

I never learned who she was but she must have caught many a man's eye. Around the feet of the easel, in their gold and silver frames, some of the well-heeled fraternity of 'Ye Fair Citie' looked out with an air of great importance at the motley crew.

Behind and above those, another white cardboard message, pinned to a turquoise green curtain, offered this dubious advice:

Bring your sweethearts here
and we shall be looking out for you.

As poor old Jimmy O'Dea used to say "I'd be nervous of that". So would I. Would you?

Extending from the right front of Fox and Greenhawk's there was a long high wall with a footpath at its base which joined up with Dunphy's newspaper and sweet shop as it was then.

The back-warmer wall

THE WALL THAT WAS A BACK WARMER

From October to March, year in and year out, that wall was used as a back warmer. It was a familiar sight to see six, seven or more men standing side by side with their backs to the warm wall in heated conversation.

And you might chance to hear some poorly dressed old-age pensioner enquire from a friend in jest as he stepped onto the footpath: "Is the fire out, Bill?"

"Out, how are ya, an' Jim Hudson after puttin' in a car load of coal from Castlecomer."

JIM HUDSON AT FOX AND GREENHAWKS

Jim Hudson was a big, tall man with a hard hat and a swallowtail coat, which he got as a pension from the parish priest. His coarse homespun trousers contrasted strangely with his above the waist apparel.

Jim was a collier's helper and he lived with his wife and child in a little thatched house near Jame's Green. He had a plausible manner and a ready wit. His movements were awkward in a 'Handy Andy' kind of way and he loved the pint of porter. A light-hearted war of words went on between Jim and the P.P. over alleged monies due for work already done.

But in the interest of fair play it must be said that Jim wasn't always too sure of his ground, on account of the 'bottle'.

And it was often a case of 'right or wrong remain steady'. Jim liked to describe himself as a free agent and could be seen doing a variety of jobs between Monday and the half day Saturday.

Although he was no Michelangelo he was a dab hand with a whitewash brush and if stony broke he would not hesitate to mend walls or build ditches. But it was as a collier's helper that Jim excelled.

Into the bargain, there was more money and less work involved, all because of the 'system'.

THE SYSTEM

The 'system' was Jim's very own brainchild and he had perfected it as time went by. It never failed him and this is how it worked: When a shop-keeper or other well-to-do person bought a cart load of coal from a 'Comer collier, Jim was paid to put it in. In those days the collier would heel up his load outside the shop or house and Jim equipped with shovel and sally basket would carry it inside. And if the collier was a decent man as most of them were, Jim could be paid as much as a florin. Then with the florin put into solitary confinement in the clasped purse, Jim would finger a penny from the corner of his swallowtail coat pocket and hasten up to Dunphy's shop.

CAN SWEETS

In Dunphy's shop Jim would buy a pennyworth of can sweets. Diligently Mrs. Dunphy would count the sweets as she picked them from the can and placed them on the counter. Then she'd fashion a cone shaped paper bag to hold the sweets. Can sweets are the same shape and size as a 'seanblob' and were pale pink in colour and as hard as lumps of anthracite. Because of the scarcity of sugar (among other things) during the Second World War, people used buy them to sweeten their tea, after softening them up with a few blows from a hammer. The latter part was a by the by for your perusal.

In continuation of the 'system'

THE WHISTLER

Standing on top of the heeled up cart load of coal, Jim would fetch a whistle from inside his shirt, where it hung from a piece of cord around his neck.

Inserted in his gob he held it in a vice-like grip between his teeth. The sound was ear splitting as Jim blew on it for all he was worth.

Within minutes four or five young lads could be seen racing like the wind from every direction. It was an understood thing: first on the spot got the job. But those who arrived second, third and fourth were not dismissed empty handed, but were rewarded with a half dozen can sweets for their trouble. And that ingenious devise guaranteed that Jim would never be short of willing hands.

And that's exactly what happened on the day Fox and Greenhawks bought a load of coal from a decent collier from 'Comer. Jim handed over his shovel and sally basket with great decorum to his protege after instructing him not to let as much as one lump of coal fall on the shop floor.

Licking his lips, he then retired to The Bridge House to wet his whistle. It wasn't that Jim was afraid of work. His real fear was that he might die of thirst.

THE BRIDGE HOUSE

Jim called for a drop of the crathur and pint of porter from the Boss and fell into flowing conversation with Georgie Barton. The subject under discussion was how to take trout out of the river without using boat, line, lime, net or spear.

"Maybe they'd jump out for the can sweets if you blew your whistle on John's Bridge" said Georgie with a grin on him as wide as the Nore.

Jim didn't rise to the bait but went on to give an account of how an experienced poacher could catch trout in the hand while tickling them as they rested under the bank of the river after feeding.

That, and other most pressing questions, such as how to sharpen a scythe and skin a rabbit, were debated fully.

BLACK SHIRT

About two hours and five pints later Jim surfaced and went to inspect the work in progress. All that remained to be put in was one or two basketfuls. He slipped a 'kids eye', (threepenny piece), into the lad's hand saying "you've done enough. Away with you". Jim took off his swallowtail coat and rolled up his shirt sleeves. He was the picture of a hard working man.

As he carried the second last basketful through the scullery, didn't Polly Waters, the washerwoman throw her eye on Jim's shirt, which was roughly the colour of a 'black eye'. Looking up from her wooden tub she asked Jim scornfully: "How long is that shirt on you Jim Hudson?"

Jim looked at her with a grin. "Well to be truthful with you Mrs. Waters" says he. "'Tis exactly three inches below me bum". He was unbeatable!

CHAPTER TWO

JIM HUDSON – COAL CARRIER OR RACONTEUR?

JIM HUDSON - COAL CARRIER OR RACONTEUR?

When we last encountered our hero, Jim Hudson the coal-carrier, he was describing with remarkable accuracy just how long his shirt was on him, to the mocking Polly Waters. Polly, you may remember, was washerwoman at 'Fox and Greenhawk's', Photographers, John's Bridge, Kilkenny.

"To be truthful, with you, Mrs. Waters," said he with a grin, "'tis exactly three inches below me bum." Polly let out a screech like a barn-owl and flew in a blind rage out through the open back door. He must have ruffled her feathers quite a lot for she landed like a winged bird in a clump of gooseberries bushes. Jim had made short shift of Polly's sarcasm and was hugging himself with delight.

THE LAST BASKET

Finally, the last basket of coal was filled. Before bringing it in, Jim swept the street with a yard scrub and the footpath he swept with a broom. 'Twas dry work. He licked his chops and swallowed hard.

Then from the corner of his eye he spotted an old adversary approaching in the shape of a tall, emaciated man clad in a soldier's greatcoat and sporting a tartan cap. In a previous escapade Jim had described him as a "pull-through for a rifle." Because of that and the fact that he almost lived in the soldier's greatcoat, Pat Laffin was nicknamed 'Soldier'.

'Soldier', who was as inquistive as a jackdaw, was rounding the corner of A. & T. Piert, Milliners, where St. Kieran street and Rose Inn street meet. Like lightening, the two men made eye contact but broke the circuit just as quickly.

There was no time to lose for the cut and thrust of gladiator verbosity that was now inevitable. "The end is nigh", said 'Soldier', indicating the last basket of coal as he came within ear shot of Jim.

"The dead arose and appeared to many" answered Jim, pointing at 'soldier' who was on his daily visit to his favourite hostelry on the other side of the Bridge for a little liquid nourishment.

"Twon't be long now," insisted 'Soldier' standing his ground.

"That's what the fella said when he cut the dog's tail", asserted Jim confidently. 'Soldier' wasn't about to throw in the towel but was like a pup playing with a rag doll.

"I suppose you'll be called to the Bar yourself soon, Mr. Hudson?"

"I'll be trying the next case in about five minutes flat, 'Soldier'".

"Will that be a case of ale or porter, your lordship?"

"A black and tan, your honour".

The contest was over. 'Soldier' went on his way, having been rendered speechless. Jim had spiked him on his 'achilles heel'. He was beaming as he left

by Cathy Kenny

his shovel against the 'back warmer wall' where 'Heelball' Hickey stood on his lonesome, soaking up the vernacular rhetoric as well as the heat from the wall.

"You gave 'im down the banks there," said 'Heelball'. "And justly so. Sure, his oul' brother-in-law was a Tan".

"Damn well I know id," cooed Jim. "Didn't the same fella arrest yours truly on Christmas Eve night for not havin' a light an' me drivin' Dick Ring's ass-an-car'." "Where's your light?" says the big galoot. "Under me liver," says I.

"I'm arresting yourself and your long-eared friend for cantering down Clooney's Hill in the blind dark without a glimmer of light upon the vehicle."

"Two shillings or three days," says d'oul Magistrate.

"Did ya cough up?"

"Did I hell! I threw a faint and got a mouthful of whiskey for me troubles."

ACOUSTICS

It came as no surprise for Jim that as he was bending down to lift the last basket of coal he broke wind. And as he strained further to raise the basket off the ground another less personal kind of acoustics pinged and ponged in rapid succession from roughly the same quarters. That was bad news indeed.

It meant that the two back buttons on his homespun trousers had just left for destinations unknown. There was nothing for it but to proceed with extreme caution. Holding the basket hard against his belly Jim moved forward like a cat stalking a nibbling mouse. His feet hardly touched the ground. All was well.

PHOTOGENIC

Or at least that's how things looked until the 'porter' rose to the pinnacle of its fermentation in his lower abdomen. When it had combined fully with Jim's Handy Andy syndrome the custard hit the fan.

Jim struck the kerbstone an unmerciful clatter with the toe of his boot. Down he went as if pole-axed. The basket of coal shot out of his hands like a cannon firing grapeshot.

It peppered the shopfront with pellets of anthracite in a rat-tat-tat, rat-a-tat. All of which left Jim sitting in a smother of fine black dust.

Jim Hudson

If ill fortune had struck, Jim did not recognise it. He sat there with his hand extended like some great black effigy, wearing a raspberry-red smile. A few handfuls of coal formed a miniture pyramid in his lap.

"Holy Moses", screamed Polly Waters having extricated herself from the gooseberry bush. "I'm telling you that man will be the death of us all. Look at him sittin' there as unconcerned as a cuckoo laying her eggs in a sparrow's nest."

As bad luck would have it and as misfortune always travels in three's, didn't 'Inky' Brown arrive on the scene just as Jim was falling down. Now, 'Inky' was a near neighbour of Jim's and was a notorious blabber-mouth into the bargain. Being familiar with Jim's idiosyncrasies, he took in the whole story at a glance.

"I see you had your photo taken sitting down, Jim", shouted 'Inky' and he bursting with hilarity.

"Aye," said Jim blandly. "It happened in a flash. Didn't I come out well?"

CHAPTER THREE

JIM HUDSON AGAIN: THE GAEKWAR OF BARODA

WHEN we last pen-pictured our fabled hero "Jim Hudson, coal carrier," he was in a sitting up position on a shiney carpet of coal outside "Fox and Greenhawks".

Jim's 'Handy Andy' syndrome coupled with the demon drink had caused him to make a faux pas of the last basketful. But because of his separate frame of mind Jim wasn't the least bit perturbed. On the contrary, he was highly amused as the following scene will confirm.

Jim was sitting there in a manner more befitting the Gaekwar of Baroda upon his throne than one who had stumbled and fell in the execution of his mundane affairs, when "Inky" Brown chanced on the exposition.

Now Inky, who was a notorious blabber-mouth, was a near-neighbour of Jim's. Quick as the second-hand on 'Willoughby's Clock' he sized up the one-man circus. He was delighted at the prospect of having yet another fabulous story to tell about his rumbustious and incorrigible neighbour.

"I see you had your photo taken sitting down, Jim" says 'Inky' and he doing something of an Irish jig, like a child having to hold its water.

"Exactly," says Jim. "It all happened in a flash. Didn't I come out well?"

There was no contest, because 'Inky' was flummoxed. Without even thinking, Jim's native wit had written 'Inky' off.

THE LAST BASKETFUL - AGAIN!

Jim was up on his feet faster than it takes Kenny's Well to spout a cupful of sparkling spring water. He swept the glossy carbonaceous pellets of anthracite into a cocked heap. His deep shovel cradled them an instant before his sally basket swallowed them up like crumbs dropped into an army bread-pudding. He worked scrub and shovel, single and double, until the last basket was filled for a second time.

Being conscious of the twin buttons' desertion from the strategic position at the rear of his homespun trousers, Jim thought of a plan. Using a six-inch nail, he skewered the straps of his braces to the back of his trousers, butcher-fashion..

Gingerly he lifted the brimful sally basket and carried it awkwardly through the shop into the back kitchen and out to the coal house. Polly Waters blessed herself as Jim jostled with the kitchen dresser, laden with "willow-pattern" delph. Her prayers were heard in heaven.

MORE PORTER

By this time Jim was sweating like an overfed filly after its first fox-hunt. He reached into his back pocket and produced two square feet of calico which he called his "hanky". It was a strip of the wife's old petticoat. Jim rubbed his forehead and ran the voluminous piece of underwear round the back of his neck and under his stubbled chin. Steam rose off him like a mist off an early morning pond in November.

He looked at his hanky. It seemed like he was sweating petroleum. He deduced he must be over-worked and under-nourished. And it crossed his mind that if "Soldier", alias Pat Laffan, was wrong about the end being nigh, he was definitely right about Jim being called to the bar. His throat was as dry as an ash-box in a solid-fuel cooker. And wasn't he himself a porter – a man who carried burdens for other men. Jim wondered if it was a coincidence that the delicious dark brown malt liquor was called after him. Or was it the other way 'round?

COSTLY EXERCISE

He counted the coins in the pocket of his swallow-tail coat without taking them out. He could tell them by touch – callouses or no callouses. It could be a costly exercise to parade one's wherewithal before the public gaze, poverty having no inhibitions. There was no need to consult his clasped purse as he had sufficient coppers to slake his thirst.

As he passed through the grocery front of his favourite hostelry, Jim winked at himself in the mirror that advertised "Lipton's tea", direct from tea garden to tea pot". Jim slapped four pennies on the marble-topped counter and called for "a pint of your best porter, boss".

A HALF PIG'S HEAD

On his way home that evening Jim went shopping at the Home and Colonial Stores beside the "Hole-in-the-Wall". There he bought four ounces of loose tea, brown bread, country butter and cheddar cheese at a cost of one shilling and sixpence. At the other end of High Street he bought a half pig's head in P.J. O'Connell's, costing sixpence. Well fortified with grub, Jim turned up by the Metropole hotel into James's Street.

To his left, the Kilkenny People printing and publishing works loudly proclaimed its presence, commanding attention by the clamour of its printing presses, as it thundered out the week's news in a rhythmic cacophony of sound.

Jim was heading for home as fast as his legs would carry him. In his own words he was "wallfallen wud the hunger". The wife identified Jim as he came abreast of St. Mary's Cathedral and he giving the odd stagger like a hobbled ass. The more he tried to steer a straight course the more he strayed.

Julia was standing at the door of their thatched cabin with her arms folded like a prize-fighter. Jim thought she bore a strong resemblance to Sam Langford, the 'Boston Tar Baby', if only her face and arms were a little blacker. But before she could start in to read the 'Riot Act' Jim called out to her as breezily as he could afford:

"Did ya ever see a half pig's head wud two eyes, Julia?" And with that he whipped the half head out of the brown paper bag and held it up for inspection.

"Are you blind drunk or what, Jim Hudson? I can only see wan eye. Where's d'other?"

"In yer head, Julia. Sure, aren't ya seein' the half pig's head wud yer own two eyes!"

CHAPTER FOUR

JIM HUDSON'S ESCAPADES

JACK SPRATT

Julia boiled the half pig's head with a lock of cabbage in the black iron pot suspended over the turf fire by a chain. In the ashes under the open fire she roasted a dozen 'Kerrs Pink' potatoes. This was the main course. A large pot of tea brewed on the hob. And cheese, bread and butter and a lump of rock salt stood side by side on the middle of the oil-cloth covered kitchen table. These were for afters. After Jim and Julia had done justice to the lot, Jim became talkative. Feeling his oats, he rose to recitation.

Jack Spratt could eat no fat,
His wife could eat no lean,
Between them both they skint the goat,
And licked the dishes clean.

"Twas me poor mother taught me dat wan,
Julia, and me a lad at her knee." Overcome with the porter, the grub and the heat from the fire, a tear glistened in Jim's eye at the memory his mother.

Under his nose and all over his bristled chin grease shone like sun on silvery water and he paused every now and then to lick his chops. And he came back to himself in a little while. "But I'm no Jack Spratt, Julia. I'd ate mate, fat or lean, half-baked or boiled. Me back is strong and me belly is wide. I could as aisy down an oul' horse as a Spring chicken."

"Arra, will ya stop crowin', ya oul' Luderamawn. I knows damn well what ya could down and it 'tisn't all grub aider. 'Tis like this, Jim Hudson, yer in the wrong line iv work as I sees it. You'd be in yer element in Smithwick's Brewery, corkin' the bottles."

I'd be even better pullin' the corks out iv 'em," said Jim. "Tis a taster I should have been. Yer right, Julia for wance - I lost me trade an' callin'."

Julia shook her head until it looked like she had the noddles and kept talking to herself in whispers as one might reveal a deadly secret to a friend facing a firing squad. "Well, 'tis not that but this, Julia, if I don't go down town tonight an' see poor Georgie Barton things could work out very bad for him. Ya see, he wants me advise on some money matters. Fine-nances, he calls 'em. Said something about a golden eagle and a crock of gold."

"A right wan he'd be askin', about fine-nances, you that haven't two red halfpennies to rub together. Are ya sure it wasn't goldfinches he was talkin' about, and bird lime?"

DOWN TOWN AGAIN

Despite all the revelations and admonitions, Jim duly went down town to rendezvous with Georgie Barton on what he supposed to be a light-fingered indiscretion that put Georgie in a fix. "Tell me now", said Jim after he had invested in a pint of that widely-acclaimed conversation activator, "what's all this I hears about fine-nances?" Georgie was looking into his pint like a cat looking into an aviary. "Ya know, Jim, love of money is a terrible dangerous affliction." Well, that puts yours truly on safe ground, Georgie. Sure, I never have id long enough to be fond of id. Tell us what came over ya, poor fella?"

"Twasn't me but my brother-in-law as witnessed the whole shinanigans, said Georgie.

TAKING THE AIR

"There he was, Mooney Murphy, the lime-burner, out on the Ballycallan Road, three years ago last August, at about four of the clock an' the sun peltin' down on Drakelands. After slakin' his thirst at the pump he turned into the Castle field and made his way down to look at the auld ruins.

"Mooney said he sat there on the trunk of a dozed beech behind a hawthorn and about four yards away from the foot of the castle. At his back a pony and cart rattled along the Poulgour road and a sheepdog barked to bring the cows home for milking in Dicksboro. "In another minute all was still 'cept for the drone of the wild bees and the faint touch of the warm breeze as it pestered the leaves and grass every now and then.

GOLD PENNIES FROM HEAVEN

"All of a sudden didn't the quarest to-do start up. This great big cock magpie flew down from a hole high up in the castle wall. It landed in a fluster upon a block of limestone and to Mooney's amazement it deposited a golden guinea in a font-like gap in the stone.

"Before you could say tom-tit it was gone back up and down again with another golden guinea and dropt it into the same place.

Mooney watched, thunderstruck, as the magpie flew hither and thither for another four times, droppin' a golden guinea into the same place every time. Next the bird began counting its treasure with its beak, giving a little jump for joy in the course of events and letting out the odd squawk like a spoiled child. Mooney had to pinch his-self to make sure he was still alive.

THE GOLD RUSH

"The magpie flew up and down, down and up, four times before Mooney finally tumbled to id that the bird was takin' back the gold coins to its nest high up in the castle wall. And as id flew up with the last but wan of the coins didn't Mooney jump to his feet and run like a deer to the limestone block. He scooped up the last guinea and was back behind the hawthorn before the magpie returned. Mooney was kicking his-self for not makin' his gold-rush sooner - when the five guineas was on the block.

"But 'though he had witnessed quare goings-on, he still wasn't ready for what was to happen next.

A MAGPIE'S SWAN-SONG

"When the great cock magpie came back and saw that the last guinea was gone, he began to bawl like a Bohinta. The great black an' white bird flew staggerin' to the top of the ruins and perched there for a terrible minute.

And then it plunged down, screamin', like a stone, with the wings folded, and dashed itself against the limestone block, with a thud like a loud slap in the face."

Jim Hudson sighed as he took a big mouthful from his pint. He hadn't touched it for the length and breadth of the story. He pursed his lips and looked about him in pensive puzzlement and spoke for the first time since Georgie Barton began the story.

"The poor crathur committed suicide. It couldn't bear to loose even wan piece of its treasure. You're right, Georgie – Love of money is a terrible dangerous affliction altogether."

Short Stories

KILKENNY CAT BY SAM KENNY

A TITANIC DISASTER

JOHNNY McCarthy from Ballydehob was but a lad of sixteen years when he boarded ship for America at Queenstown County Cork in April nineteen hundred and twelve. (1912). He tried hard to hold back the tears as he said his last farewells to his aging mother and father.

"Wasn't it a shame you had to hurt you poor hand Johnny and such a long journey ahead of you," said his mother sadly. Unable to speak Johnny nodded his head and turned to walk up the gangway. His left arm was in a sling but it wasn't hurting anymore. It had gone numb as had the rest of his body, except for his heart which he felt was as big as a turnip and forcing itself up into his mouth. A hefty clatter from an opponent's hurley stick had fractured the knuckles on his thumb and index finger, a few days previously.

"Goodbye son and take care of yourself", his fathers voice was loud and clear. "God go with you Johnny and may His holy and blessed mother protect you", his mothers voice tailed off plaintively on the wind. He dared not stop to look back as he might not be able to go on again. Without turning he left down his suitcase, raised his right hand over his head and waved slowly. Blinded by tears he could barely see in front of him. He kept on walking, walking without knowing where.

"This way lad, over here," shouted a man in uniform. "Down stairs for you lad – you're travelling third class. Look, see that couple there with the three children – you're all for steerage, follow them lad."

Music and singing greeted them as they entered the ships plainest and lowest apartments. There were men and women dancing, melodians playing, children crying and much animated talking. The hubbub which was created by many hundreds of excited occupants was deafening.Their revelry was not a celebration of happiness but was raised merely to help them forget they had left forever behind, their kinfolk and the land they loved so well.

Pat O'Hara found a bunk for his wife Mary and three children just inside the doors, at the bottom of the main stairs. Johnny slumped down on a chair quite close to them, but didn't speak. After a few minutes a harrowing thought rushed into his mind and he jumped to his feet instantly. He plunged his right hand into his coarse home-spun overcoat. A sigh of relief escaped from him. All was well. It was still there. Sewn into the lining of his pocket was a £10 note. He would have to produce that for the customs at Ellis Island. Without it he would be refused entry and sent back to Queenstown on the next available ship. Johnny saw that Pat and Mary O'Hara were watching him. They had curious expressions on their faces, but they seemed to be decent people. When he told them later about the £10 note they both laughed good naturedly and Mary said it was a great idea. From that very frightening incident a friendship developed over the next few days.

"My uncle Ned is a policeman in New York. 'Twas he sent the money for me to go to America and he'll be there to meet me when I land", Johnny confided in them.Whatever about Pat and Mary, Johnny would scarcely have known that they were on board the greatest ship the world had ever seen. Built by Harland and Wolff Belfast, the gigantic white star liner of 45,000 tonnage was on her maiden voyage to New York. She was equipped with four towering funnels and driven by the most powerful engines in the history of steam shipping. Capable of a speed of 23 knots per hour, her crew boasted she would easily smash the standing time record between Queenstown and New York. Journalists from around the world who had gathered to witness the launching of the Titanic had nicknamed the vessel 'The Floating Palace."

Over the next few days Johnny was to discover there were seven hundred and nine (709) souls travelling 3rd class. Of these four hundred and fifty four (454) were men, one hundred and seventy nine (179) were women and the remaining seventy six (76) were children. It would be much later when Johnny would be told that there were two hundred and seventy two (272) passengers travelling 2nd class. One hundred and sixty (160) of these were men, ninety three (93) were women and the remaining twenty four (24) were children.

Johnny would also learn that there were three hundred and twenty two passengers travelling 1st class. These were for the most part world celebrities such as; composers, artists, statesmen, giant industrialists and property tycoons. One hundred and seventy three (173) of these were men, one hundred and forty four (144) were women and five (5) children.

The crew numbered eight hundred and ninety eight (898) in total. Eight hundred and seventy five (875) men and twenty three (23) women.

At approx. 11.00 p.m. the 14th April 1912, Captain Smith, Master of the Titanic entered the Marconi operating-room and spoke calmly to Jack Phillips who was senior wireless operator;

"We have struck an iceberg, and I'm having an inspection. You had better get ready to send out a call for assistance." Harold Bride who was second in command in the wireless room, joked about the gravity of the Captain's words, after he had gone, saying "Surely he knows better than any of us that the Titanic is unsinkable". Jack Phillips only smiled. He sent out the S.O.S. at 11.55: We have struck an iceberg, sinking fast, come to our assistance. Position Lat. 41.46 North. Long. 50.14 West".

The collision occurred off the Grand Banks of Newfoundland and in a few minutes, Phillips had picked up a steam-ship and gave her his position. The Carpathia also answered and said she was heading for them.

Soon the Captains inspection had discovered the enormity of the disaster. The iceberg had torn a 300ft. long gash in the side of the Titanic and the freezing cold ocean waters were thundering through like a thousand waterfalls. And the ship shuddered and groaned like a gigantic beast being slaughtered.

Suddenly the lights went out causing the hubbub to cease abruptly. Almost at once Johnny McCarthy and Pat O'Hara jumped to their feet. The lights flickered then came on again.

It's high time to get out of here shouted Pat, slinging their few belongings over his shoulder. He grabbed two of the children while Mary carried the third. Luckily they were just inside the doors of the main stairway that would bring them on deck. Without a word between them Johnny took one of the children from Pat and amid a throng of hysterical people they clambered up the stairs.

Up on deck there was pandemonium. There were less than half the required number of life-belts and only one quarter the number of life-boats needed for the saving of the 709 3rd class passengers.

But true to tell, the situation wasn't much better on deck's one and two, for the 1st class and 2nd class passengers. Apparently it was generally thought the Titanic was unsinkable.

By twelve o'clock midnight the situation had gravely worsened as it became obvious that the great ship was slowly but surely going down. The sheer horror of the scene was stultifying with women crying and children screaming. And always the sharp clear call rang out from fore to aft and from deck to deck. "Women and children first".

Back in the Marconi wireless-operating room, Jack Phillips was still sending out his distress signals. There was no moving him. His assistant Harold Bride strapped a life belt 'round him. The wireless signal was growing weaker with every minute.

"I'll go on deck Mr. Phillips with your permission and see if I can be of some help there". Phillips merely nodded his approval and went on sending, sending, sending, ... They would never meet again.

On the top deck the third life boat was sent swinging loose from its davits.

The women and children stepped quickly aboard or were thrown in with tender roughness, after a fleeting kiss or hesitant hand shake. And there were some who absolutely refused to leave their husbands, preferring death to defection.

Below on the middle deck the last life boat had already been lowered into the water. It was over-crowded and in danger of capsizing. There was no hope for the lives of the 162 men, women and children left on that deck.

Pat O'Hara and Johnny McCarthy had worked side by side for almost two hours on the bottom deck, helping women and children into the few life-boats available.

"I thank God you were with us Johnny, otherwise I would never have been able to get Mary and the children into the boat", said Pat. Johnny hardly heard him because of the uproar and he was already going across to help with the people into the last life-boat on the bottom deck.

Johnny didn't see Pat talking very earnestly with a senior steward. Neither did he see the two men approach him. The steward tapped Johnny on the shoulder "What age are you son? " "I'm over sixteen sir."

"I've been watching you lad, doing a mans work, aye, and with one hand badly hurt at that. You've room for one more there", the steward ordered the man in charge of the boat. "He is only a boy and his hand is hurting badly. Step in lad, you've done your duty." Johnny shook his head reluctantly, and with that the two men pressed him gently but firmly into the last life boat on the doomed Titanic.

Up on the top deck Captain Smith's voice echoed what the steward had said to Johnny. "You have all done your duty men. It is everyman for himself now. I release you."

Two hundred yards off, Johnny looked back. There she was, her great black bulk outlined against the starry sky. She looked enormous, but somehow helpless and even frightened. And yet the Band played on and on, played a hymn that Johnny had never heard before, but would remember for the rest of his life. All the people on board the Titanic were singing and the people in the life-boats were singing and crying; "Nearer my God to thee".

There was no moon. The ocean was as calm as a pond and it was freezing cold. There was an ominous tilt downwards in the bows even though every porthole still blazed with light. Johnny found it hard to take it all in. He knew what was happening right enough but he couldn't come to terms with it. He couldn't even cry. It seemed like he was frozen over, inside and out, like a great lump of ice.

At about 2.00 a.m. on the morning of the 15th April the Titanic began to tilt slowly up on end, with the stern vertically upward. And as she did so the lights went out, then went on once more and went out for the last time.

At that minute the engines on board the great ship roared through the vessel like a moaning death rattle that could be heard for miles. She remained in that upright position for a few minutes more. Then with a terrifying shudder and a slanting dive, she disappeared beneath the Atlantic ocean, taking with her one thousand, five hundred and thirteen (1513) men, women and children.

Out of a total 322 1st class passengers, 202 were saved. Out of a total of 277 2nd class passengers, 115 were saved. But out of a total of 709 3rd class passenger, only 176 were saved. The vast majority of the latter were poor Irish emigrants.

And the mystery as to why the 'California' which was well within the Titanic's flares and wireless signals, went on her way with lights glittering like a pierhead has never been answered.

It was day break when the Carpathia finally arrived. She had been fifty miles off when she picked up the Titanic distress signal. Quickly she took on board the survivors and made haste for New York.

An awful silence greeted the Carpathia as she docked at the Cunard Quay. There relatives and friends waited anxiously in fear and hope that their kith and kin had survived the worst disaster at sea that the world had ever known.

Johnny McCarthy from the Bronx was sworn in as a New York policeman on the 12th April 1916. His 'passing out' photograph appeared on the New York Herald next day. Two days latter Johnny had a telelgram from a lady in Manhattan; With warmest congratulations and a thousand thanks, from herself and the three girls. It was signed Mary O'Hara.

THE PRISONER

MOONFACE tripped as he struck the tip of his boot in a hidden crevice in the rocks and would have fallen headlong into the ravine but for the agility of the man behind him. With lighting reflexes he grabbed him by the arms and pulled him back onto the mountain path. The man muttered some obscenity. The three men walked in single file across the stone-studded back of the mountain. The big man walked in front. Gregory judged him to be well over six feet tall and weighing about fifteen stone. He looked to be as strong as a bull and as equally repelling. His big ugly moonface was constantly sullen. The belted trench-coat with bandolier and black beret gave him an aspect of calamity which made Gregory shudder apprehensively. At the rear a medium-sized, keen-eyed man had everything under surveillance. He moved with the sureness of a mountain goat. He had the fair skin of the Celt, and his pleasant face was lined with determination. A raincape and peak cap kept out the October wind. Across his shoulder was slung a Lee Enfield rifle. On his feet he wore a polished pair of hobnailed boots and the bottoms of his trousers were secured in his woollen socks.

Between these two a young man in his late teens moved reluctantly, glancing furtively from side to side. Gregory was without great coat or cap. He had lost them in the struggle. He looked pale and frightened. Behind his back, his hands were tied securely with thick white cord. Those who knew him, called him Gregory Kyle.

"Where are you taking me? What are you going to do with me?" He tried to turn and engage the keen-eyed man, who gave no answer and Gregory thought he looked through him rather than at him. In desperation he tried again. "In the name of God, what is it that you want from me?"

"Shut your blasted mouth," shouted the moon-faced man, and he crashed the back of his red-hairy hand into the prisoner's face.

"Another word from you, me boyo, and I won't wait until we get to Gorteen." "I'll Shoot you here and now." He pulled a short Webley from his trenchcoat and thrust its barrel into the gaping mouth of his prisoner.

"Give over the horse play," warned the keen-eyed one defiantly. The moon-face became livid with anger. The explosion of gunfire echoed through the valley and climbed the rocky slopes with clamour. He could still feel the barrel of the gun in his mouth. It grew thicker and thicker, until it almost choked him. The moon-face looked formidable as it waxed and wained grotesquely. A monsterous crow gave out a bray like an ass in terror. Then the sky dropped down and rested heavily upon his head and pressed him noiselessly into the earth. The sweating clay was at once hot and cold.

When he awoke it was to the sound of running water. His hair and face were dripping. He remembered he had fainted because he thought he had been shot. Somewhere to his rear his captors were arguing, about their position.

"All that shooting can mean but one thing – the Tans have routed the camp," the keen-eyed one was speaking.

"Had we arrived sooner we would have been in the thick of it. We had better go over there and see what happened."

"What will we do with him?" asked moon-face, indicating the prisoner.

"We'll take him with us."

The camp was a confusion of oil cloths, cooking utensils and sleeping equipment all scattered in disarray. Outside a make-shift hut they found the body of an old man lying dead in front of a Brazier. His clothes were still burning.

"Listen," said moon-face, "let's bump off this twerp and get the hell out of here."

His comrade looked hard at Gregory. "No definitely not! That's the O.C.'s decision."

"The O.C. is gone or maybe dead, damn it, why should we risk taking this traitor with us? He is an informer."

"That hasn't been proven. And now shut up," came the reply.

Gregory was grateful for this man's humanity and in a burst of enthusiasm he shouted, "Thank you, thank you!"

Although the moon-face eyed him coldly, Gregory still felt safe.

"Listen," said the keen-eyed one, "the Tans will return shortly to search the camp and perhaps take the body. You take the prisoner and wait for me in the grove yonder. I will bury the body and destroy anything that might be of use to them. Go now before it's too late."

Gregory felt panic grip him. He would have gone on his knees and begged not to be sent with the moonfaced man, but it would be useless. If only the keen-eyed one would look at him. If he would but … He turned away.

"Move" and the small Webley thumped against Gregory's ribs. As they walked across the rushey field, Gregory sighted an old cottage at the northern point of the grove. There was smoke, and smoke meant fire. The house was inhabited. He began to veer north, imperceptibly, he thought. He would call for help when they came close to the dwelling. He might even make a run for it. But moon-face must have read his thoughts. Suddenly he pushed him roughly to the left and away from the cottage. Gregory felt his heart pause. Death had chilled his blood with the touch of its ghastly presence.

There was a symphony of "Aeolian" sounds emanating from the grove as they approached it. A western breeze was sighing across the marshlands and whistling softly up the hazel-covered hill. It was a dreadful dirge. As if mother nature bemoaned her son. A terrible despair seized Gregory. He could not perceive his feet to touch the ground as he stepped a part of the grove, and yet, the rustling noise of the Autumn leaves in their brown and brittle decay, rang like stones on iron in his ears. The brittle twigs and rotten branches that snapped and cracked with each footfall made thunder in his head. If only he had someone to feel sorry for him, he thought, he would be less afraid to die. Or was he dreaming? He had had bad dreams before, but never so horrible. Surely a dream would never have such length. Yet he remembered having read that dreams, though they seemed to range over a prolonged period, really took but seconds to experience. He would awake presently. That was it! His father would call him to come down stairs and breakfast with him. "Gregory! Gregory!" "Yes Father, I'm coming."

He tried to bring the form into focus, but his eyes were dimmed with tears. He was speaking aloud to himself. "You gone crazy 'Britisher'," asked moonface sarcastically. "That's enough. Stand right there."

A powerful fist was brought down heavily on his shoulder. "Kneel! Kneel!"

Moonface stiffened. There was the unmistakable sound of someone or something moving through the woodland. Could someone be coming to save him? The perspiration glistened on Gregory's face like dew on a spider's web. It ran from his locks, down the sides of the jaw and flowed across the neck to meet at the adam's apple and coldly streamed down his chest.

An old woman walked into the clearing, carrying a faggot of sticks upon her head. "What's on foot here?" she asked, glancing from Gregory to moonface suspiciously.

"Mind you own affairs, woman," answered the moonface.

She spat at him and he pulled back with a mixture of surprise and fear on his face. Gregory seized his opportunity. "He's going to kill me, lady. Please help me."

"Am I to witness murder then?" she asked.

"Don't concern yourself with what happens here. This is justice."

"What has he done?" she insisted. Her instinct would not allow her to abandon the youth.

"Go, damn you, before the Tans return to search the camp."

"I know all about the camp and the Tans too and I've paid with the blood of my own."

Moonface was stunned.

Gregory saw his chance. He sprang across the clearing and was making towards the trees, when he heard the old woman scream. Moon-face had fired and fired again.

The second bullet caught him on the left side puncturing his heart. He felt a glowing warmth expand within him. Something hot and vital was percolating through his being. He was deadly tired. As the old woman lifted his head onto her lap he felt a convulsive spasm of the mouth and a warm stream of blood spurted forth. Her tears washed him of his loneliness. Her face became his mother's face and her prayer comforted him. It was her sobbing that finally sang him to sleep.

On their way back across the mountain moon-face was both sullen and silent. Once he had spoken but the keen-eyed one had ignored him. He turned on moonface ferociously, with a deadly threat – "I'll finish you, you cowardly bastard"

"You, you blasted fool," began Moonface, but he lost his footing again and in an attempt to recover himself he clutched at his comrade. The keen-eyed man drew back without a word. As he continued alone upon the mountain pass he heard the moon-face man curse and scream, as he fell headlong into the ravine.

A HUNDRED POUNDS LESS 10%

ONCE upon a time, and a very hard time it was when money was so scarce that a one pound note was enough to turn a man's head, or a woman's heart. It was that terrible time in Ireland known as; The Economic War'. Things were as bad in Ballymena, Co. Antrim, as they were in Ballycallan, Co. Kilkenny. To make matters worse, there was only one 'Fair Day' left before Christmas. 'Twas make or break time.

Seamus and Sean were brothers. They lived together on their hungry little farm of thirty acres. Two middle-aged bachelors, who preferred wine and song to thrift and good husbandry. Having squandered their hard earned money they wondered what they might do to get the 'shillings', for Christmas. "I have it", said Seamus, "we'll sell a few cattle, on the next 'Fair Day'. That will keep us going 'til Spring. We'll be back on our feet by then".

"If we're going to sell, we might just as well let the ten of them go. There's not a 'trainin' between any one of them", said Sean.

"What will we ask for them?", said Seamus, "they're fine beasts".

"We'll ask a hundred pounds for the lot. They're worth every penny of it. Or eleven pounds a head if sold single."

"So be it then" said Seamus, "and we'll buy ten calves to replace them at the right money."

Next 'Fair Day' saw the two bachelor brothers on a fog-filled 'Fairgreen', in Kilkenny, with their ten sturdy cattle. Seamus stood with the stock, while Sean searched the ground for ten healthy calves at the right price.

"You're asking far too much for them" Seamus was told repeatedly, and Sean was accusing the calf-sellers of the self-same conduct. Of course, they couldn't buy unless they sold. As the day wore on, the fog lifted and settled down again, without incident. Despite peals of hand-slapping and yarns of luck-money, no money changed hands.

Then, like an apparition, a great giant of a man came out of the fog. He wore a belted 'Crombie' coat, a deer-stalker hat, and a pair of bright yellow boots. His big face was a cardinal red, and his voice was full of authority.

What are you asking for that lot, young man?"

"Eleven pounds a head, mister, or one hundred for the lot".

I'll give you the hundred pounds for them, then, less ten per cent".

Seamus looked perplexed. "I'll have to think about it. I'll need to ask me' brother".

"Be quick about it, then. I'll be over at the sheep pens and I haven't all day". He vanished into the fog, like he had been swallowed up.

Sean arrived in a state of excitement.

"Did you sell? I have ten little beauties, over there, and at the right price too".

Seamus told him of the offer the big cattle-buyer had made, and asked him how much was a hundred pounds, less ten percent? Sean hadn't a clue.

"I'll tell you what", said he, "slip over to Sean Byrne's Public House, and ask Nancy Purcell how much is ten per cent. She's good at figures".

You're right" said Seamus, and away with him like the wind.

"I know that you have had one already. I could smell your breath", Sean shouted after him.

The pub was packed, and the din of conversation was perfumed with smoke and alcohol. Nancy, behind the counter, made eye-contact with Seamus the moment he entered. "Here he comes against, she thought. "What can I get you, Seamus?" she asked smiling.

"A drop of the 'cratur', love... but there's something very important I have to ask you first".

"What is it, Seamus, a vic?".

"Well, if I said to you, I'd give you one hundred pounds, less ten percent, how much would you take off?".

Nancy spilled half of the whiskey measure on the counter, but Seamus didn't even notice.

"Well", said he, impatiently, "how much?"

Nancy looked at him in surprise and wonder. "Seamus", said she, her voice trembling, "I'd take off every stitch".

THE PROPHET

"**B**EGOR Pakey, that's a massive problem entirely," said the school-master, as he stroked his grey goatee beard knowledgeably. "Selling out and emigrating can be a dangerous business and England is a long ways off. Once there, you might never again find the road back to Shanbally. You'd be like a pair of brown trout pining away in the Dead Sea."

"But 'tis the wife's whim, master. Peg don't like it here anymore. Not one bit, since the day her mother died, after cutting down a May-bush in the Fairy dell. She says everything we touch turns sour, and swears the worst is yet to come."

"Her mother had no right to meddle with the 'Sidhe'. You are in need of greater powers than I can command. But England will not be a solution. It is a heathen land that even God washed His hands of. Let us invoke the Oracle."

So saying, the master stuck the little finger of his left hand deep into his left ear, and shook his large head vigorously. Pakey watched in awe. He had seen this happen once before when the cream wouldn't curdle in Kate Dunne's butter-churn. It meant the master was about to make a pronouncement. Then he swiftly pulled his finger from his ear, making a noise like a cork being drawn from a whiskey bottle. P-L-U-N-K. Pakey waited anxiously for the wise words that would follow:

"Don't sell your house or stock,
Don't part with land or flock,
But fly like the wind to Dooney
And consult with the Prophet Cooney."

Although the master had spoken in the language of the Bards, Pakey wasn't convinced.

"To Dooney!" queried Pakey, in bewilderment, " a day's journey from morn 'till night, to speak with the Prophet Cooney. Sure isn't he the Magistrate as well? What would he be doing with the likes of us?"

"He settles disputes and solves problems. Some say he is as wise as Solomon sitting upon his throne."

The interview was over. The master smiled wisely, and extended a long boney hand. Reluctantly, Pakey placed a heated two shilling piece in that cold chalk-white palm.

"Mark you well," added the master, seeing fit to include a few extra words as value for money, "the Prophet's fee is an Irish ten shilling note."

Pakey was too astonished to make any reply. He nodded gravely and turned for home. That'll surely put an end to all this foolish talk about selling and shifting, Pakey thought. But as it turned out, he was sadly mistaken. The more he scorned the journey to Dooney, the more Peg was determined to go.

"Won't it be marvellous to have our whole lives laid bare before us, Pakey? Who knows, – maybe we'll fall in for money and buy a big house in England?"

But Pakey didn't share Peg's enthusiasm for looking too far into the future. He was afraid the Prophet might advise them to sell up and clear out.

"Sure wasn't it yourself said that the worst was yet to come, Peg? And who's going to milk the cow and feed the pigs and chickens?"

"What are neighbours for, if not to help one another in times of need?"

That was the end of that. He had lost the argument and he knew it.

From that day on, everything Pakey did was designed towards making the journey to Dooney, to consult with the Prophet Cooney. He had Neddy, their black ass shod, and make frisky with a few fistfuls of oats each day. He repaired the harness, and polished the ornamental medallions. Then he painted the body of the cart cobalt blue, and the wheels, indian red. Finally, the day before they left, Peg sold their fattest pig, for thirty shillings. Nothing could stop them now.

Pakey felt a tinge of regret as he looked back at their whitewashed cottage, with its' thatched roof and latticed windows. It was as if he was seeing it for the last time. His stomach tightened, and his breathing shortened. These sensations confused him.

Not so Peg. She had no such sensitivities. Her feet tapped while her hands clapped. And she sang: "Kilkenny Boys Hurrah". "Cheer up Pakey my love, we'll have a whale of a time, I'm sure. 'T' will be our second honey-moon."

She put her arm around Pakey's waist, and gave him a great squeeze. Like light'ning, he saw that they were doing the right thing. He scolded himself for ever doubting Peg's common sense. A blind man, he assured himself, could see that they must go to meet their destiny. He stood up in the cart and beat his chest, like 'Tarzan of the Apes'. He felt he could almost tell the future himself.

A few miles down the road, they came upon a Tramp, who begged to be carried to the next town. He said he hadn't eaten for three whole days, and walked a hundred miles. At first Pakey had been reluctant, but Peg persuaded him, saying; "'T'would be a sin to refuse the poor 'auld saint."

He landed in the cart with one bound, and began conversing as if they were old friends. The more Pakey heard him talk, the less he was able to imagine him in the company of either St.'s Patrick or Brigid.

"That's a strapping little 'baste' ya have there sir, – well worth his oats I'd say."

"Aye," said Pakey, curtly.

Peg turned and smiled at the Tramp.

"We'll stop for a bite and sup soon, mister."

"I'd ate the Twelve Apostles meself this minute, so I would."

And his greedy eyes devoured the contents of the food-basket.

The mid-day sun blazed down as they pulled in to the side of the road. Pakey unyoked the black ass, and let him graze, while Peg shared out the food. The Tramp grabbed his portion and devoured the lot in minutes. Then he retired under a tree, and fell to sleep, liking his chops. Pakey was next to relax into sleep, and was soon snoring.

With the two men sleeping, Peg was able to have a good look at the Tramp. He wasn't as old and worn as she had previously thought. Though his face was deeply lined and weather-beaten, he was no more than forty, and even handsome, in a rugged sort of way.

Peg was about to stretch out beside Pakey, when she caught the Tramp's eyes upon her. There was something sinister in his stare.

"Himself mustav' woke me would' the snoring'," he said with a sly grin. "I don't suppose he'd hear a Brass Band comin' up the road this minute."

"Pakey wouldn't hear the Chapel bell if he was asleep in the belfry," replied Peg, without thinking.

"Maybe ye'd like me to make a pillow of grass and leaves, fer' yer' head, mam?" He was on his feet and walking towards her. She was so surprised at this forwardness that she wasn't sure what she should do. If she woke Pakey, there would be a confrontation.

"I'm not one bit tired. If you want to be of any use, go and stand by our black ass."

She spoke with conviction. He stopped in his tracks and looked down the long white road. Twenty yards away, Neddy was grazing contentedly. Before he went, the Tramp's eyes searched her person from head to toe. Peg tightened her grip on her purse, when his looks rested there. In a minute he was gone.

Peg knew she mustn't sleep, and only lay down to relieve the tension of the close encounter. She put her purse under her head. Feeling proud of the way she had handled an awkward situation, she fell to sleep in spite of herself.

Suspended somewhere between the realms of fantasy and reality, Peg dreamed. She saw the Tramp gather leaves and grass, and bind them with wide ribbons, to make a pillow for her head.

When Neddy won the Donkey Derby at the Parish gymkhana, it was the Tramp who rode him past the winning post. The Prophet Cooney presented the winners Cup to herself, all dressed up in lavender and pink.

She heard the thrilling humming music of all the hosts of creatures in the heavens, on the hedgerows and in the earth. Far off, she heard Neddy's newly-shod hooves ring, like iron on stone.

"Neddy, come back," Peg screamed, and awoke herself with the din. She looked around her in a daze.

"What's up, what's wrong?" shouted Pakey, jumping to his feet.

"I think I must have been dreaming."

Suddenly she threw herself upon the ground, like one in a fit, and began tearing up grass by the roots.

"My purse, my God, it's gone. We've been robbed. We're left without a penny."

Pakey ran down the road like a mad-man, hoping to catch the Tramp. He was too late. The Tramp was three hundred yards down the road, and riding away like the wind, on Neddy's back. After they had disappeared, Pakey could still hear Neddy's hooves ringing in the distance.

With his head bent low, Pakey walked back to Peg, who was still on her knees, crying.

"Oh, what possessed us to give a lift to that dreadful man, Pakey?"

"What do you mean, US? Wasn't it yourself that insisted? I hope you're satisfied now. You and your poor 'auld saint."

Pakey spoke with a sarcasm that until then he never knew he possessed. Peg was devastated.

"We'll have to face home pennyless, on foot, without our lovely black ass. We'll be the laughing stock of the parish, God help us."

"Not likely. We won't be going back there until we do what we set out to do. And as for that robber, he won't go no further than the next public house, where I'll nab him."

So saying, Pakey got between the shafts of the ass's cart, and began pulling with all his might.

"Are you coming Peg?

Peg ran to the rear of the cart, tears running in channels down her dust-covered face. She pushed with a will.

They made a strange sight, plodding along the country road with an ass's cart between them. Some time later they met a drover, who told them he had seen the Tramp riding a black ass faster than a storm in full blast, through the village of Scart. That did it. Pakey broke into a trot and didn't let up on the pace. Peg was being pulled along. She felt so proud of her man. As they approached Scart, a big policeman stepped onto the middle of the road, with both hands raised.

"Whoa back there. Where do you two think you are going?"

His hostility was obvious and he stared at them with baleful malevolence.

"Did you see a Tramp riding a black ass through here, about an hour ago?" Pakey asked him.

"I'll ask the questions here. You give the answers. Now, where were you going with this ass's cart? And where did you rob it?"

"We're trying to catch the robber who stole our black ass and Peg's purse with thirty shillings in it."

"That's hard to swallow."

"'Tis true, and he rode through here about an hour ago."

"He didn't"

"He did."

"Are you calling me a liar?"

"If the cap fits, wear it."

Pakey was adamant. The policeman was furious.

"I'm arresting the two of you, for unlawful possession of an ass's cart, and having no visible means of support."

When Peg pleaded with him to trace the Tramp, he answered curtly, saying,

"I've no intention of looking for a cuckoo's nest."

He impounded the cart and questioned them closely. He tried every trick he knew to make them change their story, but all to no avail.

"You're the cleverest pair of villians I've ever come across. As this is a very serious business, I'm, taking you up to Dooney, to stand trial before the magistrate, better known as the Prophet Cooney."

To the utter amazement of the policemen, Pakey and Peg danced for joy. He had expected them to tremble in fear.

"'Tis to meet the Prophet we set out in the first place." Pakey told him jubilantly.

Completely puzzled, he looked at them, and wondered what game they were playing.

Within half an hour of being arrested, they were on their way to Dooney, handcuffed together. They walked in front, Peg leaning hard against Pakey for support. The big policeman followed, seated on his utility bike. He had wanted to put a halter on them, like wild beasts, but Pakey advised him not to try it.

As they entered the celebrated village of Dooney, the residents came onto the street. A sight like this was rare. At first the people laughed and jeered at them, covered from head to toe in the fine white dust of the road. They looked more like burners in a lime-kiln than ordinary country folk. But when they realised that the misfortunates were handcuffed to each other, and were being herded along by the big policeman, the mood of the crowd changed. Their hearts went out to the pitiable pair, and they scowled hatefully at the big bullying policeman.

It was then Packey spotted Neddy, their little black ass, at the top of the street. Head down the poor beast was tied to a pole outside a public house. It was in a lather of sweat. Pakey broke into a trot, and Peg, unable to keep up, stumbled and brought the two of them to the ground. The crowd was seething, and on the brink of creating a fracas. The big policeman was fast to interpret its' anger. His movements quickened by fear, he dismounted, helped the couple to their feet and unlocked the handcuffs. The anger of the crowd subsided.

The Tramp came rushing out of the public house as Pakey and Peg were fondling their badly abused Neddy. Seeing the jig was up, he made a dash for freedom. Pakey was on him instantly and shouting, while holding him tightly.

"This is the robber who stole our ass and our money."

The crowd was closing in.

"Keep back. Make way there."

The big policeman was roughly pushing people out of the path of a tall distinguished looking man, who was making his way towards the middle of the crowd. The man had an aura of authority about him. He wore a black serge suite, a white front and a whale-bone collar. On his feet were a pair of Norewell's all leather, black knee boots. In his hand he carried a cane walking-stick with silver handle and ferrule. His expression was mild, but full of resolution. His blue eyes, though soft, were bright with vitality, and a shock of gray hair crowned his noble head.

With a glance the Prophet took-in the whole situation. He addressed himself to Pakey and the Tramp, who with Peg and the little black ass, stood in the open space at the centre of the crowd, like pieces in an exhibition.

"Is the ownership of this animal the only cause for this disturbance of the peace?"

"'Tis that your honour, and the taking of the wife's purse 'would every shilling we had in it."

The Tramp hummed and hawed, and nervously felt his coat pocket.

"Let me see your hands," the Prophet said to Pakey and the Tramp.

Pakey's hands were large, and covered with callouses. The Tramp's were slender and soft, with long, dirty nails. The Prophet spoke directly to the Tramp,

"How long do you say you have had this ass?"

"Since 'twas a foal, 'yer honour."

"And how long do you say you have had the ass," he asked Pakey?

"I bought him as a yearling on the Fair, your honour."

Pakey thought the Prophet looked puzzled.

"Perhaps 'tis best to toss a coin to decide which of you keeps this ass. Or shall we cut him in two and each of you can have half?"

"Oh don't do that your honour," pleaded Peg. "We couldn't bear to see him hurt.""Das fair be me boss," said the Tramp, forgetting who he was addressing.

"We'll toss for it. It will be less gruesome after all," said the Prophet. "Will one of you loan me a coin?"

The Tramp plunged his hand into his pocket, and produced a fistful of coins. One fell to the ground, and rolled towards the big policeman, who picked it up and handed it to the Prophet. The great man eyed the coin. First a smile and then a frown crossed his countenance.

"What have we here – a dud half-crown?"

He raised the coin for closer inspection, and turned to the big policeman.

"Officer, arrest this man for possessing and passing forged money."

The Tramp became desperate.

"'Tis not mine at all, 'yer honour. 'Tis hers. That women there."

He pointed a long, dirty finger at Peg.

"She's 'da 'wan ta' blame."

Pakey and Peg were perplexed, but the Prophet was jubilant.

"That's just what I thought you'd say. So, you did steal their money and their ass. You ungrateful scoundrel. I'll have you incarcerated."

The big policeman took the Tramp by the collar, and made him empty his pockets. When all the money was counted, the total came to twenty seven shillings and six pence. He had got rid of the purse along the way. Still, all was well. They had their little black ass, and most of their money. Together they hugged Neddy, while the crowd clapped and cheered.

After the Prophet had heard their full story, he invited them home to tea. Pakey politely asked the Prophet if the 'Sidhe' and the cutting-down of the May-bush had been the cause of all their troubles. The Prophet told them all their troubles were over, and the reason Peg's mother had died was due to a prod from the May-bush which is poisonous when the sap is up in the thorn.

Outside on the lawn Neddy having been watered, fed and rubbed down, waited patiently to take Pakey and Peg home. He looked resplendent, harnessed to a magnificent trap, which was a gift from the Prophet.

At last came the question that had brought them to Dooney. As he asked, Pakey extended an Irish ten shilling note towards the Prophet.

"Should we sell-out and emigrate, your honour? For that's the very reason we came to visit you in the first place."

The Prophet graciously accepted the fee and smiling wisely he answered Packey's burning question, thus:

"You would have less chance of health and happiness by leaving Ireland than the sky-lark would have confined to a cage. At home, in your own place, you will become the father of seven sons, and your seventh son will be a Prophet, beyond par."

FROM PUB POTMAN TO POET LAUREATE

JOHN Masefield was born in Liverpool in the year 1875. In his early teens he ran away from home to join the Merchant Navy or as it was called then the Mercantile Marine. The "Battle of Waterloo", it has been said, "was won on the playing fields of Eton": Signifying that the inevitable success of most great men is related directly to their early education and experiences. Consequently the origin of Masefields great poetry and prose can be traced to the H.M.S. "Conway" in which the poet trained for the Mercantile Marine. Aboard this sailing ship he gained a knowledge not only of the sea and ships but of the men who went down to the sea. As a result of which he wrote his first outstanding collection of poems called "Salt Water Ballads".

Like most poets, John Masefield was a humanitarian and a defender of the under-dog. And in his introduction to the Salt Water Ballads he wrote the following under the title of, "A Consecration".

The Men of the tattered battalion which fights till it dies
Dazed with the dust of battle, the din and the cries
The men with the broken heads and the blood running into their eyes
Not the be-medalled Commander, beloved to the throne
Riding cock-horse to parade when the bugles are blown
But the lads who carried the koppie and cannot be known

Masefield worked at a variety of 'jobs', including messenger boy, poacher, carnival boxer, able seaman and pub-potman. These multivarious employs afforded him vast material for his writings. In 1902 he published the already named "Salt Water Ballads". Those were followed by "Ballads" in 1903. And in 1911 he published what is probably his greatest work. It was his first narrative poem and he called it, "The Everlasting Mercy". Many years later on the death of Robert Bridges he became Poet Laureate. That was in 1930.

A first rate American journalist whose initials were, K.B.K. Karl Benny Kitchen, was a great admirer of Masefield's poetic genius. So when Masefield invited him on a journey to visit a public house "The Columbian" in Greenwich Village New York, he jumped at the chance. Being a very astute newspaper man he had a hunch there was a story behind it.

"You know, I once worked in the Columbian", Masefield told K.B.K. "In fact it was while working there that I first became interested in poetry".

K.B.K. was ecstatic. Here was a story that would make history. He visualised the headlines: "How one of the world's greatest Poets first learned his trade".

Luke O'Connor's son Charley was tending bar when two distinguished looking gentlemen arrived at the 'Columbian'.

"What can I do for you gentlemen?", Charley asked.

"We'll have two light beers please, Whom do I have the pleasure of speaking to?", Masefield enquired.

"I'm Charley O'Connor, the governor". "That's what I thought, Charley. But tell me is your father and mother still living?"

"No, father and mother passed on a long time ago. Luke had a quizzical look upon his face. "Why – did you know them?"

"I knew them and loved them as I did you", answered the great man.

"Then you can only be one person, – John Masefield, – poet of the people" beamed Charley, as they happily shook hands.

"You've got my name right Charley, but as regards fame, I'm more fortunate than famous". Masefield turned to K.B.K. who had his jotter out and was writing furiously.

"This is my very good friend Karl Benny Kitchen who really is a famous writer with the New York Globe".

"And I've read your articles too Sir", said Charley. "This is a great day for me. You'll hardly believe this Mr. Kitchen but Mr. Masefield here taught me how to ride a bicycle, how to swim, to play cards and how to box". He turned to Masefield, "When mother and father were alive they never stopped talking about you. They were so proud when you became famous". A tear glistened in Masefield's eye.

"I never forgot them, or you either Charley and always promised myself that I'd come back one day to say thanks for your kindness".

Charley ushered the two men into the back room, taking their drinks which neither had touched, with him. He spoke again: "People from many parts of the world come in here to the "Columbian" and ask": "Did the poet John Masefield really work here?"

"I've had more than my share of good luck, God knows", said the great poet simply as they sat down. K.B.K. was jubilant. The more he heard the better he liked it. He began a new paragraph.

"Twenty years had not dimmed John Masefield's memory of his old friends. People who were kind to him and took him in when he was a run-away sailor lad eking out a hand to mouth existence. It was Luke O'Connor of the old "Columbian" public house in Greenwich Village who befriended the penniless, poet to be, making him a general factotum about the house and bar. For Luke did not employ him as a bar-keep on the first day that he gave him a job with full board and lodgings – He couldn't as the lad knew nothing of the trade".

Charley turned to Masefield, "You're famous now and I dare say rich".

The poet smiled, "As I said earlier, I've had extraordinary good fortune, an excellent wife and good friends. Soon after I ran away to sea I became convinced that there were only two careers for me – literature or medicine. And then one evening while browsing in a second-hand bookshop across the street from here, I came across a copy of Chaucer's Poems. I bought it and took it back here with me. And after having read it a second time I felt transformed. There and then I determined to become a poet. I read every book of verse I could leave my hands on after that and in less than one year I was writing my own poetry".

"It is our good fortune", wrote K.B.K., "that the Irishman Luke O'Connor was so kind hearted as to befriend a run-away sailor lad and treat him like one of the family. Otherwise John Masefield might never have happened upon Chaucer's Canterbury Tales and the whole world would be the poorer for it".

"A thousands thanks Charley. That was an expression often used by your parents", said the great man of 'Letters' as he extended his hand. Charley shook it warmly but was unable to speak. The tears flooded into his eyes as they embraced. K.B.K. hugged himself. He had the story of a lifetime for the 'New York Globe'.

THE KILKENNY CATS – NO LAUGHING MATTER

UNLIKE Charles Dickens classical novel, "A Tale of Two Cities", Kilkenny City is a tale of two towns; an Irishtown and an Englishtown. Between the two communities the River Breagagh flows swiftly on its way to the silvery Nore.

The Irishtown which is older by hundreds of years got its Charters from the Bishops of Ossory. It came into being under the shadow of St. Canices Cathedral on the Northern side of the Bregagh. Self-contained and self supporting it elected its own municipal authorities and was governed by a Portreeve or Mayor.

The Englishtown on the southern side of the river was established after the Norman Invasion in 1169, and had it's Charters from the Earls Marshall. This community was governed by a civic magistrate who held the title of "Sovereign".

In those days the only legitimate crossing from one township to the other was over a limestone bridge known as the Watergate. Armed guards jealously guarded their frontiers. Indeed the unlawful crossing of the Breagagh was said to be more dangerous than "Crossing the Rubicon".

That there was no love lost between the two towns, surprised nobody. In lifestyle and language they were as different as milk and meat. As a result they never tired of finding fault and were forever feuding and fighting over everything in creation. Not only were the people so disposed, but the animal kingdoms too, waged war with tooth and nail on their counterparts across the river. In particular the Feline brood were most confrontational.

The Irishtown cats, wore thick fur coats as black and shiney as the Castlecomer coal and had powerful tails as long as a man's arm. On the other hand the Engishtown cats wore brindled coats like the tiger. They had claws like an eagle and heads as big as cannonballs. It was freely admitted that both breeds were ferocious and would fight to the death.At that time a number of blood-sports were allowed and some were even supported by the authorities.

Bull-baiting was one such "sport". It was financed by a group who called themselves "The Councillors of the Bull ring". This "sport" was staged directly in front of St. Francis Abbey, the ruins of which are beside the present day Smithwicks Brewery. Cock fighting was another of the so called "sports" and public monies were paid to build Cockpits. There were no less than three pits between the Cathedral and the Castle. Dog-fighting was held to be illegal but a blind eye was turned to its continuence because some people in high places bred powerful dogs to fight for large sums of money.

The most vicious and brutal "sport" of all; Cat fighting, was banned under pain of incarceration and the Lash. The latter instrument, it appears, was appropriately administered with the flesh cutting cat-o'-nine-tails. Yet as life would have it and as is said laws are made to be broken, the blood letting continued. Eventually there emerged two so-called champions, one from Irishtown and one from Englishtown. These terrible Toms were the talk of the two towns and soon a contest was arranged 'Sub Rosa' to determine which Tom would be crowned king.

The venue, was fixed for the Pit under the City Wall between Lee's Lane (Abbey Street) and New Building Lane. The rules for the contest were as follows:- A rope line would be erected between two ash poles at a height of five feet above the ground. The cats tails would be tightly tied together with hemp.Then, at the drop of a hat the cats would be slung over the rope line and the fight would commence. And that's exactly what happened on that fateful day. As the battle raged the people from the two towns fell to fighting also. With the uproar of the cats and bellowing of the crowd, Patrick Darcy the "Sovereign" was alerted. A lookout spotted him running hot-foot towards the Pit and gave the agreed signal. Instantly the referee drew his sword and slashed the cats tails. The wounded but greatly relieved Toms quickly disappeared in the crowd. When the "Sovereign" came on the scene all that was visible was the cats bloody tails swinging from the rope line.

"Don't tell me", said he, "they have eaten each other down to their tails".

KILKENNY CAT BY SEAN KENNY

A CAT'S TALE OF THE UNEXPECTED

STRANGE stories about cats are legion. The Egyptians believed them to be sacred creatures, with supernatural powers. They kept them in their temples as religious symbols, four thousand years ago. Cats are the most inquisitive of all domesticated animals. Since the dawn of civilization, these fascinating creatures have been recorded in art and literature.

Some people are afraid of cats, and one either loves them, or hates them. One thing is certain – for better or for worse, cats do change the lives of those with whom they come into contact. This phenomenon proved itself especially true for us. Cats are natural climbers, and are noted for the way they always search for the highest pedestal. It was this characteristic which in the end, caused 'Fluffy's' undoing, at least as far as Aunt Harriet was concerned. Up to then, he had been playing a blinder, in the way of making himself everybody's darling, – everybody but one that is.

Fluffy is a black-and white 'tom'. We acquired him as a scruffy little kitten. The girls brought him home one black winter's night. It was December 28th, three days after Christmas. He looked more like a ragged lump of soiled cloth, than a living creature. They came upon him huddled in the doorway of a disused house, crying and shivering pitifully. A dirty red ribbon hung loosely around his neck. It seemed as if he had been loved for a time, but was abandoned when the Christmas spirit faded. We fed him hot milk, on a cotton bud, while his tiny heart raced like a mad, fast watch. At first, we thought he was black, with a few white patches, but the opposite proved true, under the agents of soap and water. He soon discovered that we harboured no ill will towards him, and in time, he settled in, as a fully-fledged member of the family. When we ate, he ate, and when we went to bed, Fluffy went too. Not to the same bed, I hasten to say, for he had his own apartment, complete with bed and sanitary tray. He even had his own 'First Aid' kit.

"What went wrong, then," you ask? Well, one fine day, Fluffy went literally as high as a kite, in the kitchen. It was his finest acrobatic display ever. In one fantastic leap, he had landed right on top of the dresser, where Aunt Harriet's precious, antique vase had rested in peace, forever, it seemed. Fluffy knocked it over, when someone screamed, and it crashed to the stone floor, in a hundred pieces. It was like an explosion in a Jeweler's shop, as silver fifty pence pieces went flying through the air, like confetti.

In a mad rage, Aunt Harriet pelted a glass saltcellar at Fluffy. It was a direct hit. He cried like a frightened child, as he scurried out the back door. He left a trail of blood behind him. No one spoke a word.

It was almost two years before we saw Fluffy again. He sauntered in, one Saturday afternoon, as our chiming clock struck three. He rolled himself up on the rug, in front of the fire. It was unbelievable. We had thought him lost, or even dead.

"Aunt Harriet will be pleased to see him, when she comes back from town", said Mam.

No one spoke.

Some time later, Dad answered a knock on the front door. It was a Garda Sergeant. Aunt Harriet had been involved in a traffic accident, down town. She was rushed to St. Catherine's hospital, where she died at exactly three o'clock.

DOGS FOR EVERYBODY

VOLUMES have been written about the dog, that domesticated quadruped that was once the full-blooded brother of the wolf. He has accompanied man down through the ages and has more than once been acclaimed as man's best friend. But I know a lame postman who would not subscribe to that sentiment at all and a cyclist or two who would vigorously refute it. I suppose it is a case of "once bitten twice shy."

Our town may have its faults, but there is one accusation that can never be levelled against its people and it is, that they have ever – even at the risk of being eaten alive – turned their backs on the animal kingdom, at least not the canine breed. Insurance men, rent collectors and milkmen excluded of course. Excuse me for just one moment, there is someone knocking at the door. "Come back here, Lassie, sit. Lie down, Lassie. She won't mind you, sir, her bark is worse than her bite. Lassie, Lassie, oh sir." Add to that list of dissenters one savaged pools-man. He shook his fist and said he was striking my name off the list.

I think some statistics might be in order, although I cannot be absolutely sure about the accuracy of my figures (the census clerk was bitten by a pug-nosed Corgi and suffered from hallucinations) nevertheless, there is sufficient evidence to prove emphatically that there is a least one dog for every man in town. So you understand there is no need to rush or foam at the mouth. Everyone can be facilitated. There is one obligation, however, – collars and leads must be provided. Muzzels are optional.

Occasionally one can see a pack of nine of ten 'growlers' roaming freely. But, more often than not they wander in lesser numbers to achieve compatibility. Of course they are not all what you might call house-broken. Indeed, I suspect it would be unreasonable to image that they should be. Having had the experience of this, I am sure that some of them have never been closer to a human being than the broken handle of a sweeping brush.

As far as names are concerned, they have none and they have many. It is safest to call them by whatever prefix comes into your head, most people do. Rex is a good title, it has an authentic ring to it. Spot is descriptive and used a lot. Towser gets a turn and there are one or two other adjectives that are yelled more frequently. I will not mention those here, some people might think me prejudiced.

Just like people, they come in all sorts of shapes and sizes. Every known breed (and a few not yet tabulated) has met in our town and married. The result of this canine cross fertilization would undoubtedly be a source of wonder to those experimenting in the field of hybrid permutations. Indeed some species are so spectacular they would seem to merit a dog-star trial in Disney Land. But one in particular I took note of for posterity. It was – as exactly as I can describe it – a cross between a Fox-terrier and a Siamese-cat.

Another nice thing that can be said about the Bow Wows, is that there is no class distinction among them. It is not unusual to see a well-bred bitch stealing a march down the Canal Walk with her jaunty mongrel male.

But it's a dog's life, isn't it.

BOY AND DOG

HAUNTED

OUR house is haunted. We know that now for certain. Otherwise how could one explain how things keep on disappearing. For years and years personal effects and ordinary household utensils have, as they say, 'vanished before our very eyes'. Bambooslem's Abracadabra: 'Now you see it, and now you don't,' would aptly describe our every-day experiences. Things such as: biros, door-keys, scissors, boot polish, scarves, razor blades, gloves, rings, tin openers, reading glasses and socks, have all taken French-leave at one time or another, from our house. To be honest though, most of these objects turn up after a week or maybe a month. But some vanish for as long as a year or even two.

And there are other articles that have 'vamoosed' and never returned. In this regard vanishing socks have been a particular vexation.

Only last week I counted seven odd socks sulking in the bottom drawer of the Dressing table. There was something incongruous about their singularity. They were in mourning for their mates, I suspected. Having walked out together for so long, they must have had great expectations. Socks are like swans; they mate for life and if anything such as death or disappearance happens to one, the other lives a life of celibacy. Don't ask me how I know that, I just do.

Woolen socks, nylon socks, knee socks and ankle socks, have been spirited away. And isn't it bizarre that they never-ever disappear in pairs, but like disenchanted lovers they part, never to meet again. Somewhere between the bedroom, the washing machine and the clothesline, they have all gone AWOL. As a result of which I am now left with the princely amount of two pairs of socks. One pair of woolen knee socks and one pair of nylon ankle socks. I cherish these like pets even though they are old and holey. And I wonder how long more these two couples will be left together. The answer must be in the 'lap of the gods'. Perhaps I should say ghosts.

My wife doesn't like to speak about ghosts and would prefer to believe the reason for the vanishing socks, is that the angles have all got cold feet.

"If anything the reverse is true", I told her, "What with global warming and all that".

"'Tis much more likely to be the work of the Boyos down under", I said

"As sure as hell the fire has gone out below and the divils are dancing in 'me socks'.

"Hey – who swiped me bloody biro."

OUR LOCAL T.D.

WE have a politician who lives out our way. The people all call him T.D. Murphy. He has a red face, and a big black car. His missus drives an old 'banger', but his own one is so big and shiny that you could see your face in it, right down to me brother's broken boots. The Murphys' don't live beside all the rest of the people, because their house has too many doors and windows.

Last week, Mrs. Murphy ran over a chicken on the widow Whelan, up the road. There were feathers everywhere. Killing the chicken, cooked the T.D.'s goose, Mam said, because that's one vote he'll never get again.

Politicians don't get up early like everybody else. They only come out at night. They're like owls in more ways than one, Dad says, because they feather their own nests too. Politicians are nearly always out, whenever you call. But, if you peeped through the crack in the garage door, you'd see the car there, hiding.

Dad said politicians go to work in the Dail, and not on the Dole, where he works. The work is much the same, only there's a big difference in the money, Mam said.

A famous Irishman, named Shaw, told our teacher that six good men could run the whole country, no bother. Dad said there's more politicians running for the Dail now, than in the 'Dublin Marathon'. If we have to depend on the politicians to run the country, Mam said, 'tis God help the human race.

TO SCHOOL OR NOT TO SCHOOL

WHEN I was seven years old mother took me to the Boys National School for enrolment. I wasn't exactly sold on the idea and only went under protest. Three years painful attendance at the Infants of St. Canice's had left me very sceptical about the merits of education.

As mother knocked on the classroom door I saw my chance and made a dash for freedom. I would have succeeded too if it hadn't been for a goggle-eyed old lady on her 'High-Nellie'. Before you could say "gotya", mother was all over me.

"Mind you Madam," said the shortsighted old lady, "if you don't chastise your little terror, there's nothing but trouble in store for you". Mother thanked her for her sinister prediction and hauled me back inside.

After knocking loud and long the door opened half way and the Headmasters bald-head and upper body pushed through the opening.

"Oh, its you is it?"

"Tis me sir, I brought P.J. to be enrolled just like his brothers before him".

"Ah, yes, I remember them well. The first lad in particular.They called him 'pick-axe'. That fellow was one thorn in my side".

"But sure 'twas only a nickname sir. He was always a bit of an Archie-ollie-jist, his father said".

A smile broke across the headmaster's face as he stepped out onto the corridor. "And this fellow here what's he going to be?"

"He has the makings of a Missioner in him sir. Knows all his prayers by heart". And with that she gave me a pinch. I didn't know what the pinch was for and looked up at her for direction.

"Go on son," said she, "show the master how well you know your prayers" I said the first thing that came into my mind, after going down on my knees and blessing myself I began. "Bless me father for I have sinned. 'Tis only one week since my last confession. I stole a..."

"Whoa back there. There's no need to make a public confession of your sins as well as your chosen career young man. Get off your knees for God's sake before the three of us are thrown in the 'loony-bin'. What's this fellow's name" he asked mother and produced a pen and paper from nowhere.

"Patrick Joseph sir – the youngest and the last of them".

He blessed himself saying: "The last of the Mohicans".

Instantly I saw that he was on the wrong track and confusing us with some other tribe

"We're not Mohicans sir," I told him proudly. "We're the Monaghans".

"But I thought you knew that sir" ,said mother.

Smiling broadly he told us he was only talking in Metaphors and that the Mohicans were a bunch of Red Indians, who were all wiped out in America. Mother said she was sorry to hear it and wiped a tear from her eye. I sniffled because my nose was running and I put on as sorrowful a face as I could to match Mother's.

The Headmaster looked from one of us to the other in disbelief and suddenly let out a great roar of laughter. I took to my heals. I could see this whole education thing was only a joke.

THREE IS A CROWD

MAEVE Barton leaned against he parapet and looked absentmindedly at the continuing mass of traffic shuttling to and fro across the back of Vauxhall Bridge. Flakes of multicoloured confetti blew from the netting around her straw hat. The tiny flakes rose high above the surging throng and faded into nothingness. It was strange how things had turned out between Stella, Joe and herself. She had not expected the outcome of their triangular affair to end like this. Yet it might not be so odd after all. Life really was stranger than fiction.

Joe Cox and Stella O'Dowd had been constant companions since their teens. Stella grew on Joe as the mistletoe upon the oak. She was an only child and lived with her widowed mother. She looked older than her twenty years but was pretty and had a good figure. The money she earned as a typist at the Worsted and Woolen Mills provided them with their needs. Any money over and above was put aside for her wedding day.

Joe Cox was twenty-one years old, tall, fair and handsome. He had just finished his apprenticeship as a mechanic at the local garage. He had a likeable disposition and more than one girl had eyes for him.

One day the manager at the mills asked to see Stella in his office. Work had been slack for some time and she feared the worst. On her way to the office she saw Maeve Barton coming towards her. Tears were spilling down her face.

"I've just got the sack, Stella. What will I do?"

"It looks as if you won't be alone, Maeve. He has asked to see me".

"I'll wait here until you come out", said Maeve, making a brave attempt at a smile.

"Come right in, Miss O'Dowd. I'll be with you in a moment".

Stella stared at the teaty wart in the corner of his mouth and wondered how his wife could bear to kiss him.

"I'm afraid I've got rather unpleasant news for you". He massaged the wart with a circular motion of the finger. "Just as soon as things improve we will send for you of course." She decided he was positively ugly. "Goodbye, Miss O'Dowd".

Joe Cox looked at his watch. Stella would be waiting for him. Mrs. O'Dowd opened the door before he had time to knock. Her usual smile touched upon her face but took off again before it could land.

"She is waiting for you in the parlour".

"Is there something the matter, Mrs. O'Dowd."

"Indeed there is, Stella lost her job and is talking of going to London. Talk some sense into her, Joe. She is too soft to be a bird alone in a foreign land."

Stella was standing by the window, gazing into the laurel hedge at the rear of the house. A shaft of sunlight lit her face making her complexion white and fantastic. She appeared to be without substance, as a thought or vision in the mind's eye. She seemed strangely out of reach. She turned as he entered the room.

"Joe, I have lost my job in the mill."

"I know, your mother told me".

"Well?"

"Well nothing, it isn't a life sentence."

"But it takes money to get married and mother has to be provided for. There is only one answer to it, Joe, and that is to go to London. Typists are paid great money there."

"But you can't possibly go to London alone."

"I won't be alone. Maeve Barton got her marching orders too. We talked about it and decided we should go together. We would share a flat and maybe even work together with any luck."

"She's the one who stole my shirt while I was swimming at the pool last summer."

"Yes, I know. She told me all about it. It think she likes you."

In a loud, black clattering, a flock of jackdaws flew into the back yard and hovered before the window like a dark cloud. They jostled and screeched at each other until their presence was almost menancing. Then in a thunderous beating of wings they had gone. A tiny black feather floated earthwards. It flittered and trembled as it brushed against the window pane. Then it paused, impaled upon the glass by an up-current of air. It peered sympathetically at the troubled faces then slid down to the waiting earth.

Joe had no answer to Stella's persuasive reasoning. One week from that day saw Stella O'Dowd and Maeve Barton leave for London. Being qualified typists made their search for employment an easy task. They found work together at a car factory in Park Royal. The pay and conditions were marvellous. Stella worked in the Accounts Dept., and Maeve worked in Dispatch.

They rented an elegant flat at Notting Hill and settled down to live in the great metropolis. They had no desire to emulate the hectic life that their contempories insistently spoke of at work. Their's was a life of ease and contentment. They marvelled at the multi-channelled coloured television programmes, the public parks, the mystique of the underground trains and magical place-names like the Elephant and Castle, Piccadilly Circus and Shepherds Bush.

They worked from nine to five, five days a week. Stella often worked Saturday as well to earn extra money to send to her mother.

Every Sunday evening Stella would sit at her typewriter and hammer out two letters. One to her mother, the other to Joe. She would ask him what he did with his spare time. Tell him that she missed him very much and it would be no time at all until she returned.

With every letter she told him that Maeve said hello. That was what she wrote week after week. Faithful as an old dog, Joe would answer her every question as if his life depended on it. But time was running on and Stella, unaware of what was happening, was beginning to feel the tug and fascination of the teeming city. Something more intimate and vital than the letters from Joe Cox had caught her attention.

It had been a mistake to stay in for so long. They couldn't have known that seeing so much of each other would eventually cause them to bicker and fall out. So it was that Stella and Maeve began going out. At first they went together to a film or dance. In less than a month they were going their separate ways.

Stella accused Maeve of being bitchy and prying in her affairs.

"What the hell has it got to do with you if I let him drive me home?"

"I didn't say that it was. I am merely telling you that he is not your type. I heard some of the girls in "Accounts" talk about his capers. He's enough to shock Lady Chatterly's Lover."

"So what! Your trouble is jealously." Stella had put her coat on and was going towards the door.

"Where are you going, Stella?"

"I'm, going to a dance at Cricklewood. Any objections?"

"Shouldn't you be writing home?"

"Writing, I just can't think any more. I have nothing to say. My imagination is already stretched to its limit. But if you are so concerned why don't you type a nice little piece of gossip for Joe Cox. You would like that wouldn't you?"

Before Maeve could answer, Stella had taken paper from a drawer and wrote hurriedly at the bottom of a page – Love, Stella. She left the flat without another word. Maeve sat for more than an hour in a bewildered daze. Then suddenly she was sitting at her typewriter with fingers poised. She struck at the keys, which formed the first words. My dearest Joe, she began. Her touch was professional.

Stella did not answer Joe's following letter, nor did she answer the second nor third. She was too busy living it up with an oily, overdressed Cockney. How she kept up the pace was beyond Maeve. Soon her health began to fail. It was obvious that she could not continue to work all day and stay out all night. There was a letter from her mother begging her to come home and scolding her for not answering Joe's letters.

Next day when Maeve returned from work she saw that Stella had gone, bag and baggage. A note on the kitchen table read: Got another job. Going to live at Hammersmith. See you around. – Stella.

Paper was left beside her typewritter. At the bottom of the top page was written in Stella's unmistakable hand – Love, Stella.

It was obvious that she wished Maeve to write a last letter to Joe Cox. But what was she to say?

One evening about a month later Maeve saw Stella boarding a bus at Marble Arch. She looked sickly and worn-out. Before she could get to her the bus had pulled away. Stella had seen her though and waved. Maeve thought there were tears in her eyes.

Joe could not understand why Stella was not returning home. In his last letter he had asked frankly what detained her. He got only an evasive answer. Stella's mother told him that Stella no longer wrote but faithfully sent a few pounds every week.

She advised him to go to London and search her out. That was all the persuasion that he needed. He sailed for Holyhead next day, unannounced.

When the door bell rang Maeve was preparing for bed.

"Who is it?" she asked.

"It's the police. Would you please open the door."

Maeve trembled as she undid the lock.

"What's the matter?"

"You're Miss Barton, are you?"

"Yes that's right."

"A friend of yours has had an accident. A Miss Stella O'Dowd was knocked down by a car on the Bayswater Road. She is at the Regal Hospital."

Maeve gasped with fright. "Is it serious, constable."

"She has head and spine injuries, I understand. She wishes to see you. We'll take you there if you like."

Maeve stepped quickly into the waiting police car.

"Miss Barton, how long have you known Miss O'Dowd?"

"For many years. We came to London together and shared a flat up to a few months ago."

"Have you any idea what she has been working at since then?"

"No, but she is a typist."

"I'm afraid she has taken up another sort of trade for some time now. You are obviously unaware of this but it is best that you are told. The women who walk the Bayswater Road are notorious."

Maeve looked at him with disbelief and dislike.

The ward was dimly lit and smelled of T.C.P. and polish. Sister stopped at a screened bed and peeped through the shades. "She is awake, but you must not stay long. She is still very weak." She pressed Maeve onto a chair beside the bed, then smiled at Stella and was gone.

Stella clasped Maeve's outstretched hand and held it against her bruised and swollen face. She tried to speak but her tongue only made a click in her mouth and her lips were stuck as if with glue. She rolled her eyes to express her gratitude. Maeve felt the warm, wet flow of tears seep into the pores of her hand. The top of Stella's head was swaddled with bandages. The blood oozed through in parts and looked like red paint spilled on snow. A circling fly nose-dived at the smell of blood and landed on her pillow. It preened itself watchfully and made short scurries back and forth, inspecting its terrain.

"Don't try to speak. I will stay with you until you can get some sleep. Don't worry about a thing."

Joe Cox hailed a taxi at Paddington Station and was quickly motoring towards the flat.

"O.K., mate, this is it. The best of British luck to you." Joe rang the bell again for the fourth time without answer. Out of the corner of his eye he saw a sign that read "Charington's Ale." He would have a pint while waiting for them to return. He relaxed with his drink in a lounge chair facing the street. Opposite him an old couple were feeding their dachshound crisps and beer off a large ashtray. When it had dined and wined it was lifted onto a lounge table and brushed impeccably by the old gent. He looked to the old lady when he had finished and she smiled approvingly.

Maeve jumped off the eighty-seven bus outside the King's Head bar. She would get some cigarettes to take to Stella in the afternoon She smiled at the old couple as she came into the lounge. She looked at Joe and when he met her gaze she dropped some coins out of her hand and stood as if stuck. Joe saw a silver coin wheel towards him across the carpet. It hit against a table leg and fell softly across a fag end.

"Joe Cox, how in God's name did you get here." Her face was as red as a poppy in a churn of milk. He stared at her in disbelief. She looked so attractive and full of life. She had embraced him before she knew it and could have kicked herself when she saw the embarrassment on his face.

"Where's Stella? How is She?"

"Joe, there's bad news. Stella has had an accident, but she is recovering." She saw the blood drain from his face. His lips trembled when he spoke.

"What happened? Where is she?"

"She was hit by a car."

Maeve told him of the accident and of Stella's injuries. At the hospital she left Stella and Joe alone and waited patiently in the lobby. When he came out his face was lined with distress. She waited for him to speak.

"She will never walk again. Did you know that Maeve. The doctor told me that permanent damage has been done to her spine. Why did it happen to her."

Maeve did not get time to answer as he went on speaking.

"She is so brave about it all. It is almost as though she doesn't care. She looks so strange and distant. I'm not even sure that she was happy to see me."

Suddenly he stopped and looked at her. She held her breath. Her womanly intuition told her he was about to say something important.

"I asked her to marry me, just as soon as she is well enough."

"She said she could never marry because of what happened."

Maeve was relieved, but only for a moment.

"I'll make her change her mind, you'll see. I'll take a job here until she is better. It is the least I can do."

He found work at Carmichaels of Regent Street and adapted to the city life straight away.

All three saw a lot of each other in the weeks that followed. On several occasions Joe took Maeve to the films. They even fed ducks together in Kensington Gardens.

Stella improved as if by magic and was speeding about the hospital wards in her wheel chair with confidence.

They were married at St. Malachy's almost three months from the day of Joe's arrival. Maeve was Stella's bridesmaid. After the reception she slipped away unnoticed. She stopped at Vauxhall Bridge and looked about her vacantly. A few pieces of confetti blew from her clothing as she climbed the parapet and jumped with quiet desperation into the Thames.

GOING TO A WEDDING

THE wedding invitation card stood spread-eagled on our kitchen table. It was the most impressive piece of communication that ever came through our letter-box. It looked like two pages from the "Book of Kells", with their gold and silver Celtic lettering, bedecked with garlands of flowers and ferns. "Two hearts beating as one", suggesting these emblems to be the seat of affections. As further proof of man's undying love, (woman's ditto)? If further proof be necessary, the angelic infant hovered above, the bow and arrow aimed at the queen and jack of hearts. I could see from the size of the arrow it would not be possible for it to pierce the Jack and queen of hearts at the same time. Cupid's arrow was too short by half.

"He will have to shoot a second arrow", I said to myself aloud.

Just as I was saying this, our five year old son, "junior" came trotting into the kitchen with the cat held in a "half-Nelson".

"Where's d'indians dad"? he asked in bright-eyed amazement and dropped the cat on its' fat head, and gingerly climbed onto the kitchen table.

"I'll get me bow-n-arrow" he said, and jumped off the table with a whoop and a holler as they say in the best American movies, and he tripped over the sore head of the cat.

"Awe –u-awe, awe-u-awe", undeterred he yodeled his Indian war-cry, in that time honoured hand over mouth, boy's way. I could have sworn the cat was using bad language as it plunged through the open window, in terror of its mortal life. Whatever about its nine lives, its present one was under heavy attack.

I glanced at the pendulum clock and got a start. It was twelve-thirty p.m., and time was a flying. At this rate, I reckoned I wouldn't be able to get a jar before we went to the wedding. I had gone to the "Stag Party" the night before and had done more staggering than partying.

A hair of the dog that bit me, was the only cure. Just then, junior came back at a dog-trot, armed with his plastic bow and arrow. He was searching for the cat. Mistakenly, I had once told him it had nine lives, and I wondered if he was trying to disprove my rash opinion.

"Hold it right there, Geronimo", I said.

"Have you seen my cuff-links"?

"Where's the cat"? he asked in return.

"Gone flying out the window", I said.

"Then maybe he took them for his other coat", replied junior.

"What other coat, son?" " Cats don't wear coats".

"They do so", he said. "Mam said she'd be putting her winter coat on soon".

Enough said. "Where's your mother, junior"?

He had his head out the window.

"She's eating out of the dust-bin, dad".

I burst out laughing and then I remembered.

My wife had gone upstairs for a jiffy, three quarters of an hour earlier to put on her hat. They weren't as long putting the dome on St. Peter's in Rome, I thought to myself.

But I knew she'd be doing her contortions before the full mirror. She might even have tied herself up in knots. It's no piece of cake trying to measure your behind from the front. You'd need a swivel neck like a barn-owl.

"Vanity, they name is woman" may well be described as a male chauvinist's bias, and that is why I would never dream of offending their intelligences by conferring upon them any sentimental bouquets of silly and undeserved admiration. I know they wouldn't have it any other way, the dear little dears. Oh dear, it looks like I'll have to beam the wife down, Scottie or no Scottie. I went to the bottom of the stairs, and bellowed in my best Rambo meets the Wolfman voice; "Woman, if you're not completely disintegrated, I'll beam you down. Are you gone back to bed or what"?

No answer. She's throwing the deaf ear, I thought.

"It's one o'clock, dear", I lied. "Where did you put my cuff-links, love"?

"They're on your bloody shirt sleeves, Hawkeye" she almost screamed, and I knew things weren't shaping up before the mirror. But she was right, the cuff-links were there. I sung dumb and was about to walk back to the kitchen when she commanded.

"Listen, plug in the electric kettle, put out the cat, and wash junior's face and hands. I'll be down in one minute. What the hell are you doing down there anyhow, dreaming"?

First it was Hawkeye, and now its Rip van Winkle. I'm being demoted, I thought. Next stop is the village idiot. But being the nice fellow that I am, I swallowed my pride and set to work with alacrity.

I plugged in the electric kettle like a flash. It was a new-fangled job, with an in-built fuse for absolute safety. I had bought it the previous week, and had connected it up myself. Who will I leave my hands to, I mused, as I swung into the next order of business. The cat, the cursing cat was back and had rolled itself up like a football in the armchair, on my "fresh from the cleaners" jacket. To make things worse, she was moulting. Faster than "Billy the Kid" could clear leather, I gave her a look at the mop where she couldn't see it and she went, post haste, to look for lodgings, I suspected. Everything is working like a dream, I thought, not a hitch. Junior was next on the list.

"Oh, junior, where are you"?

To me junior was proof positive of that established principle; " You can bring a horse to water, but you can't make him wash"? Well, anyhow, drink or wash, it didn't make much difference, I'd have to catch him first.

"What the hell is going on in the stairhole"?

I asked myself, while looking at a fist-full of the cat-hair that I had harvested from my jacket. Between sneezes (I sneezed seven times), I wondered if we might ever see the day that cats would be an endangered species. There was a God-almighty racket in progress under the stairs. Could it be junior persauding the cat to indulge in an act of Hari-Kari? The cat wasn't buying it. She rose from the stair hole like a rocket, but on a false trajectory, and ditched in the coal bucket. A junior "William Tell" shot an arrow after it, and hit "yours truly" in an unmentionable place, and I fell to my knees howling like the proverbial hound-dog. Looking back now, I think I must have overdone the semantics, because it brought my wife down in the most unlady-like fashion. Apparently, she thought something terrible had happened to junior, and she stuck one of her very high heels in the "landing" mat, and bingo, she came flying down, mat and all, just like Sinbad on his magic carpet, only, she failed to execute a smooth landing. She brought down with her an authentic imitation of a "Ming dynasty" vase, and a genuine Irish oak miniature table.

"Are you sure you're all right, dear," I asked as I extracted her from the wreckage. I knew she was indestructable, but I had to ask. She was on her feet faster than Mohammed Ali, and almost as pugnacious.

"Is junior all right? What happened to my little baby"? she bawled, like a sergeant major on parade.

"There's nothing the matter with our little terror", I assured her.

"It's your misfortunate husband that's been clobbered".

She eyed me, the same as Morriarty eyed Sherlock Holmes. Junior had the cat by the tail with both hands, and wouldn't let go.

"If that animal bites the child, it will be your fault", she pointed out.

"Who else's"? I enquired. "Elementary, my dear", and I almost said Morriarty.

Suddenly, the smell of burning rubber was everywhere. The electric kettle was doing a jig. Smoke and sparks plunged skywards, as if from an old coal-fired train engine of long ago. "You've set the house on fire. You plugged in an empty kettle, you nincompoop. The element is burned out of my new kettle. Why did I ever invest"? she asked her mother's picture on the wall, and I wondered if it was me or the kettle she was referring to.

The socket blew off the wall, making a noise like a twelve gun salute. It was almost funny, but the wife wasn't laughing, although if you didn't know her, you might be excused for thinking so.

Have you ever heard the great Australian King-fisher bird calling, the one they named the laughing jack-ass? You really couldn't tell them apart, and believe it or not, she fished more than the twelve apostles, until the Pharisees slapped on the rod licence. But I'm not complaining, I just feel like a fish out of water, at times like this.

"Oh, men, you couldn't ask them to do anything. You damn near blew us all up", and she waved her arms with superb dramatics, until you'd think you were looking at Desdemona, demonstrating before Othello the Hun. Then with a flick of the wrist, she produced a tissue-paper from nowhere, and neatly touched the bridge of her nose.

"Don't cry dear", I said, "you're eye-shadow will run".

I knew damn well it couldn't. She was just like an oil painting. You know that one of the lady with the mad grin and the Roman nose, painted by Leo someone or other.

"You couldn't make faces". She was still firing broadsides across my bows.

I hung my head sheepishly, pretending guilt and sorrow. "That hat looks marvellous on you", I said. She left the mirror over the mantlepiece, and demurely stepped to my shaving mirror. It was magnified.

"I like it", she cooed. "T'was worth the money". "Like hell", I thought to myself, but dared not say so. "You know what they say: If you want to get ahead, get a hat", she said.

And I looked at my delapidated old deerstalker stretched out on the telly, going nowhere. So be it. If the price of freedom is eternal vigilance, the price of peace must be eternal silence. "Will you light the gas, for God's sake, seeing as how you've destroyed the electric kettle".

What could I say? I bravely struck a match, and it broke off and fell lighting, to the ground.

"Not a very friendly one, a cara", I quipped. She gave me a look that would separate a famished cat from a fresh herring. I picked up the gas lighter, but it didn't have any flint. Did it ever? I struck another match and it lit like a torch. Bright as light. I imagined myself lighting the Olympic flame at the First Olympiad in ancient Greece.

The roar of the crowd was deafening. I put the torch to the great bowl, and wouldn't you know it, the gas jet made a noise like a cat's fart, and blew out the bloody match. "The gas is gone. Feed the meter. Have you got a ten-penny piece"? and before I could say, "no change", she was going through my trouser pockets. I held my hands over my head, like the evil Mexican, Buckskin did when Johnny MacBrown got the drop on him in the badlands of Dakota.

"I thought you said you didn't have any money, Scrooge", and she pulled a ten-pound note from one of my pockets.

"You got me busted, kid!, I joked. "But I was keeping that for your birthday".

"Oh yeah, my birthday was three months ago, remember? You don't and you didn't then either".

"Silent O'Moyle", I thought. I have a golden rule: When your hand is in the lion's mouth, draw it out very slowly.

"I have one", she shouted triumphantly, as she pulled a ten-penny piece from my other pocket. She pushed the coin into the meter and turned the knob whilst Jack-a-lantern lit the third match. Nothing happened. The coin was stuck in the slot and wouldn't go in or come out. "Well, I'll be a monkey's uncle", said she.

"Don't you mean Aunt, dear", I said and I thought she'd have a seizure. "Never fear, brains is here", I said. I grabbed a hammer from junior. He protested that he was mending the radio-gram. I made a swipe at him, but he was too quick for me, and I fell over the blasted nail-tearing cat. It sailed through the kitchen without any visible means of propulsion. It was its third time in space in less than half-an-hour.

Without further hesitation, I made a run at the gas meter and like the "Blacksmith of Limerick", I brought the hammer crashing down on the medal. That's right. It was a medal, and not a ten-penny piece at all. I realized as much just as I scored a direct hit, but it was too late to call off the attack. The meter rattled in shell-shock on it's little wooden shelf.

"That was my Confirmation medal you put in the slot", I reproached the wife.

I'll tell you one thing", she said, "you surely didn't get it for home-cooking".

Undaunted, I struck another match and turned up the burner. Lo and behold, it lit up like a holy flame. "There you are now," I said, "religion does have its' compensations after all." "Polly put the kettle on, and we'll all have tea".

That's the wife's name, – Polly.

MICKEY SPURS

THE moment I laid eyes on them, I knew there was something in the wind. There was an aura of the bizarre about them. It was as if they had stepped into our presence from another dimension. I felt sure there was more to their coming amongst us than was visible to the naked eye. Yet they were mortal sure enough and more than that their whole demeanour was strangely compelling.

I was sitting in my favourite hostelry at No Rose Inn Street imbibing a pint with my old friend Billy B. It had struck twelve midday some fifteen minutes before and already there were about twenty people on board in the public bar. A brilliant sun poured through the front window and created cartoon like silhouettes on the vacant parts of the bar room floor. A sudden gust of wind got up and pushed open the bar room door. It blew unfettered paper drip mats to the floor. One to two of the customers looked towards the door. Then the bar radio came on, seemingly of its own accord for about five seconds and then switched itself off, as it had come on. I looked around the room. The hum of conversation hadn't ebbed. Was I the only one who had heard It? Was I beginning to imagine things? No. Billy B. had heard it too. He laughed and nodded his appreciation.

"I always knew that friggen Hong Kong wireless was weird."

And where did that sudden gust of wind come from?" I asked him

"That's' the wind that shook the Barley", Billy said, full of his fun and happy with his quick witted response. Again the bar room door opened and Petey came in from the sun. Cradling a pint of Smithwicks' in his fist he sat down beside Billy, grinning like the proverbial Kilkenny cat. After exchanging vernacular greetings, we were getting down to the business at hand when the door opened once again. This time it opened ever so slowly, an inch at a time. When it had opened about a foot, a mans head appeared. His dark eyes scrutinized the customers one by one.

He must have been satisfied with what he saw because in another minute he was inside and holding the door open. Apparently he had company. He was still sizing up the place and wondering where they were going to sit. He looked over the seven men, two women and a dog, that sat up to the counter. There were three men in a corner rehearsing the 1987 All Ireland Hurling Final. On the long seat at the front window four men questioned the political strategy of Dessie O'Malley forming a new party, and then his eyes rested on Billy, Petey and me. When our eyes met I could have sworn I knew the man from somewhere. And I thought I saw a flicker of recognition brighten his face too until a frown chased it away.

He was of small stature, about five feet six inches and weighed about eleven stones. And then it dawned on me he was a dead-ringer for the film star Clarke Gable, but in reduced dimensions. He wore a grey tweed three piece suit. The jacket had a half belt at the back and was pleated from the underarms and came down at an angle of forty five degrees to be concealed behind the belt. A razor sharp crease ran down his trouser legs and his brown leather shoes were covered with a fine white dust. His matching waistcoat gave his outfit a long-ago look. He carried a navy blue travelling bag which he held in a tight fisted grip.

There was a legend printed in green across the side of the bag. It read "Viva La Spania" Two ribbons were tied to the travelling bag – one to each handle – a black and amber one and a white one. Had he just come back from Spain? Perhaps he was a Spanish tourist eager to explore the Irish psyche. But there was something strange and incongruous about the travelling bag. Its shape too was odd. Both ends were drooped while the centre was full and rigid. He caught me looking at it and I though a wave of sadness crossed his face as he looked from me to the bag. He was still holding the door as the second person came into the room.

She was of medium height, well made and full of life. When stepping into the room she moved like a cat, that was out of it's territory. She wore a belted cream gabardine overcoat. On her shoulder hung a black leather bag and her scarlet high heel shoes were covered with a fine white dust. Her dark brown hair was tied up in a bun with a black ribbon at the back of her head. She was very attractive and not a day over forty I guessed.She moved a little to the side to make room for the third member of the party.As she did so she was searching the face of the lookalike Clarke Gable for any signs of concern or misgivings. She found only a calm assurance.

The third member of the party stepped gingerly into the room. He was a low-sized red headed man with a soft white face. He smiled nervously it seemed, while trying to exhibit a casual expression. He was dressed in an expensive black Cromby overcoat which swung open, displaying a dark blue pinstripe suit which was double breasted with tiny lapels.

Under his receeding chin he sported a polka dotted cravat and his pale blue shirt had its collar peaks buttoned down on the chest. His size six black leather shoes were covered in a veil of fine white dust. His entrance was the signal for the three of them to find a place to sit. With Gables lookalike leading the way, the three of them came towards where Billy, Petey and me were sitting. He placed the mysterious looking travelling bag on the table in front of us and said:

"Would you mind if we sat here, gentlemen." Even though there were chairs available and room enough, they stood there waiting for an answer.

"Nothing could give us greater pleasure", I assured him. The fact was, I was intrigued with their presence and delighted with the prospect of observing them and their travelling bag at close quarters. All three smiled their thanks and the red headed man asked the other two what they wished to drink.

"Lizzie won't have any booze, – just a mineral water, – she's driving, – remember"! The red headed man nodded in agreement.

"I'll have a large whiskey with a little water for me eyesight and what ever your having yourself." The red headed one soon brought the drinks to the table and went back for a large gin and tonic for himself.

While the three of us sat with our backs to the wall, the three of them sat four – square in front of us. We exchanged pleasantries and were soon chatting away like old friends. I felt as if I had known these people all my life. This is an act of fate, I thought to myself. Here we are the six of us, having travelled down the years to meet in this place and time, – why? The well watched travelling bag sat solidly on the table between us, not as a check to our developing friendship but as a promotion for it, I felt.

I addressed my question to Gables look-alike; "Has anyone ever told you, you are the spitting image of Clarke Gable, give or take a few inches and a few pounds?" "All the time", he said, laughing.

"That's nothing!, Lizzie said, "he drives a bus in Dublin and the locals call it Gables Bus.

Not wanting to be left out of the conversation the red headed man continued; and before the driver only busses came to pass, Gable had a great Kilkenny man, conductor with him for years." Then the three of them placed hands upon the travelling bag, while a tear flowed down Lizzies cheek.

Gable finished off his large whiskey and after glancing around the table he excused himself and went to the bar.

"Are all three of you from Kilkenny City," Lizzie asked?

"Bred, born and reared", I answered.

The Nore flows in our blood
Black Marble is in our bones
Born with hurleys in our hands
Kilkenny City is our home

And then Gable was back at the table with drinks: Two pints of Guinness for Billy and me. One pint of Smithwicks for Petey. One mineral water for Lizzie. One double Gin and Tonic for the red headed man and a large whiskey for himself, with a little water for his eyesight, and there was an extra small whiskey for nobody at all.

"It's nice to meet decent people", I said, "thank you".

"Normally I wouldn't drink with strangers", but I'll make an exception this time, just for you, Billy exclaimed to Lizzie, and we all laughed uproariously.

Then Petey, who was three-sheets-in-the-wind but beginning to feel left out of it, promised them faithfully, that if their 'jalopy' screwed up, he'd let them have on loan -for free, three-speed racing bikes for their return trip to Dublin. I though the three of them would explode with laughter.

"Wouldn't Mickey Spurs just love to be here" Lizzie said, "he so loved the crack".

"You're forgetting," Gable said "he is here", and so saying he stood the extra half whiskey on top of the travelling bag.

I hope you won't mind me asking but are any of you from Kilkenny, – city or county? The three of them shook their heads.

"Do you have any relatives or in-laws here abouts?"

"I'm afraid not", said the red headed man, but we do have strong links with Kilkenny and know a great deal about your Marble City.

"Then it must be from Gable's bus conductor," I ventured. It was a long shot but I was trying to make sense of the whole scenario.

"You have hit the nail on the head," Gable agreed, "but there is more, much more."

"So the three of you have come to our medieval city, to see the sights as described to you by the Kilkenny man, but where is he?"

Lizzie looked from the redheaded man to Gable and then to the half whiskey resting on top of the travelling bag. "You are right about he asking us to come to Kilkenny", Gable said," and he also asked us to stop at a pub known as Andy's at Rose Inn Street and to have a drink on him. So here we are."

In the meantime the redheaded man had ordered another round of drinks and paid for them despite our objections, saying; we are only doing as we were told, its Mickey Spurs money. Its his last visit to his native city."

Gable got to his feet saying, "I would like to propose a toast." Lizzie and the redheaded man jumped to a standing position with glasses raised. Billy, Petey and me did the same. Then Gable lifted the half whiskey from the travelling bag.

"To the memory of Mickey Spurs, the best friend a man, ever had." So saying he downed the drink, leaving a timble full in the glass. We all drank the toast and then Gable did an extraordinary thing: He opened the travelling bag and poured the timble-full of whiskey into the bag.

FANTASTIC HORSE
SK

Billy, Petey and me looked at each other in blank amazement. I had thought a little earlier the mystery was beginning to unfold, I wondered now if the reverse was true?

"Please don't think me rude but would you mind telling us natives what you have got in, the travelling bag?" "I thought you'd never ask," said Gable. "It's a man," said Lizzie "A man called Mickey Spurs," said the redheaded man.

Gable took up the story; We promised him on his death-bed that we'd take him back to his native Kilkenny for burial. He also insisted that we should buy a few drinks here in Andy's. Back in 1975 after Kilkenny had won the All Ireland hurling final, he took three days off work and came down with the team. He said he spent the best three days of his life in Kilkenny that September." Gable lifted a silver urn from the travelling bag. "These are his ashes which we will bury this very day in Kilbride Cemetery outside Callan. Gable went on to relate:

Mickey and me worked together on the Dublin busses for more than twenty years. He was an only child who was orphaned at seven years of age in Kilkenny. His only living relative was his grandmother who lived at a place called Goose Hill. She was an old lady of seventy seven years, when she took Mickey to live with her. But she was strong willed and refused to die until Mickey was able to look after himself.

When she died aged eighty seven, Mikey was seventeen years of age and working as a messenger boy in Smithwicks on High Street. After his beloved grandmother died Mickey was broken hearted and without kith or kin. He decided to leave for Dublin and try to better himself. And as luck would have it he landed a job on the Dublin Busses as a Conductor. He was a real man's man and never married. A maverick you could say that was never branded. The strange thing was, that although he seldom went back to Kilkenny, he never stopped talking about it.

"Can I say something", Lizzie asked. "We drove down early this morning and took him to Goose Hill. Then we went to Saint Canices Church where we had a Mass offered for the good of his soul, from there we drove to Irishtown, up Parliament Street into High Street and down onto your beautiful Parade. We parked on the Parade and went walking through the Castle grounds. Mickey had it all written down for us, including our coming here to Andy Hendersons.

"My turn now", said the redheaded man as he brushed the fine white dust off his trouser bottoms and shoes with his handkerchief. The first thing I'll say is that you need to have your Castle walk Tarmacademed, – only joking. I personally have known Mickey for nearly thirty years. A more sincere and loyal friend I have never known. All over the South Side he was known as a sound man. When I met Mickey at first, he had two great loves in his life. One was the Kilkenny Hurling team and the other was Tottenham Hotspurs. In our part of the city he was known as Mickey Spurs.

NO NEWS IS NOT NECESSARILY GOOD NEWS

WHAT'S THE LATEST NEWS?

Some self appointed pseudo Aesop once observed: "No News is Good News". People say it everywhere and all the time. And they say it with such conviction and earnestness that one would be forgiven for believing it to be the Gospel's truth. The fact is I have used the same ill-logical expression myself a thousand times.

Lately though, I found the more I used it, the less I liked it. On examination it simply doesn't stand up. Any fourteen year old aspiring philosopher could tell you that No News is merely No News, nor could it ever presume to metamorphose into good news. One might just as well say: No bread is good bread.

And so I determined to demonstrate once and for all to the whole gullible world the utter stupidity of such a phrase. I would prove that of all the words of wisdom, maxims, pithy sayings and excellent proverbs, none save this preposter, so obviously lies through its teeth.

RESEARCH

In order to mount a well ordered attack I donned my thinking Tam (O'Shanter) and invoked the gods of controversy. I would begin by interpreting a history of ancient Greece. Once that was accomplished I would pour over the Bible and finally peruse the three volumes of H.W. Longfellow, prince of poets.

The smoke of the lamp caused by the burning of the midnight oil saw me through two pairs of spectacles and left me with a twitch in my right cheek and callouses on four fingers and thumb. And yet in none of these books did I find confirmation of the expression: "No News is Good News". Therefore I have no qualms about denouncing 'your man' (our pseudo Aesop) as a chancer of the first water.

ANCIENT GREECE

"What possible connection," you may ask, "did ancient Greece have with the reporting of News or the absence of it either"?

Well one chapter struck me very forcibly. That was the war (They did damn all else) between the Greeks and the Persians. Talk about 'Blitzkreig', this one was a 'Greekzkreig'.

It happened in the year 490 B.C. After the battle one John Joe Barry like Grecian ran all of the 22 miles from Marathon to Athens in his bare feet, with the News of their victory over the Persians (who were really Iranians and the ancestors of Omar Khayyam of Rubaiyat fame). And don't you know that some poor Persian (Iranian) ran twice as quick in the opposite direction with the news of their defeat. (Bad news always travels faster). There is no evidence there that, "No News is Good News" .

Is there?

THE BIBLE

"But what has the holy Bible got to do with News?" you ask while lifting your eyes to heaven.

Amen to that. I thought everybody knew the New Testament is properly called the 'Good News'. To emphasis that didn't a choir of angels bring the Good News of Christ's birth to the shepherds minding their flocks and they came rejoicing to adore Him. Which to my mind proves that Divine Providence also refutes the notion that: "No News is Good News".

H.W. LONGFELLOW

And now we come to the three volumes of Henry Wadsworth Longfellow, and his concern for the distribution of the News.

"Listen my children and you shall hear".

Of the midnight ride of Paul Revere".

This heroic horseman rode his trusty steed all through the night from Charlestown to Medford, from Medford to Lexington and from Lexington to Concord with the News that the Red Coats had landed and were on the 'war path'.

It was at Concord, a village in Massachusetts, in the Spring of 1775 that the American War of Independence opened with a skirmish that sent the British Red Coats running for their lives.

If you think about it, No News in that instance would have spelled disaster for the fate of the American Nation and proves beyond the shadow of a doubt that No News could never be good news.

PAUL REVERE'S RIDE

NEWSLETTER

The predecessor of the Newspaper was the Newsletter. This was nothing more than a written sheet of news sent by an agent to his subscribers. One such newsletter was published for the information of Charles I's officers. The misfortunate messenger was intercepted by some of Cromwell's soldiers and ordered to hand over the newsletter. Like lightning the loyal Royal screwed up the newsletter and stuffed it into his mouth and swallowed it down like peaches and cream. We are not cognisant as to how the brave messenger fared after his feast. Whether he suffered heart-burn or indigestion, or was relieved of such nausea with a swift thrust of a Cromwellian sword in the solar plexus, we have no news.

THE NEWSPAPER

It was Lord Burnham, otherwise Mr. I.M. Levy of the "Daily Telegraph" who gave London its first penny-daily Newspaper. He reduced it from two pence to one penny on the 17th September 1855. The same Lord Burnham who persuaded Henry M. Stanley to return to Africa where he had met Dr. Livingstone at Ujiji on the shores of Lake Tanganyika. It was there Stanley uttered that famous greeting: "Dr. Livingstone I presume". Livingstone who was a missionary as well as an explorer had discovered Victoria Falls and was the first European to travel the length of Lake Tanganyika.

In 1866 he set out to find the source of the River Nile. When Stanley found him at Ujiji he could see that Livingstone was ill and worn and didn't seem capable of completing the task.

Back in London Stanley was giving a detailed account of that historic meeting to Le Sage who was correspondent for the Telegraph. Lord Burnham accidentally walked into the room and immediately got the gist of what was happening. He confronted Stanley on the spot saying: "Could you and would you complete the task of discovering the source of the Nile? And what is there to be done?" Within minutes a new exploration of the 'Dark Continent' had begun. Next morning the headlines on the Daily Telegraph told the news: "H.M. Stanley to seek source of the Nile".

PADDING AND EMPTY COLUMNS

To give their readers their money's worth if news was scarce, editors would pad-out their newspapers with a few chapters from the Bible. At other times of scarcity they'd publish some of 'Aesops Fables' and verses of poetry. And there were other editors who would record the scarcity of news by leaving a blank column or two. These would point out that such spaces could well be used to record the reader's private news or could serve the purpose of school children practising a good writing hand.

MODERN NEWSPAPERS

The appetite of the mind for news is insatiable and its capacity to absorb it is elastic. Modern newspaper men hunt up-to-the-minute news like G.K. Chestertons Fr. Browne chased after the law breakers. Once they have captured the facts they submit them piping hot for publication. Old news is old hat and this week's news will be as dead as the Dodo next week.

But fresh news is always a tonic for the intellect. With it, readers keep themselves informed about the real issues in their own community and country and wider news from around the world. In this way the best newspapers help to mould public opinion. And so having traversed history and literature in my attempt to unmask the farcical proverb that "No news is good news". I confidently leave the resolution to your own very able powers of deduction.

A TRUE BULLOLOGIST

THE STAGE IRISHMAN

The Stage Irishman was largely a figment of the English imagination. Portrayed as a boisterous rake he was ordained to speak in the jargon of the buffoon: Uttering sentences loaded with blunders and so-called Irish Bulls. In such a farcical creation the character of the Irishman was seen to be stupid and absurd.

The worst part of it being that this theatrical invention was accepted by the broad English public as the genuine article: Shillelagh swinging Paddy and his pig. Or the more sophisticated types like Capt. O'Cutters, and Sir Lucius O'Trigger, which were possibly more damaging to the Irish psyche because of their supposed class superiority.

FATHER OF THE IRISH BULL

Even Mr. Sheridan stooped to this erroneous description of the Irish character with the above: "Sir Lucius O'Trigger". But it was the real live Sir. Boyle Roche who was said to be: "The Father of the Irish Bull". This colourful gentleman was a member of the Irish Parliament for Tralee about the year 1775. His bulls we are told were deliberately constructed so as to put the government and opposition into good humoured debate. And it is on record that his Bulls seldom failed to sire such favourable conditions.

This man's highly amusing utterances have long since reached the lofty heights of the proverbial. One such revelation in Parliament is worth repeating here: "Mr. Speaker Sir; this country of ours is in such dire straits that little children who can neither walk nor talk are running about the streets cursing their Maker".

TRANSITION

All these things happened at a time when the rich and vibrant 'Gaelilge' was in a state of transition to the more crude and cumbersome Anglo-Saxon. Linguistic scholars all agree that the Irish language contains the most abundant vocabulary in the world for the expression of the human condition in both sorrow and love. And as these two passions best declare our concern for each other, no greater proof of the communicative power of the language is needed. But because the Irish were compelled to speak a language that was alien to them, they often substituted the idiom of the gaelilge for the one that was foisted upon them. Hence the idiosyncrasies of speech.

DAN DAN THREAD THE NEEDLE

We Irish are said to have a way with words. Some call it the gift of the gab. The Americans seem to believe every Irishman and woman has kissed the Blarney Stone. And the English are so perplexed with our conversion of their 'King's English' that they pretend not to understand us most of the time. It serves them right don't you think, for insisting that we should adopt their silly language in the first place. If anything, they should be grateful for the way we revitalised it with Celtic imagination and Irish wit. By playing a verbal Dan Dan Thread The Needle and sewing the calico letter here and stitching the homespun word there, we have saved it from a fate worse than death.

The written word has a greater permanence than the spoken word. It's something to do with Ink and Gutenberg, I think. Yet the spoken word can have a more persuasive power when it pours from the mouth of a rich personality. But somehow for me, the extraordinary words of a True Bullologist are more enduring and enjoyable than either author or orator.

I do not seek to insult your intelligence when I tell you that an 'Irish Bull', as well as being the uncastrated male of the Ox family, is also an inconsistency in speech that is said to be peculiarly Irish. That said, I suppose a Bullologist could be interpreted as an authentic speechifier of 'Irish Bulls'. These rare 'Homo Sapiens' specimens are scarcer than golden nuggets in farm-yard manure. Accordingly, if you should ever meet with one, thank your lucky Mars and bend to him your ears, as it is highly unlikely you will ever meet another.

JOHNNIE

I first met Johnnie many years ago in a Lodging House in Ladbroke Grove, London. I liked him from the moment we met. There was an air of candour about him. His manner implied that we were equals and could be friends without any commitments. Though he was Irish, he looked more like an olive-skinned Spaniard than a west of Ireland 'Paddy'. But of course looks are only skin deep and it is from the depths of the heart and soul that speech springs.

Johnnie used the English Language in a way that I had never heard before. His phraseology was both unique and hilarious. One of the first indications I got of his linguistic idiosyncrasies came the day after I became a paid-up-for-a-week lodger at Johnnie's home from home.

It was snowing as we ate our poultice-like breakfast of stir-about and fried bread. Johnnie kept getting up between gulps to conduct his own meteorological survey. The importance of this will not escape you when I tell you that his trade was with the shovel and pick.

"What's it like?" I asked after his tenth return to the table. "Well 'tis like this Jack", said he. "Judgin' be the cars goin' up and the wans comin' down make a differ, for there's snow on some and ther's more on none". Was it a slip of the tongue or had I happened upon a Bullologist? Johnnie was from the West of Ireland, and like the majority of his kind, he drank, smoked, danced and generally went to the Dogs at the White City Stadium. And he was a real humdinger with the women too.

"I hit the bulls eye right on the nose would the first girl I axed to dance at the Hop in Cricklewood", he confided. Only he didn't call it Cricklewood. He wouldn't. He called it Cricketwood.

"Angela's so nice you'd hate meetin' her". He added.

The celebrated argument about which came first; the egg or the chicken always came to mind whenever I boiled an egg. But that was before I met Johnnie. Chicken fruit was inexpensive in those days 'though not quite the twenty-four eggs for a penny of the "Hole in the Wall" Kilkenny fame.

But we ate so many of them that one would be excused for describing our place of residence as a hen-house. And our landlady always used a sand egg-timer when boiling them. Now, this advanced piece of technology intrigued Johnnie no end.

"It's quite simple", I advised him. "The sand tells you when the egg is boiled". "Sure I can see that", says Johnnie. "But how does the sand know when the egg is boiled?"

For one born in the wilds of Connemara, there is little tranquillity to be found on the streets of London.

But if one were to wander into Hyde Park or Kensington Gardens, one might find a remote corner where in the words of Thomas Hardy, one would be "Far from the Madding Crowd". This is precisely what Johnnie used to do whenever a fit of loneliness came over him. And he'd sit there signing for the birds, oblivious to that asphalt multi-purposed monster as it swallowed down trains and vomited up buses and cars with an ear-bursting clang, bang and boom, from morn' 'till night.

WAN HORSE TOWN

It wasn't surprising then that our unusual friend often spoke about how peaceful life was back in his little village, in the WEST of Ireland.

"It's a wan horse town, would more asses den men – would four shop's an'two a them Public Houses, an' we have three civic guards", he boasted. – "Three!"

"But surely ther's no need for three Civic Guards in such a peaceful hamlet?" I asked.

"There's not", said Johnnie. "But there would be if they weren't there".

As we saw quite a lot of each other daily at breakfast and supper, we soon entered into easy conversation. It should be stated that this mutual respect is not always shared by fellow lodgers. In fact I suspect the opposite more often pertains, and the legend of the Lodger's Reach is far from being a myth. Indeed it is an unfortunate truth that displaced persons forced to live together around one table often find themselves competing for the last cup in the pot, the best buttered slice of bread, et cetera, to such an extent that the strength and speed of the Lodger's Reach could well mean the difference between a full belly and an empty bowel. On the Sunday morning I left Ladbroke Grove to live in Wimbledon, Johnnie confirmed my faith in him as a true Bullologist with a double decker piece of phraseology.

What happened was: The Sunday newspapers were giving front-page coverage to an incredible story which claimed that mountaineers had sighted the Abominable Snowman or Yeti on the slopes of Mount Everest. And there were photographs that proported to prove it. Johnnie was spell-bound. He had a flair for the fantastic.

"Here, have a Decco at dat", he said. "There he is for all to see. The Abdominal Snowman 'racin' across the tip of Mount Never Rest".

THE MINOTAUR SYNDROME

WHEN first I saw it I thought the horror of it would surely drive me mad. Deathly cold it was despite the choking heat. It felt as smooth as glass and hard as flint. It was jet-black and shone like polished stone, excluding its base which showed a transparent bloody root. The thing was grotesque and frightening. It was a manifestation of mans' bestiality. Outward and upward it grew: a formidable weapon against any adversary. It tapered to a point like a church steeple except it was all twisted. Its aspect was so unholy, so macabre as to strike terror into the bravest heart. And oh what a point it had! No fencing foil was ever honed to such a point. All in all it had about it the mark of the devil. The people were still leaving the city on foot. Cars wouldn't start. Those who were able packed whatever chattels they could carry upon their backs. Then with their heads down they shuffled westward without a backward glance. In their panic to get out they left doors and windows thrown open to the elements. They were beyond caring. Their one ambition was to stay alive. Shops were broken into and looted. The streets were strewn with oddments of furniture and clothing. Those too badly infected and others too old and ill to travel had gone into the churches. The hospitals were dangerously overcrowded. An epidemic was inevitable. Now and then shots rang throughout the city like distant thunder claps. One could only guess the reason for it.

I had awakened earlier than usual. My room was murky-dark and stifling. The pyjamas were stuck to me with perspiration. Yet I shivered from some unfamiliar anguish. My forehead throbbed with an unspeakable intensity. The pain was excruciating. What happened next will stay with me until I die. I raised my hand to soothe my brow and spiked it upon some sharply pointed thing: A thing that sunk into the flesh like a skiver through fresh suet. A scream pierced the burning dark: an animal like shriek of fear. Was that me? What sinister movement was afoot? What dreadful presence had taken possession?

I leapt out of bed and pressed the light switch on. It didn't work. Off, on, off and on again I pushed it, but darkness won.

I struck a match and stood there looking around the room furtively. Gloomy shadows danced about the walls as the match flickered. I went towards the mirror on the dressing table. The match burned down and out. I lit another and stood squarely in front of the mirror. Blood was oozing from the stab at the palm of my hand. I was looking at myself in the mirror. It wasn't me. Who was it? What was it? It was looking back at me. Could it be a shadow, a shaft of darkness across my forehead? Surely my eyes were playing tricks on me! But how could I be sure? I struck two matches as one and held them close against the mirror. Slowly and deliberately I leaned forward and stared. I though the horror of it would surely drive me mad. In a glimmer of white and pink light the dawn crept through the back window. Somehow, the faded red apple and green leaf design on the off-white background made the scanty curtains look obscene. It would be daylight soon. I dared not be seen like this. The landlady would call in the police.Supposing she knocked on the door and then looked in. She'd throw a fit or die of fright. It was getting brighter by the minute. I'd need to think, to act instantly. In a flash I knew what had to be done. The vile thing would have to be removed quickly. The tear of a sharp-toothed hacksaw would sever it forever. I sprang from the room in a wild glee, jumping in three's down the stairs. I met no one. The tool-shed door gaped open. I was in luck: the hacksaw blade was like new. Armed with it and a hammer I swiftly re-entered the house. In the hallway the once playful old cocker spaniel confronted me with menace. It looked like a half-cooked turkey.

It was blistered and hairless. As I closed on it it gave a yelp and scampered into an adjoining room. We had frightened each other. As if by magic the hall light came on and with it the light on the stairs. Could someone be up and about at such an unearthly hour? The radio in the kitchen spluttered into life at the end of ELGAR'S: DREAM OF GERONTIUS. I paused as the time signal gave six consecutive bips. A clear crisp voice told: "This is BBC 1 with the news at six. Read by Imogen Steward. SCIENTISTS FROM EIGHTY COUNTRIES BIZZZ CRACKLE BIZZZZ, melt down has occurred." The lights were flickering on and off. Bizz…a nuclear catastrophe at Windscale. IN DUBLIN YESTERDAY BIZZZ BUZZZ AND HALT ALL NUCLEAR BUZZZZ CAUSING WIDESPREAD PANIC THROUGHOUT EUROPE BUZZ BUZZ BUZ BUZZEE IN HUMANS AND ANIMALS ALIKE. ZEEZ ZEESSS AND MUTATIONS HAVE BEEN IDENTIFIED BUZ THE MINOTAUR SYNDROME BUZZZEEEE TEN DOWNING ST.=BUZ –BOP. The kitchen light went out and the radio went dead. Some one screamed as I went past the kitchen. It was a hateful cry. Startled, I quickened my steps. Halfway up the stairs the hammer slipped from my hand. I heard a noise like mountain rams make, in skull splitting combat at mating time. I was about to retrieve it, but something or someone moved in the hallway. Whatever it had been I was too quick for it. I laughed to think of it and detected a strange timbre in my voice.

Not being a keen student of psychology I paid no heed to that. Darkness and light now fought for possession of the room. The mirror was drawing me towards it like a river to the sea. Perhaps the whole episode was but a nightmare. Again I tried the light switch. In a blinding flash the room was filled with divulging light. Deep into the mirror I stared. It was only too true. The horn was even more grosse, more satanical than I had suspected. You heard me right. That's what I said: the horn. It was set in my forehead above my right eye. Around the butt there was a large transparent swelling of the flesh that showed its tangled bloody roots. It had enlarged the eye by pulling it up to meet it. Distorted and goggle-eyed, it looked like something Picasso might have painted. My vision was unimpaired. I determined the length of my horrendous growth to be about seven inches. I was a modern-day Minotaur. A dead silence descended on the house. My silver pocket-watch ticked excitedly on the chair beside the bed. I placed the blade of the hacksaw as close as I dared to the base of the cruel horn. Steel bit into bone. Sawn particles floated before my eyes. The pocket-watch drummed out its frantic measurement of time. It s silver heart pounding in pace with mine. Faster and faster I sawed. There was something of an uproar out on the stairs: agitated voices and galloping feet. Someone was knocking on my door. "Can I have a word with you Sir? Would you please open your door? It's a matter of great urgency". "Get lost" I shouted back. "Hump off, can't you see I'm busy". "This is the Police. Open up in the name of the law. If you don't open up at once we shall be forced to break the door down".

I kept on sawing. It would not take long. The infamous thing was hollow. Sawdust of bone mixed with sweat ran down my face in yellow streaks. They were battering down the door. With every blow the silver pocket-watch leaped like a trout for a mayfly. In a thunderous burst the door came flying in. Three men stood in the room, gaping. One was a policeman, the others wore long white coats. Their fear had immobilised them. Relentlessly I sent the blade tearing into the dread thing. Its operation sounded almost like a dirge. Something gave and I let loose a plaintive cry. It was finished. I raised the damned thing aloft in a frenzy of delight. "Free, I'm free at last", I shouted and fired it at them. "Take it. It's what you want isn't it? It's what you came for!" There was no reply. They were examining the beast-like horn apprehensively. "It's the Minotaur Syndrome", a white coat announced and the others looked from the horn to me and back again. "Shall we take it with us doctor?" inquired the other white coat. "Yes, wrap it in a newspaper or something". "We shall have to take you away from here for your own good sir....I am a doctor". The policeman moved forward: "Best be going now, there's a car waiting outside". I ran to the front window. Outside a carthorse was harnessed with rope to a span new motorcar. As we walked down the footpath a tiny white kitten waddled across the rubbish filled, blackened road. Then it sat on its hunkers and peered at me with it's two heads.

Famous Kilkenny Men & Women

FROM
ST. CANICE TO HUBERT BUTLER
By Seán Kenny

CHAPTER ONE

KILKENNY: NATURAL HOME OF THE ARTS
FROM SAINT CANICE TO HUBERT BUTLER
KILKENNY IS IN OSSORY AND OSSORY IN KILKENNY
KIERAN, PATRON SAINT OF KILKENNY
SAINT CANICE OR KENNY
OUR PAST NOW FORGES THE KEY TO OUR FUTURE

LOOKING back now it seems like yesterday that the President of Ireland opened Kilkenny's first Arts Week at the Courthouse in Parliament Street. That portentous event happened on the 25th August (a Sunday) in the year 1974.

As I recall now there were quite a few sceptics and almost as many false prophets in the crowd. The sceptics questioned Kilkenny's capability and indeed suitability to bring off such an Artistic Exhibition. The false prophets forecasted that the event would not last the week, never mind about the originators promise to make it a yearly festival. "They are just a handful of over-enthusiastic boyos with delusions of grandeur", said one knowall.

And another pseudo intellectual asked "What does Kilkenny have to promote itself as a centre of excellence for the arts? "It has no history in the Fine Arts of Poetry, Painting, Music, Sculpture, etc and is therefore unfit to host any such Arts Festival".

"Sir, I said, allow me to point out that Kilkenny has had a unique and powerful involvement with the arts down through the centuries".

"It's the first I've heard of it. You'll have to prove that mister".

"It will be my pleasure to do so Sir, I said.

Let me begin by saying that the holyman after whom Kilkenny is called, was himself a poet. I shall come back to Canice later, but first:

KILKENNY IS IN OSSORY AND OSSORY IN KILKENNY

About the year 190 A.D. the island of Ireland was divided in two. One half was known as Leath Chuin and the other Leath Mhoga.

This came about because Conn of the Hundred Battles feared that his powerful military rival Mhoga Nuada might well defeat him in an all-out war for the whole island. And so they agreed it would be wiser to share, (discretion being the better par of valour – one supposes). Conn would rule over the Northern half and Mhoga rule over the southern half. The line that divided the two parts ran from Dublin via Clonmacnoise to Galway Bay.

When I tell you that the southern half consisted of Munster, Leinster and Ossory you will have a nice idea of the importance of Ossory from the very beginning, in the whole scheme of things. Further, the territory of Ossory was decided at the Synod of Rathbreasail in 1110 A.D. and was written into Irish history as follows: "From Slieve Bloom to Milahacham (near Waterford) in the South, and from Greanarbhia (near the Chapel of Grean) in the West, to Mount Margie (otherwise the Johnswell Mountains) in the East, all of which will be subject to the Bishop of Kilkenny."

The Kingdom of Ossory was founded by Aengus Ossory about the year 180 A.D. From a poem which was translated from the Gaelic by the legendary James Clarence Mangan, we learn that King Alfred, who ruled over the Northumbrian Saxons, was educated in Ossory between the years 684 A.D. and 690 A.D. Some historians claim he was educated at Kells by the monks of the Augustinian Priory known as "The Seven Castles", which was the medieval capital of Kilkenny. The poem records the high regard King Alfred had for his educators and the indigenous peoples of Ossory:

"I found besides from Ara to Glea,
In the broad rich country of Ossory,
Sweet fruits, good laws for all and each
Great chess-players, men of truthful speech."

FROM
ST. CANICE   TO   HUBERT BUTLER
By Seán Kenny

KIERAN: PATRON SAINT OF KILKENNY

Some three hundred years earlier in the year 375 A.D., the man who was to become the first of the Saints of Ireland was born here in Ossory. Kieran was the son of a pagan nobleman named Lughaidh and his wife Liedania. When he grew to manhood, Kieran voyaged to Rome to be educated in the Classics of Greek and Latin literature.

During his instructions he became aware of a comparatively new religious movement called Christianity. He studied it with great interest and later asked to be baptised. When eventually he returned to Ireland, he did so as an ordained missionary.

It was only natural then that Kieran set about the conversion of his own people first, in Ossory. That was about the year 410 A.D. And when we consider that St. Patrick did not come to Ireland, as a missionary until 432 AD, we see that our own St. Kieran preceded him in the conversion of Irish people by more than 20 years.

Early in the 4th century Kieran established the See of Ossory which is the oldest in Ireland. Kieran, the Ossorian who played a leading role in the spread of Christianity in what became known as the Golden Age when Ireland was said to be "The Island of Saints and Scholars" throughout the whole of Christendom.

Like St. Francis, St. Kieran was a great lover of animals and birds. The fame of his monastery, where he trained missionaries to preach in Eastern as well as Western Europe, became known far beyond the shores of Ireland. It has been written that when his coffin was being carried to his last resting-place, a flock of wild birds hovered over it.

ST. CANICE OR KENNY

Next came the holy man after whom Kilkenny is called. Canice or Kenny was born at Glengiven in Derry about the year 514 AD.

The place-name Kilkenny, literally means, Church of Kenny. No Cill Chainnigh mar a deirtar as Gaedilge. Canice ruled over the See of Ossory from 578 AD to 598 AD. He built his wooden church on or near the place where St. Canice's Cathedral stands today

Far from being well-to-do, Canice's parents had a small holding with a few cattle and a little land. But his father had the distinction of being a poet and a scholar. Probably through the influence of his father, then, Canice showed a deep desire to become a man of learning like him. Determined to accomplish this, he left home and parents and journeyed to the famous monastic school of St. Cadoc at Glammorgan in Wales.

The monks at the monastery soon discovered there was a latent poet as well as a priest waiting to be drawn out and nurtured, at the heart and intellect of the young scholar.

Saint Kenny's Well
By
Sean Kenny

By the time Canice was ordained he was also an accomplished poet, thanks to the inspirational and learned Monks of St. Cadoc. Canice returned to Ireland where he preached the Gospel and furthered his studies. As well as being deeply religious, Canice was recognised as a man of great learning. So great were his powers of oratory that the famous St. Columbcille brought him on many missionary crusades to the inner Hebrides, of which the principal isles are Iona, Islay, Jura, Mull and Skye.

Written works of religious and literary excellence which are attributed to Canice are a Life of St. Columbcille, a Life of St. Patrick in verse, a Commentary on the New testament and a Selection of Hymns.

Long before Kenny's Well, at the bottom of Croker's Hill by the river Breagagh, was crowned with a Stone House, Saint Kenny baptised all those who came to listen to that great poet-priest and marvel at his eloquence in Christ.

OUR PAST NOW FORGES THE KEY TO OUR FUTURE

Not only historians are fascinated by the past. Many people look back with wonder and in awe to where great men and women brought about events that shaped the lives we live today. Did not H.W. Longfellow advise us most solemnly that:

Lives of great men all remind us
We can make our lives sublime,
And departing, leave behind us
Footprints on the sands of time;

Footprints, that perhaps another,
Sailing o'er life's solemn main
A forlorn and shipwrecked brother,
Seeing, shall take heart again.

And men as wise as Henry Wadsworth Longfellow have told us that; the key to the future can be found by a close examination of the past. Bearing these wisdom's in mind, it beloves us to look to it. Don't you think we owe it to our predecessors, to ourselvs and to generations yet unborn, to pass on by word of mouth or by written letters the authentic version of the past?

Happily, it seems to me that now more than ever before, we Irish are searching for our roots and we find that people of Irish extraction too from around the world, are writing to newspapers in an attempt to discover exactly who their forefathers were and where they hailed from. Here in Kilkenny we see such letters to the Editor, periodically, in the "Kilkenny People".

I earnestly believe that every family should construct its own "Family Tree". By unearthing old photographs, letters and newspaper cuttings and securing them in an album you will be giving your children and their children's children, the priceless gift of knowing and understanding who and what their forebears were. Having a proper pride in ones place of birth is cousin to who we are. Here again the poet assures us that even the savage loves his native soil. We easily see from this, that even though people travel great distances and set up homes at the world's end, they never loose the love for the place from which they came. I think it was Carl Jung in his "Collective Unconscious" (1912) who described this love of place to the love of the new-born infant for it's mother's womb. All of us are truly the product of our past.

And now with your permission I shall attempt to answer in full the question asked by one of the sceptics or false prophets at the beginning of this article, namely; "What does Kilkenny have to promote itself as a centre of excellence for the Arts? Everyone knows it has no history in the fine arts of poetry painting music and sculpture." We shall see!

Kilkenny has been the home of many famous and highly artistic men and women throughout the ages. Men and women who strode easily upon the worlds stage. Poets, painters, playwrights, musicians, politicians, novelists, philosophers, architects, sculptors etc.

Taking the advice given to me by that false prophet, I will now attempt to name some of the glorious throng.

CHAPTER TWO

JAMES ARCHER
RICHARD ARCHDEKIN

JAMES ARCHER was one of Kilkenny's and indeed Ireland's most illustrious sons. Born in Kilkenny in 1550, into the merchant oligarchy. He was educated at Louvain and Rome as a Jesuit.

He became chaplain to the Spanish Forces in the Netherlands and rubbed shoulders with the greatest people of Spain. Later he became the first rector of the Irish College at Salamanca, however it was in the political arena that he was to distinguish himself.

Because he advocated for the Irish Cause in Spain and Rome he drew down upon himself the wrath of the British government. And his author Thomas Morrissey S.J. tells us that he so terrified officialdom, that the State Records described him as a man of superhuman strength and stature and capable of any and every mischief against the State.

James Archer returned as a missionary to Ireland during the Counter Reformation period 1596-1603. The 'greats' of the Elizabethan period in Ireland all figure in the life and times of James Archer. Men like, Hugh O'Neill, Ormond (Black Tom), O'Sullivan Beare, Kinsale and Dunboy, Mountjoy and Carew.

The faithful Kilkenny man stood tall amongst them all, inspiring the bitterest hate for the government, while being given the love and trust of the Irish people. He had so many narrow escapes with his life that the Lord President of Ireland said he must have been helped by witchcraft. From the moment of his arrival back in Ireland he had been a marked man and was accused of planning a Spanish invasion.

It was published in all the cities, towns and villages that he was a traitor and a large reward was offered to anyone who would take him prisoner or kill him. John Daniel reported to Robert Cecil on the 20th Dec 1596 that Archer was trying to persuade the Earl of Ormond's nephews to enter into a rebellion against the British Crown.

On the 15th September 1601 Archer landed in the west of Ireland and went immediately to the counties of Tipperary and Kilkenny. He was said to be in the best reputation with the Spaniards and in the Kings council. Once Philip III decided to send aid to Ireland, Archer's part in the Expedition was sealed. If the Expedition were to land at Cork Archer claimed that all Munster would rise up with him and the Spaniards. But because of some petty in-fighting a landing at Kinsale was agreed on as an alternative to Cork. The leader of the Expedition Del Aguila felt his position was being eroded by clerical interference. And so shortly after his arrival at Kinsale he refused an offer of 1,000 armed men and another 1,000 unarmed ones, from O'Sullivan Beare. Archer's opinion of Del Aguila was that he was both cowardly and incompetent. He sent the following letter concerning Del Aguila to Spain: "Del Aguila has the reputation in other parts of being a brave soldier, but here – and I voice the common opinion of all, he has shown himself the most cowardly and timorous man I have ever seen in my life." O'Neill and O'Donnell came with a good army on the day appointed for him to sally out to meet them as arranged. But he refused to leave Kinsale.

The Counts and Captains of the army asked insistently that I should go with them to the camp. With this Del Aguila would not agree and replied with disdain that it was my function to pray, teach doctrine and hear confessions, – nothing more. Now he has concluded a peace with the Viceroy Mountjoy even though we had 3,300 soldiers fully armed and fighting fit. The man is a craven coward. Mountjoy has struck camp and retired in triumph to Cork, taking Del Aguila with him".

The finality of Kinsale soon became evident even though the rumours of another Spanish Expedition remained hanging in the air. Carew sent a letter to Sir Robert Cecil from his castle in Bantry Bay, it was full of the 'arch-traitor' Archer: "Archer's activities in this barren pitiless place, swept by rains and storms seems to have brought about a stirring of superstition. 'Archer the priest conjures the foul weather, which I do partly believe, for the oldest in the land have never seen the like in May. If he remains in Dunboy I hope to conjure his head in a halter. He has a fellow devil to help him, one Dominic Collins whose brother was last year mayor of Youghal."

In June 1603 a Spanish ship did arrive with a little powder, lead and money and the news that O'Donnell was coming with a large force. Owen McEgan, Bishop of Ross, was on board. He promised that an army of 14,000 men was being prepared to land in Ireland. One of the functions allotted to Owen McEgan was to report back to the King on the situation in Ireland or else to send back James Archer. McEgan was a bad sailor and so Archer went in his place. "He and others arrived in Groyne on 17th July in a small French ship with only one mariner and without compass, card or glass. Is he some kind of magician or madman?" So wrote Sir William Monson to Sir Robert Cecil.

The long hoped for Spanish Armada never came and James Archer the great and good Kilkenny Jesuit died at the age of 70 years at the Irish College of Santiago Compostella in Spain.

Given his affinity with both Anglo-Irish and native Irish and in particular with Ormond and O'Neill, as well as his contacts with the Spanish Court, one could easily assume that had the Catholic Confederates been successful in war, James Archer the Kilkenny priest would have been one of Ireland's most influential men.

RICHARD ARCHDEKIN

Richard was born into a merchant family in Kilkenny in the year of Our Lord 1618. He was educated at Louvain where he became a Jesuit. In his day he was considered to be one of the Catholic Churches most able theologians. He was a famous controversialist and lectured in the principal colleges of Antwerp and Rome. He was a brilliant writer who wrote fluently in four languages, – Irish, English, Latin and Flemish. His most masterful works were: A Treatise of Miracles and A Life of Saint Patrick. Richard Archdekin died in Antwerp in 1693 having reached his 75th year.

CHAPTER THREE

THE BANIM BROTHERS: MICHAEL AND JOHN

MY FATHER was fond of saying: 'Give every man his due'. On the face of it this seems to me to be an excellent piece of advice and a laudable principle. But it is not always easy to put into practice. If for instance one is singing the praises of two brothers who have collaborated in the production of works of genius, how does one give each his 'just deserts?' Well that's my dilemma when attempting to sum-up the creative powers of John and Michael Banim!

Michael Banim was born in Kilkenny in the month of August 1796 and his brother John in April 1798. All the evidence would seem to suggest that John the younger brother was far and away the most gifted writer of the two. As was said about another writer (Dylan Thomas), at a much later period: 'He was a precocious child and a compulsive writer.'

As a seven-year-old John wrote a lengthy story about a family of Fairies who lived at the end of their garden.

His nine-year-old brother did all the spade-work. When John was ten he wrote a poem of a thousand lines which he called 'Hibernia', an old name for Ireland.

John followed his brother into the English Academy in the city which was owned and run by the notoriously eccentric Charlie Buchanin, said to have been a Don at Oxford before he got a 'brain-storm'.

At thirteen Michael entered the famous Kilkenny College, alma mater of Jonathan Swift, George Berkeley and William Congreve. Two years later John followed in Michael's footsteps and soon became the leading-light for English Poetry and Composition at Kilkenny College. When he was sixteen years old Michael was withdrawn from College, as his father needed him to help in their Hardware and Gun Shop. But when John reached his sixteenth year he was sent to Dublin to study as an artist.

Before he left for Dublin their father had taken John and Michael to the Kilkenny Theatre, where (the National Poet) Thomas Moore who was then called the idol of Kilkenny, was reciting his 'Monologue on National Music'. The same Thomas Moore who composed The Last Rose of Summer at Jenkinstown House.

Later in Dublin John fell madly in love with an Art student, named Anna. Anna died tragically and the over sensitive, John, suffered a nervous breakdown. Once out of hospital he refused to paint and instead returned to his poetry and prose. He set himself up as a writer and was soon contributing articles to the leading newspapers both Irish and English. A London Editor who liked his work wrote and invited him to come and work for his newspaper, – the 'London Gazette'; all expenses paid and pocket money. It was an offer John Banim couldn't refuse. His work on the London Gazette brought John into contact with the artistic milieu of the greatest city on earth. He was invited into the social atmosphere of the finest literary persons on life's stage, where: "All the men and women are merely actors and all have their entrances and their exists." John Banim's first play, The Prodigal, was accepted for production at Drury Lane with the great Thespian Kean, playing the leading part. In everything that he did in the world of Literature he sought and got the advice and expertise of his brother Michael. It was he who produced the raw material, as he stood behind the counter of their father's shop in Kilkenny. And now they were planning a work that would be their greatest collaboration to date. They were in the process of producing; "Tales from the O'Hara Family". As the Banim brothers saw it, it was high time to write-off the silly, stage Irishman and replace him with the real live authentic Irish men and women of modern times. Hadn't Gerald Griffin done it with his Collegians, and William Carleton too in 'Traits and Stories of Irish Peasantry', in four volumes no less, and Maria Edgeworth, also in her 'Castle Rackrent'. But now the genius of the Banim brothers from Kilkenny was to become known to the English speaking world of literature. The fist of the 'Tales from the O'Hara Family', series, was published on 7th April 1826. It was an instant success and was hailed as a work of great creative writing. Later as the series continued, the literary 'apostles' proclaimed it the 'gospel' on Irish customs and habits in the moral, political and religious sense.

But which of these two is the greater genius, critics were asking? Some ventured opinions that Michael was the one who was unearthing the stories locally in Kilkenny and serving them up, as it were, unadulterated for John who then proceeded to adorn them in a more literary vein that appealed to the more sophisticated London publishers. Who can tell whether it was Romulus or Remus who was the greater? Was it Rodgers or Hammerstein? Who cares if the work gets done? 'Croohore of the Billhook' was a very powerful and important novel by the Banims. And subsequent novels such as 'The Nowlans' and 'The Boyne Water', all give testament to the genius of this great duo.

The 'Tales of the O'Hara Family' were dedicated to Thomas Moore: 'To Ireland's True Son and First Poet, Thomas Moore Esq. with the Highest National Pride in his Genius as an Irishman, these Tales are inscribed.' Moore was later staying at Jenkinstown House, around 1830 when one day he walked into Kilkenny City to meet with Michael and his father who was still alive.

Thomas Moore, wrote the 'Last Rose of Summer', while staying at Jenkinstown House:

"Tis the last rose of Summer, Left blooming alone;
All her lovely companions Are faded and gone;
No flower of her kindred, No rosebud is nigh,
To reflect back her blushes, Or give sigh for sigh.

I'll not leave thee, thou lone one, To pine on a stem;
Since the lovely are sleeping Go, sleep thou with them.
Thus kindly I scatter, Thy leaves o'er the bed,
Where thy mates of the garden, Lie scentless and dead.

So soon may I follow, When friendships decay,
And from loves shining circle, The gems drop away!
When true hearts lie wither'd, And fond ones are flown,
Oh" who would inhabit, This bleak world alone?

John Banim had married a Miss Ruth in his earlier days in London, when the money was flowing in from commissions. But he was something of a spendthrift and he liked to socialise with his peers. Of late his health had deteriorated and a trip to the continent only exacerbated his condition. By 1833 his illness was so severe it caused him to call a halt to his writing. He soon found himself in debt, and this compounded his ill-health. But his friends did not forsake him. Instead, they set up a fund for him. Samuel Lover who was the author of the hilarious novel 'Handy Andy' saw to the collection and administration of the fund. By 1835 John was in constant pain. He returned to his native Kilkenny City and was welcomed by the Mayor and members of the Corporation and a great number of citizens. He took up residence along with his wife at Windgap Cottage overlooking the silvery Nore and facing the Ormonde Castle on the other side.

John Banim was only forty-four years old when he died in 1842. A fund to help his widow was set up, but it dwindled away soon after, despite the fact that its members were Daniel O'Connell, Isaac Butt, Thomas Davis, Samuel Ferguson etc. A public meeting was convened to erect a monument or memorial to John Banim on 15th Dec 1852. A bust by the sculptor Hogan would be installed in the City Hall. His biographer told the Mayor and members of the Corporation, there wasn't much value in a bust, which was not one bit like him, while his widow was left in poverty.

CHAPTER FOUR

GEORGE BERKELEY:
ONE OF EUROPE'S GREATEST PHILOSOPHERS

GEORGE Berkeley was born at Dysert near Thomastown County Kilkenny in the year 1685. He was educated at Kilkenny College, John Street and later at Trinity College, Dublin. His studies at Trinity, alongside the traditional subjects were the new learning of Newton and the philosophy of John Locke. In 1707 George Berkeley was elected to a fellowship of Trinity. It was within the next six years that he published the works on which his fame as a philosopher rests.

We are told that before he was thirty years old he had made his mark. His first major work was "An Essay Towards a New Theory of Vision". Later in the "Principles of Human Knowledge" which he published in 1710 he developed a theory of perceptions: "To be is to be perceived".

And his one other main philosophic work is "The Dialogues of Hylas and Philonous."

Along with the philosophers John Lock (1632-1704) and David Hume (1711-1776) George Berkeley made up the three great representatives of the theory known as British Empiricism. This movement spanned the period from the Civil War in England to the French Revolution.

From 1713-1721 Berkeley lived in England but was constantly travelling to and fro around the continent of Europe. He seems to have channeled his main energies into other causes such as religion. He returned to Trinity and took up a Senior Fellowship. Then in 1724 he became Dean of Derry.

It was about this time that he began a work for the founding of a missionary college in Bermuda. Apparently the British Government had assured him of its financial backing. In high spirits he sailed for America in 1728 hoping to enlist support among the New Englanders. He soon discovered that Westminsters' promises of financial assistance were but empty rhetoric and he was forced to abandon the project.

Weird and wonderful stories about George Berkeley abound: He did not feel himself in love with feasts and parties, and crowds were anathema to his natural temper. Neither did he promote visits, nor late hours nor strange faces nor moaners nor groaners.

And when some wag heard the latter part of that assembly he said "He makes no bones about it: he doesn't like the human race one, bit". I suppose it is inevitable that when men of the calibre of George Berkeley come into vogue, stories about their lifestyles and general behaviour are born and grow in proportion to their stature. And as is often the case some of these stories can be strange, weird or even illogical, yet they grow and grow. By welding half-truths and fictions onto facts, the real state of affairs can be easily obliterated, as the following tale reveals:

"George Berkeley was a man of immense knowledge who once had a school in Kilkenny. He taught his students that there was neither spirit nor Immortal Soul. But that when the body died, annihilation followed. In order to bring this strange doctrine to life he made his students leap over their school desks until striking against them, their shins were red with blood." Which proves absolutely nothing, except perhaps the stupidity of the inventor of the lame story.

I read somewhere that George Berkeley and Jonathan Swift were friends. Not a bit of it, but I suspect this was said on the basis that the two great men got their earlier education at Kilkenny College. The fact is that Swift couldn't stand the sight of Berkeley. The dogs in the street knew that on the occasion of Berkeley securing preferment to the Bishopric of Cloyne in 1734, Swift had canvassed every senior cleric and politician in Ireland, in the hope of landing that distinguished and lucrative post for himself. And when Swift said that he hated to look into a coach fearing he might discover a bishop inside, it was Berkeley he was speaking about.

In his pamphlet titled "Querist" Berkeley was a courageous exponent of the long suffering Irish peasants. In 1752 he went on a visit to Oxford where he died at the beginning of the following year, aged sixty-eight years. He had held the post of bishop right up to his death.

He truly was one of the greatest of European philosophers and his works are still widely read and quoted. He gave his name to a city on the east shore of San Francisco bay. The University of California moved there in 1873. This university is now called Berkeley. By his industry in righting wrongs and his genius as a philosopher, George Berkeley brought honour and distinction upon his native Kilkenny.

CHAPTER FIVE

ANCIENT ANNALIST OF KILKENNY
CONFEDERATION OF KILKENNY
CATECHISM OF CHRISTIAN DOCTRINE
YOUNG IRELANDER
RENOWNED PORTRAIT PAINTER
ARCHITECT OF WHITE HOUSE
GREAT IRISH SCHOLAR
POET & HISTORIAN
FENIAN CHIEF
ONE OF IRELAND'S GREATEST PAINTERS

THE people of Kilkenny City and county can be justly proud of their heritage as the following grand parade of its most distinguished men and women are remembered and commemorated.

ANCIENT ANNALIST OF KILKENNY

Clyn, Friar John – a good honest man. A Franciscan of note and a great Kilkenny Annalist, did reside at Saint Francis Abbey near the Bull Ring where he once prayed and wrote his Annals in Latin comprised; "Memorable Things of Which I was an Eyewitness", was subject to Richard de Ledrede, Bishop of Ossory and a contemporary of the Witch Dame Alice Kyteler, about whom he wrote in his writings. Born about the year 1300, he compiles his Annals up to the year 1348, containing "the dry bones of history without any local colour".

John Clyn's Annals are said to be the authentic and most revealing version of the Plague knows as the Black Death, which ravaged Ireland and indeed Europe during the 14th and 15th centuries. He claimed that Kilkenny suffered more than most other centres.

Writing about the Plague which the Crusaders brought back with them from the East in 1348, Friar John Clyn recorded: It was so contagious that anyone who touched the dead or stricken was as often as not infected and soon died: so that the penitent and confessor were carried off together to the grave.

As he continued to write his Annals he became aware that he too had contracted the dreaded disease and wrote: "I John Clyn of the Monastery of Kilkenny do write these notorious events which have taken place in my own life time, fearing that these events may fade from the memory of future generations, I have committed them to writing. I have given the truth of what I have heard and seen in every instance. Therefore lest the writing perish with the writer and the work disappear with the workman, I am leaving a role of parchment for the next writer." In his record of events he wrote on the Great Famine in Ireland and terrible pestilence of 1271. Then in 1316 he wrote that Ireland was devastated by famine and fever. Again in 1324 he recorded there was a great plague in cattle in many parts of Ireland. Again in 1325 Friar Clyn wrote in his Annals: There is universal discord and unrest amongst the poor religious of Ireland which reflects the tumult outside, where some uphold their own nation, bonded by blood and language while others selfishly solicit for the offices of prelates and superiors.

Friar John Clyn was an early and very important source for Kilkenny Mediaeval history. Five hundred years after his death from the Black Death in 1849 the Irish Archaeological Society published his Annals.

CONFEDERATION OF KILKENNY

David Rothe Bishop of Ossory was born in Kilkenny in the year 1585. He was the prime mover in the Confederation of Kilkenny. An illustrious scholar, a distinguished theologian and a historian of note. He was the author of 'Analecta Sacra'. David Rothe, chaired the conference of bishops at Kilkenny in 1642, to discuss the implications of the 'Rising'. He was badly treated by the Cromwellians and died in Kilkenny shortly after they had laid siege to the city in 1650. At the time of the Confederation of Kilkenny, Kilkenny was recognised by Spain, France, Belgium, Holland and Italy as the Capital of Ireland.

CATECHISM OF CHRISTIAN DOCTRINE

Stapleton, Theobald, was born in Kilkenny in the year 1589. A great scholar who went to Salamanca to further his studies in 1609, and was ordained in Flanders. He had a unique place in literature because his Catechism of Christian Doctrine was the first book in Irish that was printed in Roman letters.

YOUNG IRELANDER

Cane Robert, was born in Kilkenny in 1807. He was a patriot even though he did not take part in the actual 'Rising' of 1848. He was a prominent Young Irelander and was later imprisoned for his politics. Robert Cane was Mayor of Kilkenny in 1844 and he founded the Celtic Union in 1853. He was a remarkable writer whose principal literary work was; The History of the Williamite and Jacobite Wars. He died in Kilkenny in 1848.

RENOWNED PORTRAIT PAINTER
Comerford, John born in Kilkenny in 1762. He became a member of the Royal Academy and exhibited with them in London, Paris and Berlin. He gained a formidable reputation as a portrait painter of male sitters.

John Comerford began his artistic vocation by copying portraits in the Picture Gallery in Kilkenny Castle. He died in Kilkenny in 1832.

ARCHITECT OF THE WHITE HOUSE
Hoban, James was born in 1762 at Desert Court Co. Kilkenny. He is reckoned to have been the greatest architect Ireland has ever produced because it was he who designed the White House in Washington D.C. This world famous building was opened as a residence in 1800 by President John Adams who was the 2nd President of the USA and father of John Quincy Adams who became the 6th Presentiment of USA

GREAT IRISH SCHOLAR
O'Donovan John was born at Attateemore in Co. Kilkenny in 1809. Undoubtedly he was one of Ireland's greatest Irish scholars. He will long be remembered for his version of the Annals of the Four Masters. He died in Dublin in 1861.

DRAMATIST AND PATRIOT
Sheil, Richard Lawlor. He was born in Drumdowney Kilkenny. Richard was a dramatist first and a lawyer second. Several of this plays were very successful and were staged in Kilkenny, Dublin and London.

He was an ally of Daniel O'Connell and a tireless worker for Catholic Emancipation. He became a King's Council in 1830 and was successively a Member of Parliament for Louth, Tipperary and Dungarvan. He died in Florence in 1851.

GREEK SCHOLAR, POET & HISTORIAN
Bibby, Thomas was born in Kilkenny City near St. Canices Steps in the year 1799. He was a leading Greek Scholar, poet and story teller. For his two dramatic poems 'Gerard of Kildare' in 1854 and 'Silken Thomas' in 1859 he achieved recognition as a poet and historian. He became something of a recluse and eccentric before his death in 1863.

FENIAN CHIEF
Stephens, James was born in Kilkenny in 1825. He was the founder of the Fenian Movement and was with Smith O'Brien at Ballingarry where he was wounded and was reported dead to the British authorities.

He escaped to France dressed as a ladies maid while his 'mock funeral' marched in great 'mourning' through the streets of Kilkenny. It was one of the greatest charades of the century, that 1848 'funeral' of the 'Fenian Chief'

Later he went to America with John O'Mahony where he founded the Irish Republican Brotherhood. James Stephens died in Dublin 1901.

If ever you go to Kilkenny
Enquire for the Hole in Wall
You'll get twenty four eggs for a penny
And butter for nothing at all.

ONE OF IRELAND'S GREATEST PAINTERS

Butler, Mildred Anne was born at Kilmurry outside Thomastown Co. Kilkenny in the year 1858. She went to London in her early twenties and studied under Paul Jacob Naftel. Later she studied under William Franck Calderon who founded a school of animal painting in 1894. Her greatest animal study is said to be her painting of the three crows and the calves feeding with her two brothers flying a kite in the background. The Crows was her first Royal Academy work and the calves was exhibited in the Watercolour Society of Ireland Exhibition. Mildred Anne was a regular exhibitor at the Dudley Gallery Piccadilly. Her works were seen in Liverpool. Birmingham, Bradford, Glasgow etc. In 1911 a group of Irish and English artists hung an Exhibition in Darmstadt where the Grand Duke of Hesse bought two of her paintings.

Her first major sale was bought by the Chantrey Bequest. It was her magnificent painting 'Morning Bath'. In 1893 she had been included in the book of water-colours given by the Lady Artists to the young princess later to become Queen Mary. Her reputation was made. Mildred Ann Butler continued to paint and exhibit in Dublin and London right up to her death in 1941. Her reputation continues to grow on the world's easel.

CHAPTER SIX

KILKENNY'S MEDIEVAL WITCH: DAME ALICE KYTELER

Dame Alice Kyteler was born at Kyteler's House, Kilkenny, where her father carried on a Banking business in the year 1280. Her father was a wealthy Norman Banker who came over to Ireland after the Norman conquest of 1169. When her father died in 1298, Alice who was an only child inherited his business and properties.

After his death she married one of his former associates. William Outlawe who was also a highly successful Banker from Coal Market St. and like her father of Norman stock. This man was the brother of Roger Outlawe, Chancellor of all Ireland whose position and power would one day play a dramatic part in the saga of Witch-craft and Heresy with which she would be charged, found guilty and sentenced to death.

William Outlawe was twenty years older than Dame Alice when they married in 1299. She bore a son for him a year later, whom they called William junior. Shortly after that, Dame Alice decided to build an addition to their house extending it to Kyron St. (St. Kieran St.) and develop it as an Inn. She was a good-looking highly sophisticated woman who could manipulate men to lavish gifts of money and jewels upon her. Because of this Kyteler's Inn soon became the rendezvous for wealthy men, both young and not so young, who craved for the attentions of the alluring Dame Alice.

But there was a darker side which was beginning to manifest itself in rumour and hearsay of Satanic rites, practised by their fascinating host. And then William Outlawe died suddenly under mysterious circumstances. It was said that upon forcing open a cupboard in the basement he had discovered a terrible assortment of 'Malaficia'. Jars and bowls of evil smelling entrails of cocks and eyes of ravins, horrible worms and sprays of deadly night-shade, dead mens hair and fragments of unbaptised babies, cooked in a pot made from the skull of a beheaded thief.

DAME ALICE KYTELER
BY SEAN KENNY

Months later Dame Alice married another Banker from Callan named Adam Le Blont. It is believed she had a daughter by Le Blont whom they called Basilia. In 1310 Dame Alice was once again a widow as Le Blont died after a 'drinking spree'. As her first husband Outlawe had left her a wealth of money and property, so too did Le Blont leave her all he possessed. Dame Alice was fast becoming one of the wealthiest women in Kilkenny and if gossip was to be believed the most wicked woman alive.

She had gathered a bevy of young maidens around her to help with the running of the Inn which was the busiest in Kilkenny. But reports were rife that they were also used as participants in Dame Alice's experiments in Demonology. One maiden in particular, pleased her more than all the others. She was named Petronella of Meath. Petronella would eventually pay the ultimate price for her expertise in the art of Witch-craft and Necromancy. Dame Alice married her third husband in 1311. He was a wealthy landlord who owned extensive properties in and around Clonmel. His name was Richard de Valle. Richard departed the land of the living long before his appointed time. It seems he grew suddenly ill while in the prime of life and died after a sumptuous supper.

He had bequeathed all his land and properties to Dame Alice in his last Will and Testament. She was now one of the wealthiest persons in the Province of Leinster. Only the Princes of the Church could command greater wealth and resources. All the while Dame Alice had been indulging herself deeper and deeper in the art of Demonology. Her favourite Demon was Robin Son of Artisson, who was also her lover. And she presided over nightly gatherings at the cross-roads where living animals were cruelly dismembered and offered to Demons.

A verse from W.B. Yeats poem, "Nineteen Hundred and Nineteen", comes to mind.

There lurches past his great eyes without thought
Under the shadow of straw-pale locks;
That insolent fiend, Robert Artisson,
To whom the love-lorn Lady Kyteler brought
Bronze peacock feathers, red combs of her cocks.

RICHARD DE LEDREDE

The "Narrative" is a Latin MS which was written during the time of the 'Kyteler Excommunications'. The manuscript was published in 1843 under the title "Contemporary Narrative of the proceedings against Dame Alice Kyteler, Prosecuted for Sorcery in 1324 by Richard de Ledrede, Bishop of Ossory". Forty pages of close packed print is proof positive of the terrible events that necessitated the inquisition (Harley MS 641 British Museum).

Dame Alice married her fourth husband around the year 1320. This man was also of Norman stock as were all his predecessors. John Le Poer had been a constant customer over many years at Kyteler's Inn and had fallen into the snare of Dame Alices spell, wherefore it was claimed she could infatuate men and bring them to such a state of mind that they gave her all the riches they possessed. John Le Poer was brother of Arnold Le Poer, Seneschal or Major-domo of Kilkenny. By 1323 John found himself suffering from many different sicknesses. Although he was only middle-aged he became feeble and slow. His hair fell out in patches and what remained turned silvery grey and his finger nails fell off. Fearing that it was Dame Alice's doing, he went just before he died to the Friars at Saint Francis's Abbey for help. They in turn contacted Richard de Ledrede Bishop of Ossory giving him full account of Dame Alice's coven of witches and her alleged responsibility for the deaths of her four husbands. Also there was the charge that she abjured the faith and claimed that Christ was a mere man who was justly put to death for his own sins.

Richard de Ledrede made every attempt to have this coven of witches arrested but was hindered because they were very influential people. Remember Dame Alice's former brother-in-law was Roger Outlawe, Chancellor of all Ireland. The Bishop did however hold an inquisition in 1324 at which she was found, by common agreement of all the judges secular and religious, to be guilty of Witchcraft and Magic, of Heresy and of having sacrificed to Demons. For all of which she and her faction of sorcerers were excommunicated from Mother Church and their goods confiscated and they were to be handed over to the secular authority.

But it was in fact the Bishop who was arrested and put under lock and key in Kilkenny jail. And there he remained for seventeen days on bread and water. This scandalous treatment says the "Narrative" was something unheard of in Ireland until then.

It was only after John Darcy the Lord Chief Justice travelled from Dublin to Kilkenny, that the Bishop was released. Darcy proceeded to examine the facts put before the 'Inquisition' and declared the sentence just and proper. And so the tables were turned once again on Dame Alice.

In those medieval times, for one to be found guilty of Witchcraft was a most serious offence and one that carried the sentence of death.

Dame Alice and her disciples were condemned to be whipped through the streets, tied at the back of a horse and cart after which Alice, as chief priestess and instigator would be burned at the stake. But by the political power of the Chancellor of all Ireland, her former brother-in-law Roger Outlawe, her escape was organised. Her guards were beaten senseless and Dame Alice was released from the dungeons beneath Kilkenny Castle and freed from the sentence of death, that hung over her.

But her hand-maiden, Petronella of Meath wasn't so lucky. To placate the howling mob that had gathered around the huge bon-fire in front of the Tholsel in the centre of Kilkenny, Petronella would be sacrificed. Already badly shaken from the whippings, she confessed her guilt to everything she was charged with. She told them it was at Dame Alice's instigation she had denied that Jesus Christ was the son of God. Also that she had called up Demons and received responses from them and performed many abominations of the flesh. But she rightly claimed that Dame Alice's demonic powers by far exceeded her own and she begged for mercy. Petronella of Meath, was burned alive at the stake before a brutalised, chanting mob, as she screamed in vain for her mistress to come to her aid. But Dame Alice had begun a new life in far off London, never again to set foot in her native Kilkenny.

CHAPTER SEVEN

STANDISH O'GRADY:
FATHER OF THE IRISH LITERARY RENAISSANCE

"Through all the centuries, Ireland labouring to bring forth the Irish Nation, and that nation yet unborn. But when Ireland at last emerges, standing out clear on the world's horizon, her conscience will be Irish indeed, – that will never fail, – but it will also be the conscience of the Earth. And none can hate her; none ever will or can. Because of her own millennium – enduring tragedy, she will love this suffering world, and because of her sufferings, her patience, her faith, her hope, and her heroic and unconquerable resolve, the world will love her too."

THE above was written about one hundred years ago by that unique Man of Letters, Standish O'Grady who was an Historian, Novelist, Playwright and Editor. He was the son of a Protestant Rector who was also a substantial land-owner. Born at Berehaven West Cork, one year before the Famine 1846. He was educated in the Classics at Trinity College Dublin. Studied for the Bar but became a leader-writer for the Daily Express and later became its editor. And how prophetic his words have turned out to be! "The conscience of the Earth."

Let's hope we can continue to play that role on the "World's Stage" by taking our full part in the E.U. Everyone knows that although we are in the lightweight division of the world's powers yet we have proven we are not afraid to take on opponents well above our weight when it comes to defending the underdog and the downtrodden. That's what we do best because we wore that tattered coat ourselves for so very very long.

But we must go back to our patron Standish O'Grady: "And if our history is often a disappointment, our Legends are not. Our heroic literature is bound to repeat itself in action and within the constraining laws of time and space and the physical world. For that prophecy has been always and will be always fulfilled. The heroes are coming. Their advent is as certain as time; they are on the road."

"Or if we must consider this our semi-mythical heroic age, from a more mundane and entirely rational point of view, here at least is food for the never-sated, impervious, and domineering imagination. Because here if never elsewhere, we are permitted to see the majestic shapes of Kings and Queens, Chieftains, Brehons and Bards of the heroic age of Ireland".

The heroic age in Irish folklore tells about a semi-mythical period when heroes or demigods were shown to have lived among men. And although these faulted men and women who were identified as mythical by the wise, yet O'Grady assured us that Cuchulain, and Laegh, Queen Maeve and Fardia and Fergus Mac Roy and all the hosts of the Red Branch Knights, have never suffered death at all; "but are very strong and well as I write. And yet how many millions that belonged to the historical ages are today forgotten like last year's snow. And see how it comes to pass that Ozymandias, King of Kings is quite dead."

OZYMANDIAS
    BY PERCY BYSSHE SHELLEY
    I met a traveller from an antique land
    Who said: Two vast and trunkless legs of stone
    Stand in the desert...Near them on the sand,
    Half sunk, a shattered visage lies whose frown,
    And wrinkled lip, and sneer of cold command,
    Tell that it's sculptor well those passions read
    Which yet survive, stamped on these lifeless things,
    The hand that mocked them, and the heart that fed:
    And on the pedestal these words appear
    My name is Ozymandias, king of kings.
    Look on my works, ye Mighty and despair!
    Nothing beside remains. Round the decay
    Of that colossal wreck, boundless and bare
    The lone and level sands stretch far away.

CUCHULAIN, THE HEROIC AGE
Standish O'Grady's first book on the heroic age in Ireland was about the coming of Cuchulain or Setanta, son of Sualtam. His second book told the story of Cuchulain's manhood. And the third book told of the Passing of the mighty but meek warrior. The name Cuchulain is indeed a strange one especially for a mild-mannered benevolent youth. In truth it sounds almost barbaric. Translated it means, Hound of Chulain. And how did our kind and well-behaved hero come to be given such a dog-like designation? Well, according to the ancient storytellers of Irish legend, Setanta, son of Sualtam, loved to play with his camán agus sliotar (hurley and ball) in the fields around his home.

The game of hurling as every Irishman knows is the authentic national game of the manly sons of Erin. By comparison the lesser skilled sport of football is a mere two hundred years old and was introduced into this country by the Sasanochts. Furthermore, the Ossorians were practising their hurling craft on the Fair Green by the Windy Arbor, in preparation for the Tailtean Games, when Aengus Ossory ruled this Kingdom in the year 180 A.D.

But to get on with the story about how Setanta, son of Sualtam, got the name Cuchulain: As he played with his camán agus sliotar he habitually hurled the ball ahead of him with great force and then he would race after it faster than a bolt of fork-lightening and catch the ball before it cold hit the ground. The youth was so engrossed in his sport that before he knew it, he had hurled the ball into a compound that belonged to a minor chieftain named Chulain. Setanta jumped the ditch and caught the ball as it fell from the sky. But out of the corner of his eye he saw a huge Irish Wolfhound bounding towards him with great menace. What was he to do? The beast was as big as a small horse and as ferocious as a lion. Other than being eaten alive he had no option but to defend himself.

Setanta took deadly aim and as the great beast opened it's enormous jaws he struck the sliotar with his camán with unerring accuracy and powerful force. Like a cannon ball the sliotar was driven down the wolfhound's throat and it dropped dead to the ground, as if it had been polaxed. Being well instructed in the virtues of honesty and good behaviour, Setanta went immediately to the house of the chieftain Chulain and told him what he had done. "Henceforth", said the chieftain, "you must guard my house in place of my great hound". And so Setanta son of Sualtam was from that day forward known as Chulain's hound or Cuchulain.

A YOUTHFUL W.B. YEATS
BY SEAN KENNY

STANDISH O'GRADY COMES TO KILKENNY

O'Grady came to Kilkenny City in 1898 to become owner and Editor of the widely read culture conscious "Kilkenny Moderator". As he saw it he could use this prestigious newspaper to broadcast his ideas for a social and economic conversion among the Landlord class. He would do this by outlining their poor management of their estates and deplorable treatment of their workers. He would also make his newspaper available to his friends to express themselves on not only the day by day vital issues but also on matters of art and literature. We know that Standish O'Grady's first Christmas publication of 'The Kilkenny Moderator', had articles that were contributed by W.B. Yeats, George Russell (AE) and perhaps T.W. Rolleston.

It seems that neither W.B. Yeats nor A.E. could understand why on God's Earth O'Grady had chosen to go to Kilkenny when he already had the Editorial chair of "The Daily Express" in Dublin. Nor were they pleased that he had gone. But I suspect they figured they could at least keep in touch with him by contributing articles to the 'Kilkenny Moderator'. In Dublin, W.B. Yeats had been a constant caller to the home of Standish O'Grady at Earlsfort Terrace. We know now that Yeats was profoundly influenced by O'Grady's passion for the Heroic Age. It rubbed off on W.B and expressed itself in his poetry such as; Cuchulain's Fight With The Sea, Song of the Wandering Aengus, The Hosting of the Sidhe and very many others. Indeed, Yeats freely plumbed the depths of Grady's reservoir of knowledge. But nowhere have I read that he thanked him for availing of his scholarship, giving him a free ticket as it were into the world of Irish mythology. W.B. Yeats had also gone down another road, one that O'Grady did not approve of. He was delving into the arts of the Occult and was regularly attending Seances. O'Grady scorned Yeats for his, 'practice of Black Magic'. Nor was George Russell A.E. exempt from the barbs of Standish O'Grady's tongue concerning his (A.E.'s) preoccupation with Mysticism.

AN ASIDE

And here is a curiosity for you that has intrigued me since I first came across it some years ago in an old Argosy Magazine dated October 1935 Vol XVII No. 113. In that edition of the Argosy there is a poem by a man named Louis Golding titled 'Cabins of Innisfree',

In some small cabin shall I hide
Of clay and wattles made;
Wrapt in my robes of poet-pride
Lurk in the moon-mild shade
Musically afraid.

Immediately I was struck with the poem's similarity to W.B. Yeats poem 'Lake Isle of Innisfree.' Not only was there a similarity about the romantic place-name Innisfree, but also there was the highly imaginative poetical phrase; Of clay and wattles made, which is exactly the same as; W.B.'s:

I will arise and go now, and go to Innisfree
And a small cabin build there, of clay and wattles made:
Nine bean-rows will I have there, a hive for the honey-bee,
And live alone in a bee-loud glade.

What do you think? Is it a case of great minds think alike? Are poets capable of interpreting the live ether, where we are told every noble poetic utterance made, reverberates in the upper air? Or is it a less romantic case of plagiarism? Standish O'Grady had hardly had a change of socks in Kilkenny when W.B. and A.E. began missing him.

Russell wrote to Yeats asking: "Did you know that O'Grady has gone down to Kilkenny? He has taken over the 'Kilkenny Moderator' and is determined to make it into an organ for All Ireland. How the mighty are hurled from their podiums." W.B. wrote back: "As you well know, Kilkenny was once the Capital of All Ireland. Where better to preach to All Ireland, than from its ancient Capital." "I find myself brooding over the books that have profoundly affected me. I find none that excited my imagination more than Standish O'Grady's epic narrative of Cuchulain... As I read I felt exalted as one who learns, he is among the children of Kings."

ELLEN LADY DESART

Some say it was the Countess Dowager of Desart who first invited Standish O'Grady to Kilkenny. When he saw what this great lady had done for the people of Kilkenny, he knew he had arrived at his ideal location, like a Moslem arriving at Mecca. Together with her cousin, the Hon. Otway Cuffe, the Countesss (she supplied the money and the goodwill, – he the inspiration) undertook to found a Woolen Mills, a Woodwork Factory, a Tobacco growing industry, a Theatre, a Bookbinding shop, a Village built from the ground to house the workers (Talbot's Inch) a Suspension bridge across the River Nore and a Ball alley adjacent to Talbot's Inch for the recreation of the workers. Was it any wonder then that Standish O'Grady wrote to George Russell (AE) after his first Christmas in Kilkenny: "I take this opportunity to thank your good self and our mutual friend W.B for your excellent contributions to the 'All Ireland Review which is a periodical I have instituted alongside the Moderator, for its literary content and the promotion of all things good in Ireland.' "Here in Kilkenny, I find myself in the midst of greatness. The munificence of Ellen Lady Desart and her devotion to the welfare of the working class in Kilkenny has to be seen to be believed."

HISTORIAN, NOVELIST, PLAYWRIGHT AND EDITOR

Standish O'Grady, Historian, Novelist, Playwright and Editor, came to Kilkenny as Editor/owner of the Kilkenny Moderator in 1898. It is generally believed that he came at the invitation of Ellen Countess of Desart. And it is more than likely that her partner in business as well as in social relations, Captain, The Hon. Otway Cuffe, had a hand in that invitation. The Countess was the daughter of a millionaire Jewish banker in London. The Captain was the youngest son of the Fourth Earl of Desart. He was once a dashing officer in the Royal Rifle Brigade and had been aide-de-camp to the Duke of Connaught. There can be no doubt but that he was something of a genius when it came to building foundations, overseeing constructions and establishing contracts. With absolute good will and a great deal of money this dynamic duo transformed the social as well as the industrial life of Kilkenny City, in the early years of the 20th century.

Never before or since has anybody done so much to enhance the lives of an entire community with such life-supporting and life sustaining innovations. Their likes will never be seen again. Wouldn't it be a gallant gesture from the people of Kilkenny to erect a monument or plaque to commemorate them. Especially, the Countess of Desart, whose selfless generousity and humanitarian concern for the welfare of the working class people of Kilkenny will never be forgotten. Lest we forget, I will once again outline and number for everyone of us what the Countess especially, and the Captain too, bestowed upon the people of Kilkenny: A Woolen Mills, a Woodwork Factory, a Tobacco growing industry, a Theatre, a Bookbinding Shop, the Desart Hall, (dancehall), Talbot's Inch (a Village built from the ground to house the workers), the Suspension Bridge across the River Nore a Handball Alley for recreation and a Hospital Aut Even (Ait Aobhinn i.e. a beautiful place). A beautiful place indeed and all the noble enterprises founded for the people of Kilkenny were to my mind a reflection of the magnificence of the soul within Ellen, the Countess of Desart. Was it, any wonder then that Standish O'Grady felt himself to be in the midst of greatness in Kilkenny?

For some strange reason known only to himself, O'Grady, had, an intense dislike for the 'stage'. That is to say the theatrical stage. Because of this inordinate aversion he absolutely refused to allow anyone to stage his Heroic historical dramas. And he was equally dismissive of other peoples' attempts to 'stage' such dramas. When W.B. Yeats and George Russell A.E. were about to 'stage' the Heroic drama Diamuid agus Grainne which they had collaborated to write in 1900, O'Grady was furious. He castigated them: "You two are my friends and yet I tell you to drop this process at your peril for it demeans the legend. You can dramatise Irish history as much as you like and with all the freedom of expression that you want, but do not interfere with the original form of the Heroic legends and do not reduce them to the level of the crowd, not at least through drama and the 'stage'". But he did contrive to present his Heroic age dramas in another environment – through a different medium. Ingeniously he would present his dramas in Pageant form. And this he did with great success in the open air on the banks of the River Nore, near Aut Even. With Captain the Hon. Otway Cuffe in charge of production, they raised a platform on the grassy meadow at the bottom of the woodland hill (later know as Brannigan's Wood). The wood was the ideal backdrop for the Pageant with lighted lanterns hanging from the branches. The drama was performed in the twilight whose mysterious shadows promoted a heightening of the sences. And with a couple of great mastives yelping first near then far off as if in a dream. Some of those who witnessed the spectacle told how they felt they had been transported to another place in another time. It was a spectacular success. The mystery and the magic was all part of Standish O'Grady's dramatic abracadabra.

He was so pleased as was everyone else with the result of the Masque of Fionn that he decided to write another Heroic drama; "Hugh Roe O'Donnell." And strange to tell the vast majority of the actors were from the Kilkenny Players guild. These were a group of very talented men and women who were under the patronage of the Countess of Desart. They had been called into existence at the founding of the Kilkenny Theatre. And though they were all amateurs yet they acquainted themselves with the 'art' of acting in Dublin and London.

A LIBEL ACTION

Meanwhile, just when it seemed that his Editorialship of the Kilkenny Moderator and his literary periodical: The All Ireland Review, was beginning to bear fruit, a blight fell over all: A scandal split the local aristocracy right down the middle. O'Grady took the side of the weaker section in his editorials and there were no half measures about his denunciations. As a result a libel action was brought against him by the Protestant Bishop, and Kilkenny's Master of Hounds. Once that was initiated (Libel action) O'Grady's days in Kilkenny were numbered. The big-moneyed land owners refused to support the advertising in the Moderator and the All Ireland Review. The jig was up. Standish O'Grady was forced to step down and when he left Kilkenny he was bankrupt. Back in Dublin he continued with the publication of "The All Ireland review." This was the literary Periodical he had founded in Kilkenny. O'Grady was not only the Editor-owner but was the main contributor also. And he frequently published the works of unknown poets and writers giving them advice and helpful critical analysis. But he also published the latest works of the established writers and often hung the haughty out to dry.

SAINT ENDA'S

The twenty-nine year-old Headmaster of Scoil Eanna (Saint Enda's) at the Hermitage Rathfarnham, wrote a brilliant congratulatory letter to Standish O'Grady, with a request. The Hermitage had once been the home of Thomas Addis Emmet, brother of Robert Emmet. It was here that Padraig Pearse moved his school after two marvelous years at Cullenstown House in Rathmines, where the numbers of students enrolling had by far exceeded his greatest expectations.

Padraig Pearse, called the British educational system, the 'Murder' Machine. He was the Headmaster at Saint Enda's which he claimed was an Irish school for Irish boys. As a very small boy Padraig had been introduced to Irish freedom politics by an old aunt who would take him on her knee and tell him stories about great Irish patriots of long ago, such as the Fenians, the Young Irelanders, and the greatest of them all; Wolfe Tone.

His mother too, who was a Miss Margaret Brady from Co. Meath, was also steeped in the tradition of Irish nationalism and had more than a smattering of Irish folklore and legend.

PÁDRAIG PEARSE
BY SEÁN KENNY

From childhood then he loved the heroes of Erin like Fionn Mac Cuhaill and Cuchulain. In time, these fabled champions became his ideal models for Irishmen. Growing up he identified with them and eventually emulated their high ideals and moral standards as our history confirms. It was no wonder then that Padraig Pearse wrote to Standish O'Grady congratulating him and asking him most sincerely to bring his Heroic age drama to Saint Enda's. The one we should like to see most is the 'Masque of Fionn". O'Grady was only too delighted to accommodate him. The first performance was received so well by students and teachers alike that they asked for a second one a week later. This time Lady Gregory came in the company of W.B. Yeats. The performers all excelled themselves. W.B. and Lady G. gave them the height of praise. And then they turned to O'Grady and lavished praise upon the great man for his unique production. But their commendations were nothing compared to the glorification of the work that Padraig Pearse gave.

He spoke with such passion and conviction that O'Grady, sitting at the back of the audience watched and listened enthralled, with tears of gratitude burning his eyes. He said later, he knew then that Padraig Pearse was a man marked out by destiny – a man who would gladly suffer political martyrdom for the freedom of his country. I do believe that Standish O'Grady had a much greater influence upon the revolutionary ideas that motivated Padraig Pearse than W.B. Yeats ever had. And although W.B. asks in one of his celebrated poems: "Was it some words of mine that sent out all those young men to die?" I think not. The dye was already cast by O'Grady and had coloured the aspirations of the master of Saint Enda's long before W.B. thought of putting pen to paper for that poem.

"But at the same time I will say that those who instinctively, or by resolute study, learn to like this grand old story of how Cuchulain, son of Sualtam, though alone and forsaken and encompassed by thousands of enemies, held the 'Gates of the North' against a host of invaders, and like a true champion and patriot, spent himself – his youth, energy, blood and young enthusiasm – in defence of his native land and his otherwise defenceless people – they, I say, who read and like this tale will never like it by halves. They will like it well and never forget it, if they like it at all; and of how few modern novels, even the most brilliant and most graphic, can this be truly said? For it is a great story, one of the greatest in the whole world." The above paragraph was written by Standish O'Grady in his 'Introduction' to 'In The Gates of the North.' The same Standish O'Grady who was Editor/Owner of the Kilkenny Moderator and the All Ireland Review from High Street, Kilkenny City.

CHAPTER EIGHT

REVEREND J.K. FIELDING:
FOUNDER AND FIRST PRESIDENT OF GAELIC PARK CHICAGO
PRESIDENT OF THE IRISH LITERARY SOCIETY CHICAGO
NATIONAL CHAPLAIN GAELIC LEAGUE OF AMERICA

JAMES Kieran Fielding was born in the year of 'Our Lord' 1872, in a little hamlet called Rathkieran in Mooncoin Co. Kilkenny. He was educated at Saint Kieran's College Kilkenny City and was ordained to the priesthood at Maynooth on the 15th June 1899. He was selected for the Foreign Missions and was sent to Chicago Illinois, U.S.A. At that time in the history of the emigrant Irish, most of those who left our shores for North America, settled in the great cities of New York, Boston and Chicago. The Irish were not always well received in America because most of them were poorly educated and could not communicate with any great degree of confidence.

As a result the likelihood of finding meaningful and profitable employment was greatly diminished. Instead they were forced to stand-in-line for inspection as potential pick-and-shovel men and hod-carriers on construction sites, like the Spailín Fánachs of the 18th century Ireland. And the young Irish women worked as domestics; child-minders and washer-women. Some of these had a live-in status, which greatly enhanced their prospects. All in all, but more especially for the men, it was a tough joyless life with little or no social or monetary advancement. It was no surprise then that many of the men turned to alcohol to relieve the pain of loneliness and despair.

Into such a challenging world went the young Rev. James Kieran Fielding from Mooncoin Co. Kilkenny. But this was no ordinary enthusiastic young novice priest with notions of world conversion. This was a man apart, a great man, with a good head and an even better heart. As the Pastor of Saint Justin Martyr Church, he was responsible for all his parishioners, – the vast majority of whom were Irish (first and second generation). And what a pastor he turned out to be: A tireless 'Shepherd of his flock'. Those who knew him intimately told of his almost superhuman exploits amongst the poorer sections in the Irish Ghettoes of Chicago.

He was often seen trudging through driving rain and blinding snow even in the pitch darkness of the back streets, to kneel beside the deathbed of a poor parishioner. In order to save his Irish parishioners from 'going under' due to loneliness, boredom and despair he wondered if he could create another Ireland in the great city of Chicago. And so he gathered around him twelve staunch followers to begin with. His aims were: To found the first Irish American Gaelic League in the Mid-Western state of Illinois. Being an excellent Irish speaker himself, he was keenly aware of the ancient Dutch proverb: "No language – no nation" (As Gaelige: Nil Tir gan teanga) The Rev. J.K. Fielding was only months in America when he established the Irish

Rev. J.K. Fielding

Language League in Saint Bernard's Hall, Chicago. That was in 1899 and he could not have been aware then that he had begun the first real Sinn Fein movement in America. But he didn't stop there. Great head that he had, he realised that he should try to help fill the void in the hearts of the exiled sons and daughters of Ireland. It would be an enormous task, but a stupendous undertaking. If the ambitions of this youthful priestly colossus were to become a reality, then the great city of Chicago would be the first city in the 'New World' to play host to a Culture more ancient than Babylon. Wouldn't it be like another piece of Dublin, another part of Kilkenny or another corner of Cork, to see and hear Irish traditional tales told through the ancient channels of folklore. And to listen enchanted to the old songs and sit spellbound as the heroic legends were performed and Gaelic bards reciting monologues.

If an Irish Ceile band could be constructed, with fiddle and bow, flute and bowrán, bagpipes and melodeon, how many Irish lads and lassies would dance hornpipes, jigs and reels? How many indeed? But the great Kilkenny priest was a marvelous orator too, – a man whose words could inspire his hearers.

He rose to his feet and looking confidently upon his staunch followers he said: "It is my considered opinion that if we are to be successful in uniting all the Irish here in Chicago, we must not only pray together and learn together, but we must also play together. And to that end this is what I propose we should do.

Together we should bring about the revival of the ancient Tailtean Games, which have been buried in the vaults of history for more than 750 years. We will raise funds to purchase a plot of land and erect a playing field with dressing rooms and other facilities on it."

"And Father", interjected Patrick Francis Holden, his fellow Kilkenny man, "we will call it Gaelic Park". And so they did. Gaelic Park is at the South California Avenue and West Forty-Seventh Street. There, thousands of exiles from Ireland meet their own kind. And as the stadium was developed and the crowds could see again the games and dances of their native land, their loneliness and despair slowly but surely subsided.

THE TAILTEAN GAMES

The Tailtean Games were established in Erin two thousand five hundred years before the birth of Christ (2500 B.C.) and flourished in all their glory right up to two years before Richard de Clare otherwise Strongbow, brought about the Norman conquest of Ireland in 1169 A.D. The traditional date of the first Olympiad in Greece is 776 B.C. The Tailtean Games were hoary with age when the Olympic contests of the Hellenic race were just beginning. There hurlers, runners and jumpers, vaulters and weight-lifters, hammer-throwers and wrestlers all competed to win glory and honour for their own tribes. The Tailtean Games flourished longer than the glory of Assyria, Egypt, Greece or Rome.

There was a little booklet published by the Mayer & Miller Company, Chicago on the occasion of Father Fielding's Sacerdotal Silver Jubilee on the 15th June 1924. In it the publisher tells us:

"Father Fielding is known as the father of Irish athletics in Chicago. He was founder and first President of Gaelic Park, which is an institution that has brought health and happiness and great joy to thousands of Irish boys and girls in our city. It was there as a boy that I first leaned to dance an Irish horn-pipe, to sing an Irish song, to watch the prowess of Irish athletes, to listen to Irish oratory and admire the many happy matrimonial contracts that were made there. Gaelic Park must always remain as a lasting monument to Father Fielding in the City of Chicago.

In 1904 Father Fielding invited Tom Kiely from Tipperary to come to America and compete for the world's championship in the Olympian Games in St. Louis. Kiely entered three events and won all three, and then he insisted that Father Fielding whom he had well known on the field of athletics in Ireland, should take off his coat and compete for the sake of old Ireland. This he did and emerged with as many gold medals as Tom Kiely.

A man's man we might style him, also a scholar and always a gentleman. His well-known greeting to the stranger who visits his parochial house, which was called by all his parishioners "Kilkenny Castle," proves the lavishness of his hospitality:

Come in the evening or come in morning,
Come when you're looked for or come without warning,
A Cead Mile Failte you'll find at the door
And the oftener you call here, we'll love you ever more.

PREHISTORIC IRISH SETTLEMENT CARBON-DATED AT 4,000 YEARS OLD

I distinctly remember reading with great interest some years ago about an "archaeological dig" on a hillside near Killadoon, Louisbourg, Co. Mayo. Some weeks later R.T.E. got hold of it and it featured on a programme called Newsbeat, I do believe.

In any event, evidence was brought to the surface that proved conclusively that a whole and entire community of people had settled there in pre-historic times. Famed archaeologists came over from Britain, France and America to investigate the "Settlement" along with Irish experts. Together they were able to establish that a community had in fact settled there. And there were all the trappings of human, life-sustaining necessities in evidence. There were dwellings with animal shelters, artefacts, pieces of pottery etc. But here is the mother-lode: The "Settlement" artefacts were carbon-dated to be more than 4,000 years old. See if you can assimilate exactly what this implies. Personally I can understand and measure its vast depth of time more easily by simply telling myself that communities of settled peoples lived in Ireland 2,000 years before the birth of Christ. I think that puts the perplexity into a better perspective – don't you? To my mind the above proves beyond all reasonable doubt that the Irish nation is one of the oldest in Europe, if not the world. So when I pointed out earlier in this character sketch, that the Tailtean Games were established here 2,000 B.C., I was not engaging in any flights of fancy. On the contrary I was merely attempting to put before you the prehistoric facts.

BRINGING HOME THE BODY OF FATHER O'GROWNEY

In the Autumn of 1903 Father Fielding was appointed by the Gaelic League of Ireland to bring back from America the last remains of Father Eugene O'Growney. Along with Dr. Douglas Hyde, Father O'Growney had co-founded the Gaelic League. Now, four years after his death in Los Angeles, Father Fielding felt honoured to accompany his body back to the land he loved so well. It was the renowned Father Yorke of San Francisco who was largely responsible for making this possible. Prior to his going to America Father O'Growney had held the Irish Chair at Maynooth.

Earlier there had been a quarterly session of the State Board of the Gaelic League at Holy Angels Hall, Oakwood Boulevard and Vincennes Avenue. The hall was filled to the ceiling because very many of his parishioners had come to wish Father Fielding bon voyage before he sailed for Ireland.

On the platform was Patrick Francis Holden, National Secretary who was a poet and a born Kilkenny man. Also there was John C. Gillespie, State Vice-President; Joseph Mulhearn, State Secretary, John O'Grady, State Treasurer; Daniel Sheehan, & Mrs. Rose McHale, State Directors, and Rev. Brother Finan from Notre Dame University, Indiana – whose American football teams have historically been known as, "The Fighting Irish".

A MESSAGE TO REV. J.K. FIELDING
Founder and First President of Gaelic Park Athletic Club, Chicago, President, Irish Literary Society Chicago, National Chaplain Gaelic League of America.
From Patrick Francis Holden.

They tell me you're going to Ireland,
Oh, Father pray wait just a while
And take for this exile a blessing
With love to the Emerald Isle.
When first your eyes rest upon Erin
When cliff after cliff comes to view,
Then whisper it soft to the breezes,
The heart of the exile is true.
When love from the grey mist uprises
And smiles on you over the sea,
Dear Father, I beg of you ask her
If ever she'll smile upon me?
Alas! From her bosom for ages
Have wandered the faithful and few,
Still, still – and forget not to tell her -
The heart of the exile is true.
Should you visit my own fair Kilkenny,
With fields ever bright, fresh and green,
And hedges of fairy whitethorn,
The whitest that ever were seen!
There dewdrops like diamonds are flashing
The streams wear the sun's golden hue -
Tell them, and the trees, and the flowers,
The heart of the exile is true.
You're going, kind Father – God bless you,
Bid Erin raise up her poor heart
And dash from her eyelids forever
The tears that her sufferings start.
We've sworn an oath on the gospels,
By Heaven we'll stick to it too!
And prove with our deeds stout and steady
The heart of the exile is true.

CHAPTER NINE

WILLIAM KENEALY: THE PATRIOT POET AND EDITOR OF THE KILKENNY JOURNAL

How many of you reading me now, have stood in Croke Park at an All-Ireland Hurling Final and listened to the Artane Boys Band playing, 'The Moon behind the Hill'? It used to be known as the Kilkenny Anthem. That spirit rousing air was composed by a patriot poet named William Kenealy, Editor of the 'Kilkenny Journal', newspaper and it first appeared in the New York edition of John Mitchel's 'Citizen', published in 1854. Our patriot poet contributed many articles to the 'Nation', 'Duffy's Fireside Magazine' and many other nationalistic publications.

Brian Kenealy once told me that in order to trace the history of the Kenealy family and their involvement with the 'Kilkenny Journal' newspaper, it would probably be best to begin with the Madden family, who owned the famous Supper House, known as the 'Hole in the Wall'. This establishment stood in the High Street and has gone down in song and story as a place where Makers & Breakers of Empire ate and supped. Men such as Arthur Wellesley, Duke of Wellington, Jonah Barrington, Henry Grattan, Daniel O'Connell, the Great Liberator, Thomas Moore, the National Poet, Henry Flood, orator and Parliamentarian, born in Kilkenny 1732. James Stephens, the Fenian Chief, born in Blackmill Street, Kilkenny in 1825 and very many other celebrities. The shell of this medieval hostelry is still standing. One wonders if we shall ever come to our senses and restore this marvellous link with our past. Surely there are many historically minded people in this ancient capital of Ireland, who would dearly love to see it restored to its original state. Just think, what that would do to promote tourism not to mention the restoration of our pride in our own place.

Matthew and Judith Madden employed a French chef named Louis D'Oly in the 1770's. Matthew and Judith had one daughter Mary Anne who married Louis D'Oly the year before her father's death. And when her mother died in 1800, Louis and Mary Ann D'Oly became owners of the famous Supper House.

They had five children, one of whom, Mary Anne junior, married Cornelius Maxwell in the year 1819. He owned the establishment on the Parade where the Irish Permanent Offices are today. In those times it was known as Maxwell's Corner House.

In 1830 Cornelius Maxwell bought Finns Leinster Journal and changed the name of that newspaper to the 'Kilkenny Journal'. Even so, Maxwell had no experience at all in journalism and was in fact an estate agent who owned a considerable amount of land and property. He died as a youngish man in 1851, leaving his wife Mary Ann to 'run' the Kilkenny Journal until her death, twenty-five years later. But before that she had appointed a young patriotic poet named William Kenealy from Cork as the Editor of the Kilkenny Journal. That was in 1856. She had to choose between William Kenealy from Cork and another great patriot writer named Charles Kickham from Tipperary. The same Charles Kickham who was sentenced to fourteen years for his involvement with the Fenian Movement and who wrote the two fine novels on Irish rural life: 'Knocknagow' and 'Sally Cavanagh' and the even more famous poem 'Rory of the Hill'.

I don't think I shall ever forget that kindly old Christian Brother, named Coffey (nicknamed 'Goll',) who taught us English literature – standing at the head of the class and reciting for our motley crew:

RORY OF THE HILL
   "That rake up near the rafters,
   Why leave it there so long?
   The handle, of the best of ash
   Is smooth and straight and strong.
   And, Mother, will you tell me,
   Why did my father frown
   When to make the hay in summertime
   I climbed to take it down?
   She looked into her husband's eyes,
   While her own with light did fill
   "You'll shortly know the reason boy",
   Said Rory of the Hill."

Notwithstanding the fact that William Kenealy got the job and Charles Kickham went home empty-handed, the two men remained friends all their days.

William Kenealy married Mary Anne Maxwell's daughter Rose and in doing so took over the Kilkenny Journal. The newspaper was now in the hands of the Kenealy family. William and Rose had five children, three boys and two girls. Two of the boys went into journalism.

Con succeeded his father as Editor of the Kilkenny Journal while Willy went to Dublin to work on the 'Irish Independent'. And their sons went into the newspaper business too.

Then there was Margaret Kenealy who married yet another journalist named James Doheny and they had a son named Francis who was what one might refer to in modern terminology as 'something else'. In absolute terms Francis was an eccentric genius. He qualified as a solicitor gaining first place in Ireland in his final examination. Francis then joined the British Civil Service and became a most controversial figure, picking all kinds of loopholes in the Law. In fact he once threw a brick through the G.P.O. front window here on High Street in Kilkenny City, just to prove a point of law. And the same Francis was wont to making speeches and giving pointers from an upstairs window at the Globe Hotel, John Street. As well as being a marvelous orator, he had a ready wit and within minutes of his 'speech to the nation', a hundred of more excited citizens would gather for the uproarious entertainment. There was no topic he could not speak on.

As it was common knowledge that Francis Doheny went swimming every morning, winter and summer, one wiseacre contrived to make fun of Francis, asking: "Was the water wet this morning Francis?" To which he quickly replied "O yes my friend, the water was wet, but your joke is exceedingly dry". And that put paid to your mans' jocularity for that Saturday night.

Back to the Kenealy's. Con who was the oldest was the first to join the firm. He went straight in from school and Billy joined a little later. Con then married Philomena Row, whose family owned Cloth Hall where W.H. Good's department store stands today. Con and Philomena had three children: Con jnr. and Mary who were twins and Brian. Philomena died while still a young woman in 1940. Some years later Con remarried to Mary Harte and they had one son Louis. Louis who owned the Arts and Crafts shop at 25 Patrick Street has sadly left us, but happily gone back to God. He was the husband of Mary Kenealy who presently oversees the Arts and Crafts business and who was once President of the Kilkenny Arts Festival Committee. It was Con Kenealy who managed the Kilkenny Journal from 1922-1963, when he retired due to ill health. He died in 1969. It was Brian who took over the management of the Kilkenny Journal after Con's retirement and continued to do so right up to its final 'stop press' in 1985.

Let us go back now to the progenitor of the Kenealy's of Kilkenny, namely William, the Poet and Patriot. He was born in Cloyne in 1828 and was the son of a Blacksmith and small farmer. He was reared in the revolutionary tradition. In those times Blacksmiths and school teachers were among the people most feared by the authorities, because both groups had excellent opportunities for meeting people unobtrusively and 'many a plot was hatched in a blacksmiths forge'.

William became a schoolteacher and was later appointed Headmaster in Churchtown South Cloyne. It was the year of the Young Irelanders and there was great political upheaval. He got into difficulties with a local magistrate for publishing 'inflammatory writings' that he had addressed to Saint Colmans Club in 1848. He lost his teaching post but was contacted by the Coadjutor Bishop of Derry, Dr. Maginn, and offered a teaching position in the Diocesan College there.

Leeds was his next stop where a large contingence of Irish people had relocated. There William edited the Catholic newspaper 'The Lamp' for a time before he returned to Ireland to become editor of the Tipperary Leader. But his patriotic leanings coupled with his stalwart integrity would once more land him in trouble with the law. It came about when a writer for the 'Leader; wrote an article that reflected badly on a Protestant clergyman who had taken a libel action against that newspaper. William refused to give the writer's name and assumed all responsibility for the article, as the Editor. He was jailed for libel in Clonmel, and damages of £200 were awarded against him.

As I previously said William Kenealy became Editor of the Kilkenny Journal in 1856. He was elected Mayor of Kilkenny in the years 1872 and 1873. He died on the 5th September 1876 at the early age of 48 years and was buried in Saint Patrick's' Cemetery Patrick Street, Kilkenny City. Unfortunately he did not live to see the achievement of the goal which he had striven for so long: the implementation of the three F's: Free Sale, Fair Rent and Fixture of Tenure.

THE MOON BEHIND THE HILL
By William Kenealy
I watched last night the rising moon
Upon a foreign strand
'Till memories came like flowers in June
Of home and Fatherland.
I dreamt I was a boy once more
Beside the rippling rill,
Until my eyes could see no more
The moon behind the hill.

It brought me back the visions grand
That purpled boyhood dreams
It's youthful loves, it's happy land,
As bright as morning beams,
It brought me back my own sweet Nore
The Castle and the Mill
Until my eyes could see no more
The moon behind the hill.

CHAPTER TEN

PETER DE LOUGHRY: THE KILKENNY PATRIOT-POLITICIAN (WHO MADE THE KEY THAT SPRUNG DE VALERA FROM LINCOLN JAIL)

The De Loughry's first came into Kilkenny City from Tullaherin in 1780. Tullaherin lies between Bennettsbridge and Dungarvin, County Kilkenny. Peter De Loughry was born in 1882.

He was the 5th child of the family and it was he who took over the management of the large family business which had been established in 1816 by his father Richard.

To give my readers some idea of the magnitude and excellence of this establishment, I will give you an advertisement published in an old book on Kilkenny that reads as follows: R. De Loughry and Sons of Parliament Street and Newbuilding Lane. Established in 1816. Casting in Iron, Brass etc. of every description made to order. Plough parts a specialty. Also Builders; Contractors, Millers etc. will find it to their advantage to consult us when requiring castings of any kind. Our Foundry was established in 1816. Engineering in all its branches including motor repairs. Agents for Swift Cars Cycle Depot and Hardware Store. Telephone DeLoughry's Kilkenny 43.

LOUIS PASTEUR

Peter De Loughry's wife was a lady named Winifred Murphy. Winifred was born in the Union House which was in fact a poor house. It stood where the old Central Hospital stood later. Later still this building was taken over by the Kilkenny Products, an Engineering firm now defunct. Today it is Government Offices.

The reason Winifred Murphy was born in the Union House was that her father, Thomas Murphy, was the Master of the Union. This mans job of work was similar to that of Mister Bumble's in Charles Dickens novel "Oliver Twist". But I hasten to add that unlike Mister Bumble, Thomas Murphy was a most humane man, as the following story will reveal.

Written into the records of the day to day running of the Union House was the following: "It has come to the notice of myself Thomas Murphy, Master of the Union on the Hebron Road that 3 young male inmates were today bitten by a mad dog, that showed signs of rabies. I have sent for the Union Physician." Some time later it was diagnosed that the 3 boys had in fact contracted the terrible disease of Rabies. You must remember that in those far off days Rabies was a certain killer. There was no cure for it. Not in Ireland, England, Scotland nor Wales. And so it became a foregone conclusion that the 3 boys would surely die and under the most horrific circumstances at that.

As well as being a true humanitarian, Thomas Murphy, was also a well-read man. Some, time earlier he had read in a "News Letter" that a young nouveau scientist in Paris, named Louis Pasteur, was founding a special branch of science, which he called "Bacteriology". High on Mister Pasteur's research list was a cure for Hydrophobia, otherwise known as Rabies. As Thomas Murphy saw it, he must take the 3 boys by boat and train to Paris. This he did without delay. Nothing further was found in the Union House records. But we do know with certainty that: the first "Vaccination" Louis Pasteur performed on a human being was on a boy who had been bitten by a mad-dog. Who can tell? Perhaps it was one of the boys from Union House Hebron Road, Kilkenny, that had been the worlds 1st receipient of Louis Pasteur's "Vaccination" against Rabies.

The group includes the Civic Dignitaries in the midst of whom is Senator de Loughry, then Chairman of Seanad Eireann, who was the principal agent in having the Bell restored to its ancient place in the Abbey Tower.

JOSEPH MARY PLUNKET.

Winifred Murphy later married Peter De Loughry. She became Head of the Cumann na mBan, here in Kilkenny. The poet and freedom fighter Joseph Mary Plunket was a great friend of Peter and Winifred De Loughry and often stayed at their home in Parliament Street. Joseph Mary was the son of Count Plunket. He was born in 1887 and was educated at Belvedere and the National University. His poetry abounds with the symbolism of the mystics. Among his few literary friends were Padraig Pearse and Thomas Mc Donagh, both of whom were poets like himself. I need hardly tell you that all three men shared the same glorious though sad ends: they were executed for their parts in the "Easter Rising" of 1916. Following is a little poem by Joseph Mary Plunket. I trust it will give you a greater understanding of the man behind the words, bearing in mind what I said about the symbolism of the mystics. It is called:

THE PRESENCE OF GOD

I see His blood upon the rose,
And in the stars the glory of His eyes,
His body gleams amid eternal snows,
His tears fall from the skies.

I see His face in every flower.
The thunder and the singing of the birds,
Are but His voice; and carven by His power,
Rocks are His written words.

All pathways by His feet are worn
His strong heart stirs the everbeating sea
His crown of thorns is twined with every thorn
His cross is every tree.

Joseph Mary Plunket was married in prison, shortly before he was executed. The priest who performed the ceremony was that great Kilkenny patriot priest Father Albert. I'll tell you all about him at a later date.

TAKEN HOSTAGE BY THE BLACK AND TANS

Peter De Loughry was a staunch member of the Irish Volunteers and was arrested and imprisoned on numerous occasions. He was an ardent member of Kilkenny Corporation and County Council. He was chairman of Kilkenny City and County Technical Committee and was elected Mayor of Kilkenny on seven occasions. In fact he was in jail when first he was elected to the Mayoralty. Peter De Loughry was the first to be taken Hostage by the infamous Black and Tans.

At that time he was driven through the streets of Kilkenny while standing in the back of an army lorry, blind folded with his hands tied behind his back and a rifle aimed at his head. Following on that he was jailed in Dublin and his home was occupied by the British Forces. Over the years of the "Troubles", Peter was imprisoned in Mountjoy, Ballykinlar, Frongoch and Wandsworth. He said the latter was worst of all.

THE KEY THAT SPRUNG DE VALERA

History recalls that Peter De Loughry was also imprisoned in Lincoln jail, as was Sean Milroy, Sean Mc Garry and Eamon De Valera. It was Peter who cut the Key that led to their eventual escape. He got the idea for their escape from stories told to him by his mother who was a cousin of the man who had helped the Fenian chief to escape from Richmond Jail. The Fenian chief of course was our own James Stephens from Blackmill Street, Kilkenny City. The man who helped Stephens was J.J. Breslin, who had infiltrated the prison staff by becoming a prison guard.

But here is what actually happened at Lincoln Jail: As De Valera regularly served Mass in the church jail, it was an easy matter for him to pocket a few candles. He melted these down and took an impression of the Chaplain's master Key. As there were double locks on every door the master Key was a must. There were two ordinary Keys made that didn't work. De Valera made the first impression and had it smuggled out of prison and sent to Gerard Boland in Dublin. Boland sent back the Key in a Christmas cake but it didn't turn the lock. A second impression was made which was sent to Manchester where craftsmen cut what they thought was a true replica. It too was a fiasco.

At that juncture Peter De Loughry, told Dev to have a blank Key sent into the prison with a file, saying; "I'll cut it myself". The blank Key and the file arrived this time in a birthday cake. Peter who was an expert locksmith easily cut a perfect replica.

Outside waiting at the last gate to freedom were, Michael Collins and Harry Boland. As Collins spied Dev, Milroy and Mc Garry coming towards the door he inserted another Key, which he believed, would open the last door to freedom. He attempted to turn the lock, giving the Key a powerful twist. It broke in the lock. Collins was raging. I've broken a Key in the lock Dev-what are we going to do now? Dev muttered something while inserting the Key Peter De Loughry had cut for him. It knocked out the broken part and with one turn the lock clicked open.

The five men shook hands and disappeared into the night. Peter De Loughry did not escape with the others as he had but a few weeks left to serve out his sentence.

WHAT REALLY HAPPENED READS LIKE SENSATIONAL FICTION

Some years later a national newspaper ran this story:

The true story of the "Escape from Lincoln jail", reads like a page of sensational fiction. De Valera as an altar server picks up the Chaplains master Key and in moments has taken the impression of it in the wax of a melted candle. This impression is cunningly reproduced in a comic drawing on a postcard by another prisoner. One side of the drawing depicts a drunken man fumbling with a latchkey at a door, and underneath is written; "I can't get in." The other side shows a prisoner trying to fit a big Key in a prison gate and underneath this sketch is written; "I can't get out". The Key on this side is an exact replica of the actual master Key. There is a stringent censorship over the prisoner's correspondence, which has to pass both ways through London for inspection. But this postcard, regarded by the censors as a harmless joke, gets through and eventually reaches Michael Collins in Dublin

A Key made to the required dimensions is baked in a cake and sent to the prisoners, but it doesn't work. Paddy O' Donaghue a former civil Servant, then in business in Manchester has a second Key made, but this one also fails. A third Key which is a blank is then sent in with a file in yet another cake, and this one is expertly cut by one of the prisoners, – Alderman De Loughry of Kilkenny, who had made an exhaustive study of all the locks in Lincoln Jail. The rest is history.

Eamon De Valera restored the Key to Peter De Loughry many years later in Dáil Éireann. Again the newspapers took up the story: Mr De Valera returns the Key. Alderman Peter De Loughry T.D, C.C., P.C. Kilkenny has been presented with the key which was made by himself when he was a prisoner in Lincoln Jail, which enabled three of his fellow prisoners, Eamon De Valera, Sean Milroy and Sean Mc Gary to unlock the prison gates and gain their freedom.

The Key was restored to the artificer, a week ago in the Dáil by Mr De Valera, accompanied by a letter in Irish in which Mr De Valera stated he was returning the Key in pursuance of a promise made to Alderman De Loughry some years ago.

SINN FÉIN

Peter De Loughry was chairman of the first Kilkenny Sinn Féin club. He took part in the 1916 rising and was subsequently jailed. He was a member of the 1st Senate, as was Lady Desart of Kilkenny in 1918 which was the occasion of his election to Dáil Éireann as T.D for Kilkenny, he was a prisoner in Lincoln jail.

In 1925 he brought the Black Abbey bell back from the Market House at Dunlavin Estate where it had been used to summon the workers on the Estate.

Alderman Peter De Loughry, T.D. C.C. and P. C. Kilkenny died at his sisters residence, Mrs. Henry Mangan, Richmond Ave, Dublin, on the 24th October 1931 aged 52 years.

He voted for the approval of the articles of agreement of 1921 and was a member of the Cumann Na nGaelheal, later known as the Fine Gael Party.

Richard De Loughry, who was a son of the fabled Peter, was himself an Electrical Engineer. He was the 1st Kilkenny man to volunteer for the Irish Army during The Emergency. He held the rank of Ordinance Officer with the Southern Command- a position, which he held with distinction all through The Emergency. He relinquished that position in 1948 and returned to Kilkenny to take up the management of the family business in a hardware shop, Petrol Pumps and Electrical components shop at 18 and 19 Parliamentl Street. At that time the foundry in New Building Lane was still operating with the famous Leahy brothers, Jeff and Jimmy doing the castings.

Anna Teresa Hennessy became Richard De Loughry's wife. Better known as Cis to her friends, Cis claims with conviction that she comes from one of the oldest native business families in Kilkenny. Her father Pat Hennessy was proprietor of a Saddliery and Harness Shop at Rose Inn St. Pat had a great singing voice and was a life long member of the Friary Choir. And Pat and Ciss's father had a Butchers shop also at Rose Inn St. Seanie Mc Grath from the Pound; Ballycallan later worked there for one of the Hickeys.

Patricia De Loughry is the daughter of Richard who died a comparatively young man. She is a Gaelic scholar and school teacher. She teaches at St. Canices co-ed on the Granges Road. A foremost member of the Gaelic League. Patricia is totally committed to the restoration of the Irish Language. She lives at Parliament Street with her Mother Cis, in a house that has been the family home for all of two hundred and twenty two years.

CHAPTER ELEVEN

THE FIRST MAN TO FLY WAS A KILKENNY MAN

"If God intended that man should fly, He would have given him wings. And those blasphemous meddlers who attempt to do so are flying in the face of God."

So said some stick-in-the-mud, self-styled philosopher, in the first years of the 20th century. Some few months later, in 1903, Wilbur and Orville Wright, two obscure bicycle-mechanics, from Dayton, Ohio, having built a flimsy machine of wood, cloth and wire, attempted to fly.

Over a deserted beach at Kitty Hawk, North Carolina, in December of that year, Orville did actually fly through the air in the frail ship, powered by a tiny petrol engine.

They had done what was thought to be impossible, and no-one would believe them. How could the people be expected to believe that two bicycle repair men, who had never gone to college, could conquer the force of gravity.

Had not the world famous astronomer and mathematician Simon Necomb, proven with unassailable logic, that to fly a heavier-than-air machine was absolutely impossible. It seemed that the Wright brothers' story was only for the birds.

It was five years after their first 'Hop' at Kitty Hawk, that the owner of the New York 'Herald', James Gordon Bennett, sent his star reporter, Byron Newton to investigate the 'rumour'. Along with two other reporters and a photographer, Newton witnessed the brothers Wright in magnificent flight, high above the deserted beach at Kitty Hawk.

All those events happened in the United States of America, between the years 1903 and 1908. History assures us that the Wright brothers were the first men to fly, but this is not entirely true as there were some aviation historians who claimed it was a Kilkenny man, in fact who was the first in the world to fly.

A FLYING START

Some 47 years earlier (1856) in Ireland, in a place called Swiftsheath in Co. Kilkenny, Godwin Meade Swifte, a Kilkenny man, built his 'Aerial Chariot'. He invented, patented and constructed this 'Apparatus For Navigating The Air' almost half a century before the flight at Kitty Hawk. But, because there was no engine powerful enough or light enough in existence at the time, his machine had to be manually operated and could not remain airborne for very long.

But the Aerial Chariot did FLY according to documented accounts by competent aviation historians. The propeller blades from this First Ever Flying Machine can be seen at Rothe House Museum, Parliament St., Kilkenny. "The Letters Patent, No. 2993, dated 1856 can be seen for the asking."

The body of the Machine was constructed like a small boat and made of wooden laths. This was covered with strong light-weight cloth. It had a screw propeller which had been invented by Swifte himself, and was rotated by a winch, acting on three multiplying wheels. Operated on the principle of the racing bicycle gear-shift, or something close to it, it seems, and absolutely ingenius. The wings were covered with silk, and produced 'the effect of birds' wings'. It had a tail for changing altitude and this was manipulated by a string from the pilot's seat, also a rudder that resembled a sail.

GODWIN MEADE SWIFT IN HIS 'AERIAL CHARIOT'

Illustrated by Cathy Kenny

Swifte built his flying machine in Swiftsheath dining room, and had all doors enlarged so that the Aerial Chariot, could be wheeled in and out whenever necessary.

About the whole apparatus, Swifte himself says;

"This may give some idea of the small force required to continue the flight of the Aerial Chariot, nor will it be requisite to be continually turning the winch or working the pedal with the foot, for when a certain altitude is attained, the Chariot may go several miles perhaps fifty or sixty as it were, upon an inclined plane of air, and if the person be expert, he may take advantage of it for the distance stated or even more, or according to the height he has attained".

And so Godwin Meade Swifte, from Kilkenny, was truly a man before his time, and must go down in history as the first man ever to invent, build and fly an 'Aerial Chariot' or 'Apparatus For Navigating The Air".

However, that is not the whole story of Kilkenny's involvement with the history of aviation. In 1909 Denys Corbett-Wilson, an English man, rented Darver House near Jenkinstown. Mr. Corbett-Wilson was an air-pilot who was to make aviation history, when on the 22nd April 1912, he became the first man to cross the Irish Sea by powered flight.

Luck must have been with him because after an hour and thirty minutes he ran into storm-force winds, and bank after bank of blind-dark clouds. He had no idea if he had reached Ireland or if he was still over the water. Suddenly there was a break in the cloud and he glimpsed land.

He landed safely near Enniscorthy. The trip from Fishguard to Enniscorthy had taken him one hour and forty minutes. Three weeks later, he made a victorious flight to Kilkenny City and the citizens turned out in great numbers to cheer him and welcome him back.

It was generally believed that Corbett-Wilson was killed in the Great War (1914), he being one of the first pilots to join the Royal Flying Corps. But this seems to be untrue according to an old newspaper cutting which I came upon in recent years.

The heading states:

THE FIRST MAN TO FLY THE CHANNEL D. CORBETT-WILSON

Under the heading there's a photo of the famous air-man and a communication that reads as follows;

Corbett-Wilson "I think I am right in stating that in Kilkenny it was widely believed that Mr. Corbett-Wilson, the great air-man, whose aeroplane was first seen in Kilkenny, had been killed in the Great War.

As far as I can recollect he was reported "Missing – believed killed," and I cannot recall having read any subsequent announcement confirming or contradicting that report.

Hence my surprise the other day on reading in a newspaper a paragraph stating;

"The first aeroplane flight across the Irish sea is recalled by the appointment of Wing-Commander Corbett-Wilson to the Headquarters of the Coastal Area of the British Air-Force for technical staff-duties."

"Being convinced that the Mr. Corbett-Wilson who lived at Darver House, Co. Kilkenny, and who before the outbreak of the Great War, thrilled the people of Kilkenny and elsewhere by his flights, was dead, I might have been pardoned for thinking that the author of the paragraph referred to, was confusing names, and that the Mr. Corbett-Wilson we knew, and the gentleman of that name mentioned in connection with the Air-Force appointment, did not refer to the same person. However, my doubts on the point were somewhat dispelled though I must confess, not altogether removed, by the fact that following the paragraph was a brief account of incidents and dates which undoubtedly refer to the Mr. Corbett-Wilson that lived in Kilkenny".

There you have it – a fine piece of history. But did Denys Corbett-Wilson die in the Great War or did he survive it? Whether or which, the ace pilot was a well-known figure in Kilkenny city and county in those far off days. When he arrived back in Kilkenny, after having flown the Irish Sea, thousands turned out to greet him. He landed in the Old Golf Links behind the Butts' Housing Estate. The Old Links is still there and is presently owned by Willie Brennan of Bishop's Demense, who was an old school pal of mine.

All in all, don't you think that Kilkenny can be justly proud of its association with those magnificent men and their flying machines?

CHAPTER TWELVE

THE GENIUS OF HUBERT BUTLER
IS A NATIONAL TREASURE

HUBERT Butler was born at Maidenhall, Bennettsbridge, Kilkenny on 23rd October 1900, to George and Rita Butler. His early education began at Bigshotte Rayles preparation school near Wokingham, England in 1909. Three years later he entered Charterhouse on a scholarship. In 1918 he matriculated at Saint John's College, Oxford, as a Senior Classical Scholar. Hubert returned to Ireland in 1923, having been recruited as a Librarian by Sir Horace Plunkett and George Russell (AE).

At that time the Irish County Libraries were controlled and administered by Plunkett and A.E. Hubert was put to work at first in Ballymena, – next in Coleraine and later in Portstewart.

I first met Hubert Butler at the home of James Delahunty, College Road, Kilkenny City in the company of two wonderful writers, Frank McEvoy and Tom Lyng. It was James Delahunty who introduced me, a poor prentice poet, to that great man of Letters!

I was taken aback by Hubert's cordiality and his willingness to accept me, as he all too generously put it himself; "a fellow scribbler". Later on as some other writers arrived, I was introduced to each in turn. All of us had been invited to James' home to celebrate the 'Launch' of the Kilkenny Magazine, which was subtitled an All Ireland Literary Review.

On the last page of that book James Delahunty (Editor) wrote under the caption:

About Our Contributors. "Hubert Butler. Born in Co. Kilkenny in 1900. Was Review Editor of The Bell for a time. Contributes regularly to The Twentieth Century, The Manchester Guardian, The Irish Times and other journals. Has given many talks on the B.B.C. Third Programme and Radio Eireann, which broadcast his translation of 'The Cherry Orchard', this year to mark the Chekhov centenary. Is a staunch supporter of the principal of regionalism."

Being a typical thinking Irishman, Hubert began his writing career about 1927, by emigrating to Alexandria. There he taught English literature for a time before going on to Italy, Greece, Vienna and Yogoslavia. He taught as he went, dispatching and accruing knowledge like a true student of the art of communication and learning.

In June 1930 Hubert married Susan Margaret (Peggy) Guthrie, and they went on honeymoon to Latvia, Estonia and East Prussia. They were refused entry to the Soviet Union. One year later he translated Leonid Leonev's classic novel 'The Thief' which was published in London. Later he was allowed to teach for a time in Leningrad even though the politics of the Red Terror were then very much in vogue.

In 1933-34 he translated Chekhov's world classic The Cherry Orchard, already mentioned which was produced at the Old Vic and published also in London. Between the years 1934 and 1937 Hubert Butler travelled extensively having been awarded a Travelling Scholarship to Yugoslavia by the School of Slavonic Studies in London. He was based in Zagreb, Belgrade and Dubrovnik.

In the meantime a daughter was born to Hubert and Peggy in Kilkenny in 1935. She was Christened Julia. Julia married Richard Crampton, in 1959. He is Professor of Medicine Emeritus at the University of Virginia. They have four children. I spoke with Julia and Richard briefly at Hubert's Centenary Celebration in Kilkenny Castle.

I do believe that if Hubert, from his couch above turns his spy-glass upon this page of the 'Kilkenny People', this Arts Festival, he will be highly amused. Seeing himself in the celestial company of Saint Canice in sketch about whose Christian origin there is no doubt. In his 'Decay of Archaeology' Hubert says that "the second Marquis of Ormond who was President of the Kilkenny Archaeological Society, edited the Life of Saint Canice (from whom Kilkenny took it's name) from the Salamanca Codex and made a gift of a free copy to all members of the society."

I shouldn't be at all surprised if the journals in the Salamanca Codex were compiled by our own Fr. James Archer, born in Kilkenny 1550 who was first Rector of the Irish College at Salamanca, (about whom I have written elsewhere).

Spying on that pen and ink sketch he might recall his first published book in 1972 namely, "Ten Thousand Saints".

But Hubert's saints were not the holyman of God, that we normally associate with hagiography such as the Life of Saint Canice. These were the pre Christian chieftains of continental tribes, – some good and others not so good who landed on our shores long before Saints Patrick, Kieran and Canice were born. Some were fearless warriors, who protected and provided well for their subjects thereby carving for themselves such fame that legends grew about their names, making them synonymous with the place they ruled over.

But of course one must conclude that it is possible to be holy without being Christian. Take Mahatma Gandhi for instance.

Hubert sensibly sums up "Yet for the Irish people to forget their saints is for them to forget their childhood. We are emotionally and intellectually committed to them. They beckon us along a private road that leads not only to the Irish past but to the past of Europe. It is through them that we can learn about the youth of the world and the infancy of religion.Whether they really lived or not, they belong to use more than to anybody else."

I have often wondered why it was that Hubert Butler left it so late in his life to publish his first book. Could it be that this consummate intellectual was a reluctant hero, – a bashful genius? He certainly was not in any hurry to reveal himself to the masses, notwithstanding the fact that he loved to communicate. Perhaps it was because he was happy in the knowledge that he had already committed to writing most of what he wanted to say on the subject of man's treatment of his fellow man. Having read Hubert early and late I do believe that in the main he subscribed to the philosophy that man is often a beast to his fellow man. One only has to read, "The Children of Drancy" to fully appreciate that!

PART OF THE FINAL SOLUTION

"The Children of Drancy were part of Hitler's 'Final Solution' Two of the writers I consulted said it was in July, a third said it was in August 1942 that 4,051 children were sent off to be killed in Poland from the transit camp at Drancy, north of Paris. Were they French Jews or foreigners? Were they girls or boys? It is usually said boys, but sub-urban residents on the outskirts of Pairs who heard them wailing at night say they were little girls, and there is a story of a bleeding ear torn by a harried police inspector as he removed an earring."

They spent four days without food at the Nélodrome d'Hiver (the winter cycling-racing stadium) before their mothers were taken from them; then they were loaded three or four hundred at a time into cattle trains at Gare d'Austerlitz and taken to Auschwitz... "But to kill and burn 4,051 children after transporting them to Poland was a huge co-operative endeavor in which thousands of French and German policemen, typists, railway officials, gas fitters and electricians were engaged." The noted French Catholic writer Francois Mauriac in 1942 said he saw thousands of small boys and girls between the ages of two and fifteen crowded into cattle wagons at a Paris railway station, crying their hearts out. However, some twenty years later the same Mauriac wrote that he did not see the wailing children in the cattle wagons himself but that his wife did and she described the scene to him. One wonders had he developed a guilt complex twenty years on at not having done enough to bring world attention to focus upon that terrible tragedy.

In the early 1960s Francois Mauriac wrote "Nothing I had seen during those sombre years of the Occupation had left so deep a mark on me as those trainloads of Jewish children standing at the Gare d'Austerlitz. Yet I did not even see them myself. My wife described them to me, her voice filled with horror. At that time we knew nothing of Nazi methods of extermination. And who could have imagined them? Yet the way these lambs were torn from their mothers, is itself exceeding anything we had so far thought possible. I believe that on that day I touched upon the mystery of iniquity whose revelation was to mark the end of one era and the beginning of another".

In Vienna in 1938 Hubert made contact with a Viennese Quaker organisation that worked to secure the freedom of refugees from Hitler's Nazi Anschluss Camp. He succeeded in winning freedom for many through hard graft and gifted negotiation. He worked with the Quaker organisation through 1938 and 1939 with much success.

At home in Maidenhall Bennettsbridge, Hubert's father died in 1941 and he inherited the Butler house and grounds. He returned to Maidenhall with his family.

Almost immediately he immersed himself in Kilkenny's literary milieu. Later he revived the Archaeological Society in 1944. Between 1945 and 1947 he visited Yugoslavia a number of times where he investigated the war time genocide.

It was as a result of these 'investigations' that Hubert Butler supported in his writings in the Church of Ireland Gazette, Serbian Orthodox against the Croat Catholics. It must be said though that few, in fact very few agreed with his estimation of what really happened. My opinion on the rights or wrongs of what happened is unimportant. But I do defend his right to publish his conclusions one way or the other. Yet Hubert was not hung out to dry, because two men of genius supported him, namely, Sean O'Casey in 'Sunset and Evening Star' and Sean O'Faolain in 'The Bell'.

As stated earlier Hubert himself had been Review-Editor of 'The Bell' for some years. At a public meeting in Dublin in 1952 Hubert had a disagreement with the Papal Nuncio about the role of the clergy in the Croatian genocide. He was boycotted and censured by many civic bodies and was forced to resign from the Kilkenny Archeological Society. That same year he organised the first Kilkenny Debate.

In 1955 Hubert stood for election to the Kilkenny County Council under the slogan "A minority voice" and was heavily defeated. One year later he went on a visit to China and the Soviet Union under the patronage of an Irish cultural delegation.

The American South was his next stop in 1962. While in Atlanta, he met with Wyatt Tee Walker who was Martin Luther King's second-in-command.

He called his office boy – "Get me a sandwich please from the café next door and one for this gentleman too! I am sorry that I can't ask you to lunch there, as it is segregated. However, we're tackling that problem next. I am giving them an ultimatum. If they don't desegregate within thirty days I'll organise a sit-in".

In Jackson he met another Negro leader. He claimed he was the Editor of the only Negro newspaper in the United States that was not an Uncle Tom paper. In parenthesis, Mrs. Beecher Stowe, like most conciliatory people, annoyed both sides. She wanted the Negroes to be free, but expected them to be simple and merry like Uncle Tom and very deferential to the 'good' whites. So to be called 'an Uncle Tom Paper" is to be damned.

Hubert had an embarrassing question for the Editor: "I was told by an official of the White Citizen's Council that young Negro leaders are partly white and therefore quite untypical. Is this so?" He answered quickly, "More than 65 percent of American Negroes have white blood. I myself am part Indian and had a white grandfather." In fact the average Negro integrationist is not interested in racism and Africa. He smiles sardonically when he hears the whites talk of a basic physical repugnance between black and white, for he knows that the white man invariably took the initiative in the creation of the 65 percent.

Hubert founded the Butler Society along with Lord Dunboyne in 1967.

In 1985 he published his first collection of essays in book form which he titled, Escape from the Anthill. For this he was given the American Irish Foundation Literary Award. He published the Children of Drancy in 1988. I have already spoken about that. In 1989 came the Irish Book Award Silver Medal for Literature and in 1990 Grandmother and Wolf Tone.This was followed by The Sub-Prefect Should Have Held His Tongue: Selected Essays published by Penguin in October to correspond with Hubert's 90th birthday. His literary greatness is in direct line of descent from Jonathan Swift, Oliver Goldsmith and George Berkeley. The great man of Letters died on 5th January 1991 in Kilkenny. We feel both proud and privileged that we can claim his genius for Kilkenny.

CHAPTER THIRTEEN

THE SMITHWICKS OF KILKENNY:
WHO BEFRIENDED AND SUPPORTED
DANIEL O'CONNELL

THE now world famous Smithwicks Brewery, properly called Saint Francis Abbey Brewery was established by a member of the Smithwick family about the year 1710. Apparently the family had come to Wexford from Hertfordshire in the year 1580. But during the Insurrection of 1641, a terrible tragedy struck, – the entire family, with the exception of one young lad, were killed by marauders. When the house was raided John Smithwick hid on a loft and escaped with his life. To remain in the locality would mean certain death. He decided to clear out of the county Wexford while the going was good, and under the cover of darkness he ran as fast as his feet could carry him. He rested by day and travelled by night. Into south Kilkenny he went, and up and into Tipperary town. There it was easy for him to melt into the population and secure employment.

Having grown to manhood he married a woman named Le Hunte. She was the daughter of a Cromwellian Colonel.

Later on around 1709 a prosperous young man named John Smithwick came out of Tipperary and into Kilkenny city to live. He set up a business about the year 1710 and got married to a woman named Jane Dunphy. There must have been an epidemic or some such outbreak, because Jane and five of their children all died and were buried at Saint Canices Cathedral. John married again, - this time to a woman named Mary Grace from Lazybush, near Bonnettstown on the Tullaroan Road.

It was from this second marriage that the Smithwicks of Kilkenny as we know them descended. They had three sons, the eldest named Edmond and he became Parish Priest of Saint Patrick's in Kilkenny city. This misfortunate man was murdered while trying to settle a faction fight near the Market Yard in Nov. 1776. Their second son Peter married a woman named Margaret Murphy and left four children after his death in 1773.

The eldest son John married Catherine Butler who was the daughter of Edmond Butler of Dangan county Tipperary in 1789. A younger brother Paul married Eleanor Murphy. This union produced one child, – a son who again entered the priesthood and became Canon Paul Smithwick Parish Priest of Howth.

The son of John Smithwick and Catherine Butler of Dangan, named Edmond was born in 1800. He became a Director of the National Bank. Along with Richard Sullivan owner of Sullivan's Brewery Kilkenny city, Edmond Smithwick set up a Soup Kitchen to relieve the starvation of the poor during the 1847 famine. Edmond was Mayor of Kilkenny on four occasions.

I feel sure most of you reading me now, will remember with affection the cast-iron plaques fixed to stone walls on bridges and roads outside the city, announcing the Borough Boundary. In iron letters it told the legend: Edmond Smithwick Mayor of Kilkenny 1849. The plaque that adorned the White Bridge – that is to say the original and true White Bridge, on the Kenny's Well and Ballycallan Road, was stolen by some trophy hunter some years ago. It seems to me it must have been the work of some clever dick or pseudo citizen, as a true Kilkenny man would never stoop to defacing or removing such a souvenir of old Kilkenny relique."

Edmond Smithwick first purchased the free-hold of the Brewery in the Court of Chancery when it was a Distillery (alcoholic spirits such as whiskey) as well as a Brewery in 1827.

DANIEL O'CONNELL

The Great Liberator, Daniel O'Connell was a life-long friend of Edmond Smithwick. He stayed at Kilcreene House every time he came to Kilkenny. And whenever the two friends ate out, it was as often as not at that famous Supper-House, The Hole in The Wall on High Street. Daniel was the God-father of one of Edmonds sons who was Christened Daniel O'Connell Smithwick. O'Connell who was known as the uncrowned King of Ireland was the champion of Catholic Emancipation.

This international, giant political figure, got rid of the Penal Laws against Catholics and campaigned endlessly for the restoration of Ireland's own government and parliament which had been abolished by the Act of Union in 1800. The liberation from the Penal Laws and the right to self government is summed up in the slogan; Emancipation and Repeal".

In some ways O'Connell was an odd sort of patriot. Although a born Irish speaker he continually advised the people to adopt the English language, saying it was the language of progress. And though he advocated for Irish independence, yet he still preached she should stay loyal to the British Crown. He was born in Cahirciveen Co. Kerry in 1775.

Later he was forbidden to attend Trinity College Dublin, the only Irish University at that time, because he was Catholic. He was sent to an English speaking College at Saint Omer in France. He returned to Ireland in 1796 and was called to the Irish Bar. Two years later the 1798 Fight for Freedom got underway, but O'Connell did not support the cause of the United Irishmen. Many great Irishmen were dismayed and angered when he said, "The Irish are not sufficiently enlightened to bear the sun of freedom". Because of this Thomas Davis and the Young Irelanders would later sever all connections with him.

He stood for election to Parliament in 1828 and won the election but was not allowed to take his seat because he was a Catholic. A year later he was elected again but this time he took his seat as the British Government had changed and an Act granting Catholic Emancipation was passed. Although he deplored the spilling of blood O'Connell fought a duel at Bishopscourt, near Naas and shot dead his challenger, a man named de Esterre. A short time after he had a raging argument with the then Chief Secretary for Ireland Robert Peel, and only after the intervention of mutual friends a second duel was avoided. O'Connell was a hot-head who always said, what he thought and in a very robust language at that.

The Great Liberator gave a fiery speech to the people of Kilkenny from the first floor of the offices at Smithwicks Brewery on Parliament St. That was in 1830 a year after Catholic Emancipation had been granted. Now he was agitating for Repeal. By 1834 the Vote at Westminster on Repeal was 523 against and 38 for. He didn't stand a chance of achieving the second part of his twin objectives.

But there were new and younger men who were ready to fight for Irish freedom. Men like Thomas Davis, Thomas Francis Meagher and Smith-O'Brien. By 1843 an ageing O'Connell organised his famous monster rallies in protest again the Act of Union. The first of these was at Trim Co. Meath. And then on August 15th it was estimated that more than one million Irish men and women came together on the Hill of Tara. Never before had so many men and women gathered in one place to listen to and support one solitary politician. Remember he had already achieved Catholic Emancipation.The British Government was dumbfounded and frightened. On the following year in January 1844 O'Connell was arrested and convicted by a Dublin jury that was made up almost entirely of Protestants. After having spent three months in Richmond Jail the House of Lords reversed that conviction. But it was too late for the ageing O'Connell.

Things came to a head in 1846 when the Young Irelanders to a man walked out of one of O'Connells meetings. Thomas Francis Meagher took the floor and savagely attacked O'Connell's peace-at-all-costs, policy. One year later a seriously sick Daniel O'Connell left Ireland for France. The Great Liberator and Uncrowned King of Ireland, died in Genoa, Italy on the 15th May 1847. As was his wish, his heart was taken to Rome and left at the church of Saint Agatha and his body was brought back to his beloved Ireland and buried in Glasnevin.

BACK TO THE SMITHWICKS OF KILKENNY

John the eldest son of Edmond Smithwick went to live at Kilcreene House after his marriage to Christina Devereux of Bishopswater Wexford. The Devereux family owned a Distillery at that time in Wexford. John, who had been Chief Justice of the Peace and Deputy Lieut. of County Kilkenny and High Sheriff of both city and country, died in 1894. His eldest son, another Edmond died as a boy of seven years and his second son James was born in 1869. He, James married Gertrude Boland of Boland Mills fame in 1900 and they had three sons, namely, Arthur, Colonel Harold, M.D. O.B.E. and Walter K.M. It was Walter who owned Smithwicks Brewery, prior to the take-over by Guinness Group.

Walter Smithwick K.M. married his good wife in 1934 and their union produced a family of six, – four sons and two girls. The girls are Ann and Judy and the boys are named Peter, Paul, Michael and John. As well as owning Smithwicks Brewery, Walter K.M. was a practising Solicitor with offices at Parliament Street. His eldest son Peter, also practised Law at the same offices. Peter Smithwick like his father Walter was a prominent Fianna Fail activist and served as a member of the National Executive. Later he was appointed a Justice of the District Court and fulfilled that role with courtesy and distinction. Peter is now President of the District Court, which is one of the highest judicial posts in the country.

SMITHWICKS NO 1 ALE

It wasn't always called Smithwick Beer. Originally it was known as Smithwicks No. 1 Ale and was sold in bottle and on draught. The old advertisement for that famous brew featured a hefty middle-aged smiling man with his cap on the Tullaroan-side, holding aloft a pint tumbler of that distinctive and unique blend of alcohol. Underneath was written this rousing refrain: "The more we are together, together, together, the more we are together the happier we will be."

My old friend Paddy Cody (RIP) from Wellington Sq. was one of the old timers of Smithwicks Brewery fame. Paddy, who was a lorry driver was a man amongst men and was truly in body and soul a gentle giant. He worked for the best part of fifty years at the Brewery and knew all the Smithwicks – that is to say the three sons of James, i.e. Arthur, Harold and Walter. According to Paddy Cody one of the three sons was a great boxer and had boxed for Ireland and won against an English middle-weight. Paddy said it wasn't Walter KM but thought it was Col. Harold M.D. and OBE.

And on a cutting from an old newspaper the following death notice: Capt. James A. Smithwick J.P. of the 4th Battalion Royal Irish Regiment. Died on 7th November 1915, aged 34 years, from wounds received in the battlefield. Obviously this man must have been a first cousin.

Another larger than life Smithwicks Brewery man was Big Dick Cantwell from Fatima Place. Dick saw the two eras, the horse and dray, and the lorry and trailer. He was a great character and the stories about him were legend. Dick knew Smithwicks Brewery when it stabled twelve Irish draught horses at the bottom of the yards, close to the stony skeleton of Saint Francis Abbey. He 'followed' a huge, fiery, jet-black horse that was the finest of them all. This great animal was nick named 'Blackman Doyle'. The story went that Dick's horse, hadn't been fully 'broken' when bought and was as likely to break into a gallop under a full load as when pulling an empty dray. And he did just that early one Monday morning with a full load heading for Thomastown. Fortunately there weren't too many people around as Dick and Blackman Doyle careered up High Street and onto the Castle Road. 'Twas said there was many a Bumper at Gowran Park that wasn't run as well. But he wasn't getting away from Dick. And by the time he topped the Black Quarry Hill he was 'broken' at last.

And Paddy Cody, remembered when the 'bone-shaker', solid tyre lorry was bought to take the cinders from the Boiler. It was driven by Con Scully, with Ned (Scrap) Dunne, riding shotgun.

And of course, one couldn't talk about old timers at Smithwicks Brewery without calling to mind Tommy O' Neill from Rothe Terrace. After his retirement, having worked for fifty years, Tommy went back and did another ten years as yard foreman.

These days, Smithwicks Brewery is one of the finest and most up-to-date breweries in Europe. Gone are the Mineral Water plant, the old Boiler House and the Scald, not to mention the Stables where the finest draught horses in Ireland were lovingly looked after.

Time moves on and waits for no man, neither commoner nor king can halt its march. And the name Smithwicks, that was once a National Institution, now echoes around the world as people from every race and culture, call for Smithwicks Beer, to celebrate the feast of life.

CHAPTER FOURTEEN

THE DUGGANS OF THE MONSTER HOUSE, KILKENNY CITY

MARGARET PHELAN (NEE DUGGAN): ARCHAEOLOGIST, FAMED LECTURER, HISTORIAN & FREEMAN OF KILKENNY CITY

Kilkenny born Margaret Phelan was the daughter of Richard and Henrietta Duggan from William Street, Kilkenny. She was educated at the Loreto Convent here in the city and later attended Our Lady's Bower, Athlone. Later still she studied at U.C.C. where she got her degrees in Arts and Commerce. Margaret was destined to become one of Kilkenny's most famous daughters; as an Historian, Archaeologist and Lecturer extraordinary (without notes), and was given the Freedom of the City.

Along with her husband Dr. William Phelan, County Surgeon, she was a founder member of Kilkenny Archaeological Society.

Margaret Phelan (nee Duggan)

She had the honour of being elected as President of that truly beneficial body on two occasions.

When the unique medieval dwelling known as Rothe House was purchased by the Archaeological Society in the 1950s she said it was: "a dream come true".

The first section of that famous House was restored and opened to the public around 1965. Rothe House is fully restored now and stands as a monument to this lovely old city but also to the memory of a great lady whose dedication and commitment made this restoration possible.

I'll always remember approaching Margaret Phelan at the time when a group of us were attempting to bring about the restoration of Kenny's Well. She gave us every support and encouragement. She told me how fond she was of Kenny's Well and how her son Bill, as a boy used to accompany her on a regular basis to the Well and take away with them containers full of that salubrious water.

On the week before the Well was about to be re-dedicated and blessed by the Bishop of Ossory, Laurence Forristal, four of us went to visit the Well: Margaret Phelan and Sue Nunn from Radio Kilkenny, Brendan Corcoran and myself. We went on a kind of pilgrimage to that enchanting place. And I was minded of Chaucers "Canterbury Tales" wherein the Knight, the Merchant and the Miller etc. all told their stories of great events to their hearers. You see, Kenny's Well too, was once a place Pilgrimage, to where people came from the four corners of Ireland seeking cures and for reasons of piety and penance too. There in that old Well House of history Margaret Phelan recited for us a part of the poem written by Paris Anderson about the year 1845. The poem is actually about Kenny's Well.

E'en the Well's old arch was brightening
And it's cross with sunny lightening
Seemed as if it e'er was frightening
Misery from our Isle away
Till the old land, tho 'he leaves her
He shall see this in the spell
Which into the persons thinking
Comes again by simply drinking
If his faith be all unshrinking
From Saint Kenny's Holy Well.

By the way, it was Margaret Phelan who officially opened Kenny's Well after the Bishop of Ossory had blessed and re-dedicated it. And Mick (Moc) Lawlor was Master of Ceremonies.

THE MONSTER HOUSE

Directly opposite "The Thosel" (City Hall) stood the Monster House; the first departmental store in Leinster.

It was a fabulous trading establishment by any standards. This colossal store once dominated the commercial life of Kilkenny City. It was big by name and nature and sold everything from shoelaces to Astrakhan coats and from kerchiefs to Boudoir furnishings.

The Monster House was originally founded by a man named Henry Potter around the year 1853. Henry was the father of Maggie Potter who was a fine artist. Her forte was the painting of flowers, often with a fable or anecdote.

Henry was also the father of Michael L. Potter who later owned the "House of Seeds; where the High Street Shopping Arcade stands today.

Another son of Henry Potter's was William Vincent Potter. He was the last of the Potters to own and manage the Monster House.

On or about the year 1875 a family called Mc Stays bought the Monster House from W. V. Potter and ran a very successful business there. Twenty one years later in 1896 the Mc Stays sold out to Richard Duggan. Prior to that Richard Duggan and his brother Ned had been trading at 104 High Street, where Paddy Allen's Home Decorations and China Shop is at the present. This establishment was simply called Duggan Brothers. Richard Duggan was born at Innisnag near Stoneyford. He was trained in "Cocks" of Kilkenny and in Henry Street Dublin. A more astute business man and progressive trader would be hard to find. The story went around that some Puritan elements in old Kilkenny's so called aristocracy had declared it was vulgar and immodest to sell women's underwear and men's vests and shorts under the same roof. Richard pooh-poohed them saying "Please observe Ladies and Gentlemen, these are merely pieces of cloth. We have here real live men and women working together. Some of whom are living-in and sleeping under the same roof? Would you have me get rid of those too?"

I must confess I am not absolutely certain if that ludicrous complaint took place under the management of the Mc Stays or The Duggans. But rumour and folklore would seem to suggest that that ingenious reply was most likely the response of the indomitable Richard Duggan. But look how far we have come since those days. It makes your head spin. Now anything goes. I'm told some men buy their wives lingerie. Others wear them. One doesn't know whether to laugh or cry. Best to say nothing perhaps. Or concur with the words of the late Paddy Crosby: "Let that be as it may." It will anyway.

A RAGING FIRE

Ten years after Richard Duggan had bought the Monster House a fire destroyed most of the building and the goods. Fortunately no lives were lost even though many of the staff lived-in. There was a great to do as Kilkenny Fire Brigade apparatus was pushed across the High Street from its shelter beneath "The Thosel" by stalwart citizens. Pandemonium ensued as many of the living-in staff were forced to jump into sheets and blankets from up stairs windows. There was no shortage of sheets or blankets needless to say, or willing hands either to hold them.

Richard Duggan was on business in Dublin when the fire broke out. He knew nothing about it until he landed at Kilkenny train station next morning. It was only when he spotted his two old friends standing together on the platform that he guessed something terrible had happened.

His old friend Dr. White from Medical Hall Rose Inn Street and his brother-in law Michael Shelly from Callan gave Richard the bad news. The Medical Hall was where Michael O'Connell's Chemist shop is today.

There was a huge "Salvage Sale" in a draper's shop across the street that was owned by a man named Wall. The poor of Kilkenny city were able to buy clothes, boots and bed linen for a fraction of their original price – for pennies in some cases.

A BORN FIGHTER

Good business men like born fighters don't lie down and so Richard Duggan rebuilt the Monster House and did more business than ever. In 1906 he had an ornamental tower erected on the front of the building at the William Street end. The tower remained until 1980 or thereabouts. Most of you will remember it.

Richard Duggan had four sons and two daughters. These were named Peter, Dick, Jack, Paddy, Nin, and Margaret. It became my good fortune and privilege to know Margaret personally.

Richard Duggans son Dick was father of Tommy Duggan who owned and managed the Monster House, prior to SuperMacs setting up a fast food outlet on part of the premises. History we are told often repeats itself and these days we find Tommy's two sons Richard and David still in the Drapery trade in a section of the old Monster House like their grandfather and granduncle did in the Duggan Brothers at 104 High Street long long ago. Tommy Duggan's wife now runs a boutique on William Street. Their daughter Barbara has a business there also – all on the premises of the old Monster House.

I'm sure I would be thought negligent if I were to fail to name at least some of the old Monster House staff. Those fine men and women who worked so diligently to promote the image and prosperity of one of the finest departmental stores in Ireland in its day. I know everyone will understand when I name Leo McAdams, as the first among equals.

LEO MCADAMS

As well as being floor walker, Leo McAdams was also manager at the Monster House. In fact Leo was a many talented man. He was a first class photographer and a classical biographer. He wrote a wonderful account of Corbet Wilson that great airman who landed his aeroplane on the Old Golf Links behind the Butts houses, in the 1930's. Leo also wrote a biography on Ellen, the Countess of Desart. It was so well written and researched that the scholarly Sean White said of it: "This little book should be read by everyone who loves Kilkenny city." It was developed from a talk that Leo had given earlier to Kilkenny Archaeological Society. He was in great demand as a lecturer and gave frequent talks around the county.

I feel sure that most Kilkenny people would at least have heard of Lady Desart. She was the daughter of a Jewish banker who left London and came to live in Kilkenny. She endeared herself to the people of Kilkenny by her generosity and absolute humanity. Year after year she devoted her money and her time for the public good. Never before or since has anyone done so much for so many people. In all of this she was encouraged and aided by the Hon. Otway Cuffe, the youngest son of the Fourth Earl of Desart. And in the words of Leo McAdams: "They got on well together – much better, one hazards, than if they were married to each other, – she provided the wealth and he the dreams and both the enthusiasm needed to fuse those forces into action."

I hope to elaborate on Otway Cuffe at a later date and to tell you about Thomas Count O'Loughlin who was the donor of Saint John's memorial church opposite the train-station, also the life and times of the Airman Corbet Wilson.

Leo McAdams father was an Ulsterman but his mother was a Downey from Conahy. It was she who instilled in him that great love which he had for Kilkenny.

Other great Kilkenny men and women who worked at Duggans' Monster House were:

Peter Quinn, Toddy Pembroke, Jimmy O'Brien, Wm. Kerr, Watt Cody, Tommy Stapleton, Mary McEvoy, Tommy O'Neill, Sean Minogue, Bob Doherty, Molly Comerford, Ted O'Grady, Sean Jones, Joe Kelly, Cissy Hayde, Jimmy Conway, Joe Bollard, Jim Kennedy, Sean McDonald, Georgie Byrne, Mick Bourke, Jimmy Hayde, Marie Minogue, Dick Coogan, Gerry Doyle, Paddy Sunderland, Mary Purcell, Danny Rowe, Paddy Kenny, Ted Kenny, Phil McEvoy, B. Phelan, Paul Fennelly, Paddy Bourke, Denis Nyhan, Mick Maher, Bridie Purcell and Peadar Malone.

CHAPTER FIFTEEN

CAPTAIN WILLIAM HENNESSY FROM GREENSHILL, KILKENNY CITY CHICAGO POLICE CHIEF DURING THE REIGN OF NOTORIOUS GANGSTERS AL. CAPONE, BUGS MORAN AND JOHN DILLENGER

THE life and times of Captain Wlm. Hennessy, originally from Greenshill, Kilkenny city, who was Police Chief Chicago, during the reign of the notorious gangsters Al Capone, Bugs Moran and John Dillenger.

CHICAGO

Chicago is the fourth largest city in the world and hub of industrial America. Situated in the Northeast of the state of Illinois, at the mouth of the Chicago River. No city on Earth has grown at the speed of this great metropolis. It is said to be America's most American city. Up to two hundred years ago, it was little more than a settlement called Fort Dearborn. It had a population of just a few thousand inhabitants who daily fought off Indian raids and lived by trapping furry animals on the western shores of Lake Michigan.

Chicago, is a city of great contradictions with it's stockyards and slaughter houses, producing meat products that feed most of America. In juxtaposition here also there are institutions for the Fine Arts, Museums of Science and Natural History, Universities like the Circle Campus Chicago, which is a branch of the University of Illinois. Here also can be found gangsters and rogue dealers from penny arcade crooks to multi-millionaire racketeers. But Chicago is also a city with high ideals and noble aspirations. In truth it is not unlike Joseph's multi-coloured coat in its portrayal of the very many races one would encounter upon walking along the sidewalks of Michigan Avenue know as the magnificent mile or down on the clamorous State Street.

Chicago is a city of enormous energy and positive disposition. Nobody saunters along Jackson Boulevard or wanders aimless down around Wells and Orleans Streets. The vast majority are either going to or coming from work. Chicago is dynamic because it is the home of the youthful and courageous men and women who arrive on a daily basis from every corner of the world.

Its driving force is relative too, to its stimulating climate whose variations in temperature can be as hot as India in Summer and as cold as Siberia in Winter. Like the latter part: When the wind blows across the city off Lake Michigan from January to March, one would need to wear a protective facemask to prevent getting frostbite. And there must be fifty miles of Boulevards, – Western Avenue alone is probably 25 miles long. But for all its beauty and grandeur it does have its ghettos and ghastly slums where conditions can sometimes be almost as bad as parts of London's East End.

Broadly speaking though Chicago came alive on 7th August 1803 as an army outpost called Fort Dearborn. Officially it stretched its legs on the 4th March 1837 as a sprawling cow-town and railroad centre. Both of these descriptive designations have stayed with Chicago and grown with it over the years. The Stockyards grew out of the cow-town and Union Station fast tracked it from its original railroad centre. Chicago is the largest railroad centre in the world today. In America they say: All roads lead to Chicago.

Some of the most imposing landmarks of Chicago are the Adler Planetarium on Northerly Island, the Picasso Sculpture on Chicago Civic Centre, the Marina Towers, the Merchandise Mart which is the worlds' largest business building located on the north bank of the Chicago River, First National Bank Building, White Sox Park which is the home of Chicago White Sox Baseball team, Arlington Park Race-Track, said to be a city within a city and is the most modern race track in the United States. And finally the fabulous Hancock Centre. "Big John" as it is affectionately called, houses a Bank, hundreds of Offices, 705 apartments and has parking facilities for 12,000 cars. Standing over 1/4 of a mile high, the building itself is 1107 feet, 100 stories in height and is topped by two 344 foot television antennas. Nowhere else on earth could one see such awe-inspiring man-made, masterpieces in concrete, steel and stone. But when speaking about landmarks it just strikes me now that I have left out Chicago's greatest and most advantageous asset – it's gateway with the world; O'Hare Field. This airport has grown into the world's largest transportation centre, with as many as 100,000 passengers moving through O'Hareport every day of the week. With flights leaving and arriving at a rate of 100 per hour, the air traffic control is nothing short of mind-boggling. All of these magnificent and spectacular developments have taken place since Mrs. O'Leary's contrary cow kicked over a paraffin-oil lamp in a milking shed in 1871. The fire that followed burned for 3 _ days and levelled 15,000 buildings. But like the fabled Phoenix, Chicago rose from the smoking ashes and red-hot rubble as the invincible Chicagoans rose to the task of building an even bigger and a better city. A city that is today the pride and promise of hope for all freedom-loving people everywhere, who arrive on a daily basis to win for themselves a permanent home in the fabulous and friendly Windy-City.

KENNYSWELL KILKENNY CITY (1912)

"What's the name of that place in America that poor Billy is going to today?" Katie looked at her sister Lizzie as she climbed out of bed in Kennyswell Street above the River Breagagh.

"I can't remember the name of that place now, – but I wrote it down on the back of a letter from Paddy. It's the same place where Molly got married to Billy's father, John Hennessy. In any case, what's poor about Billy? He's a fine strapping young lad of 17 years and as big and as strong as any grown man of 21 or 22 years. And hasn't he got two or three uncles over there all doing well for themselves."

"I wonder if Billy will meet our Paddy over there?" "Have sense woman, Paddy is in New York, hundreds if not thousands of miles from where Billy is going. There, it came to me now – Billy is going to a place called Chicago. I remember Molly wrote to us after she married John Hennessy, there."

"What time is Billy leaving for America today?"

"Soon. We had better have breakfast and go over to Greenshill, to say goodbye to him. Get a move on, Katie and get Bob out of bed – quick"

Lizzie was the 'boss'. She had been running the family since her father and mother had died. Lizzie was the oldest and Bob was the youngest. In between there was Paddy, working in New York now, Mary (Molly) Billy's mother was married to John Hennessy a local Coal Merchant now living on Greenshill with their family. Katie was a cook in Kilkenny Asylum, (Psychiatric Hospital), Lizzie as a nurse at the asylum, Bridget was housekeeping at home, Richard was an Attendant in the Asylum, John was a stable hand at Fitzgeralds of Nore Mount, Ned was an odd-jobs boy at O'Rourkes of Greensbridge, and young Bob had just finished school at the Butts National on Butts Green. He was particularly happy when he awoke, because Lizzie had told him before going to bed "Starting from Monday next you will be employed as a boy companion to Master Frank Fitzgerald".

"What does that mean?" Bob asked Lizzie.

"It means you will play with him and accompany him on outings".

"But sure I'm doing that already. Am I to be paid for it now?"

"Never mind, – get ready for bed.

Next morning: "Be sure you wash you face and hands and don't forget to wash your neck," Lizzie warned Bob, now out of bed.

"We are going over to Green's Hill just as soon as you've had your breakfast".

Frank Fitzgerald would later become one of the leading show-jumping horsemen in Ireland. He was a member of the Olympic team that represented Ireland on at least one occasion.

GREEN'S HILL

Billy Hennessy finished his breakfast and went out the back door to stand in the yard that overlooked the river Nore and Bishop's Meadows. There were tears in his eyes as he scanned the grey ribbon of the Nore from Greens Bridge to the Third field. How often he had swam its length right up to the Suspension Bridge and on to the Weir beyond Greenvale Woollen Mills. Would he ever come back from America? Was that the reason people called the goodbye party before leaving for America, an "American Wake"? Would he never see his mother and father, sisters and brothers again?

Inside sitting at the fire, Billy's mother Mary (Molly) was busy sewing a ten-pound note into the lining of his overcoat. This money would be needed to present to the Officials of Ellis Island New York, to prove he was capable of providing for himself until he got work. Billy's father and mother had told him they had seen emigrants being returned, who didn't have funds. But his uncles Pat and Mick who were Freight-car managers with the B/O and legendary Sante Fe Railroad Company would claim him into the USA. They had promised to get him a job in the U.S. Mail Department Dearborn Station, in the middle of the famous "Loop". He tried to imagine what kind of place was called a "Loop" and then he heard someone knocking on the front door. He recognised the voice at once, it was his aunt Lizzie and a boys' voice shouted "Where's Billy" – it was young Bob. Within minutes there was another knock on the front door and another and another. Half of the Greens Hill community were coming through the front door. It had been but a few hours since they had gone home after, the all-night 'American –Wake' and here they were back again for more of the same.

And then a cheer went up from a dozen or more children outside on the street as they spotted Andy Burroughs coming up by Sonny Teehan's Public house driving his spic and span ass and cart. Andy came to Green's Hill every other day to sell milk, country butter and eggs. His ass Neddie stopped outside Hennessy's door as was its wont. Andy turned to the children. "O who is the youngest, the supplest and the most obliging as to get a wisp of hay for the poor ass. Is it you Kavanagh?" There was no shortage of hay at Hennessy's. Billy's father John was a Coal Merchant and had a horse and a mule for drawing anthracite contract coal from the Deerpark Mines Castlecomer, to deliver it to the business establishments all over Kilkenny city.

ELLIS ISLAND, NEW YORK

Billy was met on Ellis Island by his uncles Pat and Mick. They laughed when he told the Emigration officer he had a ten pound note sewn into his overcoat. That was on the 8th June 1912. It was Friday afternoon and New York was in the throes of a heat wave; 75 in the shade. Chicago was one thousand miles away in the Midwest.

He made up his mind there and then that just as soon as he earned his fare he would return to Kilkenny come hell or high water. But hell stayed where Dante Alighieri had left it in Dis and the next high-water he saw was a high tide coming up the Chicago River. Although he was often homesick for family and friends by then, he was determined to see it through. And as promised, his uncles got him a job sorting the U.S. mail in the 'Loop'. Every Sunday he went to the Rev. J.K. Fielding's Gaelic Park to meet the lads and lassies from home and to give and get the latest news from Ireland. As the Seannachies of old used to say 'Things rhested so', until Jackboot-Germany began to march across Europe rattling its sabres and then Britain let loose the dogs of war. America went to the aid of the Allies, who claimed it was a war to protect the rights of small nations. Bill wondered if that promise also applied to his beloved homeland. He was among the first to volunteer for the front, in France and further afield. He was a full grown man now and answered only to the name of Bill. He received three citations for bravery above and beyond the call of duty and was in command of a Landmine unit responsible for making the roads safe for advancing armies. Bill fought in the Battles of Bar Le Duc, St. Mihiel and the blood bath of Verdun. He saw many of his unit blown to kingdom-come and narrowly escaped death himself many times. But he was wounded and had to be hospitalised on two occasions in France. It was after his second hospitalisation that he was give a 72 hour pass to visit his parents and family on Green's Hill Kilkenny city, Ireland.

A banner was strung from the top window of Sonny Teehan's Public House to a wireless pole owned by John Kerwick. John, known as Gentleman John was a wealthy business man who owned a number of businesses throughout Kilkenny. The banner read "War Hero Comes Home". It was John Kerwick who owned the Wheat Sheaf Inn later known as Powers of The Parade and was again called the Wheat Sheaf Inn when Pat Henderson owned it years later. Pat was Managing Director of Fit Remoulds, and later still of Good Year Ireland. Today the premises is owned and managed by Willie Henderson, Pat's younger brother.

Needless to say the celebrations on Green's Hill went on with singing and dancing and story telling for nearly all of the three days.

THE WAR SONG
  The yanks are coming, the yanks are coming,
  So beware.
  We won't come back till it is over.
  Till its over, over there.
It was time to say another goodbye and return to his base on the borders of the French frontier. When he arrived his unit was in a state of euphoria. Word had it, that the end of the war was imminent. The American army would soon be Stateside again.

Back in his hometown, Chicago, Bill was missing his 'buddies' who had lost their lives on the battlefields of France. But he was missing the hectic hustle and bustle of living dangerously too. Sorting US mail would be too monotonous from here on. And so Bill applied to become an Officer on the Chicago Police Force. He couldn't believe it when he got a letter by return.

His discharge papers from the army had been so complimentary that he was called to duty within days. And so began the action packed career of the Green's Hill garsúin, with the Chicago Police Force. But before he donned the famous Police garb he would marry his girlfriend Rita Meade whom he had met before joining the army.

Rita and Bill had been in communication while he was over seas. All of her family were 'railroad people' and so the wedding was a society affair. Once the honeymoon was over Bill was back in uniform once again and ready for whatever ensued.

ROARING TWENTIES

There is great publicity now in the media for the latest blockbuster film to come from America, called "Gangs of New York". Everywhere there is animated talk that this film is the Alpha and Omega of all films made about early American life, – New York in particular. The box-office super stars such as Daniel Day Lewis of My Left Foot fame, and Leonardo de Caprio of Titanic's terrible tale look out at us from television screens and newspapers in dramatic pictures reminding us we cannot afford to miss this extraordinary movie, said to be historically factual. But one very good thing about it is that there are a number of outstanding Irish actors and musicians featured in the film.

What this film attempts to portray is how gang warfare developed from feuding families fighting to take over territories where gambling dens, liquor saloons, and vice joints predominated in amassing wealth. The principal contenders were the Irish, the Germans and the Italians. That was in New York.

But in Chicago, early-on, in the year 1881 there was a different twist to gang warfare. The early gangs in Chicago were in fact school gangs who fought for the supremacy of the classes, or the schools, – their Alma Maters. The Walsh School in particular seems to have 'Lorded' it over all the others for mayhem and murder. For instance, between the years 1881 and 1905 several students were killed in bloody battle and many more were stabbed and shot. Using guns, knives and clubs these early gangsters fought it out in the school playgrounds and afterwards on the streets.

This diabolical behaviour went on in Chicago for almost a quarter of a century. It was brought to an end only after school managers, teachers and police searched every student at the school doors each morning before admitting them into the classrooms.

Chicago Police Chief Cpt. Bill Hennessy welcomes superstar Humphrey Bogart to town.

There is much concern now about people's drinks being 'spiked' while socialising. Especially young women are fearful of this dastardly act being perpetrated upon them. Society considers that those who indulge in these horrific practices be quickly apprehended and given the maximum jail sentences. The origin of spiking drinks is said to have been at The Lone Star Saloon at State and Harrison in Chicago. This infamous 'dive,' was owned by an even more infamous man named Mickey Finn. Hence the correlation: "Slip him a Mickey Finn".

The concoction was said to have been given to Mickey by a black voodoo doctor from the Southern United States as a reward for sheltering him from the law.

The drink consisted of raw alcohol with a dash of white powder which was according to the Voodoo doctor, the crushed teeth of a crocodile. And so any out-of-town misfortunate who strayed into the Lone Star Saloon was slipped one of Mickey Finns' knockout drinks, robbed of his possessions and was dumped in the nearest alley or side street. You guessed it, – Mickey was a rogue Irishman. Not exactly a Céad Mile Fáilte – was it?,

It is indeed true to say: there is nothing new under the sun. It has all been done many times before; the good the bad and the ugly.

PATROLLING THE BEAT

Because of his expert army training in the handling of landmines and every kind of bomb and explosive device, Bill Hennessy was detailed to take charge of the Bomb Squad in down-town Chicago. But before he could be appointed to head that deadly dangerous job, he would have to do six months patrolling the 'Beat', on 'Shanks's–mare'. While doing this Bill got to know many of the young up-and-coming small time crooks. One of these was a young tough guy named Alphonso (Al for short) Capone and there were his brothers Frank and Ralph. The Capone family lived on North Clarke Street where the father had a Barbers shop. But he could not interest any of his sons in becoming hairdressers "There's no percentage in it", they all insisted. They were only interested in making 'a fast buck'. Their mother was a Seamstress and like her Barber husband worked very hard for little money. Al always maintained that one day he would become the wealthiest man in America. And so he did. In fact, he would one day make more money per annum than the Ford Foundation (Cars and Trucks), in Detroit.

Because Capone's Barber shop was on North Clarke Street it was part of Officer Hennessy's 'Beat' and Mrs. Capone got to know Bill. One day she spoke with him and said "Officer, my husband and me are concerned about our boys. We would be right proud if you would come to visit some Sunday for a boiled dinner after 12.00 p.m. Mass at Saint Leo's". (They were Roman Catholics and knew that Bill was a regular churchgoer). Bill didn't go to dinner but he did call now and then and had a cup of coffee and a slice of blueberry pie. During his visits Mrs. Capone often referred to her sons and more than once asked Bill if he would speak to them, especially Al: "He's mixing with the wrong sort of people and he don't pay his father and me no heed. Thanks for coming by, Officer Hennessy".

GANGLAND BOSS AL CAPONE

Al Capone was only seventeen years old when he went to work as a strong-arm man for a notorious Bootlegger during the "Prohibition Era". Because of his absolute ruthlessness, Capone climbed the ladder of dominance among the Gangland leaders. And whereas it had been the policy of gangsters to force their own brand of booze upon the owners of the Speak Easies (illicit saloons) and make them pay protection money into the bargain, Al Capone took it further. He bought out the owners at his price, or if they refused he bombed them out and took over the business in many instances. His 'mouthpieces' (attorneys) purported to make this legal and above board, by giving payoffs to crooked officials. So that Capone made his own brand of spirits and hooch (beer), owned the Saloons and managed their own protection racket with the machine gun. Of such was the "Roaring Twenties". It has to be said here that Chicago was not the only American City to be involved in such decadence.

New York, Boston and even San Francisco were but a few of the great cities that had suffered because of 'Prohibition' and gang warfare. And there can be no doubt about it but that the banning of alcohol by the United States Government, had been ill-conceived. All too soon it was as plain as the nose on the face of Cyrano de Berjerac. One had only to look around to see the terror, the mayhem and murder that was the result of making such laws.

Into this maelstrom of murder and madness the young (now sergeant) Bill Hennessy from Green's Hill, Kilkenny City was thrown, like a piece of dry kindling wood into a furnace. But this man was no rookie. Remember he had been through the battles of Bar Le Duc, St. Mihiel and the blood bath of Verdun. He wasn't about to crack up or cry off, Hennessy would see it through.

At that time there were two murderous mobs jockeying for territorial possession in Chicago. One gang belonged to the Irish mobster Dion O'Banion and the other was run by Al Capone, – an Italian mob. This period was known as the 'Roaring Twenties'. The roar of death and destruction was echoed by bombs and machine gun bullets as the feuding gangs were forever evening the score for the previous nights incursions. Al Capone's murderous empire was reckoned to have topped the financial earnings of the Ford Automobile industry of America. If the Saloon owners refused (few did) to buy Capones' booze or failed to pay "protection money", they were bombed and killed without pity. If today, the bombing was on O'Banion's 'turf', tomorrow it would be evened-up on Capone's 'turf'. It was Sergeant Bill Hennessy's job as leader of the Bomb Squad to investigate and document the sundered bodies and shattered buildings, never knowing if the next dismembered remains contained another bomb or explosive device under it that could blow up in his face. The gang wars were Old Testament stuff: "An eye for an eye and a tooth for a tooth". The saga of death and destruction was so devastating that many of Hennessy's squad cried off or broke down under the threat of being blown into oblivion or murdered in their beds with their families. But still Hennessy wasn't intimidated. On the contrary, when AL Capone gave the order to have Dion O'Banion eliminated it was Bill who volunteered along with five of his best men to arrest Capone. Immediately after O'Banion's murder, Capone fled with the two assassins to one of his 'safe houses' on South Prairie Avenue.

DAY LIGHT MURDER

What had happened was: Two of Al Capones' most murderous assassins parked their luxurious 'Chevy' by the sidewalk at O'Banion's Flower Shop. It was still daylight although it was a misty November afternoon on a Friday 1924.

Two elderly women had come from the Parish Priests house to purchase flowers with which to decorate the altar in the nearby Catholic Church for Sunday masses.

The two middle aged murderers watched as O'Banion handed over two large bouquets to the admiring church decorators. There was no charge. "Say a little prayer for me ladies," O'Banion begged the women. "You'll go straight to heaven sir," one of the women said smiling broadly. Then one of the assassins closed the shop door while the other stepped forward and pushing the women to one side, mowed down O'Banion in front of them.

"Round up the usual suspects" the Captain of the Precinct told Sergeant Bill Hennessy "and bring in Capone. This has gone as far as it's going. Pick your own men." Sergeant Bill picked his five most trusted men and after making enquiries drove in two unmarked cars to South Prairie Avenue and parked one car to the front of the house and the other to the rear. Hennessy called out on a loud speaker to Capone to come out with his hands above his head and to bring with him any other members of his gang. "The house is surrounded", Hennessy told him. To everybody's surprise Capone walked out smiling, hands above his head. The two assassins came out with him. Of course Hennessy couldn't know at that time these were the two who had gunned down O'Banion in cold blood. All three were taken back to Police Headquarters at 11th and State. Another thing Hennessy couldn't know was that before exiting the safe-house Capone had contacted his mouthpiece (Attorney) to be at Police headquarters with an eye-witness who would prove conclusively that he (Capone) was nowhere near O'Banion's Flower Shop on the day of the murder. But would swear on a stack of bibles he was elsewhere on that day and at that time.

This was only to be expected. So another plan was devised to put Capone out of circulation. They would hold him and his two henchmen until the 'Feds' (F.B.I.) could be brought on board.The Federal Bureau of Investigation after congratulating sergeant Hennessy and his men, recommended that Hennessy be promoted to Lieutenant forthwith and that Capone be charged with tax evasion. It was the only way the Law could get at Al Capone. Try as they might the Police couldn't pin O'Banion's murder on him. Nor could the two old ladies who had witnessed the cold blooded murder in the flower shop, be coaxed or cajoled into identifying the assassins. Who could blame them after all? Nobody but nobody would rat on Al Capone. To do so would be tantamount to signing one's own death warrant.

Shortly after O'Banion's death Hymie Weiss took over the Irish mobsters. But within a few months Hymie was himself gunned down. Next in the order of 'clout' came Bugs Moran. Bugs was second generation Irish and was better educated and more sophisticated than his predecessors. Moran moved the Irish gangsters headquarters downtown to a huge garage and bus depot. Bugs had this huge building converted into a small distillery and brew house. He had offices installed along with a loading bay. This den of thieves and murderers was situated at 2122 North Clarke Street.

THE SAINT VALENTINE'S DAY MASSACRE

I'm sure that many of you reading me now will remember seeing the award winning film "The Saint Valentine's Day Massacre". It was shown on TV 3 only last year. That converted garage and bus depot at 2122 North Clarke Street was where the massacre occurred. Just minutes before Bugs Moran was due to go down town to gang headquarters, he got an urgent call from the owner of the speak easy across the street from headquarters. He told Bugs there were six 'hoods' armed to the teeth and dressed in police uniform, playing poker in the back room. "They have a tout posted out front, watching for the arrival of your truck load of booze". Bugs looked sick when he heard the news. He picked up the phone quickly and frantically asked the operator to put him through to his H.Q "The phone is ringing sir, but there is no answer".

"What the hell were they doing?" He asked himself. "Was it already too late?" He waited another half a minute and dropped the phone without returning it to its receiver. Then shouted at his chauffeur "Start the effin Limo, we're goin' down town now." As they neared their H.Q. Bugs told his driver to go slow and to wind down his window. As they crawled past H.Q. the thunder of machine gun fire was deafening as it roared and screamed from behind the steel-clad doors. Bugs looked like a dead man when he shouted "step on the gas Pat, get the hell out of here, - go, go go."

As they rocketed down North Clarke Street Bugs heard the screams of fear and pain reverberate in his ears even above the thunder of the murderous machine guns. He knew now it was too late. He had become too complacent where Al Capone was concerned. Without being told Bugs was able to figure out what happened: When the tout spotted the truck load of booze rounding the corner at the top of North Clarke Street he immediately alerted Capone's gangsters. Then as the steel doors of Bugs H.Q. swung open, Capone's men ducked in behind the truck and entered Bugs' H.Q. undetected. And when the truck came to a halt at the loading bay, Capone's machine gunners sprang into action. All seven of Bug's men were mowed down without a chance to fight for their lives. Literally, they didn't have a prayer. Shortly after this terrible massacre, Capone said: "There will be no more contenders for the territories under my jurisdiction." Further he boasted "Everybody knows now that I am the most powerful man in Chicago."

But Hennessy had arrested him and called in the 'Feds' (F.B.I.) who had charged him with millions of dollars in tax evasion. And they made it stick. He was sentenced to twelve years imprisonment. Some seven years later he became very ill but wouldn't allow the prison doctors to prescribe medication for him. neither would he allow them to operate on him later still when he became seriously ill and was in danger of dying. He feared they would do away with him. Al Capone died of syphilis in prison in terrible bodily suffering.

SAINT PATRICK'S DAY PARADE

Chicago Police Chief, Captain William (Bill) Hennessy was the originator of the Saint Patrick's Day Parade in Chicago. It began on 79th Street, but Richard J. Daley who then worked as a clerk at City Hall promised Capt. Bill, he would move the Parade downtown the following year if he got elected, as Mayor of Chicago. "Together", he told Capt. Bill, "we will make it the biggest and best parade in America", and so they did.

Starting from West 84th Street and South Ashland Avenue it now takes almost three hours for the parade to pass at any given point. This gigantic celebration of our Irish culture now features 15,000 Marchers: men, women and school children, 40 Bands, - Brass and Reed, Pipers and Drummers and 50 very colourful and highly imaginative floats, each depicting a different era in Irish History. All of which brings thousands upon thousands of eager spectators from all over the State of Illinois, onto the streets of Chicago. People of every colour, class and creed, line the Parade route, to witness the greatest show on Earth, of faith and fatherland.

THE KILLALOO BIRD

Capt. Bill Hennessy like all great men had a wonderful personality and great sense of humour. Riding the lead car, perched on its podium between Mr. Hartigan, the automobile tycoon, and Capt. Bill Hennessy, Police Chief, stands the Killaloo Bird – prouder than any peacock. Capt. Bill who is protector and patron of this native Kilkenny – Irish bird, told the story of his very first encounter with this fabulous creature.

But first says he "I've got to tell you that the Killaloo is a compound Kelly-green in colour, from the tip of its tail to the needle-like point of its long curved beak. And it doesn't take kindly to heretics either but glares at them with wicked intent. So much so that it has converted many a Doubting Thomas and sobered up quite a few pagan newspapermen. But be not alarmed, it doesn't eat human flesh but much prefers Irish Stew and its favourite beverage is an egg-cup full Smithwicks Beer, - it being a bred, born and reared Kilkenny bird, you understand. It has one other very unusual characteristic; it prefers to fly backwards, being more interested in where is has been than where it is going to."

The newspaper reporters and columnists of the many Chicago newspapers flocked to hear more about this Killaloo creature from Capt. Bill. Bill's views on all matters that impinge upon the lives of the citizens of Chicago, are always in demand, be they political, criminal or even comical. His opinions are always news and as often as not are sensational.

An old newshound approached the Capt. "Tell us about that time when you first made contact with the Killaloo Bird Capt. Hennessy".

Congressional immunity for Kilaloo bird.

A beam of good humour flashed across the Captain's face and settled in the bright blue eyes of the legendary Kilkennyman. "Well, if you have even one drop of Irish blood in your veins, I'll tell you all about that".

"Believe it or not Capt." said the wordy welder, "my great grandmother came from a place called Dublin, about a mile from Ballingarry County Tipperary".

"I know it well," said Cap. Bill "and here is the story for you: Before coming to America I worked on the farm of an old couple who had neither chick nor child, in a place called Killaloo County Kilkenny. Killaloo is about six miles as the crow flies southwest from Kilkenny City. Each night I slept on the loft over the stables that housed an ass and a cob. But these weren't the only occupants of the stable. There was a big bird that I thought at first was a goshawk in a nest as big as a bowler hat above my head in the rafters. I regularly brought it fistfuls of corn bread dipped in a mug of warm milk at night.

The old farmer spotted me taking the bread and milk to the loft. "I see" said he "you have befriended the Killaloo or rather he has chosen you and as a result you'll never see a poor day again and you'll live a long and happy life". And every day I went out on Ballykeeffe Bog to cut turf the great green bird flew with me and I shared my midday meal with him.

I had just about forgotten the whole episode until about a month ago, didn't the self same bird (or one exactly like him) fly out of an Irish oak down on South Emerald Avenue, here in Chicago. Having heard me speak many times about the Killaloo, didn't two of my detectives capture him and brought him safe and sound to myself at headquarters. And the minute he laid eyes on me he hopped up onto my shoulder like Long John Silver's parrot and began to coo in my ear. But what it said to me is not for publication at this time. That's all for now. Thank you Mr. Copy".

JOHN DILLENGER PUBLIC ENEMY NUMBER 1

Long before Capone's slow and tortuous death in prison, Lieutenant Bill Hennessy had become a local hero. Many other gangland leaders had come and gone. Some had gone out of circulation after severe sentencing. Others had gone down forever by the bullet. Al Capone's brother Frank was gunned down in a confrontation with the police. His other brother Ralph, known as the Enforcer took over the Liquor Establishments but cleverly kept the lid on all-out gang warfare, while the tit-for-tat bombing of the 'Speak Easies' went on apace. As Lieutenant Bill Hennessy confided "It was a tough time for all who attempted to enforce the Law, but it was even tougher for the Police Bomb Squad. Just staying alive was an ongoing ordeal, as the bombing of the saloons became a near-nightly affair". In the early 1930's, the then famous Kilkennyman was asked to support the F.B.I. (Federal Bureau of Investigation) in the capture of John Dillenger, known as Public Enemy No.1. Dillenger, had killed more men and robbed more banks than Doc Holiday, Jesse James and Billy the Kid rolled into one. He was hunted for in every State of the Union, – Mexico too. His capture was beginning to look like an impossibility. The F.B.I. were being attacked and humiliated by a scoffing media, from Midway to Maine. But his detection would be nothing short of miraculous it seemed, because he had burned off his fingerprints, got a crooked plastic surgeon to work on his face and had shaved all the hair off his head. As well as that his so-called friends and his enemies too, were blind, deaf and dumb to any interrogations about his whereabouts. This man was lethal and would deal out death at the drop of a hat. Early one Friday morning in July, the Captain of the precinct asked Lieutenant Hennessy of the Bomb Squad to come to his office as a matter of urgency. "Come on in Bill and take a seat", the Captain said. There was a big middle aged man sitting in his shirtsleeves at the end of the Captains table. "This is Victor Polaski of the F.B.I. He is here on a matter that concerns the security of the entire State of Illinois". He turned to Polaski: "This is the man that I told you about, Commander, Lieutenant Bill Hennessy of the Bomb Squad." Hennessy and Polaski shook hands. "It's over to you Victor", the Captain of the precinct said. The F.B.I. agent got to his feet, and began talking: "Sightings of Public Enemy No. 1, one John Dillenger have been reported over the last eight weeks, – first in Des Moines, next in Milwaukee and then Toledo. Two weeks ago he was reported seen in Indiana and last week he was definitely seen in Cicero. We know this for certain because we arrested and interrogated an illegal emigrant named Anna Saige. She is one of Dillenger's scarlet ladies. We arrested her during a raid on one of the "Strip Joints" in Cicero called the Bunny Club. Under interrogation we discovered she was an illegal emigrant and warned her if she didn't co-operate we would let her cool her heels in the 'Pen' (Penitentiary) for six months before shipping her back to Veracruz for good. She has agreed to collaborate with us."

"But where do I come into all this?" Lieutenant Hennessy asked.

"This woman will accompany Dillenger to a movie called "The Manhattan Melodrama" starring Clark Gable, Loretta Young and William Powell. It will be screened at the Biograph Theatre on Sunday night next.   Anna Saige will be wearing a red dress with a pink carnation and a white shoulder bag and white high-heeled shoes. She will walk beside Dillenger." He turned to Bill Hennessy "What do you think Lieutenant?"

"Well for one thing, he won't stay too close to her dressed like that. He'd be too much of a target More than likely he'll let her go in on her own and meet her inside. And coming out he will probably walk behind her".

"That is one of our scenarios too" confided the F.B.I. agent. "Now as we see it, there should be no more than fifteen men, perhaps less involved in the stake-out. How many of your men do you hope to involve, Lieutenant?"

"Five along with himself", the Captain needed to have his say. After all the stake-out was in his jurisdiction, even if the F.B.I. were involved.

"As we see it now it might be hard to hide six policemen and nine F.B.I. agents even though the agents will all be in civvies. Six a side should be sufficient and easier to command and above all easier to control" Hennessy volunteered. "And nobody can be allowed to shoot unless the order is given, - otherwise some member or members of the public may get shot".

"I agree entirely", said the Commander. "The whole operation must be highly disciplined. The arrest of Dillenger should be timed to take place after the movie when the public are leaving the Theatre, – not before. We told Anna Saige to hang back at the end of the film. Are you happy with that Lieutenant Hennessy?"

"Yes indeed Victor, that's fine by us", trumped up the Captain of the Precinct.

THE STAKE-OUT

It was about 6.45 p.m. on the Sunday night in question and all twelve Lawmen were in position. It had been a sweltering day with the mercury just above 100 degrees in its glass tube. There wasn't a breath of air that a midge could launch on nor enough to rustle a single sweat-clotted strand of peroxide blonde hair. Anna Saige wiped her forehead with the back of her hand. "Phew, its suffocating. I hope the air ventilation system is working inside". Dillenger turned his head towards Anna Saige "You go on in, I'll join you inside," he said as he pressed a ten-dollar bill into her hand. She purchased two tickets and waited for him in the foyer. A moment later Dillenger entered the Biograph Theatre and the twelve undercover Lawmen outside breathed a sigh of relief. So far so good.It was 8.55 p.m. and the film called Manhattan Melodrama was in its dying moments. A trickle of people were walking towards the exit some looking back over their shoulders at the tear-jerking finale.

With a musical crescendo came the words The End. Then the trickle of patrons became a steady stream overflowing onto the street. The eyes and ears of the Law strained to take in the effluence of the crowd. Suddenly an eye-catching colour of red stood out like a beacon burning on a hill at the dead of night. The tall good looking woman who wore it walked quickly towards an ice-cream Vendors van. Behind her walked a medium sized malicious looking man with a crew hair cut. He was looking left then right, then left again. He walked cautiously like a hunted animal. Dressed in a white silk shirt open at the neck, and white canvas shoes. He might have been a Tin-pan Alley Faro dealer. His right hand was in his pants pocket. Dillenger shouted something at Anna Saige. She panicked and began to run.

Out of the corner of his eye Dillenger sighted one of the "Feds" dashing from his undercover position when Anna Saige began running. She saw him too and instantly dropped to the ground believing he was about to shoot them, despite the F.B.I.'s promises to the contrary. Dillenger crouched as he ran toward the Ice-cream Vendor's van. Lieutenant Bill Hennessy quickly summed up the situation: "If he succeeds in getting over amongst the people around the Ice-cream Van, Dillenger might well take one of them hostage and that could prove to be deadly dangerous." As he ran he took his right hand from his pants pocket faster than Wyatt Earp might have done, revealing a shining Colt 45. Inside a split second the order rang out with ear-bursting clarity; "Fire!" Four shots rang out in rapid succession, shattering the otherwise ordinary Summer Sunday evening. Dillenger was hit by two of the four bullets and he slumped head first to the sun-baked asphalt. His mouth dropped open as if to speak. But no words came only a quick flowing stream of blood that mingled with sweet papers, torn up tickets and cigarette ends, – the debris of any street outside a cinema. The third bullet ploughed into Anna Saige's handbag, burying itself in her metal make-up kit which more than likely saved her life. The fourth bullet was never found.

Within minutes the news that John Dillenger, Public Enemy No.1 had been shot dead was flashed across the nation. A huge crowd gathered on the street outside the Biograph Theater. A thousand people asked a thousand different questions: How many bullets did it take to put him down? What were his last words? Did he ask for forgiveness? Can we sleep safe in our beds tonight? Who did the stake-out along with the F.B.I.? Was it Lieutenant Bill Hennessy and the Bomb Squad? Are they sure Dillenger is really dead?

John Dillenger's body was taken to the Alexian Brothers Hospital at West Belden and North Racine and was pronounced D.O.A (Dead On Arrival). Because most people figured Dillenger was the last of the "Badmen" they went to the city Morgue to view his last remains. And the city officials understanding their need-to-know, placed his body on a slab tilted at a 45 degree angle for better viewing.

The Lawmen, who had stopped forever this savage beast of a man, became famous overnight. Lieutenant Bill Hennessy became a celebrity and was promoted to Captain, even though he always played down his own part in disposing of America's deadliest killer. Even so, US Newspapers and moviemakers could not get enough data to publish on the fabulous Kilkennyman. And the fact that not one member of the public had been hurt or injured during this most dangerous operation appealed to the American peoples sense of propriety and humanitarian concern.

Bill Hennessy financed and brought out to America two of his brothers; Ned, who became an engineer and John who became a "Chicago Transit," Authority. His brother Pat along with his newly wedded wife Eileen paid their own way. Eileen was sister of the late great Kilkenny All-Ireland hurler and G.A.A. Secretary, Paddy Grace. And Pat became first Chairman of the GAA in America in 1949. His other brother Richard (Dick) stayed at home, got married and reared a family at Lord Edward Street. Bill also brought to America his sisters, Mausie, Nell, Chriss and Ann. Two other sisters settled in New York, and the youngest sister Kitty, married and went to live in England.

In his time Capt. Bill has been proclaimed the Instigator of the Saint Patrick's Day Parade in Chicago, Chicago Man of the Year, Honoured in The Hall of Fame as Ambassador of Goodwill. He was awarded many Medals for Bravery, received many Citations and Commendations by the Chicago Police Department. Bill was given Honorary Membership of Chicago's foremost organisations: 'Le Roy', 'McCullough,' 'American Legion Post', The 40 and 8 Honour Society of the Legion, The V.F.W., Police Captains Association, The Elks, The Lions Club, The Kiwanis, The Knights of Columbanus and The Ancient Order of Hibernians. After his retirement from the Police Force he became Vice President and Director of the Circle Chevrolet Co. owned by Mr. Hartigan the Automobile Tycoon.

An old friend of Capt. Bill's said at his passing: "His like will never be seen again".

Ar dheis Dé go raibh a ainm!

A resolution

adopted by **The City Council**

of the **City of Chicago, Illinois**

Presented by ALDERMAN MICHAEL F. SHEAHAN   **on**   SEPTEMBER 11, 1985

Whereas, Former Chicago Police Commander William Hennessy, was born on January 1, 1895, in the county of Kilkenny, Ireland, came to the United States in 1912 as a young man of 17. He served with distinction and honor in World War I, worked for the B and O Railroad, joined the Chicago Police Department in the early 1920's, expired at the age of ninety, on August 27, 1985; and

WHEREAS, Commander William Hennessy worked his way up through the ranks of the Chicago Police force, serving at the Woodlawn and finally Gresham police district, (better known as "Hennessy's Parish"), retired in 1958; and

WHEREAS, Commander William Hennessy was instrumental in forming the first St. Patrick's Day Parade in Chicago at a meeting of the Ancient Order of Hiberians along with 25 others in 1953; and

WHEREAS, The St. Patrick's Day Parade, which began at South 79th St. and Ashland Ave., was moved downtown by the late Mayor Richard J. Daley, is still in existence today and highly successful; and

WHEREAS, Commander William P. Hennessy was a much sought after speaker, who had an illustrious gift as an orator; and

WHEREAS, Commander William Hennessy symbolized the essence of the American dream, served his Family, Community and City unselfishly and provided an invaluable service to his fellowman; and

WHEREAS, The name of Commander William P. Hennessy will be memorialized eternally by those who lives he touched by his inspirational presence, now, therefore,

Be It Resolved, That we the Mayor and Members of the City Council of the City of Chicago, gathered here this 11th day of September, 1985, do hereby officially and personally mourn the loss of Commander William P. Hennessy and extend our deepest sympathy to his family and innumerable friends; and

Be It Further Resolved, That a suitable copy of this Resolution be prepared and presented to William P. Hennessy's family.

_____
MAYOR

_____
CITY CLERK

CHAPTER SIXTEEN

PAT HENNESSY, KILKENNY CITY AND CHICAGO IRISHMAN OF THE YEAR : WE SALUTE YOU

TALKING about life in general: There are givers and there are takers. There are makers and there are breakers. And I have found that nine times out of ten, the givers are the makers and the takers are the breakers. If you think about it, it makes sense.

Regarding generosity, I read somewhere recently, that he who gives of his wealth gives little. But he who gives of himself gives all. Generosity is nobility of spirit, and it's opposite frame of mind is selfishness. Correct me if I am wrong, but it seems to me there is quite a lot of selfishness doing the rounds these times. And the selfish theory of morals tells us, that man acts from the consideration of what will give him the most pleasure. Whether his actions cause pain or distress to others doesn't seem to trouble him over much.

It is not that I consider myself to be a student of psychology or indeed philantrophy, but it occurs to me that most of us go through life with the sole purpose of taking care of number one. Nothing or no-one else really matters. Love of self supersedes all. Just as long as: 'I'm alright jack', every thing in the garden is lovely. But despite that and fortunately for mankind, the spirit of philantrophy takes a hand. Every now and then in different countries and amongst different cultures, benevolence raises its fair face. The inevitable happens when destiny brings into play men of extraordinary character and unique capabilities. When such men are called forth our faith in our fellow man is once more restored.

The 1920s in Ireland saw the beginning of the Civil War. It was a war that went to the heart and soul of the Irish people. A terrible war that pitted brother against brother and father against son.

On the 26th April, 1920, a man child was born to John and Mary (Molly) Hennessy from Greens Hill, Kilkenny City. He was the youngest of a family of 10 and was christened Patrick.

Patrick was sent to the Lake School, off Michael Street, at the tender age of four years. As he remembers it, Mister Danny McEvoy was Headmaster and Mrs. Andrews along with a Mrs. Reid taught first and second infants. He attended the Lake School until the age of seven years when he made his First Holy Communion, in Saint Canice's, Butt's Green.

After that he went to the C.B.S. at James' Street to continue his education. Pat remembers dedicated teachers like; Brother Wattie O'Brien, Brother Byrne and Master Mick Fogarty. He was a willing student and just like fabled Achilles to whom Phoenix said after Peleus had chosen him as tutor to his son:

Therefore he set me by thee
To guide thee and to teach
To make thee a doer of deeds
And a master too of speech.

So too did Pat Hennessy go on to become a doer of deeds. He hurled for his native Kilkenny and even captained one All-Ireland hurling team. But there was more to come, much more. And a master too with words. for half a hundred years he has written for four North American newspapers, especially on Irish American affairs.

Pat went on to tell me about what he considered to be the greatest thrill in his young life. It was going by train to Dublin to witness the world encompassing religious event called the Eucharistic Congress, in 1932. He was twelve years old and accompanied his mother to the Capital for the week long ceremony. It looked like the whole world was participating in that once in a lifetime event. The clergy of the world were there from humble priests and nuns to Bishops and Cardinals, speaking every language under the sun. The flags of every nation lined the streets of Dublin. Especially his mother kept pointing out to him the Stars and Stripes, alongside the Green, White and Orange. It seemed like half of the young men and women of Ireland must be working in America. Of course, his mother had married his dad in America, all those years ago.

Now it was widely hoped that the Eucharistic Congress would help to heal the terrible wound the Civil War had opened in every town and city in every segment of the population. And the churches were left open all day and all night and Masses and Retreats were continually offered to heal the gaping wound.

Pat remembered Cardinal Laurie, who was the Pope's Representative, with Monsignor Spellman of New York, who later became a cardinal. And Cardinal Fardini from Rome, who came to Dublin by Mail Boat from England. "We were fortunate to be at Merrion Gates where the Papel train stopped for the very popular Dublin Mayor, Alfie Byrne, to welcome the visitors in Irish, English and Latin", Pat recalled.

"On the Saturday over 80,000 boys and girls many with their parents joined in the singing of well-rehearsed hymns as the Most Rev. Dr. Kelly Archbishop of Sydney, Australia, celebrated the Mass. There in attendance was Ireland's beloved Cardinal Mcrory. And two legendary Irish patriot politicians from opposite sides of the Civil War were there, to show that it was both possible and proper for all factions of Irish men and women to reunite, were Eamon De Valera and William Cosgrave."

"The following day was Sunday 26th June", Pat recalled, "which by the way, was the 1500 anniversary of Saint Patrick lighting the Pascal fire on the hill of Slane. More than half a million people converged on Phoenix Park for the Pontifical Mass. There was a procession afterward to O'Connell Bridge for Benediction. And the legendary Irish tenor Count John McCormack is said to have pierced the heavens with his renowned rendition of 'Panis Angelicus'. It was a once in a lifetime, never to be forgotten experience. it must be remembered, Pat insisted, that the Gaelic Athletic Association played a major role in bringing about a reconciliation between hurlers and footballers and camogie players from every county in Ireland on the playing fields.

Later, back home in Kilkenny it looked like Pat would have to cut his education at the C.B.S. short. His now widowed mother was making plans to take him to America. Except for his brother, Richard (Dick), who was married and living at Lord Edward Street and his sister, Catherine (Kitty), who was married and living on Greens Hill, all other brothers and sisters were living in New York and Chicago.

And so Pat and his mother sailed from Queenstown the cobh of Cork, late in 1932, bound for America. It was a nine day voyage via Boston. Their cousin Mrs. Holland claimed them at the notorious Ellis Island and took them to her home in The Bronx, New York. They were given a wonderful welcome but declined to stay more than two days as they were anxious to meet their family in Chicago. Mother and son boarded the New York Central train having said their thanks and goodbyes. Great was their surprise when their train stopped at Gary Indiana. Sergeant Bill Hennessy of the Chicago Police Bomb Squad had come on board to welcome his mother and younger brother to America. Next stop was Dearborn Station, Chicago. There brothers Edward, John and sisters Mausie, Ann, Nell and Chriss, were all waiting with open arms. An Irish night was all set up and ready to roll at Sergeant Bill's house on South Ada Street.

Pat's education had only been interrupted for two weeks when he was enroled at the Visitation Grammar School. As hinted at earlier, he was an apt student and easily assimilated all knowledge laid before him. He excelled in the physical arena too, and by the time he graduated in 1935 he had represented his school on its baseball and football teams. In his final year at visitation, Pat won a Scholarship to Saint Leo's C.B.S., South Sangamon, Chicago.

Halfway through 1935, Pat's mother decided she would like to return to Kilkenny City in the dear old Emerald Isle. And, of course, she would take her youngest son, Pat, home with her. Now Pat would continue his education at the Vocational School, Parliament Street. Pat recalls that Mr. Walsh was C.E.O. and Mr. Jim Henry and Mr. Gibbs taught second and third years. He left the Vocational School in 1937 and took up employment at Statham's Garage, Patrick Street. He remembers with great affection most of the fine men who worked in that reputable establishment: Paddy Murphy, foreman; Jim and Mick Conway, Martin Ward, Phil Treacy, Kevin Ruth, Davy Gaffney, Joe Hynes (boss); Seamus Hayes, Larry Reide, Lar Kealy, Bill and Mick Brophy, Johnny Kelly (Callan), Marty Brett, Tommy Muldowney and Yankee Kelly. Pat confided: "I could tell you great stories about all those fine people that would fill a book and make you laugh 'till you cried. It was a wonderful place to work".

"And during those years I had the privilege of wearing the Eire Óg jersey. In 1936 I was on the panel that won the minor championship in Thomastown. There were powerful men on that team. Men like Jimmy Langton, Jack Mulcahy and Christy Bollard and many others. And because I was under 18 years on the following year, I was fortunately picked to play centre half back on a team that was captained by Seanie O'Brien which included Pat Fahey, Pat Burke, Tommy Murphy, Neddie Brett (in goal), Jimmy O'Dwyer, Ned O'Connor, etc".

Pat married Eileen Grace from Palmerstown in 1948 and they both emigrated to America. For Pat it was his second time to emigrate and because most of his family were domiciled there he was in a sense going home. His wife, Eileen, was a sister of the late great Paddy Grace of Kilkenny All-Ireland fame and G.A.A. County Secretary for many years. Sadly Eileen died in 1996, 2 years before their 50th anniversary. Their lovely daughter, another Eileen, is a happily married woman with a fine family, now living in Indiana.

The newly married Pat went to work for the U.S. Mail at Dearborn Station. Immediately he made contact with any and all G.A.A. activists in Chicago. But because of a major Depression which was the result of World War II, U.S. Immigration Laws had become very restrictive. The result of that in turn meant there were few if any young Irishmen available to play their national games of hurling, football and handball in Chicago and wider America. The organisers, the few of them that were, would have to start from scratch by once again putting Chicago on the G.A.A. map.

Pat Hennessy told me he was elected Chairman of the Board and was responsible for publicity and the co-ordination of the associations activities, which covered everything from selling flags to driving the players to all the venues and reporting to the newspapers and radio. Pat started with the Irish World in New York which was the only national newspaper in existence at that time.

"And we had no typewriters either. So that everything had to be written by hand and a carbon copy kept for the Chicago Irish Radio programmes. It was an uphill struggle all the way and there were plenty of complaints if we made an error, even in spelling. And of course there was always the problem of getting permits to play. But despite all the obstacles we came through. And whereas it seemed to take forever to get four teams established and playing matches on a regular rota in hurling and football we now proposed to increase our standing army of players to eight teams with a committee capable for implanting such a burst of activity during the G.A.A. season.

EDMUND IGNATIUS RICE

At the invitation of an old school pal, Seamus O'Brien from Callan (R.I.P.), Pat became involved in promoting the Canonisation of the marvellous Callan Christian Brother, back in 1968. As is typical of Pat he soon got a committee together to work for the cause. He told me: "We have three big C.B.S. schools here in Chicago and it is not too difficult to work with the Alumni. We marched under the banner of the legendary Callanman in the Saint Patrick's Day Parade. We had 1,000 marching men in 1966. And we were able to fill two 'planes leaving chicago for the Beatification ceremony at the Vatican and we had them all visit Kilkenny Castle and Callan before returning to Chicago." With a smile Pat said: "We are still hoping for that elusive third miracle".

The foregone is only by way of telling you what Pat Hennessy did in his spare time. Briefly, his day job was at the Mayor's Office in charge of Public Relations including dealing with the media and others for everyday news on neighbourhood projects, ongoing and forecoming. His team also handled the Mayor's private business regarding complaints etc., employees, Police, Fire, Health Dept., Dept. of Streets and Sanitation, composing of more than 40,000 workers. As head of Streets and Sanitation Pat Hennessy won the All-American Cup for Chicago seven times in-a-row. Pat began with Mayor Richard J. Daley when he first entered Office in 1955 and was by his side until he died in 1976. and Pat finished at City Hall with Richard Daley's son, Richard M. Daley, in 1990. In between Pat had worked with a lady Mayor Jane Byrne, who was, in fact, a niece of the original political supremo, Richard J. Daley, also two black Mayors, Washington and Sawyer, and Mike Bilandic, who took over when the original Mayor Daley died suddenly.

Usually, new incoming administrations bring their own people with them to hold important positions. But Pat Hennessy was retained by all incoming Chicago Mayors, thereby creating a unique record, never before witnessed by any administration. The $99,000 question was: Why was Hennessy retained while everyone else got the sack? And the answer usually given was: Because he knows where all the bodies are buried.

When I asked Pat what exactly it meant, he said with a grin: "It must be some kind of compliment, I guess", and he went on to elaborate. 'Anyway, I enjoyed my work. It was exciting to be always meeting new people and new challenges, wrestling with new ideas. After 35 years of service I learned how to deal with people and the media. The answer would seem to be – It's nice to be nice".

By way of concluding I asked Pat to name one or two of his most memorable occasions in that great city of Chicago and here's what he told me: "Being present at Soldier Field Chicago in 1957 for the Pan American Games which was opened with a hurling game before 60,000 spectators, most, if not all, of them seeing our national game for the very first time. Seeing how they loved it as they cheered every puck of the ball. American teams vied with each other for the honour of escorting the Irish teams off the playing field. And another memorable occasion was introducing the Kilkenny hurling team to Mayor Richard J. Daley, in 1963. Newspaper men that day were running up and down the sidelines calling the great Ollie Walsh 'The Bambino for Babe Ruth'. They were excitedly comparing Ollie to the greatest hitter in American baseball history.

Again, meeting all the great U.S. political leaders who came to see Mayor Daley at his private office, numbered 100, at City Hall. There was Lydon Johnson, John, Ted and Bobby Kennedy, Hubert Humphries, Jimmy Carter and a host of others. I remember in 1980, when Ted Kennedy was campaigning for President, Bobby Kennedy's wife, Eithel, was campaigning for him in Chicago and I got nominated to escort her to all the Catholic schools in the city. At the end of the campaign I got an invite from her for Eileen and myself to visit Hynannis Port. But we didn't go. And a last one: Having to deputise for Mayor Daley one morning at a reception of U.S. Toastmasters. Their convention was held at the Conrad Hilton Hotel. Mayor Daley was due to be the main speaker after Governor of Illinois, Al Shapiro. The reason why I got the nod, you guessed it – I knew where all the bodies were buried."

"Just before I finish I'd like to pay the highest possible tribute to two of the greatest Kilkennymen I have ever met: Liam O'Brien from Goresbirdge and Geoff Butler from Windgap, these marvellous men led a fundraising marathon to raise enough money to purchase land for a Chicago Gaelic Park: 'A Green Patch of our Own'. Enough money to buy nine acres just outside the city. Today those nine acres have grown into a 50 acre athletic arena, thanks to Liam and Geoff and a host of other great men. All of them are a credit to their country".

OFFICE OF THE MAYOR

CITY OF CHICAGO

RICHARD M. DALEY
MAYOR

PROCLAMATION

WHEREAS, Pat Hennessy has been actively associated with the Gaelic Athletic Association for over sixty years; and

WHEREAS, during that time he has been honored by his county, Kilkenny, to represent them in All-Ireland hurling finals and to captain the team in 1938; and

WHEREAS, for the past forty years he has actively promoted Ireland's national games of hurling, football and handball in Chicago, both as a player and administrator; and

WHEREAS, in 1949 he was elected Chairman of the Chicago Gaelic Athletic Association and entrusted with the task of re-activating the Association in Chicago and the midwest; and

WHEREAS, in 1965 he was the Chairman for the successful promotion of the United States fund-raising effort to erect the President John F. Kennedy Memorial Park in Wexford, Ireland; and

WHEREAS, as national organizer of the American-Irish Immigration Committee he has actively promoted legislation in the United States Congress for the past twenty years, to amend the present Immigration law and allow more Irish to come here; and

WHEREAS, in 1980 he was founder, member and first president of the United Irish-American Society of Illinois, an organization seeking to have the President of the United States help bring peace with justice and reunification in Ireland; and

WHEREAS, he has covered Chicago Gaelic News in the Irish World, Irish Echo and Irish-American News for the past 36 years:

NOW, THEREFORE, I, Richard M. Daley, Mayor of the City of Chicago, do hereby proclaim Saturday, January 27, 1990, to be PAT HENNESSY DAY IN CHICAGO and urge citizens to join in the salute to him as he is honored by the Chicago Galway Fellowship Club as "Chicago Irishman of the Year," at Gaelic ceremonies at the Martinique.

Dated this 16th day of November, 1989.

Richard M Daley
Mayor

IRISH ECHO, SATURDAY, JANUARY 13, 1990

STAND UP PAT
AND TAKE A BOW

Columnist for the Irish Echo, Pat Hennessy, has been named "Chicago Irishman of the Year" by the Galway Fellowship Club. A 30 year veteran with the Mayor's Office of Inquiry and Information, he will be honoured at the ninth annual dinner dance of the organisation scheduled for Saturday night, Jan. 27, at the Martinique, Evergreen Park, Illinois.

To mark the occasion chicago Mayor Richard Daley issued a proclamation designating Jan. 27 "Pat Hennessy Day in Chicago", urging Chicagoans to salute him for outstanding and dedicated work for many causes, over the past 40 years. Pat is being cited for actively promoting Ireland's national games, hurling, Gaelic football and handball, as a player and administrator since 1948.

Pat was elected chairman of the Chicago Gaelic Athletic Association in 1949, and entrusted with the responsibility of reactivating the association in Chicago and the Mid-West. In 1965, he was elected chairman of the successful national fundraising program to erect the President John f. Kennedy Memorial Park in Wexford, Ireland. He received recognition from the Kennedy family for this work.

Two years later, he was elected National Organiser of the American-Irish Immigration Committee to promote legislation in the congress of the United States to amend the Immigration law and make it fair and equitable for all people.

Pat is also being cited for his work as founder-member and first president of the United irish-American society of Illinois, and organisation seeking the help of the president of the United states in helping to promote peace with justice and the reunification of Ireland.

Pat is also being recognised for his writing of "Chicago Gaelic News" in the Irish Echo. The irish World. And Chicago Irish-American News, over the past 36 years.

"It's a great honour to be recognised by your peers", says Pat, "particularly the chicago-Galway Fellowship Club, one of the finest organisations of its kind in the Gaelic world".

Poetry

Sounds of Sadness

BY SEAN KENNY

A Poor Poet

A penless paperless poet
A vagrant scribbler I
Would trace in the clay
With my fingers
Symbols and shapes for joy.
By lovingly rearranging
A fistful of fertile dust
Could discover some common wonder
Of myself at the paps of earth.

With dust for page
With fingers for pen
And with no art that's my own
I write on clay
As a simple man
To prolong the living poem.

Sad Remembering

This secluded road winds nowhere
Aimless as my turning thoughts
And almost as hopeless
Nobody comes out here anymore
To break this cruel repose
Not even a dogs distant bark
Nor the neigh of a tired horse
To shift my attention away
From this ancient sorrow
With its gone forever complex.
And its long as I live regret.
Event the birds have flown
And left these dim fields
To the winds cry and the rains
What am I doing here
Sky watching and weeping inwardly.

We In Autumn Wood

For Ann

Come white-faced with me
Having dreamed this act
A heaped up hundred ways.
It is this and it is now
Shivering in our desire
Here in this autumn wood.
List-looking the burnt umber cause
That branches crick crack make.
On yellow ochre haws
A robin red sharp chirps
The sky-high wood-walled place.
His sing song throbs
And pulses through the breeze
Electrifying our delight.

I mouth your name
It is Ann.........Ann
Black-haired blue-eyed woman.
No sound will come
Above the creaking tongues of trees.
The aspen and the rust down leaves
Applaud your fame.
Oh let your indecision's creep
Between the heart-broken stones and
Nailing your confiteour

To the shrunken willow
Be in with me.
Wood woman see
The image that is you, in me.

Under oak and jackdaw croak
We nest naturally,
'Neath yellow leaf and black feather fall
Down from shaking sticks
That scratch against grey flying clouds
Free wheeling down black Blunden's wood.
Amid fern and laurel trill
Wood pigeon with plover bill
Tell the talk-singing wood
That you and I have met
And it is good.

The Nobel Prize for Hoping

Aye
I say to myself
Why not now
At thirty three.
My clip clop feet complaining
The implacable track
Of my fameless years
Without respite.
And
The hope
That was hammered by hope
To the shape of a capital D
For despair.
And from spice words like pity
To race from that bled shadow
Of the cross-tree
Bearing its terrible truth.
To emerge
To good day meet
My genesis.

But aye
What have I done
With my days
Hopping about like the sparrow

Water henning
In and out of the swim
Being consistently narrow
Mea culpa beating
The belly from sin
And from drunken debate
And what have you
Where
Do I aim my treadmill feet
Used in the past
Only to meet myself
On the way
Coming back.

Crossly I am fastened
To an evergreen tree
Of mediocrity
But
With hope I go on
From past hopeless decades
Related to myriads
Of Our Fathers
Forever and never
Amen
My sin body flabbergasted
Always imbibing the acid cup
In an urban Gethsemane
Being certain
That I must win
The nobel prize
For hoping.

Little People or The Hosting of The Sidhe

I know that you have been hiding
All the long long day.
I know that you want
To come out to play.
And wise-welcome the august moon
With some fairy ancient tune.
But you fear that my human eyes
May not see beyond the guise
Of the world's banality.
And you dread that my clacking
Tongue
Might misrelate such a scene
As the hosting of the sidhe
On the lawns above Kilcreene.

I own that my life is turning
From woodland bog and lea
Past the point of no-returning
To compass the Irish sea.
Muse of Brighid ever ready
Summon on the noble sidhe
From Callan fields and Comer
And from Kells in Osraighe.
From Inistiogue and Gowran
To the swards of Dickboro high.

And as you celebrate brown autumn
To me say a green goodbye.

So come out from under
Your sandy dunes
And play about these ivied ruins.
Your fun I'll not hinder
By my stay,
I'll not return for many a day.
Come out little people
I'm going away
Come out little people
Come out and play.

If She

If she came back to me
I'd set her free.
Free from the memory of me
I'd lie to tell her why
I never said goodbye
She'd cry and so might I
To see her cry

The day before she left
I penned a poem
A silly piece of
Nonsense verse she said

We swore we'd never part
Like sun and flower
And when she laughed
I knew the thing was dead.

And she being so like me
Could not consent,
To come to me to run
And so I went.

And now its far too late
I'll mend my net
And boat again and fish again
I'll fish to forget.

And now with the minimum of words
I door you key
You fruit I tree
I pod you pea
You ocean I sea
You and Me
We.

Christ at my Lai

My Lai, My Lai
My village and my life.
Deadly still my people lie
All twisted limb and face.
In agonizing huddled heaps
Their slaughtered human frames
All bloodily gashed they gape
In wide-eyed tearfilled death.
Stopped forever in their tracks
Struck dumb this expressive race.
Father mother brother world
Crushed before my face.

Like giant prehistoric birds
High in the morning sky
The swishing helicopters swooped
Above the hamlet of My Lai.
With armament and combat drill
As thunder across the plain.
Those so-called saviours of mankind
Those savage soldiers came.
With grenade belt and gun in hand
Sardonic men or war
Equipped to storm a citadel
Not to massacre and maul
Poor innocents.

The horizon was a black line
Scratched across an amber sky.
Sunrise was an orange
Poised upon the rim.
Motionless it stood, as though
It had forgotten its ascending path.
And when it trembled remembering its cause
The great plains shuddered.
Time had slept behind the junction of the earth
Reluctant to begin that terrible day.
Then with convulsive jerk
Its first lights ran
Red riot through the sky.
Awful in its silence it paused
Looked back and caused
A purple mist to creep across
That (earmarked-for-doomsday) land.

The march sun flashed between the huts
In haloed hoops of light.
Compassing a poorly village
Patient in the lap of sleep.
Calm, though one hour would discover
It's entire inhabitants dead.

A mongrel pup-dog whined
And barked to make itself alive
And from inside his crib
A frightened boychild cried
A brief complaint to God.
Father if it be possible-
Let this chalice pass.
The village yawned
Stretched and got up
To grope at another day,
Eager alive, man woman with child
The compliment of the earth.

Decidedly made in God's image
To labour to love to make happy.

The armed platoon of soldiers
Steel sealed the hamlet, My Lai.
Whilst heart-thumping elders shielded
The innocents of their race
Measuring the intruders manners
Searching to discover a trace of humanity.
My Lai, My Lai
On the brink of genocide.

It was at My Lai
The multitude died.
Babes in their mother arms.
Old men cried and died
Side by side girls and boys
Astonishment, terror, disarray
Clutching each other for shelter
Begging, beseeching, dismay
On their artless faces
All bloody their heads were bowed
Their bodies torn with bullets
The rape of the pure and the proud.

And Jesus in His mother's arms
Convulsed when the bullets hit.
Then spouted His red hot crimson blood
Like wine through His golden skin.
Like wine through His golden skin.

A mound of massacred man
Was their horizon.
Their sun like a piece of yellow paper
Hanging out in space.
The earth and sky were one
In a blood-red disgrace.

Sowing The Words

This is the poets season.
He puts on his considering cap
To ply the stiff acres of clotted words,
Making them pliable as wet clay.

The ground wants breaking.
Let the silver sock of his deliberations,
Carve the crust of some experience
That moved him, beyond words.

Letting us peer into the earth womb,
Of man's machinations.
Marking the maggots gluttonous race,
For the rich man's graVe.

Praying with tattered lips,
Looking fish-eyed at the fray.
Had the worms but working hours,
They could not be constant.

The rusted iron of the will.
The abcess of the withered flesh.
The paradox, that from evil issues good.
The words would lief be sown.

He a satirist,
Could pluck from live ether
A galley of Aesop's Fables.
Exposing that foolish ass
In its gammon as a ferocious lion.

Being wrongly ashamed
Of its poor bothered self.
Until it was sticked and stoned,
Into the acute fact of its own perfection.

Copper Eyes Wise

How will I look when I'm dead?
Wax fingers and wax face
With copper-brown pennies for eyes
Bare footed and out of the race.

And who will come when I'm dead
To view the lifeless Kenny
To shake solemn hands and heads
And comment on the value of pennies

A Poor Gift I Sing You

I have no powers that can make you well
Only to sing for you
And hope my song rings true
Telling you old wisdoms
In the present tense fixing
Hope upon hope to the end
Of your pain filled day translating
Born and dead, to love and peace
Scaling the inch tape of my mind
To measure ages.

Before my time
Your father drove the 'Iron Horse'
For the Great Southern before
He took the Kings shilling, and
Blew it in the boozer
Forgetting to enlist, the R.I.C.
Pressed him into Over Seas Service
Somewhere in Kimberley. Tied
To a field-gun for three days and nights
The Boers and the flies feasted.

Why some people are born to suffer
All their days is Biblical
And smacks of eternity
'Tis a poor gift I sing you
Relating the torment of your years
To the abandoned Christ on the cross.

Chesterton Road Odyssey

Then sadness sat down beside me
And whispered that I should depart
From that lovely spot on the mountain
Lest the beauty should hurt my heart.

A new begin now; this notion that brought me
Here to Ladbrook Grove, out of Wimbledon S.W. 19,
One day after my twenty seventh birthday,
Carrying a suitcase full of shirts and socks
And a haversack packed with second-hand books,
Bought on Petticoat Lane, pouring over stalls
Of half forgotten paperbacks: The Inferno Of
Dante Aligheri, Paternally inscribed: To Will
From Father, June 6 1908. Tempus fugit.
My father used to say: "Time nor tide waits for
No man." Like a charmed boy delving into
A chest full of comics and shining clockwork toys,
I discovered Alexandru Sahia, great Rumanian
Writer who militated against Fascism sweeping
Europe like a plague. His peasant people subjected,
He learned to read and write at terrible cost:
His freedom cut off His family intimidated refused
To yield. Bloodied but not broken, he resumed
Studies later at Saint Savas College, Bucharest.
Even so, "The Literary Truth" his first book
Was confiscated. A long short story "Rain in June " describing the
absolute misery of a poor
Peasant with a wife and nine children, has lived with me all my
life.

When he died August 12
Nineteen thirty seven Alexandru Sahia was 29 years young.

What a kin is sadness thought I
To beauty the bird that flies,
If sorrow is but the estuary
That beauty overjoys?

Then across o'er the stirring mountain
Flew echoes of germane sound
Could the cheer I had loosed in gladness
Return with sadness found?

Disillusioned in the face of beauty
I, who had sketched the scene
Repelled for my doglike devotion
And the eulogies of my hymn.

If its lodgings you're looking for, mate
Take a left at the Elgin pub. Never Mind the Eagles Nest, down
the road, Mick O'Shaughnessy's the best for grub.

Each night before he goes to bed,
In Godless London town,
Poor Paddy on his knees will pray,
His alarm-clock won't let him down

Thursday is the day, Our Lord spoke to Mosses:
"Pay the men", He said, "remember, the labourer
Is worthy of his hire, even though he might
Throw his hard earned money to the wind like rain.
In the Pub down Chesterton Road last week
A free-for-all, a punch up that hospitalised two Paddies
And a Policeman who swallowed his false teeth
Having bitten off more than he could chew

An Irish Navvy broke them in two. Another
Said, me ribs are busted to bits, Skinner. Wire
Me poor Mother over in Fenner. Tell her
I got the Priest, and died sober and game
And like Ashes Aegans greyhound, I
Didn't die without fame.

See here G.K., look what they did with your name
Near Notting Hill Gate like Lots Wife
They turned you into stone, as black as
Porter, polished marble like Kilkenny Limestone
Chiselled out: Chesterton Road (Gilbert Keith,
British Novelist 1874-1936) When you snuffed it
The ascendancy rushed in, refusing to let you be
Your anti-imperialist self, Claiming you for their
Own - they turned a blind eye toward your
"Napoleon of Notting Hill", that was their Waterloo.

At "The Elgin" public house on Chesterton Road
Cherry Trees blossom in pale pink, like
A painting by Pierre Bonnard,
And lavender-Lilac grows and here
And there an Aspen shivers,
And a red rosebush blows.

Like a biography of Kensington Gardens
Written Eighteen Ninety Two, when you
A prentice poet of eighteen years sat
By the Central Pond rhyming and feeding
Black and white ducks quacking with
Brown bread, composing green ballads on
Flapping pages of yellow Foolscap, making
A brave attempt to poetically take wing.
Was it there you saw with the psychic eye
A far off Christ riding a colt ass?

In your own words: "With ears like errant wings."
Proudly stepping down the Bayswater Road
Strewn with laurel branch and palm,
Chock-a-block with Londoners enchanted.

While double-decked buses conveyed, excited
Passengers pressed tighter than the seal
On the Bank of England safe, more frightened
Than early Christians herded together in
The Colosseum, prayerfully waiting
To be fed to the roaring lions.

These giant red omnibuses read like pages
From a childs school-book teaching
With highly imaginative phrases
In blank verse and pertinent prose:
Billy Graham will preach at Marble Arch.
Drink a Pint a Milk a Day and Be Sure
To Go To the Dogs Every Friday Nite at
The White City Stadium. Always Travel Light
And Go To Town On An Egg. Beware,
The Kingdom of God is at Hand. (Scripture)
These street ships chug and hug
Their teeming cargoes all over town,
Belching them out and sucking them in,
From Bus Stop to Bus Stop interminably.

Look back no more G.K. Go On
With God in your Parnassian heaven.
These London highrise buildings stifle me
And I'm stuck in claustrophobic streets,
Like a three-legged war horse,
In a gully in no mans land. Oh
To be high as a kite over Daley's Hill
Or bobbing for eels down in the Breagagh Valley.

My Talkative Foot

I think what started me on this road was when I first read Swift's "Gulliver's Travels." The idea of being a giant for a time among midgets and later to be a midget among men fascinated me. The psychological shock of shrinking from the physical bigness of Titans to the terror-filled littleness of dwarfs was surely devastating. Gulliver must have developed a dual personality as a result of his escapades.

This then is the story of a foot. The personification of a foot, to be exact. I have found that altbough I am attached to it, it and I do not share common opinions. Morally and ideally we are at opposite poles.

On the third reading, while 'Gulliver was still in Lilliput, I had a sudden urge to take off my shoe and sock. Then to my flabbergasted disbelief, I heard a voice coming from my foot. Hoping that my imagination had not eclipsed my reasomug, I listened and felt as if thunderstruck.

My big toe was wagging
and wriggling up and down, circling and fencing
around and about.
Listen to me, it said,
I am the foot that feels.
"Let me gaze awhile on the countenance
of your serrated physiog.
That valleyed and mountainous orb of flesh,
that great cave that is your gob.
At that bulbous elongated smeller,
wide nostrilled triangular nose.
Tell me, chum, is it
the work 'of a Pharaoh, or just a pyramidal pose."
And under the slopes of the brain bulge

that from black ringed caverns peep,
identical sad spectators,
what sorrows do they keep.
And your brow, that barren hill of furrows,
scratched by many a plough
of thought, for fertile poetic imagery.
Imagery my foot, and how your
whole life is a whirl
of kaleidoscopic topic.
And the way you reckon things
with your brains up there in the clouds.
And those mad sad preoccupations
that send you out from the crowd,
into vacuums of loneliness,
away even from away.
Where no human feet can follow
where the hapless ones betray,
their true selves to silences.

If some gay verse gate-crashed
that dumb glum reverie,
its happy song would tremble
into janglings. of despair.
From shuddering to shattering
lisping into whispering
softening by saddening
dying by crying.
Until a new song is born,
limp, soundless and sad.
Product of the gloomy mind.
You are a sorry looking chap.
Cheer up, you haven't elephant ears.
But bigger than their owners
are all your foolish fears.
I regret having made you grieve,

but your face provoked my scorn.
Yet, I'm still as much attached to you
as the day that you were born.

I lament that your reason is shadowcd
and by competition confused.
That you haven't found yourself as yet.
That your intellect is illused
by bad opinion.
Let me broaden that narrow noodle nook
that you erroneously call a brain.
Drive out conceit, open your eyes
and tell your friends the same.
Tell them that your foot knows more
than the grand total of their knowledge,
for all their books and bachelorhoods
of arts, parts and college.
I am the pace-maker, the dancer of acres,
the march of time.
My prints have kissed the sand of ages.
I am the rhythm and the rhyme
of rambling years.
Foot of the feet of Adam,
Heel 'of the heel of Achilles.
By Olympian feats I be well
as swift as deer or gazelle.

Had I not sketched from heel to toe
the alphabet of what I know,
you would have thought me mute
and out of reason.
That I was your shanks-mare,
your silent slave
asleep to all reality.
Deaf, dumb and unaware

you'd put your foot in it.
I am the foot that feels.
While the body sleeps
and the drowsy brain dreams
in the warm darkness :of linen sheets,
I foot-sore scheme.

There must be an end
to the abuse of feet
torture of toes
and absence of heat.
An end to barbarous broken boots
water-logged boots and shoes too narrow.
Oh how I fret for feet
that are cut to the marrow
with great leather lumps
of the crudest hide.
And for poverty's feet
ever cold and wet-wise.
For feet that were severed
because of the gout
by some sawbones
with sharp hacksaw clout.
Murdered and buried in pine wood chests.
No coffin it is called,
but a final foot-rest.

I say away with the tyrant
maker of clogs
hobnailed boots and stilletoe jobs.
Off with Wellington and his rubbery breed,
there will be no rest until feet are freed.
This is the slogan of my invent
that from heel to toe by foot was sent.
A gawk behind a bawk,

eyes stalk, squint talk.
A riggle and a giggle
a size six for kicks,
wha's the time, 'sgetting late
retreat attack. retreat.
A ride beside the slide
a clout about the snout.
Toe's red, do 'as I said
take off your boots and fly in bed.

Attention all you feet
from instep and ankle street,
the time of liberation is at foot.
Stir yourselves when the feet
of the clock shows eight.
When the big foot counts the hours
and the little foot is in debate
with minutes, mark your time.
Mush, mush, away you go,
scuffle, shuffle; clip clop
into the street, feel, feet in thousands meet.
Hurry Harry ho!
Helter skelter High street
high heels and low.
Look up, look down
the shoed and booted town.
The population is on its feet.
Black and brown and white all meet
On clatter patter natter street.

A Silver Hope

In a lime kiln near the lios
I spied a silver hare.
The sidheoga told me this
to want is to own care.
A silver hare
in a lime stone lair
to hansel the sidhe oh then.
A silver hope
round a quarry's ope
keep away from the ledge
little men.

The Psychic Womb

With June's fifth sun eleven high
and climbing
And the twentieth century thirty four years
learning the ropes
of life's peculiar battering ring.
A world dispeopleing war behind
A war to end all wars ahead.
Hard times from Killiney to Kilkenny.
My father out of work.
My mother in labour.
I in full tune with nature.
at the earth edge of infinity.
On the human brink of existence.
All knowing through the senses
Waited and measured my time
between the hearts red throbbings.

As the convent cattle chewed the cud
in Empson's rushy field
my mouth watered in the womb
and Breagha licked her banks sensuously.
I heard with muffled ear
the larks throaty song

splitting the vast silence
sky high over Daley's hill.
I made my lips into an. O and blew.

At the nettled end of our garden
Christy tried to bribe Hickey's horse
With a chunk of steaming bread
bridle behind his back.
A nod was as good as a wink
Tom backed off
tired before he was tackled.
I bucked and gave a horse-laugh
at the very mouth of the womb.
Next door the old woman
pulled strings of warm milk
from her spanseled goats
to make tea for the waiting.

I felt the whip of pain searing
through the cancerous world
and bawled in pity.
I saw my mother fasten
a white ribbon to her auburn hair.
Saw her dying face.
Heard the death rattle in her throat
And lay transfixed and choking in her womb.
Christ disentangled the umbilical cord
and placed His saving spit upon my tongue.
I saw my father borned
fight for ideal and fame.
Beget me and die.
I saw clearly from out the psychic womb
Lazarus's ghost walk the room.
Christ live and let die.
At the sickening thud of violent death

my hands and feet were holed.
I gulped their foggy blood.

As the sun threw its shining arms
Octagonally.
Piercing my womb walled life
like wheel spokes enter in the hub
my shape was cruciform.
Through the torrent of corporal waters
I heard Kitty's call near and far
reverberating the length and breadth of Breagha.
Come quick she called
Sean is about to be born.
Breagha paused outside our door
in ponderous abstraction
then flowed on by Kenny's Well
to Black Mill bridge
with its prophesy
Another belly to fill.

Nore in Flood

Swollen with persistent rain,
your waters thundering down.
Cruel your surge, harsh your tone.
Sweet Nore,
I'll call you that no more.

Flowing muddy, flowing wild,
rushing on, fierce ocean child.
Mind not me, nor give a glance.
For I am but in solemn trance,
marvelling at your might flow,
wondenng where on earth you go.

Tell the trees along your way
the havoc you unleashed today.
Compose yourself, don't be so brave.
In your wake you have left a grave,
of sally trees and structures lank,
your fern clad your danewort banks,
burst and uprooted, building and bower,
that pleasured generations,
crushed in one hour.

Who calls you on this fleeting chase?
Whence begot this rapid pace?

What escapee with cunning bound
eludes your rush oh flowing hound?
Even now I hear the knell
sing sad song in plain and dell.
With hissing leap and turbulent clatter,
gushing gurgling drowning water.

But to my ears you have related
and with tragic operettas stated,
a symphony of sights and sounds,
unfolding in orchestral rounds.

When I Am Old

When I am old
I'll sit and watch the grass grow
and listen to the leaves blow.
And count dead years.
on crippled fingers.
And daydream dead dreams again
and make images out of dreams.
and talk and laugh and play with them
When I am old.

When I am old
when my back's bent like the bow.
And my arms like half sawn
boughs hang low.
And my feet are made of lead
with legs of straw.
When I but nod and wink my way
through all the dream filled days.
And nevermore may wander
proudly free, mid hill and sky.
That seeking I might chance to see
God's handy-work, in
some twisted elderberry tree, or trace
His foot-print sunk
into a stony pass.
When I am old
I'll know the bone in all things

man needs knowing.
From the maker to the breaker
everyman that struggles
from the belly of a woman
is made alive to puzzle
out God's plan.

When I am old
my young face will have grown
a wrinkled flesh.
The glad will be a sad smile
ear to ear.
A white beard I will set
against the north wind.
Then my weary eyes won't sin to see
a flash of lace from
some feminine place.
The passions then in me
will be outdated
And all the while my heart run on
like a mad-fast watch
to its winding hour.
To beat its last in this clay tower
When I am old.

When I am old
I'll treat death with much respect
and call him by his Christian
name of peace.
My soul and body I'll bleach well
and wear white linen next
the skin
For fear he might drop in.
to measure me dead accurately
against my bag of sins.